The Ethical Condition

I0889917

The Ethical Condition

Essays on Action, Person, and Value

MICHAEL LAMBEK

The University of Chicago Press
Chicago and London

Michael Lambek is professor of anthropology and a Canada Research Chair at the University of Toronto Scarborough. He is the author of several books, most recently *The Weight of the Past*, and editor or coeditor of several more, including *Ordinary Ethics* and *A Companion to the Anthropology of Religion*.

The University of Chicago Press, Chicago 60637
The University of Chicago Press, Ltd., London
© 2015 by The University of Chicago
All rights reserved. Published 2015.
Printed in the United States of America

24 23 22 21 20 19 18 17 16 15 1 2 3 4 5

ISBN-13: 978-0-226-29210-6 (cloth)
ISBN-13: 978-0-226-29224-3 (paper)
ISBN-13: 978-0-226-29238-0 (e-book)
DOI: 10.7208/chicago/9780226292380.001.0001

Library of Congress Cataloging-in-Publication Data
Lambek, Michael, author.
The ethical condition : essays on action, person, and value / Michael Lambek.
pages cm
Includes bibliographical references and index.
ISBN 978-0-226-29210-6 (cloth : alkaline paper)—ISBN 978-0-226-29224-3 (paperback : alkaline paper)—ISBN 978-0-226-29238-0 (ebook) 1. Ethics—Anthropological aspects. I. Title.
BJ52.L36 2015
303.3'72—dc23
2015006388

♾ This paper meets the requirements of ANSI/NISO Z39.48–1992 (Permanence of Paper).

For Jackie

CONTENTS

PREFACE

This volume contains a selection of my essays that attend ethnographically to ethical life, to the action entailed in becoming and being a person, and to the relationship of acts and persons to value. The essays address central questions of social theory from an assumption and by means of a demonstration of the pervasiveness of what I elaborate as the ethical. *The ethical* in my vocabulary is not an object, not a distinct compartment of the social, so much as a force, dimension, or quality of human existence. To attend to the ethical is to look at social life in a certain way and to put it under a certain kind of description. Ignoring the ethical leaves ethnographic description thin and risks caricature in place of social analysis.

Ethics as an intellectual pursuit concerns reflection on how to live. This must include reflection on how we live in relation to others (to past and future generations, contemporaries and consociates, humans and nonhumans), how we live in relation to our language and our conventions, and how we live in relation to our individual voices and to our particular selves. Some thinkers consider the (fully) human life a hard-won achievement or even an unreachable goal. Other thinkers want to examine how it is that we do in fact live a human life, that the life we live is already human. Thus ethics may be seen as attending primarily to the realm of the ideal or to the realm of the real, to ends and goals or to means and everyday life. If philosophers and proponents of religion sometimes prefer to explore the ideal and the extraordinary, it is the province of anthropologists to consider the real and the ordinary. What is ordinary life, and in what sense does it fulfill the human? If ethics qua intellectual pursuit concerns reflection on how to live a human life, ethics qua practical activity is the actual living of it. How does life come to be so and what do we need in order to see it in this way?

These observations contain within their province—do not disregard—two additional and fundamental observations. First, for many people part of leading a human life is the effort to transcend it, to posit and seek ideals, certainties, or mysteries beyond the ordinary (efforts that are also the province of anthropological investigation); and, second, that ordinary life also contains within it much that, from certain mundane definitions of the ethical, could be readily described as non-ethical or unethical.

Ethics is currently a significant topic of conversation in anthropology, a conversation to which I have contributed. Yet for reasons that will become clear, I do not see ethics as a distinct compartment of social life and hence am skeptical about the development of ethics as a separate domain of investigation or a subfield. Ethics is not only an explicit province of intellectual activity but also a tacit dimension of practice. My interest lies in how attention to the ethical enriches our understanding of practice, of acts and action, of cultural worlds and worlding, of social value, of personhood and individual lives, and more generally, of human existence—of human being. My position, in a single phrase, is as follows: *The human condition is an ethical condition*. In chapter 1, the newly written introduction to this set of essays, published originally over a thirty-year span between 1983 and 2013, I intend to build a context for this bald assertion.

The goal is not to discover "ethics" (or "morality") as one (let alone two) discrete object or objective manifestation that could be compared, classified, and tracked from society to society but to understand the ethical qualities or dimensions of life. I take ethics as pertaining to the intentions, qualifications, and consequences of human speech and action, more specifically the entailments of acts in relation to time, person, and existence. What if we took domains of social life or anthropological inquiry, like "kinship" or "religion" and viewed them through the lens of action? That would be partly to examine the stream of practice and the way that discrete acts, some called ritual, arise within it and produce consequences for it. These consequences occur, in the first instance, in the moral realm, not the material. They change the descriptions under which people live, directly transforming not behavior but the criteria through which behavior is understood. Understanding the human situation—what we have done, who we are, where we are heading, what these things mean for us and for others—is one way to describe the ethical. Ethics in this sense is to be examined less prescriptively than hermeneutically.

Anthropology and Philosophy

If, as some authors argue, ethics has been an implicit topic of anthropology all along, that is because it is embedded in the best accounts of other people's lives, ethnography that observes the richness, complexity, and ambiguity of experience; the directions people take; their engagement in their lives, projects, relationships, and communities; and how they surmount or fail to surmount obstacles or seek newer horizons. To take two eminent but now neglected examples, consider the essays of Meyer Fortes on how West Africans understand varieties of moral luck within their world or the account by Kenelm Burridge of how Melanesians imagine transcending the moral limits of their world (Fortes 1983, 1987a; Burridge 1969, 1970).[1] But the implicit was rarely made explicit. It was long a truism of the anthropology in which I was trained that we should observe the difference between what people say they do and what they actually do—yet the assumption behind the instruction was fairly cynical; the question that never came up was how people themselves actually live that gap or what it means to live in a world with ideals, rules, or criteria that cannot be met completely or consistently. Anthropologists also wrote a great deal about what symbols mean but relatively little about what people mean by what they say and do. How do others (or they themselves) know that they "really" *mean* it? Must we, as Stanley Cavell famously asked (1976), *mean what we say*? All these questions have profound significance for the quality of life—life lived with others and with ourselves. And they are profoundly ethical.

Attention to ethics is in a way simply a redescription or foregrounding of subjects and questions that have interested anthropologists all along. But to speak about it explicitly does attune one more closely both to what I call the underdetermined features of the human condition (taken up below) and to the kinds of questions asked by philosophers. One of the things that anthropologists and philosophers share, as Cheryl Misak says specifically of philosophy, is that "we unwind complexities and we take things that one might have thought not complex, and we show that they are in fact complex" (quoted in Lanthier 2013). It is easy to be overawed (or dismayed) by the erudition, intricate language, or analytic precision of philosophers, but they have been thinking explicitly about ethics for a very long time. I do not think anthropology should give ground to philosophy or be shy about its own contributions, but we can and should learn from our neighbors—not

1. I borrow the phrase "moral luck" from Bernard Williams (1981).

least by attending to the debates that divide philosophers.[2] For example, one of the debates or divisions in the philosophy of action is whether acts are conceived as things that can be *explained*, drawing on a language of *cause*, or whether they are things (actually not "things" at all) that can be *interpreted*, by means of *reasons*. Can reasons be reduced to causes? Is it interesting to do so? How readily one jumps on the bandwagon of evolutionary psychology will depend on how one answers such questions.

Anthropology has much to learn from philosophy but perhaps also something to teach it. Unlike philosophers who give hypothetical examples or have the privilege of drawing from prior texts, anthropologists begin with the messiness of actual life, which does not divide up into neatly demarcated and internally consistent cultures, domains, or time periods nor readily produce universal categories, unambiguous statements, or discrete events. Where philosophers have often turned to literature for empirical substance, they might also turn to ethnography—but only when ethnographers provide the thick description and the close inspection that approximates good literature. A step further is to follow Wittgenstein's admonition to "*look and see*" or John Austin's request for "field work in philosophy" (1970, 183). This is, in effect, what philosopher Ian Hacking has accomplished in his studies of psychiatry (1995) or Jonathan Lear, in drawing from his psychoanalytic practice (2003) and more recently his ventures into Crow history and ethnography (2006). But it also describes the practice of contemporary anthropologists like Veena Das (2007) or Michael Jackson (1989, 2013) (see also Das et al. 2014) and could serve as a retroactive description of work by figures like E. E. Evans-Pritchard (1937) or Maurice Leenhardt (1979), not to mention Claude Lévi-Strauss (1966) or his eminent successors (Descola 2013; Viveiros de Castro 1998), albeit the latter are not concerned directly with ethics.

In describing the ethical worlds of their subjects, anthropologists have to account for such things as ambiguity, ambivalence, uncertainty, hope, regret, compromise, compensation, rationalization, humiliation, and the lived gap between fact and value, but also, more positively, love, conviction, dignity, ease, determination, insight, and wisdom. Anthropologists, notoriously, offer up the evidence for cultural difference, raising the twin specters of ethnocentrism and relativism but also, I think, providing ways to address, work through, or transcend them.

2. By contrast, my friend Maurice Bloch (personal communication) has complained that words like *ethics* and *morality* are useless to anthropologists and that my references to Aristotle serve (only?) to intimidate those who haven't read him.

Ethics All Along

About a decade ago I took up ethics as an explicit question. I held graduate seminars together with two inspiring colleagues, Paul Antze and Jack Sidnell, and I organized a small workshop on what I called "Ordinary Ethics" that later became a book. But upon reflection, I came to realize that, rather like Molière's *bourgeois gentilhomme* who discovered he had been speaking in prose all along, I had been highlighting the ethical dimension of social life from the start. It is evident in each of my ethnographic monographs and most of my articles.[3] In compiling the present collection, I have selected the articles that address the ethical most explicitly. A collection is something of a recollection. Rereading the essays, I am not sure whether to be pleased about the consistency of thought or dismayed at the lack of innovation exhibited in them, but it has been surprising to me to discover the continuity not only in general theme but also in the terms by which I have approached it, in particular through addressing questions of personhood and the nature of social action and value. If there is progression, it is of working through the particulars of ethnographic cases to levels of increasingly broader abstraction. In that sense the collection is iconic of how anthropological thought as a whole (at least that of my fieldwork-based generation) works.

Speaking with the rationalization and excess clarity that a retroactive account implies, there were three concerns driving my work, attuned respectively to reason, dignity, and freedom. (I find I cannot disentangle the ethical from the epistemological or the personal from the scholarly in these inquiries.) First, like most anthropologists before me who have conducted research outside their own societies and especially in places that have been undervalued by the West, I wanted to put the practices I observed in the best possible light, to understand them in ways that showed the sense they made to their participants and then to make them sensible to readers.[4] Indeed, I

3. The monographs (Lambek 1981, 1993b, and 2002a) provide much richer pictures than can any of the essays provided here. The limits to all of them are, in the first instance, the limits of my linguistic abilities in Malagasy (Kibushy).

4. To put a set of practices in the best possible light is not, of course, the same as saying that they are "best practice" (a phrase now swallowed up by the audit culture) nor to put them above criticism. But it is a commitment of the ethnographer and one of the criteria that establishes a practice as ethnography rather than, say, travel writing, to try to do so. That said, there is little agreement as to what "best light" would mean and certainly no current agreement to understand it in functionalist or utilitarian terms. In addition, things might have been different, certainly much more compromised for me, had I encountered a community pursuing projects I fundamentally disagreed with, like settlers in the West Bank.

wanted to show not only why they are compelling but *that* they are. This meant showing how the concerns that informed the practices I encountered in the field were not, in the end, so different from the kinds of things that concerned people at home and everywhere; to slowly increase, in Hans-Georg Gadamer's terms, the fusion of horizons. More abstractly, people reasoned, made and kept commitments to values and to other persons, and led complex, reasonably virtuous, and interesting lives.

My accounts were deeply cultural, or at least I tried to be finely attuned to cultural difference, but my conclusions did not rest with the demonstration of difference but tried to show that through difference, and by the very act of acknowledging difference, one can glimpse similarity. At the end of the day, things come down to the human condition, not to radically different ontologies. We live in distinct and distinctive cultural worlds, and we construe the relationship of the human to the nonhuman or extrahuman differently from one another (Descola 2013), but we do live in the same human world or at least share some part of the horizon. I follow Stanley Cavell when he says, "Each life is exemplary of all, a parable of each; that is humanity's commonness, which is internal to its endless denials of commonness" (1996, 11).[5] Anthropology extends this philosophical insight to the range of human cultures, showing with precision other lives, ones we might not have thought about or could not even have imagined, and their exemplarity for all of us.

Phrased this way, it should be clear that I am not arguing that if we dig deeper, we find the human universal beneath the cultural particular, or if we look further, we find it at a horizon beyond the cultural; Clifford Geertz (1973c) long ago was able to dispatch such fallacies. Implicitly, his argument is that it is a category mistake to try to separate the humanly universal and the culturally particular as mutually exclusive domains; rather, we find the one within and not beneath, behind, or beyond the other. The problem is formally similar to that of mind and body (Ryle 1949). In any case, a well-performed interpretation shows how foreign practice speaks to us, much as Shakespeare made earlier figures like Julius Caesar speak to the first audiences of his plays and much as a good reader, actor, or director can make Shakespeare speak to us (and by "us" I mean a very broad and heterogeneous audience) today.

5. The passage is discussed by Richard Eldridge (2003) and further by me in Lambek 2014.

Second, I wanted to acknowledge the personal dignity of the people I encountered in the field, a dignity predicated on an understanding of their practices as just described. This is not to say that I found everyone equally dignified, or dignified all of the time, but that people had a certain dignity, wished to be treated with dignity, and tried to treat others that way; they understood themselves as reasonably autonomous creatures, trying to live well and exercising their human capacities in order to do so. (In my very first months of fieldwork, people reflected on why they could not just as well come and practice ethnography reciprocally in my home; many of them began to record vocabulary in English as I did in Kibushy.) They were, in this sense, no different from me, and asserting as much, and in some respects they were more dignified and privileged (and in others less so; as they said, they could not afford to travel to Canada). For me, the rubric *ethics* covers this broad observation about the human and is not, in the first instance, to be reduced to anything less, that is, to anything narrower or more precise.[6]

The third factor was the need to acknowledge something like what some anthropologists of ethics call freedom (Laidlaw 2002; a seminal essay), but that I think is better described as being underdetermined (chapter 1). While I do not dispute the fact that some societies, conditions, and circumstances provide more opportunity for human flourishing than do others, or for some classes of people than for others, or the fact that cultural context shapes the direction that flourishing is likely to take, there is no human being whose life is fully determined. Such underdetermination holds for cultural productions as well as individual experience. The underdeterminism of his interpretations that so irritated many of his interlocutors was for me a central attraction of the work of Clifford Geertz. Although I am less sure than they are about the label, the point is beautifully put by Michael Jackson and Albert Piette (in press [a]) who say, "Existential anthropology is less a repudiation of any one way of explaining human behavior—academic, scientific, religious, humanist—than a reminder that life is irreducible to the terms with which we seek to grasp it."[7]

The underdetermined quality of human action became especially salient for me as I thought about spirit possession and saw how inadequate it was

6. *Dignity* is a word that for Kant refers to the "rational, morally sovereign human being for whom there is no equivalent" (Asad 2003: 137). Although the approach I develop is not a specifically Kantian one, I take his universalism seriously, and I do not see it as directly opposed to an Aristotelian position.

7. See also Jackson's many wonderful expositions; among his recent works, see Jackson 2011 and 2013, as well as Simmel 2011.

to reduce it to a variety of causal and motivational factors that entirely failed to do justice to the complexity of the genre, the unique combination of passion and action, or the integrity and creativity of the spirit mediums. But this inadequacy of theory was characteristic not only of relatively obscure corners of anthropology like spirit possession; it extended more broadly through varieties of functionalism and, subsequently, through the versions of Marxism and post-structuralism that (partially) replaced it. Concerns for human dignity and the underdetermined qualities of human action do have their place within the history of a more specifically cultural anthropology, but the concept of culture, for all its virtues, has not had the theoretical means to address the subject very strongly.

Despite being trained to think in terms of structure, both social and cultural, I have also always had the urge to understand individuals. This can be phrased as an interest in *character*—here understood simultaneously in an ethical and a psychological sense and always in relation to the social relations and cultural forms available. To date, I have addressed character not by attempting full portraits or life histories of individuals, and certainly not by attempting to depict discrete character "types" or by elucidating what constitutes *good* character, but by following individuals as they address contingencies and face challenges, acting in the world, reflecting on their actions, and, in the process, growing in maturity.[8] I have been lucky enough to meet some remarkable people—kind, intelligent, imaginative, self-reflective, actively pursuing particular paths, and passionately engaged in their activities. While the paths they took—notably spirit mediumship (but also Muslim scholarship or musical performance, cultivation of kin ties, etc.)—were initially foreign to me, I grew close to many of them and felt that our ethical and psychological understanding transcended our cultural differences. This was especially the case as I followed my mentors Tumbu Vita and Mohedja Salim (pseudonyms) as they pursued and reflected on their own lives and as they worked as healers, attempting to understand and meet the needs of numerous other individuals. In following episodes in the lives of Mohedja and Tumbu, as well as those of several other people, I have been able to reflect on various ethical principles and challenges as they emerge in practice.[9]

8. For a beautiful elucidation of a person-centered approach to ethics, see Mattingly 2014. See also Kleinman 2006.

9. On Mohedja and Tumbu, see especially Lambek 1993b and various essays. For other strong spirit mediums in Mahajanga, notably Mme Doso and Kassim Tolondraza (their real names), see Lambek 2002a. See also Lambek 2014.

Goodness Has Something to Do with It

Combining these various concerns into one observation, I made the point that insofar as fieldwork shows that people act "ethically" or with ethical criteria in mind (i.e., that most of the time they try to do what is right or good, or want to think that what they are doing is the right thing to do), we need to take this into account in social theory, if only to understand why goodness is not always the outcome (Lambek 2010b). To clarify, I am not saying that people always do good—however that is conceived—or always want to do good, but that (*a*) they frequently act with the good in mind; (*b*) they generally want to do good, and they feel frustration when they cannot do what is good or guilt (or shame) about not doing good or failing to do good, or when they imagine they have done something that is not good; and (*c*) they apportion responsibility for acts, both good and bad, and extend informal judgment over their own practice, character, and lives as well as those of other people. These matters need to be placed alongside motivations like competitiveness, aggression, and desire, forces like power and self-interest (but also love), and objective conditions of inequality and exploitation, sometimes naturalized to those who live with them, when explaining or interpreting social life.

But in addition to these relatively commonsensical observations, which may be as revealing of my own sensibility as of anyone else's, there is a further and more profound observation, namely, that (*d*) fundamentally, *human beings live in worlds in which it is impossible not to evaluate action with respect to the good*. Here the weight of the argument no longer turns on human psychology, on what people think, want, or need, but on the way the world is, and specifically, the nature of human action. The psychological need or desire to be good or to be thought to be good is distinct from the structural necessity of being subject to evaluation.

The insight that ethics is fundamental to social life—to human being in the world, and in a structural or ontological, not a functional sense—includes the corollary that we ought to pay attention to its limits and constraints and to failures not only to act, but also to know what is right or good or how to live well. Limits and failures are not only products of human selfishness, or willfulness, or of individual badness but functions of the ways in which criteria and commitments are socially instituted. If lapses are open to moralizing or political critique and redress, limits may be of deeper structural or ontological import. These matters are complex. They will not be resolved in the essays to follow, but they might be illuminated.

Insofar as my attention has been to the openness of social life and its contingent and inconclusive qualities, a question that some interlocutors have posed is, Where then do I find order, logic, or predictability? Am I, to use the excessive term of one of them, a nihilist? Nothing could be further from my position than nihilism, unless one wants to place skepticism as its close neighbor. I am interested precisely in what engages people. I take dignity, engagement, and openness to be features of human life itself. I also take structure to underlie language and a large variety of cultural and social domains or practices (only not to *determine* them). I would say that explanation (and this is probably the wrong word) is found within human activity itself, understood as a form of life (and taking into account the cumulative weight of history). Such activity includes ritual, and here I draw on Rappaport's conception of liturgical order (1999). At least, these matters of social and cultural emergence and self-sufficiency hold within relatively stable and undamaged communities (as demonstrated by both the culturalist and the structure-functionalist streams of ethnography). Moreover, as Veena Das has shown, recently damaged communities often show a remarkable ability to revive (2007).[10] As she says, these are matters of the ordinary. Just as philosophers need not rely on a metaphysical language, so too perhaps anthropologists do not need an elaborate theoretical armature. And so, in a way, the tilt or turn to philosophy, as I take it, is not a turn to *theory* in the currently salient sense of that term.

A second criticism one could make of my approach, and it is one that I take seriously, is its possible naïveté. A perusal of history or the current state of the world shows an enormous amount of suffering, exploitation, injustice, repression, anomie, anxiety, and depression. The world, taken as a whole, is not a happy place, and human history, taken as a whole, has not been a happy one. A turn to ethics can too often be a way of avoiding hard political questions, in both theory and practice (Muehlebach 2012). In any case, the relationship of ethics to politics is by no means evident. Ethics and politics were likely the same or a continuous subject for Aristotle,[11] and their connection is evident in strong thinkers like Hannah Arendt (1998) and important recent contributors to anthropological conversations like Didier Fassin (2013). Nevertheless, many traditions attempt to maintain a distinction between ethics and politics precisely in order to be able to have

10. Life, as they say, goes on. I hope it is evident that I am not speaking here about some utopian world characterized by complete peace, justice, and positive engagement.

11. Thanks to Simon Lambek for the reminder. James Faubion (2011) lucidly unpacks the Greek terms.

a relatively neutral means or standard against which political actions, aims, methods, and motivations can be judged. This was the case in Mayotte in the 1970s where, as I recorded (Lambek 1990a, 1993b), the authority of Islamic scholars was seen to erode the more they engaged actively in the intense political debates of the day.

For better or worse, the latter questions are not quite the ones that animate the essays in the present volume. I would add that once one discusses politics, everything rapidly becomes political; yet it would be as unbalanced to turn everything into politics as into ethics—and indeed the turn to ethics within the discipline has been in part a reaction to this perceived imbalance in recent theory. Especially in the dark times, to take Arendt's phrase, of late capitalism, other visions are needed—in particular, intellectual visions that do not resort directly to the transcendental realm or the hopes and certainties of millenarian religion or ideology. One of the insights I have gained from reading and life is that there *is* no single or best path to advocate, and no fully adequate one. I take Heidegger's image of the forest paths that sometimes go nowhere and sometimes, for a time, open out into a clearing. Heidegger's own life is proof of the dangers of moving out of the forest to engineer an autobahn (especially with the goal of renouncing technology).

What I am describing ultimately has less to do with motivation, freedom, or power, whether to do good or bad, in the abstract, than with *situated context*, with the fact that all human action occurs with respect both to criteria that are already in place and to criteria that performative action is putting into place. For the most part and from a certain perspective, these criteria are in themselves ethically neutral, but they form the means through which any state of living and any course of action are described and evaluated, prospectively, concurrently, and retrospectively. Every act falls under a description,[12] and performative acts put things under new descriptions or clarify which of several possible descriptions are relevant. Practice is understood according to whether it lives up to its descriptions and the criteria set for it—Is a promise met? Is a relationship acknowledged? Is a name recognized? Every act is also subject to adverbs; is it carried out well or badly, graciously or grudgingly, completely or incompletely, and so forth. We cannot escape this.

My usage of the term *criteria* is drawn from Cavell's reading of Wittgenstein's *Philosophical Investigations* (without attempting to do justice to either thinker). Criteria, says Cavell (1999, 16) citing Wittgenstein (1973),

12. That is also to say that every act occurs in relation to other acts and to persons and their prior, current, and future relations to one another.

"are the means by which we learn what our concepts are and hence 'what kind of object anything is' (§373)." Criteria in this sense do not depend on standards or reduce to scores (as might be the case in judging a diving competition or a flower show.) "To have criteria . . . for something's being so is to know whether, in an individual case, the criteria do or do not apply" (Cavell 1999, 13). Such knowledge is based not on any external authority but simply on "what we say when." (Of course, describing or authorizing who "we" are is itself fraught.) Ethics in this primary sense is concerned both with establishing or acknowledging what kinds of objects specific *acts* are and then with whether our conduct or practice conforms to the criteria to which we are committed through these and prior acts. Ethics is therefore constituted and expressed through how specific acts are defined, what descriptions such acts put persons and things under, what people say and when about acts in given instances and eventually about the persons who have committed certain acts or engaged in such practice over time, and ultimately how people come to understand themselves and their engagement in the world.

Ethics is a complex topic on which it would be impossible to construct a theory that was at once fully comprehensive, systematic, and true to life. Indeed, that very inability itself serves as a subject of some ethical thought. I take that as a warning and invite you to read these essays as just one among many possible ways to think about the ethical in human life.

The essays are presented in the order in which they were first published, with the exception of chapter 1, which is new and takes up many of the points raised in the preface. The essays have been selected with respect to how explicitly or centrally they make ethics their subject. Read together, they form a reasonably comprehensive and unified narrative.

Chapter 1 offers a highly selective *tour d'horizon* of the study of ethical life, examining key terms or concepts, such as freedom, judgment, and action. There is much that it excludes, notably attention to the ethical ruptures and concerns that late capitalism and recent technologies bring with them, matters of human and animal rights, radical inequities and injustices, bioethics, humanitarianism, and the like. The ideas advanced here may be useful in discussion of such topics, but they are the subjects of bodies of work not directly mine. A late rereading of the chapter suggested a surprising omission of a different order, namely, the concept of culture among the key terms. I suppose that is because it implicitly underlies much of the argument. *Culture* is a word that covers the symbolic vehicles and traditions available for constituting persons (actors), acts, and actions as such, for enabling particular forms of orientation and engagement in and with the world, and for drawing fine discriminations of virtue and value. Culture, much as Geertz saw it, affords meaning, before, during, and after the fact, or the act. Ethical action and judgment are enabled by, and contribute to, vehicles of and for action, person-making, self-understanding, value-production, relating with multiple kinds and recursive levels of "others" (akin to what used to be called "social structure"), and the like.

The chapters that follow illustrate how my general view of ethical life has emerged from attempts to understand the ethnographic particulars encountered in fieldwork. They describe a particular cultural world, beginning with the way women's autonomy was constituted at a certain historical period in Mayotte through the seemingly unlikely (for most readers) vehicle of virgin marriage, and continuing with an account of the underlying practice of following taboos (prohibitions, the negative) in Mayotte and across the Mozambique Channel in northwest Madagascar, the two places where I have conducted most of my fieldwork. Several chapters draw from my encounter with "spirit possession" (a cultural form, activity, system, vehicle, technology, and art of living) as it is found in this region; possession has shaped how I think about ethics, but it is not the main subject of, or extensively covered within, this volume. What shapes and gives substance to the arguments I make is reflection on a variety of cultural practices, from the conduct of Muslim rituals to the imagination and enactment of Sakalava sacrifice and through what Sherry Ortner (1978) has termed local "reciprocity scenarios." That said, my ambition here is to abstract beyond the ethnography to more general questions of human life.

In several of the chapters the question of human action is linked specifically to that of ritual. The implication is that what happens in ritual and religion ought to inform how we understand ordinary life, and conversely. General questions of human ethical life—what it means to act with conviction or what it means to begin a new course of action—crosscut the divide we make between what is "inside" or "outside" religion—a boundary that is too readily taken for granted when we begin by asserting that our subject *is* religion. Cumulatively, the chapters circle around the intersection of two dimensions of temporal experience: discrete acts, whether understood as original or iterative, and continuous practice. Moreover, insofar as the essays argue that the ethical is a dimension intrinsic to human action, they suggest that attending to action in this way offers an original means to transect society and grasp it as a whole, rather than breaking it down into institutional domains like "kinship" and "religion" (domains that admittedly are useful for other theoretical exercises). They speak to the human condition and of how the grasping of that condition is simultaneously the manifestation and making of it. But they carry out this work in the distinctive anthropological manner of working through ethnographic particulars.

The essays are presented as first published, although I have consolidated a single style and set of references, removed small mistakes and most of the original acknowledgments, and occasionally made slight changes in the interest of clarity, coherence, and editorial consistency. There remains a certain amount of redundancy, and even repetition, which could be helpful for the reader who wants to take an individual chapter on its own. Some of the phrasing is dated, but of course each essay is to be understood in relation to the time and context in which it was written. Each essay is preceded by a short preface to address that context. This preface serves that function with respect to chapter 1.

ACKNOWLEDGMENTS

Deep thanks for very thoughtful and generous readings of the manuscript to Veena Das and James Laidlaw. They are each exemplary scholars with whom I consider myself very fortunate to be in conversation. Thanks to James, I was able to discuss parts of chapter 1 in the works-in-progress seminar at King's College, Cambridge. Through the auspices of anthropologists Maria Louw and Cheryl Mattingly and philosophers Thomas Schwarz Wentzer and Rasmus Dyring, I participated in two exciting interdisciplinary workshops on ethics at the Institute for Advanced Study at Aarhus University during 2013–14. I've benefited from presenting talks that partially overlap with chapter 1 at Aarhus and at the Institute for Advanced Study at Princeton, the Department of Anthropology at Berkeley, and the Institute on Culture, Religion, and World Affairs at Boston University, thanks respectively to Didier Fassin, Nancy Scheper-Hughes, and Bob Hefner, as well as at McMaster University, courtesy of the undergraduate Anthropology Society.

I have removed the original acknowledgments from the articles reprinted here, but the gratitude remains. I must continue to thank for their ongoing support the Social Sciences and Humanities Research Council of Canada for research grants and eventually a Canada Research Chair, as well as the Department of Anthropology at the University of Toronto, the University of Toronto at Scarborough, and, for a significant period, the London School of Economics, for providing congenial and supportive homes. My teachers, in particular Roy Rappaport and Aram Yengoyan, have deeply informed how I see the things discussed in these pages, as have the scholars I have collaborated with most closely, Paul Antze and Janice Boddy, and now the wonderful younger cohort of anthropologists at Toronto. At critical moments in recent years the following additional mentors and friends have also given me the insight, provocation, confidence, or encouragement I needed to write, present, rethink, or republish these essays: Sandra Bamford, Joshua Barker, Maurice Bloch, Girish Daswani, Naisargi Dave, Didier Fassin, Jane Guyer, Ian Hacking, Olivia Harris, Keith Hart, Michael Jackson, Wendy James, Saba Mahmood, Birgit Meyer, Sherry Ortner, Alan Rumsey, Jack Sidnell, Charles Stafford, Helen Tartar, Andrew Walsh, Hylton White, and Donna Young, among many others.

Taking time from his own fieldwork in philosophy, Matthew Pettit ably produced a consistent set of references and comprehensive bibliography and index. He, along with Anna Kruglova, Arie Molema, Marco Motta, Seth Palmer, Victoria Sheldon, Letha Victor, Shirley Yeung, and other graduate students are conducting exemplary work. Carey Demichelis proofed the manuscript with her usual professionalism.

In Mayotte and Mahajanga (Majunga) I am enormously grateful to those who have been family, friends, teachers, mentors, and just good conversationalists. Full acknowledgments have been and will be given in more appropriate locations.

Nadia and Simon Lambek have been interlocutors in conversations that only deepen with time. Hanna Lambek was there at the beginning, and Jim Lambek until almost the end.

As these chapters form a transection of a life's work, there is every reason to thank my closest partner in that life. Jackie Solway is a full coauthor of one of these essays and has played a significant role in the gestation, development, critique, and enthusiastic teaching of many of the others. The book is for her.

Permissions

"Virgin Marriage and the Autonomy of Women in Mayotte." *Signs: Journal of Women in Culture and Society* 9, no. 2 (1983): 264–81. Reprinted by permission of the University of Chicago Press.

"Taboo as Cultural Practice among Malagasy Speakers." *Man* 27, no. 2 (1992): 245–66. Reprinted by permission of John Wiley & Sons.

"The Past Imperfect: Remembering as Moral Practice." In *Tense Past: Cultural Essays in Trauma and Memory*, edited by Paul Antze and Michael Lambek (New York: Routledge, 1996), 235–54. Reprinted by permission of the Taylor & Francis Group.

"The Anthropology of Religion and the Quarrel between Poetry and Philosophy." *Current Anthropology* 41, no. 3 (2000): 309–20. Reprinted by permission of the University of Chicago Press.

"Just Anger: Scenarios of Indignation in Botswana and Madagascar." *Ethnos* 66, no. 1 (2001): 1–23. Reprinted by permission of Jacqueline Solway and of Taylor & Francis. See http://www.tandfonline.com.

"Rheumatic Irony: Questions of Agency and Self-Deception as Refracted Through the Art of Living with Spirits." In *Illness and Irony*, edited by M. Lambek and P. Antze, 40–59 (New York: Berghahn, 2003). Published concurrently in *Social Analysis* 47, no. 2 (2003): 40–59. Reprinted by permission of Berghahn Books.

"On Catching Up with Oneself: Learning to Know That One Means What One Does." In *Learning Religion*, edited by David Berliner and Ramon Sarró, 65–81 (Oxford: Berghahn, 2007). Reprinted by permssion of Berghahn Books.

"Sacrifice and the Problem of Beginning: Reflections from Sakalava Mythopraxis." *Journal of the Royal Anthropological Institute* 13, no. 1 (2007): 19–38. Reprinted by permission of John Wiley & Sons.

"Value and Virtue." *Anthropological Theory* 8, no. 2 (2008): 133–57. Reprinted by permssion of Sage Publications.

"Toward an Ethics of the Act." In *Ordinary Ethics: Anthropology, Language, and Action*, edited by M. Lambek, 39–63 (New York: Fordham University Press, 2010), 39–63. Reprinted by permission of Fordham University Press.

"Ethics Out of the Ordinary." In *ASA Handbook of Social Anthropology*, edited by Richard Fardon et al., 2:141–52 (London: Sage, 2012). Reprinted by permission of Sage Publications.

"The Value of (Performative) Acts." Special issue on value, edited by Ton Otto and Rane Willerslev, *HAU* 3, no. 2 (2013): 141–60. *HAU* is an open-access journal.

"The Continuous and Discontinuous Person: Two Dimensions of Ethical Life." *Journal of the Royal Anthropological Institute* 19 (2013): 837–58. Reprinted by permission of John Wiley & Sons.

ONE

The Ethical Condition

Ethics is intrinsic to human life and can be understood as immanent within it even while it is frequently claimed to transcend it. In this chapter I make the case for this claim. I do so less by means of direct argument than by a kind of survey or glossary of what have become some (but not all) of the "key words" in the emerging conversation that is the anthropology of ethics. It matters whether the central issue is conceived as one of action, freedom, goals for living, judgment, justification (the giving of reasons), responsibility (or responsiveness), or subject-formation (or self-fashioning), let alone the following of rules, convention, or a professional code. At the same time, these words or concepts need to be understood in relation to one another; they each orient us to interesting paths through the forest but are better seen as diverging and converging at various points than as heading out in radically different directions. Moreover, to speak of immanence at one level is not to deny, overlook, or contradict the prevalence of ethical declaration, elaboration, rationalization, experimentation, and disputation evident at another.

The aim of the chapter is not to survey the range of achievements and arguments within the anthropological conversation on ethics (for which see the outstanding work by Laidlaw [2014]), but to unpack concepts that point in the direction of what I call the ethical condition. I have reached the position developed here as a result of working through the arguments in the chapters that follow. But unlike the chapters that start from something distinctive about ethical life among Malagasy speakers in Mayotte or northwest Madagascar, and hence develop frameworks for thinking about particularity or difference, this one is unabashedly general, broadly anthropological rather than specifically ethnographic. Additionally, the goal is to begin to describe things simply as they are; a few lapses aside, the argument is not (consciously) normative.

Underdeterminism

Where some authors emphasize freedom as both an existential condition and the precondition (necessary and perhaps sufficient) for ethics, I prefer to speak of being underdetermined.[1] Human beings have a degree of autonomy, in some domains and from some social locations more than others; nowhere is our behavior programmed, fully rule-bound, obligatory, or predictable. People can surprise us—and we can surprise ourselves. We are shaped and constrained in all kinds of ways, but we are not fully determined by circumstances, rules, forces, or causes, known or unknown to us, genetic, neurological, cognitive, hormonal, or psychological (whatever that means); never fully determined by destiny, the unconscious, culture, class or other economic forces, oppression, self-interest, or the search for power, esteem, food, or sex.[2] And even if we *were* so determined, the fact that we are not aware of it (even when we claim it) is critical for human experience.

If we were fully and knowingly determined, life would be mechanical and dead boring—indeed, it would be *dead*. But if we were fully free, and free of criteria, we would have no way of knowing what we wanted or how to orient ourselves, and no means to keep us on the same path long enough to achieve satisfaction of anything but immediate wants. At either extreme we would be akin to that vegetable-like state that Geertz described of a human organism devoid of culture (1973b; Faubion 2011, Lear 2011).

The insight is not that people are absolutely free but that as our actions are not fully directed or determined, they require the exercise of some form of judgment. Arguments of freedom and determinism must confront the fact that we are constantly faced with the challenge of alternatives, free to choose but also forced to do so. Do I turn right or left at this crossroads, address you in one language or another, propose or not propose, extend my hand or avert my eyes? I am free to choose but not free not to choose. Socialization is never complete, not so much or only because of the continuing power of nature, sexual drives, and aggressive urges, but because it imposes or proposes multiple, incommensurable, competing, or inconsistent paths, relationships, responsibilities, goals, and solutions. Moreover it raises the question of

1. In anthropology, the arguments for freedom have been best and most elegantly put by James Laidlaw (2002, 2014).

2. As Cambridge philosopher Jane Heal articulated it in oral remarks on a draft, people are neither free nor determined but "wobbly"; different forces and reasons complexly pull us here and there.

consistency; once I set forth along one path, how committed to it am I, how readily can I change paths, and with what consequences? Freedom is premised on prior commitment and hence, as it were, unfreedom.[3]

In sum, we should examine both the manner and consequences of our being (relatively) underdetermined and the manner and consequences of our being (relatively) unfree. What I find most significant with respect to our unfreedom is how we are always already committed—to an identity, a particular language, a mode of life, an orientation in the world, and to particular relationships with significant others. We can abandon these commitments, but not without consequences. The steps we are free to take next draw force and meaning from the steps we have already taken (or that have been taken for us).

These arguments by means of negation (underdeterminism, unfreedom) are ones I learned from Madagascar, where states of affairs are frequently described by what they are not and people by what they do not do, rather than what they are or do. Thus, the name Tsimihety, referring now to a large ethnic group in northern Madagascar, means "those who do not cut their hair," recalling an original refusal to follow a deferential mortuary observance on the death of a Sakalava overlord. It describes not what people do or must do, but a once politically salient refusal to do something (a historical event) and what, since then, they do not do. This leaves a space that is underdetermined or underdefined, albeit not a space that is free in any absolute sense.[4] Taboos (prohibitions, or *fady*) are widely prevalent in Madagascar, indexing many levels of identity and ascription but always by defining a small space of proscription rather than a specific prescription. Malagasy are, in effect, free outside the limits imposed by their taboos.

This is akin to a theory that emphasizes constraints over rules. Or, starting from a positive rather than negative direction, we could speak of affordances, as does Webb Keane, or of capacities, as so well set out by C. B. Macpherson.[5] Affordances and capacities shape our condition, enable our projects and actions, and perhaps invite us to turn in one direction or another (tennis or track, sport or music), but they do not determine anything or enable

3. As George Steiner writes, "Although the path chosen will be one of many, it must lie inside the forest" (1978b, 20; cited in Booth 1988, 420).

4. This space of freedom formed a puzzle for their ethnographer (Wilson 1992). See chapter 3 below.

5. On affordances, see Keane 2008, drawing on psychologist Gibson (1977). On capacities, see Macpherson 1973, also discussed in Lambek 2007c.

everything. One could also start by thinking of ethics along the lines of play (or playfulness).[6]

Any discussion of human freedom sits in an interesting place between what *is* and what *ought* to be, which is what some consider the true realm of the ethical. What "is" is the realm of fact, the way the world is now; what "ought to be" is the realm of value, as we imagine something better (perhaps "freer" or perhaps less free). "Ought" can be stultifying (you ought to act respectfully, keep your front lawn free of weeds, and not do anything that will cause the neighbors to gossip) or wildly utopian (the world ought to be a place where we can all live happily ever after, with equivalent life chances, in flourishing, just societies, without conflict and undue hardship but not boring or without goals, where we can all exercise our capacities as we desire, grow organic vegetables in the morning, and play violin, football, or computer games in the afternoon). Any reasonably realistic vision of the good life must lie between these; we do want conventions, goals, and directions as well as the freedom to reject them. In fact, conventions and goals are meaningless in the absence of alternatives, freedom is meaningless without constraint, and life is boring without challenge.

Making freedom the centerpiece of a depiction of ethics runs up against two further challenges. First, behind any advocation of freedom there always looms the question of whether my freedom is not at someone else's expense. The tragic history of Zionism (and perhaps of all nationalisms) exemplifies this point. Second, any depiction of freedom as a universal existential or ethical condition needs to be purified of the connotations that come with "freedom" as a particular value. The word carries a great deal of ideological baggage since at least the Cold War, with respect to both politics and the market. It has hardly been a salient term beyond the sphere of the West, and to say this is not to join in the triumphalism of the West but to express a genuine doubt about its universal value.[7] It is certainly one of the tasks of an anthropological approach to ethics to question the prevalence and salience of freedom as a concept or value and to show how flourishing lives can be lived in the absence of such a concept. In Madagascar, as I briefly indicated, freedom is a practical outcome of the system of prohibitions, but it is hardly an explicit value in itself. Indeed, there, as in many places, perhaps especially in kinship-based societies, the idea of pure freedom would

6. But not on the analogy of games. See the remarks by Cavell cited below.

7. See also Mahmood 2005. In any case, by what neutral measure could we ascertain or compare actual freedom, even when broken down as "freedoms from" and "freedoms to"? (Berlin 2002).

be quite shocking and the condition a radically unethical one. To be free would be to repudiate others.

Freedom and Convention

If freedom is contrasted by some thinkers with determinism, for others the first thing to establish is the difference between the obedient following of rules or convention and the freedom, courage, and imagination to refuse or escape convention. Frequently these are distinguished as *ethical* and *moral*. However, the two terms are applied inconsistently in the literature and at times to opposite effect. The need for making such a distinction central comes from a particular approach to ethics and a history that are not mine. The distinction figures in interesting debates between Kantian and Nietzschean positions, the one premised on reason and rule and the other on imagination and freedom. The Kantian position enters social theory via Durkheim, while the Nietzschean one is developed in Foucault.[8] Those who adopt a version of the latter position do so in part from a resistance to the former that stems from one or more dissatisfactions with the idea of ethics or morality understood narrowly and normatively as the following of rules (albeit such adherence to rule is to be taken up *freely*, according to Kant).

Some thinkers seem to start from an intuition of the difference between doing what you are told and thinking for yourself. That is a fairly shallow distinction, since what you are told may sometimes be to go think for yourself, and thinking for yourself often leads to the conclusion to do what you have been told or what others are doing. External "conventions" often become internalized "principles." But more than this, it is impossible to simply do what you are told, since this doesn't take into account contingency, contradictory instructions, or the formation of a human self. Conversely, you cannot think entirely for yourself if you inhabit a common language with others—if you exist, as humans do, within some kind of community. So while this tension between accepting convention and, let us say, self-fashioning may be part of ethical experience and even of great salience in particular cultural contexts and historical circumstances, which might be periods described as revolutionary (say, recently in Egypt), neither pole can

8. Fassin (2012) observes in the introduction to his very useful collection that *moral* is the word of preference for those in the Kantian/Durkheimian legacy and *ethics* of those in the Aristotelian/Foucauldian legacy. Laidlaw (2014) offers a lucid and informative discussion of the two perspectives. See also Faubion's (2011) relinquishment of the term *moral* for *themitical*. I do not pursue a Foucauldian perspective here, but it is an extremely useful one, as work by authors such as Faubion (2011), Heywood (forthcoming), and Mahmood (2005) attests.

be justified intellectually as an absolute position. In philosophy, as might be imagined, the debate has been more complex than I have presented it here and takes diverse forms in particular intellectual contexts—for example, in the various ways in which mid-twentieth-century British analytic philosophers like Elizabeth Anscombe, Philippa Foot, and Bernard Williams rejected the narrow ideas of a prescriptive moral system held by some of their teachers—or, comparably, in French existentialism, German phenomenology, or American pragmatism.

While I share the urge to question bourgeois complacency and, of course, the pleasure in doing so, I think that one of the lessons of social theory (in contrast to abstract or passionate philosophy) has been that the distinction between convention and freedom is a false or limited opposition. Existential freedom of the kind idealized by Sartre is rarely encountered in ordinary life (and what he dismisses as bad faith can often be viewed with a good deal more charity). There is an inextricable connection, or productive tension, between freedom and obligation in practice, a relationship that is easier to see when approaching the subject ethnographically than by means of reified abstractions in theory.

Hence, while I remain skeptical of any idealization of absolute freedom, I do not see human action as an unthinking following of rules either. For that matter, neither did Durkheim. For Durkheim, despite all the attention given to his emphasis on the obligatory, rules exist not simply to curtail animal-like individuality or to enforce social order but to produce a kind of self-transcendence that makes human freedom possible or that *is*, in effect, human freedom (1973; see Hatch 1963). Ethnographically, it is also evident that people, both collectively and individually, often freely and deliberately submit to specific kinds of discipline in order to cultivate an ethical disposition in themselves or their children, as though the ordinary social rules or conventional cultural ends were not enough, but equally as though sheer freedom was at least as dangerous an alternative. We cannot think how to live in the absence of postulated ends and instantiated criteria, and we cannot actually live in the abstract or only in our minds.

The relation between freedom and rule or convention is evident also in the mundane fact that people are regularly faced with deciding among several competing or incommensurable conventional commitments or obligations. We might feel relatively obligated to spend holidays with family but relatively free to decide whether to spend Christmas with our own parents or those of our partner, and free also to rationalize the fact that we've decided to stay at home this year, go to Mexico, or convert to Islam instead. This entails practical judgment, which is a more useful and realistic concept than either freedom or rule, especially when the latter are understood as mutually exclusive alternatives, or distinct provinces of social life, or moments of social history. In other words, we are not free to live outside any rules or obligations, but we are both free and obliged to distinguish among them. Rather than speak of rules that we follow or break, it is more precise to talk about multiple criteria, diverse commitments, and incommensurable values. And rather than speaking of choosing among them, I think it is clearer to say that we exercise some kind of judgment with respect to them.[9]

My theoretical inspirations have been, on the one side, various modern interpretations of Aristotle's discussion of practical judgment and virtue (chapters 4 and 5 below) and, on the other side, ordinary language (chapters 8 and 11).[10] In neither of these conversations is the following of rules central; hence there is not an obvious or necessary distinction to be made between the two modalities of convention and freedom, to be distinguished as ethics and morality. Even when the distinction proves useful, for example, in observing social change, the further step by some to objectify ethics and morality as distinct entities of a quasi-positivistic social science is nothing short of absurd.[11] I use the words somewhat interchangeably but have come over time to prefer *ethics*. I cannot justify this on rational grounds; perhaps I prefer it because it is the word first and most commonly used in philosophy, the word with the Greek rather than the Latin root. Nevertheless, I do use the words *ethics* and *ethical* in more than one sense, and this needs to be clarified.

On the Meaning of *Ethical*

By *ethical* I do not mean, in the first instance, what is good or just, nor the kinds of prescriptions or theories that have been developed to tell us what is good or just; rather, I mean the simple but profound fact that our actions and words are susceptible to judgment according to whether and how they fit established criteria. So the ethical is not in the first instance what is done right or what ought to be done, but the conceptual possibility of doing right and of discriminating right from wrong, or better from worse. To go further, it is what marks the near impossibility of acting in ways that do not

9. On judgment, see further below. On incommensurability, see Lambek 1993b and chapter 10.

10. On the Aristotelian stream in anthropology, see the useful essay by Cheryl Mattingly (2012).

11. Hence, too, I start with the adjectival forms *ethical* and *moral*; ethics and morality are historically situated objectifications.

fall under, or are not susceptible to, description or evaluation according to such criteria. Not all human acts are ethical in the sense of good and just, and no human beings, a few saints possibly excepted, are good or just all of the time. But we are all always (almost always) subject to criteria, to acting, thinking, and being thought about with respect to them. Some would say the most salient ethical moments are when we no longer have criteria, but then we are responding precisely to their absence.

To be subject to evaluation, by ourselves no less than by others, with respect to how we meet criteria indicates a kind of passion or patiency that should offset any strong theory of action or agency (see below). Furthermore, it is to be subject to a sense of frequently failing to meet criteria adequately or of having to compromise between distinct criteria. We cannot be good and just consistently and completely. And we can certainly never be complacent about criteria. Or rather, complacency or obliviousness itself is a vice in the Aristotelian sense, its counterpart being over-scrupulousness or over-anxiety. Complacency may even be the master vice, just as *phronesis* is the master virtue.[12] (And if so, there may be a connection back to Nietzsche after all.)

The fact that we cannot meet all criteria fully, equally, and consistently produces difficult situations. These are the subjects of ethics in a second, more familiar sense or register, as it addresses "What we are to do when . . . ?" or "How can I do what is right . . . ?" Equally difficult are situations where there appear to be no criteria, where criteria fail us, or where the criteria are absolutely in contradiction to one another. These diverse kinds of situations are the subject of ethics qua reflection and of tragedy qua genre (certainly as Hegel described it), and they add a tragic dimension or shadow to life.

It is in these first two senses most fundamentally that I speak of the ethical condition; that is, I affirm that the human condition is an ethical condition.

In a third and more usual sense, *ethics* and *ethical* refer to acting correctly, judiciously, or virtuously according to established criteria, or at least attempting to do so, seeking the right actions to meet the criteria or the right criteria to meet the situation. Ethics in this sense is a manifestation of judgment, and an assertion about the positive value of certain actions. However, judgment itself is by no means always straightforward, especially with respect to the almost inevitable presence of competing or incommensurable criteria. The Kantian maxim of sticking absolutely to a universal

12. Can I say that I mean this remark in an abstract and descriptive rather than a normative sense?

rule or categorical imperative does not work in practice; judgment is practical insofar as it must continuously respond to changing situations.

In a fourth register, *ethics* refers to the body of established objectifications concerning what to do when and to the codification of judgment—proverbs, admonitions, codes, and rules. In a fifth sense it refers to the specialized work of ascertaining, discerning, or declaring authoritatively what *is* right and good, often performed by experts who draw on or develop the body of objectified knowledge and rules.[13] Sixth, and somewhat differently, the term is used to refer to visions of the good life to which the judgments and rules are meant to lead and to which they respond. Seventh, it refers to practices of self-cultivation and to educating others regarding a vision of the good life. And, in an eighth sense, it refers to reasoning and reflection on all these matters as they are developed in conversations within specific traditions, such as those of Western philosophy or in this introduction to a book of essays by an anthropologist. Such traditions can of course be oral as well as written and can be reproduced in embodied practices as well as reiterated words, or in some combination, as the variety of Asian arts like yoga illustrate. *Ethics* can also be used to refer to a particular attitude or approach to life, whether that is understood as one of disciplined self-improvement, deference to or care for others, ascetic withdrawal, or revolutionary ardor.

This enumerated list is of course an artificial and contingent product, running against my inclination not to objectify. In the end, and most generally, ethics is about how to live a human life and how that question is a part of the living of it.[14]

While the blurriness of these distinctions in practice can lead to a certain amount of confusion, it is also evident that when philosophers or anthropologists try too hard to distinguish or defend one from the others, the conversation quickly becomes stilted and produces systems that are simply untrue to experience. Some of the uses of "ethics" can be understood as different degrees of objectification or levels of generality or as different forms of interpretation of common human issues.[15] There is something about the

13. In light of the increasing prevalence of "audit culture," it is important to emphasize the shallowness of ethics in this sense. Ethics is not only about prescribing, adjudicating, monitoring, or criticizing, but also about understanding—and about exercising judgment as to which of these functions should carry more weight in any given context or how, over time, one comes to supersede another.

14. James Laidlaw has rightly queried whether the second phrase might be overly intellectualizing. I leave it in place for its provocation. Whether the question is intrinsic to ethical life is at once a matter for philosophical and empirical investigation.

15. Webb Keane (2010) has been particularly careful to describe the chain of objectification.

ethical that requires a sense of the whole, and discerning the relation of part to whole or token to type is part of the work of ethics itself. There is virtue in keeping things in perspective.

Action

The essays that follow bring a stream of thought from Aristotle—on ethics as practical activity (doing things) and on the centrality of judgment or practical reason—together with a stream of thought from J. L. Austin and Ludwig Wittgenstein on ordinary language, performative acts, and their affordance of criteria and judgment. I consider the relationship of the two modalities of action that I call *practice*, which is continuous, and *performance* (i.e., the performance of acts), which is discontinuous and discrete.

As I elaborate in chapter 11, I take *practice* as the relatively unmarked flow of action, including the habitual; it is action viewed or experienced as ongoing and, in effect, intransitive, the doing rather than the done. I use *performance* to describe action understood to be divided up and marked as specific and often deliberate and consequential acts—action viewed as discrete and transitive (chapter 9). These draw respectively from Aristotle's conception of practice and Austin's of performative acts. Although their insights work well together, Aristotle and Austin are often understood to contribute to quite different conversations.

Aristotle divides human activity into the theoretical, the practical, and the creative—that is, contemplation, action, and production—thinking, doing, and making. These are not discrete, mutually exclusive categories or phenomena, but they are good to think with, different ways of transecting a more complex whole. For Aristotle, ethics is an attribute of practice (praxis). Extending this a bit, we can say it speaks to what we *do*, rather than what we make or think abstractly, but also to the ways in which we understand and talk about what we do, and to the meaningful, effective, and consequential dimensions of acts. Ordinary language philosophy also talks about words in use—that is, in action—and one of the great insights of Austin (1962) is how in speaking we are also doing things. What we do in speaking is by no means restricted to things like referring, describing, or asking questions, but includes addressing, responding, exclaiming, greeting, naming, accepting, refusing, excusing, and the like—utterances that Austin called performative acts or described as carrying illocutionary force. Most interesting to Austin are those utterances that in saying what they do are actually doing it, as in promising, apologizing, thanking, and so forth. Austin was interested in describing and clarifying the different kinds of acts that can be carried out by means of speaking. While his work illustrates speech acts from a particular time and place and in a single language, the approach should be widely applicable. Thus in *Argonauts of the Western Pacific*, Bronislaw Malinowski (1922) described a whole set of quite specific kinds of acts that comprise the serious and great intercultural game of *kula* (the formalized yet strategic exchange and circulation of particular valuables) and that are identifiable in part by the performative utterances that announce and initiate or enact them, utterances that he called "spells" and that, interestingly, are structured like poetry (and to which we could compare various forms of prayer in the Abrahamic and Vedic traditions).[16]

Austin also wanted to understand the factors that make specific utterances legitimate and effective. He referred to these factors as "felicity conditions" and shifted the primary distinction from one between true and false sentences to one between happy and unhappy utterances, the latter missing or violating some felicity condition or conditions that would make them fully acceptable (1962).[17] Thinking about language in this way has profound implications for how we understand the ethical in human life, beginning with a consideration of the limits of "truth" as a criterion, or perhaps with a formulation of different kinds of truth (Rappaport 1999, 293–97), and with the fragility of action (a pervasive theme in Stanley Cavell).[18] Practice, in the sense of ongoing, relatively unmarked action, draws on criteria established performatively, but it can also violate them and is evaluated accordingly as "infelicitous" or as "untrue"' to one's word or acts rather than with respect to some external conditions, and is sometimes evaluated as "evil" in the sense of undermining the very mode of establishing criteria and commitment (Rappaport 1999). Performance, understood in Austin's sense of the performative, establishes the relevant criteria, but it can be infelicitous (ineffective, invalid), sometimes seriously so, leaving practice ambiguous. Austin (1970) also took up the different kinds of ways we can qualify or excuse our

16. Work on the poetics of performative utterances has been elegantly summarized and elaborated by Fleming and Lempert (2014). However, their project is at some level at odds with the one presented here. Arguing that reference to Austin is out of date betrays a deep misunderstanding of philosophical inquiry (are Plato and Aristotle also "out of date"?) and an ignorance of the ways in which Austin's ideas inform those of Cavell and Rappaport, among others.

17. Some obvious examples are a marriage ceremony conducted by someone without the authority to do so, where one of the parties is already married, or where the utterances are incorrectly pronounced, and so forth. The analysis of various kinds of felicity conditions is quite fascinating and should be read together with Austin's famous paper on excuses (1970). There remain many underexplored avenues here.

18. It also demonstrates how dependent the force of utterances is on extralinguistic features, as noted by Fleming and Lempert (2014), among others.

acts, as in the difference between saying "I did it by mistake" and "I did it by accident."

Thus, although starting from different premises and constituting different traditions, Aristotelian practice and ordinary language philosophy each place their central focus on human action—on the kinds of things human beings do, the ways in which we do them, and how we describe and evaluate their doing or being done (whether done by us or by others). Beginning in this way, we can then continue to think about how doing is related to making (poetics, creation, aesthetics) and thinking (reflection, abstraction, reason) and how it fits into living (being) more broadly. Thus, for example, Geertz (2000) titled an important early essay on fieldwork "Thinking as a Moral Act."

Once ethics is understood in relation to action (or, more strongly, as intrinsic to action), we can also grasp its temporality. We can attend to what is entailed in initiating acts and in executing (accomplishing) them, as well as in what they engender, what the consequences are. Ethics can be understood prospectively—*what shall we do?*—(intentions, goals, values to live by), retrospectively—*what have we done?*—(justifications, excuses, guilt, regrets, recriminations, retroactive descriptions, but also satisfactions), or as fundamentally present and of the moment—*this* is what are we doing!—(indexical, current, Heideggerian dwelling). Evaluation or judgment occurs before, during, and after the act. The consequentiality of performative acts is critical; here, in effect, acts become fact. Practice is the field of action in which new and successive acts and judgments arise and whose manifestation and interpretation are shaped by such acts and judgments.

We can compare consequences in various ways. I suggest that one critical axis of comparison is how long the effects or consequences of an act last or are expected or judged to last, how long a shadow they cast over subsequent practice and practical judgment, and, in a related vein, how long specific forms of responsibility hold, how long specific acts remain tethered to specific persons or persons to acts. How long before that favor you did for me or that insult I gave you can be explicitly returned, forgiven—or simply forgotten? This is a question that is raised in work on the gift (Mauss 1990) and addressed in practice theory (Bourdieu 1977); I take it up in different ways in chapter 13 with respect to the generation of value and in chapter 14 with respect to responsibility and the constitution of persons. I suggest in chapter 4 that memory itself is constituted through ethical judgment.

Some acts are indicated as more consequential than others through the circumstances of enactment; the elaboration of formal circumstances and heightened felicity conditions is one of the ways to define or describe what we call ritual (chapters 2, 8, and 9). But as Das shows (2012), the very slightest of actions, even those whose direction is concealed rather than flaunted, have consequences (see also Sidnell 2010). Consequences can also be divided into two kinds as indexed by Austin's distinction of the illocutionary and the perlocutionary functions of speech, each to be discussed further below. The illocutionary, one could say, operates at the level of the cultural and the public; it brings something new into being or puts things under a description. This can be a radically new description, as in a declaration of independence or a peace treaty, or it can be a reiteration or renewal of a description, as in daily greetings. These can be ranged according to the span of consequentiality just mentioned. The perlocutionary operates at the intersubjective or emotional level, shaping the tone and quality of response and relationships. One could speak of effects and affects, respectively.

Judgment

To develop the understanding of action, I build on two additional concepts, one drawn from Aristotle's account of virtuous practice and the other from Cavell's reflections on Austin on speaking. The first concept is that of judgment, or practical reasoning, *phronesis*. Practical judgment describes what is entailed in initiating and conducting a specific action—whether you jump in the floodwater to attempt to save a drowning child, at some risk to your own life; whether you give money to a registered charity or donate your time, and how much; whether you spend the evening working on tomorrow's lecture or playing with your children; whether you smile at the person sitting across from you or refrain from contact. In reflecting on these matters, it readily becomes apparent that practical judgment is at issue all the time and at issue with respect to matters large and small, broad in scope with respect to the entirety of our lives and narrow with respect to seemingly trivial, immediate, and everyday matters. Judgment in this sense can be extremely consequential or not. It also becomes clear that judgment ranges according to how immediate or deliberated and how tacit or explicit it is—shifting from relatively pure (cultivated) habit (or possibly built-in "nature") through agonized reflection. This is a continuum, and there seems to be no good reason for dividing it up and saying, for example, that on the one side, let's say the habitual, lies morality, and on the other side, let's say the explicitly reflective, lies the ethical.[19]

19. Compare the discussion on convention above.

The concept of judgment or practical reasoning speaks to the fact that whatever the scale, level of awareness, or consequentiality of an act, there are always alternatives, and selection among them may range in difficulty. Aristotle suggested that at any given moment there is a balance to be struck, for example, between being too generous and too mean, and that we can learn, more or less well, how to size up a situation and adjust an appropriate response accordingly. Excess on either side becomes vice, whereas acting just right in the circumstances is virtue. Given that every circumstance is different and all circumstances are changeable, we cannot provide a simple definition or content to any given virtue or recipe for its application—what is courageous in one instance could be foolhardy or cowardly in another. The right thing to do is not always evident. Perhaps Aristotle did not give enough attention to the fact that there may be conflict over which virtue to apply in a given situation, say justice versus compassion, or nurturance versus discipline, and how to find the balance among these. Part of the difficulty, as I argue in some of the chapters to follow, is that virtues can be incommensurable with one another; hence there is no simple formula to fit them together or adjudicate among them. Life continuously challenges us in all these respects but is also for that reason engaging and interesting. As a master or metavirtue that describes the full adjudication, *phronesis* can be translated as "wisdom."[20]

Judgment in my language refers in the first instance neither to the work of judges in courts of law nor to the judges in prize competitions (nor yet to the acts of divine beings), but to the ongoing work of discernment or practical reason that draws on criteria to inform and direct practice. The concept of practical reason or judgment (Aristotelian *phronesis*) begins with the idea that the good or right thing to do in a given set of circumstances, or how to do it, is not always obvious. We may learn to exercise judgment so that it goes smoothly, almost without saying, as a matter of virtuous character, but that does not make it simple. For Aristotle it is a matter of finding the right balance to fit the circumstances. Not only are circumstances always changing, but in social life there are always diverse calls upon our attention, competing criteria, obligations, values, desires, interests, relationships, and so on. To claim that choosing among them is easy or straightforward could be understood as itself a kind of rationalization. Aristotle thought the ability or disposition to do so was not strictly natural or innate but must be

20. At other places, different translations may be more appropriate. (Translation itself entails judgment!)

actively cultivated. Our initial judgment is often poor, and wisdom is not readily achieved.

I distinguish judgment from choice insofar as choice is a matter of calculation between commensurable goods, whereas judgment is deliberation in the face of incommensurable values (chapter 10). Choice is a clear-cut selection between mutually exclusive alternatives, whereas judgment exercises a balance. These are of course ideal types. As human beings we are subject to judging or discerning in this sense as we engage or refuse engagement (or merely consider, or simply never even imagine engagement) in various kinds of acts and relations.[21] Moreover, our acts and ultimately we ourselves are subject to judgment or discernment in this sense, both by ourselves and by others. This is what I mean when I say we are fundamentally ethical beings. This is not the same as to say we always do what is good, right, or just; if anything, it is to say how difficult it is to know how to do what is good, right or just in the circumstances. Doing good is, in effect, a matter of trying to do good. Rules may be offered to help, but they don't always work well in practice, and following the rule is often an expression of bad or inadequate judgment. My view does not discount acts that are, or are judged to be, unethical in the sense of not right, good, or just; I am *not* saying that anything goes. What I claim is that acts cannot be understood as entirely neutral; any act carried out, let us say by habit, could be criticized from some angle for being thoughtless, empty, or merely conventional, or it could be praised as judicious, principled, graceful, obedient, evidence of good character, or to the point.

We can distinguish whether practical reasoning produces actions, initial intentions, concluding verdicts, or normative beliefs (Streumer 2013), but I consider this more an empirical than a philosophical question; in other words, practical reasoning can have a variety of outcomes. Again, it depends in part on how explicit the reasoning is, when over the course of a given action or within the stream of practice it takes place, and what means exist to entextualize, narrativize, authorize, or objectify the outcomes. In a number of places in the essays that follow, I discuss the role of ritual as a means of enhancing illocutionary force and clarifying and publicizing acts and outcomes.

Judgment is to be distinguished from intention—and especially from local theories of intention. The weight put on individual intention is much

21. In light of current interest in post-humanism, I clarify that in speaking about human being, I am remaining neutral on the capacities of other species (or our commitments to them) and not attempting to reinforce some kind of grand divide.

stronger in some ideologies of personhood and in some contexts than others. People in northwest Madagascar sometimes understand their acts to be motivated by specific ancestors, to whose wishes they must defer. This is manifest not only in spirit possession but in where one lives, what jobs one takes on, and so forth. Judgment is at issue, but the process is not described simply as the carrying out of one's own intention. Conversely, to describe excessively self-interested or malicious behavior as practicing sorcery (*mamoriky*) is here to emphasize and bring together intention, bad judgment, and responsibility.

Two qualifications of Aristotle, or rather, of common depictions of Aristotle, are in order. First, in contrast to some virtue theorists, I do not think that in any given circumstance the right thing to do is necessarily obvious to the person of good character nor that the virtues to apply are necessarily consistent with one another. For example, the tension between justice and compassion might remain irresolvable; *phronesis* is precisely the metavirtue of balancing among the virtues. It further entails adjusting between incommensurable values—that is, values that do not meet fully along a single dimension or criterion, as in adjusting, for example, between devotion to one's job and to one's children. This is one reason we say we cannot put a price on them; to do so would render them falsely commensurate (subject to a common measure; see chapter 10). That is exactly why judgment is called for and why it is often neither evident, nor easy, nor likely to produce common agreement. Hence this is also why it changes according to circumstances.

A further qualification to Aristotle's depiction of virtuous judgment lies in the observation that there are always disruptions.[22] This is a point developed in a variety of ways by Jonathan Lear (2000, 2011) in his confrontation of Greek thought with psychoanalysis. Such disruptions are characterized not only by bad judgment, self-reflection, indecision, retraction, or reversal, but they can produce real disorientation, vertigo, and also, as Lear insists, renewed enthusiasm and commitment. If ethics is immanent to society or sociality, this does not mean that virtuous practice goes without saying, that it appears either as mechanical or as a kind of refined sophistication in the manner of the Bourdivine (Bourdieusian) Parisian game player. Cheryl Mattingly (2012) and James Laidlaw (2014) have each lucidly addressed this point.

22. A disruption recognized by Aristotle is temporary failure of the will—what he calls "incontinence."

Indeed, for Aristotle wise judgment is not tacit but entails reflection and feeling.[23] Reflection can occur before, during, and after the act. Put another way, ethical practice entails acknowledgment of what one is about to do, is doing, or has done. As judgment is the defining feature of the ethical dimension of practice, so acknowledgment is the quintessential ethical act, a point developed in the work of Stanley Cavell. At certain moments we owe people an acknowledgment and often we owe it to ourselves.

Acknowledgment

Acknowledgment is perhaps the primary or exemplary ethical act. In my reading of Cavell, it means first of all that I must acknowledge my voice and actions, that it is *I* who have done or said this, and that I bear some responsibility, am in some relation to the intention, the act, and the consequence (chapters 11 and 13). Cavell's discussion is elaborate and profound, but it is culturally neutral. The diverse ways in which diverse societies have addressed the broader question of the allocation of responsibility is one that has long fascinated anthropologists. Anthropologists have focused particularly on vehicles for attribution after the fact, from witchcraft to courts of law.[24] There is also the very significant matter of when the *I* is actually a *we*, as in societies where I am liable for the acts of my brother and in the ambiguity of a concept like "corporate responsibility." But beneath all this is the grammar and pragmatics of speaking; the use of pronouns and other markers, as well as of bodily gestures to indicate such things as presence, deliberateness, confidence, sincerity, deference, recognition, apology, regret, pleasure, and the like.

The Azande offer a famous illustration of acknowledgment. The Azande, in Evans-Pritchard's account (1937), are stuck with witchcraft, not least when they are accused of being witches themselves. But at the same time, they are relatively free to exercise their judgment with respect to their responses to particular misfortunes, whether to put them under the inspection of oracles or not. Likewise, Azande accused of witchcraft must judge their response; if they are sensible, they are likely to say, "If it was I who was responsible, may it now be retracted." Note how the ethical intervention here

23. For Aristotle, *phronesis* entails a conjunction of doing the right thing, feeling the right way about it, and doing it for the right reasons; action, intention, and feelings have to be aligned. My thanks to Simon Lambek (personal communication) for phrasing it so succinctly for me.

24. We might distinguish acknowledging responsibility for acts done from accepting responsibility for things to be done or to happen, or for the care of others, and each of these from the immediate or concurrent acknowledgment of one's actions while performing them.

is one of speech and carries what Austin referred to as illocutionary force. It is at once an acknowledgment of the accusation, of the suffering of the Other, and of the possibility of one's own responsibility, as well as a wish for the well-being of the Other and a retraction of the force of witchcraft.

Cavell extends his reflections on acknowledgment from the tethering of the act to the *I* (the actor) to make the point that one must also acknowledge the Other. This means not only recognizing others as fellow human beings but also recognizing their difference from oneself (and presumably from one another), their autonomy, the fact that they may see things differently, have different agendas, and so forth. What makes Cavell's writing on these topics so exquisite is that he never moralizes and always recognizes (acknowledges) the difficulty of acknowledgment, the burden or weight it carries, and the temptation to see or do things differently, for example, in a form of skepticism that might deny the reality of my act or assert that I cannot know your difference or that you are separate from me.

Of course, simple acknowledgment rapidly expands (or deteriorates) into justification. Anthropologists study the reasons people give for what they do: how they describe acts of commission or omission, as committed by themselves or others; how they explain giving more attention to one set of parents than another; how they live with the fact that there are homeless and hungry people down the street or across town; how they justify killing in warfare or infanticide; how they, or we, live with moral queasiness about the state of the world and turn that into religious piety, or existentialism, or humanitarianism, or political activism, or critique of various stripes, maybe even into academic anthropology. Anthropologists study how religious people live with passionate investment in redemption while recognizing the ultimate inadequacy of any human return for divine gifts and how nonreligious people justify their own preoccupations. And they study how people abstract and objectify all these justifications into and with respect to the discursive fields and professional codes that some people take to be the actual substance of ethics.

Of course, to reiterate a point made in *Ordinary Ethics*, ethics does not enter the picture only with such rationalized objectifications as professional codes or with respect to big-ticket items or exceptional circumstances, such as abortion or warfare, but inflects our practice all of the time. Nothing could be more ordinary than hailing someone by name or kinship term or saying good morning; greetings themselves are forms of practical acknowledgment. As Jack Sidnell (2010) has shown by means of conversational analysis, judgment occurs by the microsecond.

Cavell acknowledges the fact of human ambivalence and the difficulty of finding one's voice so that one can fully mean what one says, fully acknowledge one's utterances as one's own (*owning* them, as we say), and fully recognize the separateness (but also the connections) between voices. Of course, there are many questions of cultural and linguistic difference in the characterization of voice and interaction that need to be addressed. Societies balance a forensic conceptualization of the person with what I call a mimetic one (chapter 14). For spirit possession, as I have encountered it in Mayotte and northwest Madagascar, voice is the central issue, and a given individual can speak with multiple voices. Following both Freud and Aristotle, Lear (2013) has recently emphasized the importance of harmonizing (as opposed to unifying) one's voices, but as he also elaborates, matters of voice are deeply linked to the question of irony.

Irony

In chapter 7 I offer a discussion of irony in relation to agency. When I presented it orally, I was often met with puzzlement and told that what I was describing was not irony. Hence I have been very heartened to come across Jonathan Lear's discerning account. Lear makes the very helpful observation that most dictionary definitions of irony are shallow or incorrect. "The irony about irony is that it is almost impossible to find out what it means . . . using standard resources—a dictionary, encyclopaedia, or introductory article—to come to understand the deeper and more significant meaning of the concept" (2003, 65). Irony in the deep sense is quite distinct from sarcasm or from meaning the opposite of what one says. When Kierkegaard asks, "Is there a Christian in all of Christendom?" his irony is in earnest, neither feigning ignorance nor implying that he knows something his addressees don't. Both Socrates and Kierkegaard are asking genuine questions and recognizing that "genuinely living with these questions as continually renewed questions—is a lifetime task" (75). Irony, for Lear, is deeply ethical, in the sense of being concerned with how to live; it prompts one to continually interrogate oneself about the gap between the pretense of being who one claims to be and the aspiration to become that person.[25]

Following Alexander Nehamas (1998), I argue that irony encompasses the recognition of one's own uncertainty and of acknowledging at times

25. Describing a "moral peculiarity" of fieldwork as "anthropological irony," Geertz asserts that "Irony rests, of course, on a perception of the way in which reality derides merely human views of it, reduces grand attitudes and large hopes to self-mockery" (2000, 29). Later, he elaborates, in a way that seems more useful than recourse to self-mockery, that "the relationship between an anthropologist and an informant rests on a set of partial fictions half seen-through" (34).

that one does not know what one wants, the extent of one's responsibility for certain actions, how to live, or even who one is. It names the recognition that one is subject to multiple and possibly competing, contradictory, or incommensurable aims and claims, intentions, desires, or commitments; that there are too many criteria, or too few. It entails recognition of being simultaneously both free and determined.

Kierkegaard himself is both the great theorist of irony and the great ironist. In the synopsis of his dissertation on irony he wrote, "Just as philosophy begins with doubt, so a truly human life begins with irony" (2001, 28). Kierkegaard's life exemplifies his thought, especially as he wrote under various pseudonyms, a practice he called *polyonymity* and that addresses the problem of voice from a different but complementary angle to that of Cavell and one that has striking affinities to spirit possession.[26]

At the conjuncture of necessity and impossibility, ethical recognition is not only tragic but ironic. Witchcraft, in Evans-Pritchard's argument, is supposed to explain unfortunate events. But it also raises a good deal of uncertainty. One cannot know before the fact who the witch is, or where and when a witch will strike next. One cannot know whether one may be accused of being a witch oneself—or even whether the accusation might be correct. In fact, the presumption or diagnosis of witchcraft raises more questions than it answers. Who was the witch responsible for this event? Who are the witches among us? Why, really, do they act as they do? What, actually, am *I* capable of doing? To paraphrase Kierkegaard, "Is there a person truly not a witch in all of Zandeland?"

The accused responds by acknowledging the possibility that he is a witch. The ethical scene here affords a kind of irony that is not merely the irony that we cannot know the intentions of others or that as we plan our life projects and programs, they are being undermined by other forces. Rather, it is the recognition that we cannot fully know our own intentions. This is, of course, not restricted to the Azande, or to witchcraft, or other purely negative acts. Chapter 6 addresses these matters with respect to the attribution of justifiable anger, while chapter 8 takes up the question of how one can know that one is in fact possessed by a spirit and not merely performing as if one were. As Paul Antze has aptly put it, "If it is true, as Freud says, that much of our life is driven by impulses lying outside of consciousness, and that the unconscious consists precisely in what is opposed or contrary, what is 'incompatible with the ego,' then it becomes much harder to be sure what

26. Some of the phrases in this paragraph are taken from Lambek, in press (a). See also Lambek 2010a.

our actions mean or even who is acting. To what extent are we the authors of anything we do? Can we ever know our own intentions? Does knowing make a difference?" (2003, 104). Or as I put it (after Nehamas 1998), *What irony frequently throws into question is intentionality itself.* No account of the ethical would be complete without recognizing this. The relevant issues are how ethical subjects recognize it; how discursive forms, rituals, and disciplinary practices acknowledge or conceal it; what we do with such (absence of) knowledge; and how claims to moral superiority may contain their own undoing.

Ritual

Perhaps the major limitation of focusing exclusively on practical judgment is that it does not address the question of how judgment is possible in the first place. Whence come the criteria on the basis of which to exercise judgment, render justifications, or authorize the judgments and justifications made? Whence come the criteria appropriate for a given situation, including the criteria that define a situation as such in the first place? I argue that a source of criteria lies in the act of speaking itself and especially in the utterances found in ritual.

Criteria emerge through illocutionary action. Once I perform the act of marriage, the criteria that apply to me and to my behavior henceforward change. My behavior itself may not change, but it is subject to different evaluation. Marriage is an obvious example, but the effects are equivalent for any rite of passage and indeed any ritual, or even such ostensibly trivial matters as making an appointment. Among Azande, both the ritualized accusation of witchcraft and the ritualized apology put the protagonists and their relationships under particular descriptions and do so with respect to new or renewed criteria. Performativity establishes who we are in relation to one another, to ourselves, and to the world; that is to say, it establishes the criteria by which our conduct—as a committed partner, a citizen, a Christian, Muslim, Hindu, Jew, or Zande, but also as a parent, child, friend, man or woman, or simple human being—ought to be carried out and can be evaluated. It does not determine conduct or practice, but it establishes the relevance of specific criteria to practice and the nature of our commitments to persons and projects. In its public and definitive qualities it offsets the uncertainty and indeterminacy described by irony.

If acknowledgment is the basic ethical function of speech, it manifests at multiple levels of explicitness, from the barely registered (such as the fact that even primarily locutionary utterances have an illocutionary dimension in which, at the least, we claim implicitly that our words have a meaning and that we stand by them)[27] to the most explicit, elaborated, and consequential, as found in what we call law and ritual. Most philosophers ignore or underplay ritual and the progression of formality of speech and its consequences. Hence this is one place where anthropologists can usefully contribute. Ritual acts are ones in which performativity, as Austin described it, has an explicit and central role. The acts can be deeply meaningful, consequential, and formal, with various embellishments adding weight to the performative core. As Roy Rappaport (1999), who draws heavily on Austin, notes, three key features of ritual acts are that they are embodied, highly formalized, and embedded within what he called liturgical orders, that is, in sequential and hierarchical relation to other ritual acts.

Following arguments developed by Rappaport, I see ritual, or rather the illocutionary properties it elaborates and magnifies (including specification of the felicity conditions), as being consequential for ethical relations and indeed necessary in establishing both the distinctions or criteria for ethical life and the commitment of persons to specific alternatives (relationships, roles, identities, projects, etc.) rather than to others.

In his monumental work on ritual and religion, Rappaport (1999) notes the uncertainty made available by language, namely, the fact that we can use language both to lie and to imagine alternative worlds and courses of action. Hence we may be skeptical or uncertain of what others say to us and be ambivalent, inconsistent, or untrustworthy ourselves. Rappaport argues that ritual establishes both what he calls social contract and certainty, claiming that it offsets the capacities that language gives us to lie and to offer uncertain or uncommitted alternatives. Ritual does so by offering public enactments of commitment to particular statements and particular courses of action as well as acceptance of the very means that establish such things. Participating in a ritual indicates acceptance of the terms of the ritual in general (e.g., baptism) and of the particular enactment (*this* child's baptism). It thus places the child under a certain description, identifying him as a Christian, with all its entailments, and the other participants as party to that transformation (as officiants, kin, godparents, witnesses, etc.), and simultaneously authorizes the description and the process of making this kind

27. Further discussion would include the significant question of the relationship between the speaker and the voice, a matter raised by Goffman (1959) and discussed in subsequent work by linguistic anthropologists (e.g., Urban 1989 on de-quotation and Sidnell 2009 on footing), as well as by Cavell.

of description. It is through ritual that persons, relationships, and projects are constituted and described as specific kinds and in individual instances.

Here then are two reasons, uncertainty and ambivalence, as to why ethics cannot be a purely subjective matter and hence a matter of either pure freedom or pure biology, but subsists in reference and relation to public conventional formulations, acts, and utterances that are precise, certain and unambiguous.[28] Such public acts provide criteria needed to reduce uncertainty, not just with respect to specific judgments, but also with respect to specific commitments and, indeed, to who we are.

Whereas Rappaport saw ritual as redressing certain effects of language and hence as a necessary complement to language as a constitutive element of human society or the human condition, it is more precise and truer to his source in Austin to say that if language in its semantic or locutionary dimensions generates uncertainty, in the senses Rappaport explicates, it simultaneously generates certainty or at least commitment in its pragmatic or illocutionary dimensions. This is more in line with the reading of Austin offered by Cavell, in which every utterance may carry the illocutionary entailment of meaning what we say (1976) and equally imposes an acknowledgment on the part of the addressee.

In several chapters I suggest that many of the properties Rappaport attributes specifically to ritual are characteristic of the illocutionary force of all utterances, across a range of formality and explicitness, including the relatively informal ones of everyday courtesies. Even "yes" or "I know" are acts carrying illocutionary force. As Cavell puts it, they are "*similar* to 'I promise' *in a specific respect*, . . . namely, that *you give others your word*." Cavell continues, "*this* connection (this inner connection . . .) between claiming to know and making a promise . . . reveals human speech to be radically, in each uttered word, ethical. Speaking, or failing to speak, to another is as subject to responsibility, say to further response, as touching, or failing to touch, another." (2010, 320–21; his italics).

Nevertheless, rituals are distinctive; they are marked and deliberate interventions in the stream of practice, producing definitive transformations that allow one to speak of before and after. As such, they mark and sometimes measure the passage of time.[29] As Maurice Bloch has also demonstrated

28. However, if performative acts like those of the Zande oracle reduce uncertainty or produce certainty, that is not to say they alleviate anxiety or that their very existence may not produce or enhance it. Anticipating the results of the oracle would certainly not be a matter of equanimity for anyone whose name might be invoked.

29. Some of these points are also made by E. R. Leach (1961) on time. One can also speak of the temporality of ritual enactment itself, which frequently manifests as a three-stage process,

(1989b), ritual shifts the weight or balance from the locutionary to the illocutionary function or force of ordinary speaking so that the latter comes to outweigh the former and, moreover, is usually witnessed or authorized by more than merely a single speaker and addressee. This is especially evident with respect to what Rappaport called "ultimate sacred postulates," which are in effect semantically empty ("informationless") utterances and hence devoid of locutionary function or referential meaning while charged with illocutionary force, as in blessing or cursing. As part of liturgical orders, each utterance also carries the weight of multiple invocations within the imagined past and present community.

Performance includes a spectrum from fundamental and profoundly realized but highly formalized and specific ritual acts, such as the transubstantiation and the ingestion of Christ, through those practices we refer to as simple etiquette, to the illocutionary force of any and every utterance. One can be put under a description as a fellow human being, a saint or a sociopath, an enemy, refugee, or citizen, an invited dinner guest or unwelcome interloper, dignified or shamed. Performativity can transform tacit processes or understandings into explicit descriptions, acts into facts, or the inchoate into structure, and consign to the background the range of what is possible but unsaid or not done, while foregrounding the specificity of what is said or done and must now be acknowledged *as* said and done.[30] And of course, within any given social field, the divisions can become more elaborate and the criteria more specific, producing various modes of refinement—the sorts of distinctions made evident in J. L. Austin's (1970) wonderful discussion of kinds of excuses or in Jane Austen's ironic attunement to social form.

When I conducted fieldwork in Mayotte, exchanges of acts of prayer over and on behalf of one another were very common. But performative acts are not uniformly positive. In Mayotte sorcery was sometimes depicted with lurid details of dancing naked on a new grave or bribing a spirit with a bloody animal sacrifice to do one's bidding. In the end, it was understood as someone taking responsibility for and satisfaction from the misfortunes of others through a performative act (Lambek 1993b, 262). An act of sorcery is a kind of decisive acknowledgment to oneself before the fact that, should

as famously discerned by Arnold van Gennep (1960) and elucidated by Victor Turner (1969). From a phenomenological perspective, rituals also "take place"—bear ontological significance and demarcate, ground, and sanctify places as they do times; indeed, they unify place and time.

30. Maurice Bloch (personal communication) challenges this point, insofar as "the whole point about performatives is that they create something that does not exist before the performance. So they can't possibly make explicit something which exists elsewhere." But I am saying that rendering the tacit into the explicit is precisely a matter of creating something new.

so-and-so fall ill, I am happy to consider this my doing (my responsibility). This is a deliberate act, but it is an act, as philosophers say, of placing something under a description.

As in Zande witchcraft, the act of sorcery in Mayotte is understood as distinct from the direct material causes of the misfortune, whether conceived as operating through nature, termites, malicious spirits, or God. However the performative act is at one level of abstraction from material causality beyond what the Azande and Evans-Pritchard call witchcraft; it is not spontaneous or unrecognized by the agent, not discernable in the bowels of the sorcerer. Moreover, its direct effects lie only in the ethical, not the material realm; it does not produce the misfortune, only the accountability for it, before God and oneself. In Mayotte, to take on the responsibility or satisfaction for another's misfortune is a deliberate act of judgment instantiated by means of a specific kind of utterance. And as a deliberate act, it undoubtedly occurs with far less frequency than diagnoses or cures of sorcery (themselves each distinct performative acts) would suppose. Given the possibility of schadenfreude, there is room for ambiguity as to what one might have liked to do, but unlike the Azande, who cannot be sure whether the accusation against them is unjustified, the person in Mayotte knows whether or not she committed sorcery–that is, whether she committed herself to sorcery. The catch is that if accused unjustly, she has no means to prove her innocence.

It is worth noting a difference between my arguments and the profound model elaborated by Bloch. I posit a less sharp break between what is ritual and what is everyday communication than does Bloch.[31] At the root of our (friendly) dispute is whether ritual is intrinsic to social life (as both Durkheim and Rappaport saw it) or is an accretion (as Bloch, drawing on Marx, sees it). This debate speaks to the origin and location of the criteria and values necessary for ethical life. Do rituals or the broad range of illocutionary utterances generate primary values—or do they invert, distort, and mystify them? I would say the answer is not exclusively one or the other.[32]

Put another way, does illocutionary force, as embedded in liturgical orders, constitute the worlds in which people live and establish relations, exercise judgment, make choices, and take on projects—or does it trouble and disguise their common sense? Bloch's interventions demonstrate

31. See, for example, Bloch 1989a and his other important essays on ritual (2004), as well as on deference (2005). I also belatedly acknowledge the very stimulating book by Humphrey and Laidlaw (1994), whose position on ritual as a mode of action in which meaningful intention is intentionally displaced is distinct from but close to those of Bloch, Rappaport, and the one elaborated in these essays. The same interest holds for the essay by Seligman et al. (2008).

32. I suspect Bloch would agree with me on this point.

that these worlds are constituted by means of various kinds of inequality and injustice (whatever the criteria for ethical discernment). Indeed, ritual naturalizes certain forms of inequality and injustice, so that ethical criteria will be attributed differentially. Thus, most social worlds are constituted by hierarchies of gender, birth, and so forth that do not appear to overly trouble the majority of their inhabitants. One and the same process produces the criteria both for a certain kind of ethical discernment in some relations and for its absence or denial in other relations. This situation returns us to the issue that makes some thinkers want to distinguish sharply between ethics and morality, the one indicating accepting and following conventionalized forms of relations, and the other, seeing through them and challenging them. Moreover, when the reproduction of criteria through the enactment of liturgical order gets disrupted, there is confusion and sometimes reactionary violence, but also the possibility for contestation and positive change. Here the question of public mood (Fassin 2013) also becomes relevant.

Nevertheless, even armed with an understanding of the conservative and at times repressive functions of ritual ordering, the way forward is not clear. As Louis Dumont (1970, 1986) has suggested, replacing a world of hierarchy with one of individualism is not necessarily all for the good. And as the critiques of modernity have shown, the liberal constitution of ostensibly equal persons (qua individual human beings) embedded in capitalist relations of radical economic and political inequality is hardly satisfactory. Here we abut debates about the universal applicability of human rights discourse and legislation and the relationship of ethics to politics and to law as well as to ritual and religion.

I have been giving preeminence to ritual rather than to regimes of ethics and hence putting aside the question of the sort of historical break discerned by Foucault, Asad, and other commentators to characterize modernity. As Alex Beliaev (personal communication) astutely remarks, my "framework of 'ordinary ethics' . . . suggests that action is best [or first] understood in terms of the performative criteria which authorize it rather than in terms of an external body of thought which legitimates it."

The Ordinary

One way to think about ethics that does not depend on differentiating ritual from other forms of acting and speaking is by means of the ordinary. The ordinary is a subtle concept, whose meaning is never precisely defined (perhaps it is too ordinary for that) but should emerge in what follows.

Within anthropology, no one writes with greater delicacy and perspicacity on the ordinary than Veena Das (2007, 2012). For Das (as for me) ethics lies first *within* the ordinary rather than exemplifying an attempt to escape it or making a purchase outside it. (Hence too, ritual is an intrinsic form of language, a part of ordinary language rather than parasitic on it or transcendent of it.) Ethical judgment is found among "ordinary" people in "everyday" contexts; it is simply a part of life, a necessary part of living life, life lived with others, and not the purview of metaphysicians speaking or thinking at arm's length from that life. Das points out that ethical "work is done not by orienting oneself to transcendental, objectively agreed upon value but rather through the cultivation of sensibilities *within* the everyday" and that "ethics and morality on the register of the ordinary are more like threads woven into the weave of life rather than notions that stand out and call attention to themselves through dramatic enactments and heroic struggles of good versus evil" (2012, 134). Like me, she refuses a sharp distinction between two kinds of stances and suggests that striving for an "eventual everyday" does not entail a sharp break from either convention or the exceptional events that some thinkers (like Badiou) seek and admire. One could call it slow and patient work, rather than dramatic or disruptive. Das addresses all this in a context of urban poverty and violence, but of course poverty and violence are not prerequisites for this kind of activity, which is relevant for any set of social and historical circumstances.

As Das beautifully puts it, the task of the anthropologist is to show the ethical "growing within the forms of life that people inhabit" (2012, 136) rather than to elicit opinions or catalogue practices. Sometimes such growth leads to an explicit rule or justification but not always. Ethics is "more than mere fulfillment of social obligations demanded by rules and regulations" (137) and more than the spiritual exercises or profundities offered by philosophers, lying rather in "the small disciplines that ordinary people perform in their everyday life to hold life as the natural expression of ethics" (139). Das emphasizes the tactful qualities of ethical practice. She shows too how the unethical always shadows the ethical, that "the sensibility by which we recognize the ethical in the small acts of everyday life also alerts us to the lethal ways in which our capacity to hurt others might also be expressed in completely quotidian ways" (142).

To her picture I add the way illocutionary acts generate the criteria that inform these quiet interactions and interventions. But such acts themselves can be contingent. Cavell develops this point in showing that ethical practice cannot be understood by means of an analogy with games. What counts as a move in a game is settled in advance, but this is not true of life. "In games, what the other person is doing, the goal he aims for, his way, is clear; what it is you tell him to do is defined; what alternatives he can take are fixed; what it would mean to say, the grounds upon which you say, that one course is better than another are part of the game; whether he has done it is settled. In morality none of this is so" (Bates 2003, 35–36, citing Cavell 1999, 324). Cavell continues,

> Our way is neither clear nor simple; we are often lost. What you are said to do can have the most various descriptions; under some you will know that you are doing it, under others you will not, under some your act will seem unjust to you, under others not. What alternatives we can and must take are not fixed, but chosen; and thereby fix us. What is better than what else is not given, but must be created in what we care about. Whether we have done what we have undertaken is a matter of how far we can see our responsibilities, and see them through. ("Did you help him?"; "Did you get him the message?"; "Did you really make your position clear?"; "Did you do all you could?") What we are responsible for doing, is, ineluctably, *what in fact happens*. But *that* will be described in as many ways as our actions themselves. (1999, 324)

Cavell goes on to say that this responsibility is only bearable because of the presence of what he calls elaboratives—that is, words that can be used to defend, justify, excuse, apologize for, or otherwise rationalize our acts.

The ordinary refers to "what we say when . . ." or rather, what we say when we don't stop to think too long, too abstractly, theoretically, or self-consciously about what to say, but simply and effectively say it. The ordinary points to the ground and sufficiency of our language, our ability to say what we mean and be understood by others, to rely on shared criteria even when we do not share specific ideas or arguments, our ability simply to converse and to mean what we say. However leaving things there would take the ordinary too much for granted, seeing it as a fact rather than an always fragile achievement. Wittgenstein and Cavell suggest further that perhaps we have not reached, or do not reach, the ordinary, and that perhaps we are caught up in language where we cannot mean what we say or do not realize that we cannot say what we would mean.[33]

As Sandra Laugier puts it, "Cavell shows at once the fragility and the depth of our agreements, and he seeks out the very nature of the necessity that emerges, for Wittgenstein, from our human form of life" (2005, 86).

33. Not reaching the ordinary might be understood as akin to Freud's never quite achieving "cure" or happiness.

Sometimes we are at a loss for words or cannot find in the language or languages available to us the words to mark sufficiently or precisely the differences in kinds of acts and actions that we encounter, engage in, or find ourselves engaged in, engaged with, or engaged upon. Here it is not only that words uttered performatively put events (and persons, relationships, affects, objects, acts) under a description, but also whether we are able to find the words adequate to the description of the circumstances or events.[34] We might also stop to consider the fate of those who speak a different language from those around them, say because they are lost or captured, or those, like higher functioning autistic persons perhaps, who do not share our criteria and yet somehow get by.[35]

The question is not simply whether we mean what we say in the sense of getting the words right, or right in the circumstances, but what we say in speaking the words, whether we mean what we say in the sense of really *meaning* it, of standing by our words, of what we *do* when. For some people it is easy to say "I'm sorry" or "I love you" without "really meaning" it, or with tacit acknowledgment that they mean something by it different from what their addressee will take from it.

And the question is raised, What would it mean to really *mean* it? To speak without simply conforming to convention, we must have something to say, and where do we find that? How do we develop or cultivate a voice, and how do we ensure that that voice is true to itself and finds the words that enable it to be true to itself? How does performance escape mere iteration (chapter 8 below)? If ordinary language is sufficient and simply there, what enables us to use it well? What motivates us to go beyond the ordinary to do philosophy (or anthropology or religion)? What can we mean in those language games that we cannot mean in ordinary talk? Perhaps the point of philosophy is to redirect us back toward the ordinary and to appreciate its strengths and accept its limitations, to realize that it is what we have.

Ordinary language is "founded on nothing but itself" (Laugier 2005, 87). This "revelation of a truth about ourselves that we do not want to recognize, . . . which Cavell defines as 'the absence of foundation or of guarantee for our finitude, for creatures endowed with language and subject to their powers and their weaknesses, subject to their mortal condition'—does not

34. This is a problem faced by all writers and perhaps solved by great poets. I take these ideas from Laugier's discussion of Austin and Cavell, in which she defines a form of truth as being "a *harmony* between words and world" (2005, 98; her emphasis), distinguishing this from the "traditional analytic terms of realism or correspondence" (98). Harmony corresponds to Cavell's invocation of attunement.

35. On the ethical worlds of people with autism, see Paul Antze 2010.

come here as a relief, or a deliverance, but rather is an acknowledgment of finitude and of the everyday" (87).[36] The adequacy of language is to be found in "the entanglement, the reciprocal involvement of language and life" (87).

Cavell's response is to situate the precariousness of the ordinary: "One struggle is between criteria (i.e., the ordinary) and skepticism (the desire for the empty, freedom from myself); another is between the ordinary and the aphoristic (the desire for the transcendental, for a satisfaction out of the ordinary that is not provided by the provision of language games, that indeed will eventually be disappointed by the correction in language games)" (Cavell 2005a, 170). The ordinary is precarious insofar as criteria don't establish the existence of things with certainty but merely tell us what kinds of things they are, "thus leaving open what kind of issue is posed by the sense of needing some further proof of existence—so that criteria do not 'fall short' in the specification of the real. The sense of their falling short lies in us, creates, or accounts for what I call a disappointment in our knowledge, which nothing short of a new future, a new stance of humanity, could overcome" (166).

Cavell's is a kind of post-religious stance, and one might note in comparison how ritual in Rappaport's argument is meant to contain skepticism and to provide at least moments of certainty, or a glimpse of what certainty might be, as well as how religion can afford the aphoristic or transcendental. For Rappaport, ritual itself partakes of and contributes to (sanctifies) the ordinary in the sense discussed above, and there is no sharp or definitive break between the ordinary and the extraordinary; religion is immanent as much as it is transcendental (Lambek 2013a).

Passion

A further dimension of the ethical condition is certainly emotional. How emotion is linked to action and hence to ethics is a complex matter and will not be resolved here. Just as humans are born with the capacity—and indeed the necessity—to acquire language, so too perhaps with the capacity and need for ethics, and these may be interrelated from the start. Studies of developmental cognition and infant socialization—as well as the ordinary experience of living as and with children—make this appear very likely.[37] Whether there are primary or universal ethical emotions or dispositions, say for empathy or trust, or how they can best be named, is not my subject

36. Laugier does not give a source for this quotation.

37. See the fine work on linguistic and ethical socialization by Alan Rumsey (2010).

here, although they too surely contribute to what I am calling the ethical condition.[38] Where developmental psychologist Jerome Kagan (1987, x) speaks of "a biologically based preparedness to judge right from wrong," I am interested in the tools and enactment of judgment. That is to say, I pick up the subject from language and culture, from linguistically mediated and culturally informed social interaction.

Geertz and Rappaport each emphasize the public dimension of action and the way collective symbols or rituals are able to evade the uncertainty that emotional flux and inner feelings bring to social thought and action. Where Rappaport takes Austin in one direction, emphasizing both the canonical, reiterated quality of illocutionary utterances and their placement within liturgical orders, as well as the heightened assurance such placement brings, Cavell takes Austin in another direction, emphasizing not only the everyday nature and pervasiveness of performativity but equally the unpredictability and risk of performance inflected by what Cavell in a striking phrase calls "the disorders of desire" (2005a, 185). While Austin largely ignored perlocutionary effects, these are taken up in an original way by Cavell with respect to what he calls "passionate utterances." Whereas the illocutionary has an authorized "I" (or "we") frequently uttering what Rappaport called a canonical statement or participating in liturgical order, in passionate utterances the "I" is not authorized, but speaks directly from the heart, as it were, and it is the indexical dimension that is salient. Moreover, whereas (at least in English) the illocutionary is marked by the first person pronoun, the perlocutionary is weighted to the addressee, the "you." Rather than distinguishing two different kinds of utterances then, as Cavell sometimes seems to imply, one could say that the perlocutionary function attends to the quality of reception and its rebounding impact on the speaker.

Cavell succinctly puts it as follows: "Here is the sense of language I am trying to articulate in taking Austin's picture beyond performance as ritual. From the root of speech, in each utterance of revelation and confrontation, two paths spring; that of the responsibilities of implication; and that of the rights of desire. . . . In an imperfect world the paths will not reliably coincide" (Cavell 2005a, 185).[39] Cavell wishes to acknowledge "a mode of speech in or through which, by acknowledging my desire in confronting

38. I thank both Maurice Bloch and Robert Hefner for each reminding me, in different ways, of this omission. It is also the case that certain forms of psychopathology derive from an inhibition of development of the basic ethical dispositions.

39. Coincidence of responsibility and feeling is, of course, an ideal or goal in many ethical systems, such as the Egyptian piety movement (Hirschkind 2006). Recall that this is also the case for Aristotle (see note 23 above).

you, I declare my standing with you, and single you out, demanding a response in kind from you, and a response now, so making myself vulnerable to your rebuke, thus staking our future . . ." (185).

If one could distinguish perlocutionary affects and illocutionary effects from one another, one could perhaps disentangle an emotional register from an ethical one. But Cavell suggests that the relationship between ethics and emotion is considerably more complex. He writes of "something I want from moral theory, namely, a systematic recognition of speech as confrontation, as demanding, as owed, . . . each instance of which directs, and risks, if not costs, blood. So my idea of passionate utterance turns out to be a concern with performance after all" (2005a, 187). This recognition of passionate confrontation is less an "anti-morality" than "a refusal of moralism" (187).

Most utterances have both illocutionary and perlocutionary function. Illocutionary acts of acknowledgment, invitation, or refusal are often fraught; passionate utterances are not readily rescinded. The declaration "I love you" is hardly worth saying without expectation and is followed by rapturous concurrence, awkward embarrassment, or a range of other feelings. Such declarations, Cavell emphasizes, entail substantial risk. Even seemingly trivial remarks can provoke concurrent ethical effect (affirmation, betrayal, indifference) and emotional response—relief, gratitude, laughter, indignation, and so forth. Moreover, certain genres, like prayers or healing rituals, deliberately imbricate the illocutionary and perlocutionary.

Work in the anthropology of emotions has argued that the discrimination of emotions itself draws on ethical criteria (Lutz 1988; Myers 1988) or that moral concerns are revealed in distinctive moods (Throop 2014), and work in cultural psychology (Kagan 1994) and philosophy (Strawson 2008) has suggested that ethical discrimination draws on or from emotional criteria—what emotions certain acts or inactions elicit from subjects.[40]

40. On empirical evidence, Kagan remarks that "an appreciation of good and bad is a universal, affectively toned competence that emerges early in development, like laughter or fear of strangers" (1994, xxiii). A few paragraphs later, he says,

> The ideas of good and bad will always be a critical human concern because humans insist on one outcome being more virtuous than others in a situation of choice. The criteria selected define a person's morality. The priority awarded to each of the standards treated as moral is not an inevitable product of our genetic constitution, but stems rather from the capacity for empathy with another's distress and the universal emotions of shame and guilt that are evoked by violations of the standards that each person, through processes not completely understood, has come to accept. Although humans do not seem to be

Chapter 6, coauthored with Jacqueline Solway, addresses justifiable anger, emphasizing the ways in which in Botswana and Madagascar (with some differences from each other and from contemporary North America) the attribution, manifestation, and effects of anger are understood to move between people, articulating relations of responsibility and acts of acknowledgment and repair.

Whatever place we give to emotion, the perlocutionary dimension is significant insofar as recognizing passion or patiency provides some balance to the weight placed in theory on action as agency (Mahmood 2005; Laidlaw 2010). People are simultaneously active and passionate, agents and patients (in the sense of subjects or recipients of action). Passion can be read as pathos or suffering, hence as the inverse of action, but frequently also its complement.[41] From another angle, philosophers in the continental tradition have given increasing attention to what Wentzer (2014), in a lovely rendition, terms "responsiveness" and to how something comes to matter to someone.[42] Although I do not explicitly discuss it in the essays to follow, I take responsiveness to be a significant feature of ethical life.

Conclusion

It is possible to approach ethics from a number of directions, informed by a variety of philosophers. It has not been my intention to review or adjudicate among them but to develop a line of thought that makes sense of my ethnographic material and to me. The direction I take understands ethics in the first instance less as a subject of reflection than with respect to action, and then not as a distinct field of action but as a dimension intrinsic to action. To begin with action and judgment produces a different configuration than one generated from an initial tension between freedom and convention or rule. This approach neither rejects consideration of the normative

---

> programmed for any particular profile of moral missions, they are prepared to invent and to commit themselves to some ethical mission. (xxiii–xxiv)

Note that Kagan is interested in differences between individuals.

41. For further discussion of passion as contrasted to action, see my account of spirit possession, especially Lambek 2010a. For a recent view from sociology, see Daniel Silver, who asks, "What . . . is action like when not undertaken in the mode of struggle, conflict, and strain?" (2011, 207) and answers this with attention to the moods in which situations are disclosed and actions called forth and enriched.

42. On responsiveness and moods, see also the work of Rasmus Dyring (2013). Both Dyring and Wentzer acknowledge German philosopher Bernhard Waldenfels and, behind him, Gadamer and Heidegger. In this vein, see also the remark by Ernst Tugendhat as cited in the epigraph to chapter 4: "Being a self is a matter of how things matter to us."

nor fixes upon it; the subject of ethics is deeper than its objectifications in the justifications, rules, codes, and philosophies found in particular social and historical circumstances. The approach is more attuned to adjectival and adverbial qualities (ethical, ethically) of acts and persons than to an ostensible nominal substance (ethics, morality), except when and as ethics is objectified in local talk, values, traditions, and discourses.

The argument for the immanence of ethics rests on the activity characteristic of human life (human being) and more specifically on the relationship between practice and performative acts. Practice and performance in my usage are not discrete phenomena but different modalities of action and different analytic lenses on it. While practice is conceptualized as relatively open, *performance* in the sense I use it here refers to acts that are conceptualized as discrete, finite, precise, and completed in the doing (though this does not preclude their repetition). Muslim practice is constituted through and punctuated with performative utterances, such as *b'ismillah*, which confer criteria on the segments of practice they initiate or conclude, whether a prayer, journey, or meal. To borrow from the language of cybernetics, performance is practice divided and marked digitally; practice is performance extended analogically.[43] Hence the relationship of practice to performance is one of the continuous to the discontinuous, the open to the finite, the uncertain to the certain, or the ambiguous to the definitive. By means of the performativity found in proclamations, people like uncertain brides or bridegrooms no longer need to wonder about their action or intention but receive conclusive attribution and hence also a relatively clear framework with which to guide or interpret their subsequent practice (Rappaport 1999).

I have been articulating the concept of practice, especially practical judgment, from the Aristotelian tradition, with a concept of performance, or rather performativeness, in Austin's sense. Performative acts provide the conditions, means, or criteria according to which practical judgment is executed and distinct intentions or commitments are specified and clarified (chapter 11). The utterance of a promise, say to show up for an event, is different from vague hopes that one will, and it can be further strengthened by swearing an oath. Promise and oath set up new relations between the parties involved, casting forward a moral space such that the relations between the parties are constituted by expectations and criteria according to which

43. Practice as extended performance, what I there call "continuous performatives," is the theme of chapter 3. It might be compared with Butler (1990) on gender or Goffman (1959) on everyday life. In Lear's terms (2011) they are all "pretending."

subsequent practice will be articulated and evaluated, both by themselves and by others. It doesn't mean that the promise will be kept, but it does mean that not keeping it will be judged as a more or less spectacular failure of a particular kind. It renders practice susceptible to judgment. Discrete performances emerge from and are marked within the stream of practice; simultaneously, they articulate the practice that follows from them (and sometimes retroactively what led up to them), putting people and relationships under a particular description and providing their practice with the criteria through which it may be ascertained, defined, appreciated, and evaluated.

The proclaimed marriage of Aristotle and Austin may appear to be a somewhat unusual performative event, though hopefully not an infelicitous one. My argument does not contradict the initial concern with virtuous practice or practical judgment but moves beyond mere description of judgment to grasp how the criteria that constitute specific practices and the means for evaluating them are established and instantiated—that is, to grasp the conditions or criteria that make practical judgment possible in the first place and that shape particular stretches of practice. However, if performances articulate practice and make judgment possible and necessary, it is equally the case that new performances can only arise from the stream of practice as products of practical judgment—for example, whether to address someone by a particular kin term, when to consult the oracle, how to acknowledge a gift or respond to a verbal address, whether to perform an ancestral sacrifice, and so forth. In many instances, of course, access to authoritative, consequential performance may be contested and constrained.

Social acts occur under a description or set of descriptions and initiate new descriptions, and we all operate with a set of criteria by which we can—or must—describe our own conduct, as well as that of others. One could distinguish relatively standard acts from contested and limited ones, as well as from surprising disruptions or contingent events—Anscombe's discussion of the water pumper who inadvertently poisons the household, or the arrival of Captain Cook—that have no description to begin with or whose description may be fought over retroactively, even centuries later.[44]

44. "Are we to say that the man who (intentionally) moves his arm, operates the pump, replenishes the water supply, poisons the inhabitants, is performing *four* actions? Or only one? . . . Moving his arm up and down with his fingers around the pump handle *is*, in these circumstances, operating the pump; and, in these circumstances, it *is* replenishing the house water supply; and, in these circumstances, it *is* poisoning the household. So there is one action with four descriptions " (Anscombe 1957; quoted in Sandis 2013, 13). On Captain Cook, see Sahlins 1995.

The criteria that define acts as such or that are put into play in consequence of them are not universally shared, categorical (absolute), or entirely obvious; language, culture, history, religious traditions, public institutions, retroactive narratives, circumstances, and the relative power of distinct voices and interests articulate with whatever mental structures, forces, and dispositions we have.

Many questions remain, for example, the availability and specificity of distinct performative acts, and the very large matter of the relationship of acting or doing to being, in both ordinary and exceptional forms of life. There is the perennial Jewish question of whether one is a Jew by virtue of birth, history, practice, or interpellation (Derrida 2008); that is to say, which are the performative acts—or the orders or registers of such acts—that count? The same holds for hyphenated Americans (and other social identifications) of all kinds and, in some conversations, for gender and sexuality, no less than for the matter of simple dignity. There is also the question of radically original acts and how beginnings are retroactively inscribed.[45]

The final reason I speak of the immanence of the ethical is the human recognition of the limits to, or the limitations of, what I have just said about the conjunction of performance and practice. Human beings acknowledge the inevitability of difficulty, lapses, competing descriptions and commitments, incommensurable and imposed criteria, and sometimes the inadequacy or sheer absence of any criteria with which to face a given situation. These matters have been the subjects of much philosophy, perhaps epitomized in Heidegger's diagnosis of *Geworfenheit,* our thrownness into the world. They are also the subjects of tragedy, both written and lived. A poignant instance is *Sophie's Choice,*[46] in which a mother has no criteria for selecting which of her children will die and no criteria for justifying her action; hence it is an act she is unable to acknowledge.

Thus, if the subject of ethics qua philosophical, poetic, or religious discourse must account first for the possibility and necessity in the human situation of acknowledging what we do, it must also explore the void or tragedy of the exhaustion or absence of criteria with which to exercise judgments and our skepticism concerning them. Making criteria available is part of the work of culture (or social life) and a feature of action. Conversely and concomitantly, recognizing the limits of criteria and the impossibility

45. See Faubion (2011) on radical acts and Arendt (1998) on retroactive narration; from a different angle, see chapter 9.

46. In the book by William Styron, a mother must decide which of her two children to give up to the murderers at a Nazi death camp.

of ever living completely or consistently according to them (and inevitably sometimes failing in its own recognition of impossibility) is part of the work of philosophy, that is, of ethical reflection. Both in making criteria available, unquestionable, and authoritative and in reflecting on their limits, religion—or the kinds of practices and reflections we place under the name of religion—has played a central role. The human condition, as we all know, is characterized by a certain discordance. It is not a simple state of nature, and it is not a state of innocence. In this respect, the expulsion from the Garden of Eden offers a more sophisticated account than most evolutionary psychology.

Here is a last illustration of a limit to the arguments I have made so far. In a recent essay, Didier Fassin (2014) takes up the fascinating case portrayed in a documentary film about a Palestinian mother whose child, suffering from a life-threatening illness, is taken to an Israeli hospital.[47] The mother makes some rather provocative statements, including one to the effect that she wishes her son to be cured so that he can grow up to become a suicide bomber. Fassin reads her statements as performative, but points out that it is unclear *what kind of performative* is being enacted. There is a level of irony in the sense that the mother herself may not know what she wants or means, at least not consistently, or that she is saying different things to different audiences, perhaps in different voices. While a clear performative act can establish criteria, an ambiguous one can hardly do the same. The example illustrates how one and the same utterance can look different depending on whether it is understood in reference to preexisting criteria, thus as ongoing practice, in my sense, or as establishing new criteria, and, if so, to what effect.[48] This returns us to Rappaport's gradation between ordinary acts and the more elaborate constructions we call ritual and the effects of embedding significant performatives within the latter—thereby both abstracting them more conclusively from the stream of practice and enabling participants and witnesses to acknowledge precisely what kind of performative acts they are jointly engaged in and whether the felicity conditions have been met.

My usage of *ethical* is evidently more abstract and perhaps more complicated than what is found in the work of many anthropologists. As I have noted, it comprises, in the first instance, not just what is good, or discerning what is good, but the very fact that we can, and indeed must, make such discriminations; hence it encompasses both the good and the bad, what in other usages are the ethical and the unethical or the moral and the immoral.

47. Shlomi Eldar, *Precious Life*.

48. We might also ask what kind of performative act the Israeli film is engaged in.

When I speak of the ethical condition, I mean that we are subject to ethical discrimination and to self-reflection; subject to finding ourselves in relation to others and building continuing relations with one another; subject to action; and subject to the grammar, felicity conditions, effects and consequences of speaking and of embodiment. Most important, we are subject to criteria that produce distinctions among kinds and qualities of actions, relations, and persons and according to which we exercise practical judgment, judgment that is only possible insofar as there are criteria available. Hence too, we are subject to the limits and limitations of criteria.

Mattingly (2012) is perceptive in distinguishing first-person oriented or hermeneutic inheritors of Aristotle from Foucauldian ones. But for me the central point is that we attend to the human condition and especially to our fate as fundamentally language- and culture-based animals. What Mattingly calls the first person is always mediated by culture and language, hence by performative acts and public repertoires of genres, registers, and liturgical orders, as it is informed by the insights of psychoanalysis and the capacities for poetry, and subject to regimes of power, knowledge, and various disciplinary practices. The pervasive irony of the human condition lies in the unfathomability of the sources of our judgment and action.

Our human condition is necessarily an ethical one; we are a species condemned to the ethical even as we may be transcended by the ethical. We are bound to criteria, yet we can never conform to all the criteria we set ourselves or that have been set for us, nor can we be fully satisfied by them. To say that the world is intrinsically ethical in my sense of the term is to acknowledge the kinds of quiet, tactful, practical interventions described by Veena Das (2007) or Heonik Kwon (2008), the earnest cultivation described by Saba Mahmood (2005) and Charles Hirschkind (2006), excited activism (Dave 2012), anxious search for a life of virtue through social change (Robbins 2004; Daswani 2015), forms of self-formation (Faubion 2011), attention to hope and experiment (Mattingly 2010, 2014), conscientious acknowledgment of the past (Lambek 2002a), or the moral concerns of Yemeni hostesses (Meneley 1996), Uduk diviners (James 1988), Jain householders and nuns (Laidlaw 1995; Vallely 2002), or Chinese citizens (Stafford 2013), among many other studies.

Each of these works shows ethical exertion, people trying to do what they think is right. But to speak of the ethical condition is also to acknowledge that we cannot live up to the ethical as it is more commonly defined. We are always faced with difficult judgment, often of two minds, and frequently found wanting by someone or with respect to someone or something. We mistake criteria, misunderstand each other's intentions, and misread the circumstances far too easily. We readily notice disregard and are quick to assume insult. To this we can add the fact or fatedness of skepticism—that while holding on to criteria and living by them (they give life and action direction and meaning), we can never be fully sure of their existence or sufficiency in this or any context, or of our attachment to them, and we can glimpse the possibility of other worlds by other criteria and even the void of no or absent criteria. All this—all the different ways in which we relate or can imagine relating to criteria—is our ethical condition.

TWO

Virgin Marriage and the Autonomy of Women in Mayotte

This was a relatively early intervention in feminist anthropology, and the language may appear dated, but I think the topic remains relevant. The argument fits with one made much more recently by Saba Mahmood in Politics of Piety *(2005) but with respect to a different realm of life. Here, submitting to a disciplinary regime entails entering the cycle of exchange or world of "the gift" as it was constituted in Mayotte at the time. The article also illustrates a way in which Islam was "localized" in Mayotte (an argument subsequently developed in Lambek 2000b and other essays) so that Islam became constitutive of the life cycle and personhood but in a manner consistent with local practice. Already in this essay I understood that what was critical were not so much static moral states as* acts*—in this case a woman's acts of holding on to and then releasing her virginity.*

Village life in Mayotte has changed enormously since this was written. Young women go through high school and marry much later. The display of virginity is no longer part of the public performance, but it was still salient to the bride's mother in 2009, and weddings were still celebrated with sexy dancing. Later articles (Lambek 1990b, 2004) trace some of these developments. A major work on the related but far more elaborate marriage system on the Grande Comore is Blanchy 2010; for comparison, see Lambek, in press [b].

Many of the relatively early papers in the emerging anthropological literature on women were concerned with comparing the status of women and men in a given society. In such studies, the selection of criteria for evaluating relative status becomes a central problem. Papers documenting the dominance of men are open to the criticism that relative status has been

This chapter first appeared in Signs: Journal of Women in Culture and Society 9, no. 2 (1983): 264–81.

measured by variables or described using values relevant to men but not to women. Additionally, these studies can be faulted for tending to focus on what women lack, while neglecting essential issues revolving around who women are: the social constructions of womanhood; the forms through which being female is experienced, integrated, and recreated; the models and motivations for women's actions in particular cultural contexts. Recent publications introduce more dynamic pictures of women as they are and as they fit into social wholes that are no longer defined androcentrically (see, e.g., Annette Weiner 1976).

This chapter considers one aspect of women's identity in Mayotte, an island in the Comoro Archipelago of the western Indian Ocean. My goal is to understand the place of virgin marriage in the social construction of Mayotte womanhood. Specifically, I want to unravel what to us might appear a paradox: in Mayotte, displaying the blood of a woman's defloration at marriage expresses and contributes to the autonomy of women.

Before beginning, several cautions are in order. First, in demonstrating that sexuality is central to the self-definition of Mayotte women, I do not mean to imply that women's value lies solely in the sexual sphere. Labor, political and religious activity, motherhood, hospitality, and so on would also have to be taken into account to constitute a complete picture. Second, I am not attempting to measure women's status according to a set of more or less objective criteria, but to discover what Mayotte women (and men) themselves make of women's status through the institution of virgin marriage. My focus, however, is not on individuals but on the public, social, and imaginative forms through which individual identities are, in part, formed. In this I follow Clifford Geertz, who argues that direct experience can never be our avenue to understanding the lives of others (Geertz 1973d). Instead, we must capture the image of that experience cast by the symbolic forms through which people construct and interpret their own lives. What follows, then, is an interpretation, a "reading," and it should be evaluated in that light. Finally, to demonstrate the significance of defloration is not to argue in support of its perpetuation or to deny that it may also serve to oppress. The position of women is not ideal in Mayotte, nor is it identical to the position of men; virgin marriage undoubtedly helps to maintain the difference between men's and women's status. Any social institution can simultaneously liberate and constrain.[1] Thus far in the study of women it has been necessary to document constraint; it now seems useful to describe liberation.

1. That social life is inherently problematic is a basic insight of modern social thought; see Murphy 1971.

Because notions of virginity are both evocative and semantically complex in North America, we must be especially wary when approaching the topic in another culture. In particular, as Mary Douglas has reminded us (1966), we must avoid the current predilection for confusing order with oppression. In Mayotte, virginity is not valued as a quality or condition in itself. What is of concern is the act of abstention or restraint until the legitimate moment of release. Virginity is not idealized; there is no Virgin Mary, no Immaculate Conception, no Bride of Christ, and the idea of lifelong virginity, if it could be imagined at all in Mayotte, would be a good deal more shocking than the contemplation of its loss in less than legitimate circumstances. Women of Mayotte share a degree of similarity with Trobriand women, who are, according to Annette Weiner, "accorded full respect for the power of their sexuality. That men pay women for sleeping with them both before and after marriage does not indicate men's use of women, as Malinowski and Lévi-Strauss suggest. Rather, women use their sexuality to full advantage because they and everyone else recognize the full value of sexuality" (1976, 193). Weiner suggests that the concept of virgin birth, so famous in Trobriand ethnography, "is used as a protection for the innate value of women" (193). It is precisely this function that virgin marriage fulfills in Mayotte. Sex is a resource controlled by women, and it is their right and responsibility to reserve it for socially productive ends.

Another potential source of bias in this sort of study involves viewing virgin marriage from the perspective of the men who surround the bride—her father, brothers, and husband. For example, Ronald Reminick concludes that defloration among the Amhara symbolizes "the man's jural and sexual rights of domain" and has reference to the male role in the struggle for land (1976). This would seem at best a partial analysis; surely it has some meaning for the women as well. Compare Reminick's account of defloration to John Kennedy's of male circumcision in Nubia, which he sees as a significant factor in the development of a "strong and confident self-image and sex identity" and a reaffirmation of the "general value of maleness" (1970; Kennedy also presents a balanced analysis of female excision). In Mayotte defloration is, in a sense, a form of initiation,[2] and women are the central characters—not only the woman who demonstrates her virginity but also the female members of the community who gather to celebrate the event. Just as Nubian circumcision helps to "complete the child as a person" (Kennedy 1970, 186) so defloration in Mayotte helps to complete the woman and reaffirm

2. There is a close connection between young women's initiation and marriage ceremonies in many of the Bantu-speaking societies of southern and central Africa.

the general value of femaleness. From the male perspective, satisfaction is grounded as much in the economic achievement of marrying a virgin bride as it is in the sexual accomplishment. Demonstration of male potency is important, but there is no mystique attached to the specific act of defloration (as opposed to intercourse with nonvirgins). Men do not seek the experience of deflowering virgins, they seek the experience of marrying them.

I

Any detailed discussion of virgin marriage must be prefaced with a few words about Mayotte and the general position of women there (see also Lambek 1981, 1985). Mayotte lies between and shares cultural affinities with both coastal East Africa and northwestern Madagascar. I pursued fieldwork in two rural communities of Malagasy speakers in 1975–76 and again, briefly, in 1980. The inhabitants are Muslim, although Mayotte has been under French control since 1841. Subsistence is based on dry rice horticulture, supplemented by fishing and the production of cash crops. Kinship is reckoned bilaterally—through both parents—and kin groupings larger than the nuclear family are fluid and overlapping in membership. Villages range in size from about twenty-five to twenty-five hundred inhabitants. Both men and women hold membership status in the village as individuals, and both participate in the cycles of ceremonial exchange that characterize village life.

Most women have permanent rights to subsistence land and may own plots outright or share ownership with a spouse or siblings. Spouses cooperate in subsistence production and share control over the harvest. However, with some exceptions, men manage the production and sale of nonedible cash crops, and women lack direct access to the proceeds. Women own the houses and most of the household furnishings. The majority of adult women reside in the communities in which they were raised. They maintain strong links with ascending female kin and with siblings, and they participate in the women's age groups and political organizations.

Marital relations in Mayotte are brittle. A marriage is terminated when the man leaves and fails to provide support; however, a woman can convince a man to leave, if necessary, by flaunting her infidelity. Polygyny, though infrequent, is a major source of inequality between women and men, and it is resented by women. While it is impossible to cite statistics, marital infidelity is common on the part of both women and men. Regulation of sexual conduct is primarily the separate responsibility of each sex. Infertility does not destroy a woman's social standing, and it is offset by the ease and frequency of child transfers. Through judicious planning of marriages and child-rearing, a woman can become the focal member of a cluster of kin. Women are not secluded and can engage in friendships with men.

II

There are two forms of weddings in Mayotte, distinguished from one another by the condition of the bride.[3] The wedding of a virgin bride is the longest, most expensive, and most elaborate kinship ritual performed. It entails a week or more of feasting, organized around the establishment of the bride and groom in the former's new house. A virgin wedding can also affect the positions of the participants in a number of the formal exchange cycles that govern village life. By contrast, the wedding of a nonvirgin—that is, a divorcée, widow, unmarried mother, or bride who fails the virginity test—is far shorter, simpler, and cheaper, and is of concern only to the immediate kin. Whether or not the marriage is the husband's first is irrelevant to the proceedings.

A virgin marriage begins with the transfer of legal rights in a token payment, called the *mahary* (from the Arabic *mahr*), from the groom or his proxy to the bride's father. This act is preceded by a more substantial contribution that often includes a cow, which the bride's parents transform into the cooked food consumed during the wedding. Following the transfer of rights, the groom is secretly whisked into the bride's new house. When the consummation takes place, a small cloth is placed under the bride to catch the blood. This is used as proof of her virginity. It is prominently displayed during the dancing that follows and is then left in the wedding house to show all visitors. Several elderly women are present in the next room to ensure the evidence is not simulated. The groom's grandmother is normally responsible for supervising the cloth. One wedding I attended included four witnesses: the groom's mother's mother, her older sister, and the bride's two grandmothers. The bride's grandmothers are considered only secondary witnesses, since they might be ready to substitute chicken blood in order to save the bride's honor. Together the grandmothers may encourage a nervous groom, or coax or force a bride frightened by the anticipated pain. Once satisfied, they show the cloth to the groom's mother. If the grandmothers are not satisfied, the groom can walk out, breaking off the wedding. On the other

3. For a parallel distinction between two kinds of marriage (though they carry very different implications) on the neighboring Grande Comore, see the excellent analysis by Gillian M. Shepherd (1977). Among the elite of neighboring Anjouan, first marriages appear to be key events in the lives of men as well as women. See Ottenheimer and Ottenheimer 1979.

hand, a deal will often be secretly arranged, and everyone will pretend the bride was a virgin.

When the consummation is achieved, the women begin to trill, signaling to the community that the defloration has been successful. Other women pour into the yard, dancing, beating bamboo sticks, and trilling as well. The dancing has sexual connotations, often quite explicit. The participants dance two at a time inside a rough circle, stamping their feet in short steps. They face each other, shaking their hips and buttocks, and sing joyous and erotic songs. Occasionally a woman who is host to a spirit enters trance. A female sponsor may display money and invite further donations for the bride from those pleased that she had maintained her virginity. The women enter the house singly to congratulate briefly the couple as they lie in bed. One couple that I visited shook hands with me and showed off the blood-stained cloth.

The defloration is followed by the *harusy,* a period of celebration at least seven days long. It is a time of transition for the bridal couple, during which they must not leave their house, though they receive visitors. The bride's parents bring them food, and her female siblings and cousins joke with the groom. On one occasion I observed a large, middle-aged woman sprawl horizontally over the young groom as he lay in bed next to the bride and vigorously move her hips up and down. There is a very relaxed quality to the relations between the spouses and between them and their guests.

The first day of the *harusy* is generally marked by a large ritual feast (*walima*), provided by the bride's sponsors to accompany prayers for the marriage.[4] The meal may be large enough to feed the entire village. On each day of the *harusy* the bride's mother sends platters of food to the groom's mother, who in turn redirects them on different days to various relatives. On the last day, the groom is hidden elsewhere in the village and dressed in finery. Once discovered, he is then escorted through the village to the bride's home in a large and joyous procession, bearing a suitcase or two full of presents for the bride. The gifts generally include a substantial amount of gold jewelry, such as earrings, bracelets, and combs. In addition, there are numerous outfits of clothing, and some household items, such as soap. The subsequent dancing marks the end of the wedding period.[5]

4. The sponsors are usually the bride's parents but, with their consent, sponsorship may be taken up by another of the bride's kin.

5. A few weeks later, the bride is escorted in a parallel but much smaller procession to visit the home of the groom's mother or sister, where she is ritually fed.

III

As described so far, then, a virgin wedding entails the following significant exchanges:[6] (1) payment of the *mahary* to settle the legal transfer; (2) money and beast given by the groom to the bride's parents for the wedding feasts; (3) the *walima* feast supplied by the bride's parents; (4) daily transfers of food from the bride's parents to the groom's parents and thence to the groom's relatives; (5) gifts of jewelry and clothing from the groom to the bride; (6) the gift of house and furnishings to the bride from her parents. By contrast, the wedding of a nonvirgin bride need only include payment of the *mahary*, which is small (and which, according to some informants, then belongs to the wife rather than her father). A small feast for close kin may be held as well, but there is none of the ritual, dancing, or processions described above.

These various exchanges may readily be analyzed as dowry, dower, the establishment of reciprocity between affinal parties, the opposition between wife and husband givers, and the like. But this would only give us part of the picture, since it fails to consider the defloration, which is itself the crucial element. In fact, the bride plays a major role in the exchange process. Her role can be seen more clearly when we realize that the exchanges listed above are only part of the material exchanges that take place at the weddings of most virgin brides. Such weddings are also the only legitimate occasions during which individuals can fulfill significant exchange requirements to certain non-kin groupings, namely, age groups, villages, and groups formed for the express purpose of reciprocal feast-giving. These exchanges, known as *shungu*, entail formal obligations that each member of a designated group must in time perform for other members. Thus, members of a male age group that maintains a *shungu* must each provide a feast of rigidly specified proportions on the occasion of the donor's marriage to a virgin bride. The bride may also feast her age mates at this time. The groom's *shungu* payment is built into the system of affinal exchanges. The groom gives the bride's parents a significant sum of money, which her parents then use to carry out the requirements of the groom's age group. In other words, the groom becomes dependent on the bride's parents to meet his responsibilities to his age group.

The village itself forms a single *shungu* group with a series of obligations it expects every member of the community to fulfill during his or her

6. Smaller prestations have not been included in this account.

lifetime. The precise requirements vary among villages,[7] but they are generally considered quite exacting. Each adult must produce a certain amount of food (so many kilos of rice, so many cows, so many cakes—even the quantity of salt is measured) to feed the entire village a specified number of meals. Village *shungu* are carried out in the context of life-cycle rites, primarily at a daughter's virgin marriage, a son's circumcision, or the commemoration of deceased kin. The wedding requirements may include at least one *walima* meal for the entire community and another set of meals known as the *fukatry*, which involves feeding all the members of a different age group each day for the entire length of the wedding. Thus, a wedding at which the bride's mother, her father, the bride, and the groom are all paying *shungu* will be filled with a complex of substantial material exchanges.

Not all members of a village or age group are able to meet their *shungu* obligations. To ignore the obligations is a source of enduring, although relatively private, shame. An essential condition for payment is sponsorship of a virgin wedding. At issue in a wedding, then, is not merely the formation of alliance between affinal parties but also the transformation of each. These functions are interlinked: the exchange between the groom and the bride's parents is one in which each needs the other in order to meet its own obligations to a third party, which is ultimately the entire community. Each is the vehicle for the social achievement of the other, and alliance is thus based on an exchange of services as well as of goods.

However, if the groom and the bride's parents are mutually interdependent, they are both dependent on the bride. Just as there can be no fulfillment of social obligations without a virgin wedding, so there can be no virgin wedding without a virgin. The bride is thus a highly significant party. She is not herself an object of exchange; rather, her condition is a prerequisite for the completion of various exchanges in which she, no less than her parents and spouse, is engaged. Her contribution to these exchanges is recognized: in return for preserving her virginity and participation in defloration with the groom, she is supplied with a home, furnishings, and possibly some cash by her family, and with a wardrobe and jewelry by her husband. No further return is expected on her part for these gifts; they stay in her possession whatever the outcome of the marriage. The gifts represent not a transfer of rights in her person but rather recognition of her *as* a person. From the groom's point of view, in marrying a virgin he has carried out his moral obligations and achieved his status goals. Subsequent marriages can be to

7. *Shungu* requirements are gradually disappearing in the larger villages and in those more tightly integrated into the capitalist economy.

nonvirgins, to whom he does not have to supply expensive gifts. Everyone's rise in status is completed in the performance of the wedding and cannot be reversed. Marriages to nonvirgins entail little exchange or public celebration and are morally neutral.

IV

Defloration in Mayotte transforms a woman from childhood to adulthood.[8] A young woman's parents have the right to schedule and manage this transformation, which occurs in the context of her wedding. In remaining a virgin until this point, a young woman affirms her parents' rights. She does this through an act of will, and it is in part this active adherence to the moral code that is celebrated at the wedding and that creates in the individual woman a positive sense of her own accomplishment and identity.

This act of will is better understood when we consider the area of premarital sex. In Mayotte, sexuality is openly valued. Within certain constraints of propriety, sex is a subject of joking, good humor, and a little horseplay. Mother's brothers or grandfathers attempt to squeeze affectionately the emerging breasts of young women, and the girls may fondle the men as well. Sex is considered pleasurable; girls listen to their older friends and female siblings describe it, and they doubtless overhear their parents in the act at night.

Parents and brothers strongly disapprove of a young woman's sexual experimentation because it can lead to premature defloration and because it can give her a reputation that might put off potential legitimate suitors, either because they fear she is no longer a virgin or because they assume, if she is promiscuous, that she will make an unfaithful wife. Nevertheless, sexual activity is a recognized and central aspect of early adolescent life. Children gather in the shadows to play at night, and some girls follow boys to their bachelor houses. Many of the older unmarried girls, possibly the vast majority, have lovers with whom they practice intracrural (external) intercourse. These young women are not the blushing virgins of our own myths. For some, continued maintenance of their virginity is an extreme frustration, and, accidentally or otherwise, they resolve the frustration by having intercourse. Thus there is a tension between the contradictory values of sexuality and virginity. Ideally, a young woman marries as soon after

8. More precisely, maturation occurs in a series of stages, of which marriage is the most significant. A woman is not considered a full adult until two years after her first marriage.

menarche as possible, but in practice many factors operate to postpone marriage, causing considerable anxiety on the part of mothers.

Should it become apparent that an unmarried woman is no longer a virgin—that is, if she is noticeably pregnant[9]—the main consequence is that an elaborate wedding becomes out of the question. All parties are censured. Parents question the young woman to discover the identity not of the father of the child but of the man who deflowered her. They are extremely displeased with her, sad and ashamed at the lack of respect their child has shown them. Members of the mother's age group ask her when she is going to return their invitations to sew mattresses (for the bridal house), and the mother may be moved to tears. Most of all, the parents feel disconcerted at having been excluded from participation in the transformation of their daughter, much as contemporary North American parents might feel if they learned of their child's marriage after the fact. Failure to perform in a ritual that they have anticipated and that is part of the moral order as it is constituted in Mayotte provokes a sense of anomie. The parents make a public attempt to find, accuse, and demand a cash recompense from the man who has abrogated their rights, thereby participating, in some sense at least, in their daughter's transformation. If his identity is clearly established, he must make a payment.

In addition to being considered a thief or despoiler who owes compensation to the young woman's parents (legally, to her father), the man who deflowers a woman illegitimately *(mandrubaka zanakan'ulun)* has committed a major sin, one that will lead to certain punishment in the afterworld and that brings shame in this world. However, if the man has sinned and stolen, the woman has committed a foolish indiscretion and public act of disrespect toward her parents. In general, people in Mayotte feel that a young woman gives up her virginity by her own choice—that a reluctant woman would have the strength to fight off an attacker or the sense to call for help. Men who do attempt rape are despised, but women rarely offer rape as an explanation for loss of virginity. To do so would be, in effect, to acknowledge women as passive victims of male sexuality, to deny women's control over their own bodies.[10] The pride that women express in the marriage of a

9. Nonvirgins who do not get pregnant often pass the virginity test. There may well be collusion, since the occurrence of a virgin marriage is usually of greater importance to the bride's parents than the exposure of falsehood is to the groom. Some men, perhaps urged by their mothers, do reject nonvirgins, but the significant issue for men is the distribution of the resources for a virgin wedding.

10. For an example of response to potential rape, see Michael Lambek (1980).

virgin bride demonstrates that they do indeed have such control. This is as clear when women forfeit virginity as it is when they maintain it.

The fate of an unmarried woman who has lost her virginity depends largely on the economic situation and personal disposition of her parents, particularly her father, and is expressed in the degree to which the parents choose to withhold the property a daughter usually receives from them at marriage—namely, a house and furnishings. If she has younger sisters who also need houses, she may be given a small, decrepit building and few furnishings, or even no house at all. Likewise, she does not necessarily receive the wardrobe and jewelry that a virgin bride has the right to expect from her husband. All this makes her much more dependent on her future husband(s), who may or may not choose to supply her with a house and other gifts. Often, however, the parents use the money collected from the male transgressor to provide a house.

In sum, a young woman is considered responsible for her actions and is expected to pay the price of indiscretion. This price lies more in the material realm than in the less tangible one of honor or reputation. The dishonor is neither total nor permanent, nor will it, in itself, color a woman's subsequent career. A history of this sort is not spoken about by others. The emphasis in Mayotte is much less on the negative case than on celebrating the success of legitimate defloration. Defloration and its aftermath are eagerly anticipated by most young women. They constitute the happiest, most exciting period of a woman's life. Women are sorry that, unlike men, they can go through a major wedding only once. They look forward to sexual fulfillment, to managing their own households, to starting motherhood, and to the general rise in status that adulthood brings. They also anticipate the gifts of clothing and jewelry, and the relaxation, luxury, and attention of the "honeymoon" period.

The following excerpt from my field notes concerning a conversation between a young husband and wife conveys something of these feelings, as well as the nature of the conjugal relationship: "Amina says she wishes she too could go through the wedding *(harusy)* again, although of course a woman can never do so. Bwana says that though he'd like to marry another virgin, he wouldn't do it; Amina would be too sad. Amina replies that she would get medicine that would make Bwana sad if he tried, too."

V

Defloration is not simply a test for virginity. Whereas such a test could always be performed manually, what is important in Mayotte is to lose the hymen in a prescribed act of sexual intercourse. In other words, it is not a state of purity or impurity that is relevant here, but an act of transformation. Society attempts to control the transformation of its children into adults. The bloody cloth demonstrates not just virginity but its loss, signifying the successful transformation of the woman according to society's rules as well as her acquiescence to those rules.[11] Moreover, this transformation is not from a state of relative purity to one of relative impurity, but rather from childhood, a state in which sexual intercourse is forbidden, to adulthood, in which sex is encouraged. Purity has to do with following social rules, not with sex per se. Impurity is not held to be biologically innate or considered intrinsic to womanhood or to the developmental cycle.[12]

One may ask why society should use sexual intercourse to mark the maturation and social responsibilities of its members, and why it should focus so centrally on a portion of the female rather than the male anatomy. One possible answer is that engaging in sexual intercourse is an apt vehicle for social passage, much like crossing a threshold or being immersed in water, but with more straightforward practical and psychological implications than the latter.

Moreover, in women as opposed to men, the first full act of sexual intercourse is what establishes transformation. It can be argued that this is made possible by the fact that women's genitalia provide an admirable signifier. A man's first complete act of sexual intercourse simply cannot be marked unambiguously on his own body. First, there is no aspect of male anatomy that can function as an easily distinguishable digital signal to establish when a man has successfully engaged in an act of intercourse.[13] In fact, perforation of the hymen marks a man's engagement in sexual intercourse as surely as it marks a woman's. Second, again for anatomical reasons, there is no way to demonstrate that a given act of intercourse is a man's first. The index for women is by no means foolproof either,[14] but it is relatively reliable.[15]

11. The significance of defloration for male identity is discussed later.

12. Contrast the Moroccan case described by Daisy Hilse Dwyer (1978).

13. Digital representations in communication theory are discontinuous units, such as numbers, that can clarify analogic, continuous processes, such as distance or maturation. One reader has suggested that semen could fill this function for men. A man's first nocturnal emission is considered a (private) sign of adulthood in Mayotte, but, as this example shows, semen is not an unambiguous index of sexual intercourse.

14. An index in Peircean semiotics is a sign that is nonarbitrarily related to that which it signifies, such that it is caused by or a part of that which it signifies (e.g., smoke is an index of fire).

15. Certainly some women are victimized by the custom, since it is not recognized in Mayotte that absence of bleeding may be due to causes other than previous sexual intercourse.

It should be clear that I am not attempting to ground women's status in biology. I am arguing that if one is looking for an unambiguous, digital index of transformation that can be publicly demonstrated, virginity/defloration works quite well when the woman rather than the man is established as the virgin. As Kirsten Hastrup remarks, "Only women's bodies can be used to define social states in this way, . . . because they are marked by nature in a way that invites the use of these bodies in other than just sexual ways" (1978). For men, something other than virginity is required—for example, deflowering a woman or undergoing circumcision. The point is that unambiguous, digital, and publicly demonstrable indices are highly appropriate ways to mark human transformations in the life cycle. This is so both for individuals, who have the psychological need to conceptualize the vague processes of maturation they are experiencing, and for society, which needs to impose order on its members. In speaking of the "pragmatic effects" of the Bemba *chisungu* female initiation ritual, Audrey Richards argues that a girl's personal doubts concerning her maturity are removed by "tangible proof that she is actually a 'grown-up' and can safely and successfully behave like one" (1956, 24). Likewise Roy Rappaport suggests that in their digital aspects rites of passage clarify and summarize "all of the obscure, continuous physical and psychic processes that in concert constitute . . . maturation," as well as the complex social processes that go into the scheduling and production of the event (1979b, 185). Such rituals articulate in unambiguous fashion the private processes of the individual with the public systems of order.

A young woman who loses her virginity outside of wedlock is nonetheless transformed into an adult, but the event is a good deal less meaningful outside the ritual context. The ritual uses the personal event to make a statement of wider social relevance; the collective importance, in turn, heightens the individual impact. Defloration becomes a symbol of female sexuality, womanhood, and the value of women. Victor Turner speaks of the bipolarity of ritual symbols, of their orectic and normative poles, referring to their dual source in the urges and experiences of the body and in the moral order of society, respectively (1967). This seems a particularly appropriate model for grasping the semantic complexity of defloration. In demonstrating her condition through the act of relinquishing it, a woman looks at once forward and back—forward to the acknowledged pleasures of sexuality and adulthood, and backward to a moral order of restraint. The single act of intercourse summarizes both this previous restraint and potential sexual activity. The message is reinforced by women who congratulate the bride on her successful transformation by celebrating the pleasures of female sexuality.

Restraint, order, and morality are celebrated with the expression of desire. Following Émile Durkheim, Turner speaks of the ways in which ritual operates in the interests of society to "transform the necessary into the desirable." But the act of defloration does more than this; it moves between the poles simultaneously in both directions. For women, the wedding equally renders the desirable—sex—into the necessary. Thus, female sexuality and moral order are in some sense linked, demonstrating the value and power of women.[16]

VI

If defloration is a significant event in the development of women, is there an equivalent ritual to mark the maturation of men? One parallel, explicitly drawn in Mayotte and in other Muslim societies as well,[17] links defloration and male circumcision. Each focuses on the individual, each involves an "operation" on the genitals, the management and scheduling of each is the right and responsibility of the parents, and each is preceded by an identical prophylactic ritual of smoking out evil spirits. Both events are prerequisites for sexual activity, and both contribute to the construction of the full social persona. People in Mayotte claim that they do not object to sexual activity with uncircumcised men—as long as those men do not come from societies in which circumcision is expected (e.g., French Foreign Legionnaires). In other words, the condition does not correspond to innate or metaphysical qualities. Mayotte expects men to be circumcised (just as it expects women to preserve the hymen until marriage) to demonstrate acceptance of the social order.[18] Circumcision, preservation of virginity, and defloration are moral activities.

The other act in the male life cycle that can be compared to the female preservation of virginity and subsequent participation in defloration is a

16. This point is reinforced if we consider how women contribute to ongoing cycles of social exchange by their participation in the ritual (see sec. III), or how an adult woman's sexuality becomes a major source of her strength (not covered in this chapter).

17. See, for example, Kennedy (1970, 181–83). Female circumcision does not occur in Mayotte.

18. Of course, this is not to imply that preservation of virginity is as easy for a young woman as submission to circumcision is for a boy. Circumcision takes place when boys are quite young (anywhere from about two to twelve years of age). Disregarding exceptional cases, such as when a boy passes puberty without having been circumcised by his parents and may then be tempted to present himself before the surgeon, a boy has no say in the matter and does not sacrifice in retaining his foreskin until the appropriate ritual moment. Circumcision is greeted with general rejoicing on the part of both men and women, and the boy is congratulated.

man's marriage to a virgin bride. This is something that every man should achieve in his lifetime, preferably in his youth. Like defloration and circumcision, marriage to a virgin bride is a digital process. However, here the orectic and normative poles of the event are separated in time, context, and importance. First comes the act of defloration. When the conjugal couple enters the house, the potency of the male is as much in question as the virginity of the young woman. Demonstration of potency is not explicitly stated as the aim of the ritual, but its relevance quickly becomes apparent in informal discussion. Although in theory the public does not know at what time the couple enters the house, in practice if the women's trilling is not soon heard, speculation and gossip begin. Like defloration and circumcision, the demonstration of potency must occur on schedule, in a socially established context. Many men experience extreme anxiety beforehand. In fact, it is not impossible that the man experiences more concern over the outcome and its effect on his reputation than does the woman. Male failure is often attributed to sorcery, but it is nonetheless shameful.

It is ironic, then, that in the ritual the identity of the man who performs the act is not considered very important. In extremis, I was told, the groom could be replaced by his brother. The performance of the groom simply is not as significant as that of the bride. The groom's status is not as dependent on a single act, nor does he undergo a clearly defined transformation. A groom has a second chance to demonstrate potency; a bride has no second chance to prove virginity. Moreover, a man can demonstrate his sexual status in other ways (e.g., by paternity) and on other occasions (e.g., in previous, contemporaneous, or subsequent marriages). That his potency comes into such focus is more a product of the staging of the ritual than anything else.[19] The groom is, in fact, little more than the instrument contracted by the parents of the bride to perform upon their daughter the operation for which they hold responsibility. The first day of the wedding is dedicated to the bride and to women; the man must wait until the last day to have the social aspects of his own role publicly acknowledged. Although potency is a prerequisite to success, it is the achievement of amassing and redistributing sufficient cash and goods for the wedding that is key to the groom's rise in status. A man who has never married a virgin is embarrassed because of his economic and social, not sexual, failure. For the rare man who is

19. One could also argue that the union of bride and groom makes a statement about both the future fertility of the marriage and the genitor of potential offspring. Defloration indicates that the bride is not already pregnant and that, their fertility permitting, neither partner is incapable of procreation. However, no one ever presented me with this interpretation.

permanently impotent, failure at defloration is incidental to the wider problems concerning status.[20]

VII

The wedding moves from a focus on women to one on men, and from a suggestion of opposition between the sexes to one of complementarity. With the exception of the groom, the immediate aspects of the defloration are managed and celebrated entirely by women. Grandmothers are the ones who act as witnesses, make the final decision concerning the outcome, and are willing to be bribed or to mediate as necessary. The first person to be told the good news is the bride's mother; the person most likely to react negatively toward bad news, the groom's mother.

The celebration emphasizes the positive aspects of female sexuality, while presenting a somewhat ambivalent attitude about male sexuality. Participants state that the sexually explicit dancing and lewd singing,[21] the *ladaymwana,* is an expression of "joy for the child": there is joy in her obedience and respect, and joy in the success of her transformation. More important is the joy the women express in the bride's sexual being—and in their own sexual being as well. The young woman has been initiated into the pleasures of sexual activity, moving from a period of restriction to one of relative freedom. No longer chastised by parents and brothers, it is now her own business if she seeks sexual encounters beyond the bounds of marriage. Indeed, there are accounts of women who have affairs during or shortly after the wedding. This is not to argue that such behavior is not frowned on; the point is rather the association made in Mayotte between defloration and the subsequent enjoyment of sex.

If the dancing is an expression of women's sexuality, linking them through their individual sexual histories to one another, it also derides the sexuality of men. The women dance in pairs, miming the union of the sexes. They are clearly expressing the enjoyment of heterosexual intercourse, but perhaps, in the absence of men, there is an underlying suggestion that they do not need men at all. The women also mock men, for example, by performing a grotesque portrayal of elephantiasis of the testes.[22] The men are

20. The one individual in this position whom I came across suffers profound shame and is permanently scorned and socially marginal.

21. For example, one song speaks, in metaphorical terms, about "the penis playing within the vagina."

22. One referee has made the perceptive suggestion that the women's dances contrast the sexual performance of men and women; specifically, "if women's bodies can be marked in terms

aware of the women's activities but stay away from the enclosed yard where the dance is held, claiming embarrassment or disinterest. In fact, between certain categories of men and women, such as brothers and sisters or sons and mothers-in-law, sexual joking is forbidden, and even the mildest references are considered highly embarrassing. At any large gathering of both sexes, some of the forbidden kin are certain to be present. Therefore, the abstention of men as a body is necessary if the celebration of the defloration is to proceed, and one could argue that their absence is thus a tacit acceptance of the women's activity.

The women's dancing is not unlike female rituals among various groups in Central and Southern Africa that have been interpreted as "rituals of rebellion" (see, e.g., Gluckman 1954). The rebelliousness of the women here, however, is open to question. Richards noted the weakness of this argument some time ago: "If a woman behaves submissively in a ritual, the explanation offered is that she is expressing the sex role that is proper to a woman in a society in which meekness in women is admired; if she swaggers, the explanation is that she is reacting from this submissive role" (1956, 119).

In Mayotte, ribald behavior on the part of women does occur outside of formal ritual contexts. While not precisely congruent with women's role in Mayotte society, the "swaggering" in the ritual is not antithetical to that role. It is, rather, a selective approach to the position of women, an emphatic assertion of women's general satisfaction and pride, a model of and for women's behavior.

Only on the last day of the wedding is there a parallel celebration of the achievement of the groom and of the role of the male sex in general. Women fawn over the groom and his party, lighting his cigarettes and carrying his burdens, and express their appreciation of the male role as supplier of material goods. The men dance, not simply for themselves, but for the audience of women. While the transaction concerning the bride's sexual eligibility is completed on the first day of the wedding (Goodenough 1970), recognition of the groom's sexual and domestic rights in the woman (and, correspondingly, her rights in the man) is completed only on the last day. Weddings move from opposition between the sexes to mutuality.

In the course of the wedding, an orderly exchange between women and men is demonstrated: sexuality and domesticity in return for material wealth,

of their virginity, men's bodies are *always* marked in terms of their sexuality—a man must have an erection. Thus the pressure on a man's performance sexually is at issue throughout his life, while the pressure on women (in societies where virginity is morally demanded) is much briefer and then never again questioned" (personal communication).

material wealth in return for sexuality and domesticity. Each sex vaunts the valued resources over which it claims to exercise control. Eventually the wedding suggests that married life is the ideal context for a woman's sexuality, but it takes a week to reach that conclusion.

VIII

For both men and women it is the act of marriage, not the state, that is of primary importance. A man should marry a virgin, but once the wedding is over he has fulfilled his major social responsibility and need not remain married to her. Likewise, adult men and women should, ideally, be married, but termination of marriage (initiated by either party) and remarriage are extremely common. To be single for life is unthinkable, never to have married a virgin or to have been married as a virgin is shameful, but to be temporarily unmarried is merely somewhat irresponsible as well as inconvenient. The difference between marrying and being married is neatly illustrated by the following story. In 1975 people in Mayotte claimed there was a shortage of eligible males, and so turned to kin for assistance. One man married his father's sister's daughter. The new husband then approached his wife's brother and asked him to reciprocate by marrying the daughter of his (the husband's) mother's brother. When the second man married elsewhere, the first man divorced one cross-cousin and married the other. People admired this man's social responsibility in ensuring that both his cousins went through a virgin marriage. The conflict potentially engendered by divorce of the first cousin (it would probably have been worse had he attempted polygyny) was considered minimal compared with the social good achieved in marrying the second. This story also serves to emphasize the complementary point that alliance is achieved in marriage less through the creation of a common household or offspring, or through an exchange of goods, than through the exchange of services for the permanent transformation of the separate parties.

One might argue that the groom and the bride's parents have a central role in transforming the bride and setting her up in her own household, and that the importance of their role is demonstrated in the public recognition they receive for their activities. It follows, then, that although women have control over domestic production and biological reproduction, it is society that produces such women. But at the same time, it is crucial to see the part played by the bride herself in this process.

Here one must consider the social significance of restraint. For Freud, repression is necessary in the formation of the mature ego. For Durkheim, social constraint is the means for self-transcendence. And according to Lévi-Strauss, holding back from immediate gratification establishes the potential for reciprocity and alliance, though for him the man is the central figure, refraining from sex with his sister in order to exchange her for the sister of another man. In Mayotte, however, recognition is granted to the contribution of women. In preserving her virginity, a woman makes marriage and social reproduction morally possible. Her sexual condition permits the establishment of new households, ties between affines, the social maturation of men, and fulfillment of parents' social obligations. Furthermore, it introduces her as an active participant in ongoing cycles of exchange and grants her the material means to continue participating, thereby helping to constitute her as a distinct social persona. Exchange differentiates individuals from one another as much as it links them together (cf. Weiner 1976, 81–89).

A woman's material, social, and psychological maturation are all interwoven. Ultimately, it is the autonomous nature of women as sexual subjects (selves) rather than sex objects that emerges from the cultural regulation of initiation to sexual intercourse in Mayotte.[23] It is a woman's control over her own sexual activity that is critical. Restraint from premarital sex is practiced less to please one's future husband than to please society (represented by one's parents) and, through social recognition, to please oneself. As an adult, a woman chooses to provide her husband or lover with sexual access. Whether an individual follows social rules or not, the virgin wedding establishes a model for the orderly development of women, the significance of which all women can share, and provides a way for them to emerge as strong individuals, equipped with substantial material, social, and psychological resources. In writing of virginity in Mediterranean societies, Jane Schneider claims that women are "victims of their sexuality" (1971). In Mayotte this is not the case.

23. In another way a woman's sexuality does become objectified as it becomes an object of exchange.

THREE

Taboo as Cultural Practice among Malagasy Speakers

Like the previous chapter, this one focuses on the nature of the person and gives central place to acts rather than states or objects. Likewise, it continues with the act of not doing something, in order to generalize about refraining, abstaining, withholding, or avoiding. At the time I wrote the article, Mary Douglas was a central figure and her Purity and Danger *much cited and admired, and for good reason. While generally very gracious, Douglas was also a bit annoyed with me for suggesting that my practice approach was something not already prefigured in* Purity and Danger. *However, my goal was to understand the maintenance of a taboo (like fasting or abstaining from a certain kind of food) as a kind of act rather than as a structural relation or representation. Like her work, this was also a contribution to thinking about the body, and especially how people (i.e., those in Mayotte) use the body to think with. What I call here the "dialectic of objectification and embodiment," as well as the ethnographic particulars, are elaborated in my book* Knowledge and Practice in Mayotte *(1993b). The article was also meant as a kind of homage to Arnold van Gennep, a thinker whose influence has been largely limited to his work on rites of passage.*

> The most important developments as regards social theory concern not so much a turn towards language as an altered view of the intersection between saying (or signifying) and doing.
>
> —Giddens 1984, xxii

> In the final analysis, social life is made possible by keeping a delicate balance between falling inward and falling outward.
>
> —Murphy 1987, 227

This chapter first appeared in *Man* 27, no. 2 (1992): 19–42.

Malagasy Negation

In a paper that was only half facetious, Peter Wilson recounted his despair at locating social structure among a northern Malagasy group known as the Tsimihety. The Tsimihety "prove difficult to describe because they don't take structure as seriously as anthropologists do" (1977, 26). Wilson continues:

> These are hardly the sort of tribes who can provide the anthropologist with a new model to be slotted into the anthropological repertoire or help him dazzle his colleagues with a virtuoso analysis of a new logic. The people of such tribes don't do things, don't think new thoughts, don't create new symbols; *they can, in a sense, only be described negatively,* by comparing them with neighbors who do believe in reciprocity or do practice elaborate rituals crammed with mysterious symbols; who do tell contrapuntal myths or prescribe their daily lives through kinship. But there is not much point in trying to write 200 pages or so listing all the things a tribe doesn't do. (1977, 26–27; my emphasis)

And yet there are at least two lengthy books on Madagascar which do precisely that, Arnold van Gennep's *Tabou et totémisme à Madagascar*, published in 1904, and Jørgen Ruud's *Taboo: A Study of Malagasy Customs and Beliefs*, published in 1960. Wilson's answer lies unheeded in his own words. Obsessed with positive signs and rules, he does not stop to consider that structure can be located in negation, in prohibition and restriction. Both Lévi-Strauss and Freud tell us that this is what underlies society (see Murphy 1971); the incest taboo is just that, a taboo, a negative injunction, and an absence of a specific practice. Whereas Bryan Turner (1984, 19–20) contrasts theories that see prohibitions at the heart of society and those that locate that heart in language, taboos themselves form a kind of language. Taboos transcend the distinction between language and act, since they are both enunciated and lived out—the word made flesh, and the flesh made word. So perhaps Madagascar affords a privileged view of something that is basic to society.

Whether we wish to consider universal theories of society or not, the fact is that a focus on negation provides a useful perspective on Malagasy societies. The very name of the Tsimihety, like that of a number of other Malagasy groups, contains the negative participle *tsy*. Tsimihety means "[those who] do not cut their hair." Not those who wear their hair long, but those who do not cut it. This is identification by negation; persons and groups are defined in terms of what they do not do. This process is not necessarily simply a pejorative evaluation, such as might be imposed by one group on its neighbor, but something much more general, establishing axes of dissociation.[1] Rather than prescribing behavior, it merely sets the limits beyond which action is unacceptable. Moreover, what is circumscribed in narrow, specific terms is the Other, not the self. Self-identity or self-knowledge is predicated not on substance, but on that which the Other is not. Such negation, displacement, or indirection is found frequently in Malagasy nouns; something similar occurs in verbs, which are most frequently uttered in a kind of passive voice.[2] Spirit possession, common in many Malagasy societies, is another vivid example of an indirect depiction of the self through the periodic abdication to and substantiation of an explicit other (cf. Boddy 1989; Crapanzano 1977; Giles 1987; Kapferer 1983; Lambek 1981; Lambek 1988a; Zempleni 1977). Working from Malagasy material, Bloch (1986; 1989c) has developed a whole general theory of the construction of ideology through the negation or devaluation of its contrary in ritual. At the heart of Malagasy identity, then, lies implicit affirmation by means of negation.

Negation can be most clearly articulated in the form of taboo, *fady* in Malagasy. In the case of the Tsimihety, I do not know whether their name is merely a description or an explicit prohibition, a fady, but the fact is that fadys are extremely prevalent throughout Madagascar, a matter demonstrated encyclopedically in the two books mentioned above and addressed from a theoretical perspective in one of them. In focusing on fady I have no wish to reify the concept or even to suggest that my interpretation fits all usage of the term, which ranges from the nominal to the adjectival and which covers, as one reader has remarked, reference to such mundane matters as driving through a red light. On the other hand, little seems to be gained by excessively restricting the inquiry from the start. Suffice it to say that I will be treating fadys less as facts than as acts, less as lists of prohibitions than as a local means for constituting and marking significant relationships. In this endeavor van Gennep points the way.

Van Gennep's *Tabou et totémisme à Madagascar* appears to have been extremely important in the development of his thinking, laying the foundation for the general insights in *The Rites of Passage* concerning the enactment and marking of status changes. Van Gennep made a number of important

1. The contrast between prescriptive and complex (proscriptive) marriage systems is obviously an example of what I am talking about. The marriage system of Malagasy speakers in Mayotte is of the latter sort, specifying the categories of people whom one cannot marry rather than those whom one should.

2. Another kind of linguistic displacement common in Madagascar is word taboos. The forbidden word is replaced by a new or alternate word or by a metaphoric circumlocution.

points in the earlier work. He refused to succumb to the diffusionist tendencies that to this day bedevil Malagasy scholarship. He stuck resolutely to the view that taboos were a fundamental Malagasy institution, although he was quite prepared to admit that they were also basic to Judeo-Christianity, Islam, and African societies. Although the book purports to deal with both taboo and totemism, van Gennep wrote almost exclusively about the former topic and very little about the latter. This is because there is virtually no positive identification with a totemic species. Van Gennep concluded that "one therefore finds in Madagascar none of the characteristics of true totemism. . . . It thus seems excessive to speak of the animal tabooed by the Malagasy as a totem" (1904, 314). Indeed, in Madagascar the taboo is the totem.[3] In a sense, of course, this is precisely Lévi-Strauss's point in *Totemism*—namely, that the central issue concerns the differentiation of self and other rather than the substantiation of the self.

Van Gennep also argued staunchly against the animist interpretation of taboo (e.g., concerning the supposed fear of the dead), with its separation of body and soul. With the help of van Gennep, we can see that this theory of animism is just another version of Cartesian or Christian dualism and thus quite ethnocentric when applied to other societies. Van Gennep saw taboo as an expression of a sense of pervasive, nondualistic power, known in Malagasy as *hasina*. Taboos are thus acts of separation; they serve as boundaries, spatial and temporal, boundaries between or within persons and groups, boundaries that are marked on, or within, or by means of the body. In thus delimiting and differentiating persons and bodies, they help to constitute them.

Van Gennep's view, although somewhat more empiricist, intellectualist, and less coherent, does not seem all that far from that of Mary Douglas as expounded in *Purity and Danger*. Douglas follows van Gennep in linking boundary transgression to pollution and danger (Douglas 1966, 116). Both van Gennep and Douglas can be said to view taboo from a structuralist perspective. Unlike those of Douglas, however, van Gennep's boundaries are not between symbolic categories. Likewise, his position is not reflectionist; he does not distinguish the human body as a distinct order of classification that could be used to represent that of society at one remove from it. The taboo is not merely a symbolic representation of a boundary or ambiguity.[4]

3. I am indebted to Paul Antze for this phrasing of the point.

4. At the same time, *Purity and Danger* is a brilliant attempt to rethink and synthesize the issues. The reflectionist strain in Douglas's work goes hand in hand with a strong concern for a holistic analysis in which symbols are constitutive of social worlds and basic to social action.

Van Gennep would not, I think, have seen any point in searching for correlations between social organization and representation, precisely because he does not distinguish them in the first place. Thus, for example, he argued that the taboo is an expression of social obligation and hence "creates social continuity" (1904, 27). While van Gennep's understanding of social structure was rather weak and unsystematic (a problem he recognized and, in the Malagasy case, attributed to his unwillingness to generalize from insufficient and dubious ethnographic data), it also had a strength, which was that he viewed representation as inherent in social structure. Taboos do not reflect Malagasy society because they help to constitute it; they are part of its very substance.[5]

My argument begins with this insight from van Gennep. My own concern is less with the theory of power that lies behind the taboos than with the kinds of power and of persons they make possible. Similarly, I am less concerned with the content of specific taboos (why pork rather than beef, father's brother's offspring rather than mother's brother's) than with thinking about taboos as acts or practices and the consequences of such acts or practices for society and for the persons who carry them out. If the semantic content of the taboo elaborates who or what one is not, it is the practice of the taboo that substantiates who one is. This perspective also derives from the revision of psychoanalytic language from mechanism to agency (Schafer 1976, 1978). Instead of speaking about "having" taboos, we need a language of "being" or "doing," of verbs rather than nouns; taboos can then be seen as claims and disclaimers. This recognizes the fact that taboos are lived as well as thought and that the living out of taboos is a continuous product of human agency.

Taboos are produced and reproduced in a kind of dialectic of embodiment and objectification.[6] On the one hand, taboos are objectified negative

---

Many of my arguments in this article are prefigured in her work, although I do not follow her in the direction of social typology and systematic comparison.

5. Douglas (personal communication) suggested that this argument could be taken much further; taboos negatively constitute not only society, but the cosmos.

6. By *objectification*, I refer to features that are externalized, or exist externally and at some degree of independence from particular bodies, as signs, rules or constraints of personhood. Objectification as a process follows the path of bodies and persons into and within the public realm—for example, the legal status or change in name of a new mother, or the construction and manipulation of a statuette of a nursing mother and child. Embodiment refers to features that are internalized, or that exist internally or by reason of the fact that they are located within or as bodies. A woman who gives birth, who nurses and cares for an infant in a certain way, embodies motherhood, just as teknonymy or the exchange of cattle between affines objectifies it. Embodiment refers here not merely to the woman's body as an index of motherhood, nor

rules (proscriptions) that people can acknowledge, share, dispute, reflect upon, and choose to adhere to or to transgress, and in which anthropologists may discover structural order. Taboos may originate as culturally appropriate objectifications of either (Freudian) intra- or (Durkheimian) intersubjective experience or Lévi-Straussian play of the mind. But whatever their origins, taboos are also embodied; that is, they become part of the lived experience of specific individuals. Hence, if taboos are the rules of society, one can say that society is embodied in the acts and experience of its members.

Following a taboo means both articulating a prohibition in words and shaping one's daily acts to conform to it.[7] In the most profound cases, one's very perceptions become organized around the taboo so that the absence feels right and natural, even unmarked, and the violation or possibility of violation causes distress. Incest taboos and other sexual restrictions are so well internalized by the majority of people that the lack of sexual interest in the relevant directions appears unproblematic, and its appearance brings forth feelings of disgust, anxiety, or guilt. The objective rule may appear secondary to the embodied perception. Likewise, there are Hindus and Jews for whom orthodox dietary rules no longer carry any objective value or meaning, yet who cannot overcome a visceral reaction against eating the once-forbidden substances. These are positions that, in the normal course of events, need not be articulated consciously but are held within the body.

Often, however, taboos are followed deliberately and perceived consciously. In any given society we may inquire how various taboos are reproduced and what their consequences are for those who maintain them as well as for society in general. More basically, how do we describe the relationship of persons to their taboos? The remainder of this article addresses these

---

just to her iconic representation of the particular cultural construct of "motherhood," but also to the body as the locus through which the experience is integrated and to the complex of sensations and energies generated by the embodied experience, which it then becomes the challenge of the objectified concepts to capture. The examples of cattle and statues suggest other kinds of complexity as embodied icons in the objectified realm. In fact, many acts and practices simultaneously embody and objectify; in general, this is true of ritual (Turner 1967; Rappaport 1979b) and also, perhaps, of precapitalist exchange (Gregory 1982). My conceptualization of dialectics obviously owes a good deal to Berger and Luckmann's synthesis (1971). That work prefigures some of this discussion, elaborating the matter of public existence, for example, by distinguishing externalization from institutionalization, levels of legitimation, and so on.

7. Janice Boddy (personal communication) has suggested that in a sense all embodied meanings are negations, since they preclude alternative forms of action. Hence what is significant about taboo is not that it is an embodied negation but that the negation is marked, hence also objectified.

questions, although focusing exclusively upon social rather than psychological aspects of the problem. Without dismissing a Freudian approach, I leave the question of personal motivation in the adherence to taboos, as well as the psychic consequences of such adherence, to another context (Lambek 1990c; cf. Obeyesekere 1981). Most of my examples will be drawn from my fieldwork among Kibushy speakers of Mayotte.[8] Hence one of my concerns is to depict personhood in Mayotte as it is evident through the practice of taboos. For all kinds of reasons, the result can only be partial (see chapter 2; Lambek 1990b). Just as I deemphasize the content of the taboos here, so I do not attempt to describe the content of personhood. The point is rather how personhood emerges as the product of a given kind of relationship with the world that the practice of taboos establishes and exemplifies. The anthropologist can locate structure; the content is left for individual people of Mayotte to fill in.

Negation as Affirmation

If we are to consider taboos both as acts and as rules, it may be helpful to compare them with the positive rules and acts of exchange of which, as we should remember from Lévi-Strauss's theory, taboo forms an intrinsic part. There are three well-recognized functions that I wish to explore briefly: alliance, separation, and incorporation, or union. If the first of these is generally considered the most significant dimension of exchange, the latter two may be the more relevant for an understanding of taboo. Turning to alliance first, while taboo might be seen as the inverse of exchange in the sense that it can enact the rejection of a social relationship, it does provide a means of affinity for those who agree to hold a taboo in common. In Madagascar, members of a descent group, a locality, or a polity often share taboos. In Mayotte, there is an inherited taboo, known as *rangginalu*, against hot substances. People who are *rangginalu* avoid food and bath water of high temperature as well as spicy foods. They have an affinity with cold things, and it is likely to rain when they perform life-crisis rituals. Most saliently, whether she herself is *rangginalu* or not, the pregnant wife of a man who is *rangginalu* must avoid hot and spicy foods, and especially the fire under the bed and the hot foods, drinks, and bath water that are normally prescribed for the postpartum period. This can be interpreted as a statement and legitimation

8. Kibushy is a dialect of Malagasy spoken in the French territory of Mayotte, an island in the Comoro Archipelago to the northwest of Madagascar. Fieldwork in Mayotte was carried out in 1975–76, 1980, and 1985 for a total of some twenty months.

of their joint parenthood of the new infant (somewhat akin to the couvade, but with the difference that it is the woman who takes the action); rain falling during a life-cycle ritual is also a legitimation of *rangginalu* status. As an aside, it is an indication of the cultural bias toward negation that while *rangginalu* is defined as a taboo against hot substances, its obverse is referred to as *tsy rangginalu* ("not *rangginalu*"), hence as a double negative.[9]

Exchange not only links parties; a second function is to distinguish donor from recipient and to mark the space between them. A taboo clearly differentiates between those who must practice it and those who need not. Likewise, the distinction between the promulgator of a taboo and the person who is supposed to take it up is often significant.

Hence taboo forms a basis for hierarchical relationships, as is perhaps apparent in the co-parental relationship just described. Indeed, if exchange goods may be characterized as moving up the hierarchical ladder, the imposition of taboos tends to move down. In Madagascar taboos are often issued by royalty or ancestors; their observance by commoners or the living substantiates the power difference between them. It is in this light that Bloch (1986) argues that descent forms the negation of daily life. Yet the power dimension of taboo has many twists to it. Adhering to taboos is not just, or even primarily, restrictive; nor is it simply a response to orders. Rather, it is creative and carries positive moral implications; thus the taboo grants value to the person who maintains it (see chapter 2). Likewise, as van Gennep argued, royalty themselves were often the ones most bound by taboos.[10]

In Mayotte there are no longer any living royalty nor any vestiges of kingship except what is found in spirit possession (Lambek 1981). Taboos are imposed on their human hosts by the spirits, especially the royal *trumba* spirits, who possess them. A common taboo imposed by the trumba spirits

9. Such a double negative, in turn, does have a positive content. The application of heat after birth is an aspect of humoral theory; hence, the *tsy rangginalu* option may mark the penetration of Islam.

10. Although van Gennep realized that in the more complex polities the chiefs used the fadys against their subjects and as defense against invading strangers, that is, as an instrument of state (1904, 29), it was also the case that "in reality, the chief [was] the least free of all the individuals of a given group" (1904, 78–79). The contradiction between the chief's subjection and his power was situated in the notion of *hasina*, sanctity (cf. Bloch 1989c). The taboos on royalty are not, of course, conceptualized as originating lower down the ladder of secular hierarchy; rather, they draw their source from a transcendental order. Violations by the king of ancestral taboos bring calamity on the whole country. Royal family members, especially the king, concentrate the vitality of the people within them. The chief "is precisely that individual who is the most social: far from being outside and above society, he is its incarnation" (van Gennep 1904, 118).

is that the hosts are no longer to eat chicken. At the beginning of a possession history, the taboos indicate simply the superior power of the spirit over the host. Toward the end of the ritual sequence, the taboos are negotiated; those that remain come to symbolize the contract between the spirit and the host, the ongoing nature of their relationship, and hence the power now *within* as well as simply imposed upon the host. Similarly, every medicine has an associated fady, and virtually all local medical treatments are accompanied by taboos—for example, against eating such common foods as chili pepper, lemon, or fresh fish. Some time after the success of the treatment has been established, the client will approach the healer in order to have the taboos removed. If payment for the treatment is required, it occurs at this time; hence the taboos can be said to signify the dependency and indebtedness of the client upon the healer and the medicine, conditions that end with the lifting of the taboo. Yet, because the taboos are embodied, lived out, they do more than signify the relationship; they are rather a constituent part of it. The client's continued commitment throughout the treatment is expressed through abstention. On occasion, the curative taboo is transformed into a prophylactic one and hence continues to be observed after the patient is declared well (see van Gennep 1904, 54). Such vitally experienced commitment—a marked consolidation of energies—may, of course, also entail therapeutic effects.

One of the characteristics of a gift as opposed to a commodity is that it is essentially inalienable (Gregory 1982; cf. Parry 1986). Hence a third aspect of exchange, much discussed in the Melanesian literature, is that acceptance of the gift is a form of incorporation. An aspect of the self, albeit the public persona, is offered and, where the gift is food, literally consumed by the recipient. Thus Fortes (1987b, 139) argues that "nothing so concretely dramatizes acceptance—that is, incorporation in the self—be it of a proffered relationship, of a personal condition, or of a conferred role or status, as taking into one's body the item of food or drink chosen to objectify the occasion [or, I would add, the donor]; and sharing or abstaining from the same food, means uniting in common commitment. The intangible is thus made tangible." Fortes here likens sharing and abstention. Like a feast or gift of food, a taboo can also objectify and embody status, relationship, and union. It should be clear from the earlier discussion of alliance and separation that these functions are secondary to the primary function of taboo as a vehicle of incorporation. In Mayotte taboos mark the incorporation of a spirit within a host as much as the relationship of inequality and the contract established between them. In the long term, the enactment of the taboo serves to dissolve the differentiation of host and spirit (Lambek

1990c). Similarly, the pre- and postpartum taboos suggest or index a shared substance that is uniformly vulnerable to a particular stimulus. Sexual taboos likewise identify the parties as kin.[11]

A brief discussion of one of the taboo conditions most salient in Mayotte may help to substantiate the general points made above. In *trambungu* medicine, applied when a couple has difficulty producing live offspring or maintaining them past infancy, the parents, especially the mother, must observe a whole set of taboos, often for a period of several years. They must refrain from attending funerals, from eating the food served at funerals, from washing the dead, from committing adultery, from quarreling, and the like.[12] The following example is typical.

> *Fieldnotes, July 1980.* Amina's child has grown to toddlerhood and so she has come to the curer asking to have her fadys reduced as they are too hard to follow. But the curer replies that it is too early since Amina is pregnant again. Her fadys include the following—she must avoid funerals, she cannot eat at a ritual in which the food is cooked in many pots, she cannot eat chili pepper nor fish caught with fish poison, she must not get into arguments with anyone nor go watch others argue . . . Normally one can have the taboos removed once the child starts to move around on its own, away from the mother; the toddler itself would not be able to maintain the fadys, the argument goes, so why should the mother?

In their symbolic content the taboos create a barrier or counterweight to the forces of destruction and excessively dispersive behavior. But more important are the relationships that the observation of the taboos establish. These are not restricted to the renewed sense of identity and common purpose between the prospective parents, nor to the identification of mother and infant, whose separation is subsequently recognized in the removal of the taboo when the child becomes ambulatory. The taboos are entered into through the mediation of a powerful senior curer, either an astrologer

11. More precisely, as Héritier (1982) notes, the brother-sister taboo marks both identity and difference.

12. One explanation offered locally concerning the content of the taboos has to do with a theory of contagion in which the fetus is felt to be extremely susceptible to the experiences encountered by its parents. This impression (*tuhingy*) is evident in stories such as the following. A man died with his eyes open, and they were shut by the man who laid out the corpse. The latter's wife was pregnant at the time; subsequently, their infant son was born with his eyes shut. Similarly, it was often suggested that the pregnant women among whom I spent time might give birth to infants with my complexion.

or a spirit who manifests itself in the body of a known medium. The curer establishes the taboos and serves as a kind of guarantor of the wager that the prospective parents make; a relationship of clientship is thereby established. Not only can the observance of the taboos last several years, but even when procreation has been successful and the taboos have been dismantled in a ceremony directed by the guarantor, the relationship continues. Guarantors, whether astrologers or spirits, ought to retain a benevolent, if rather distant, interest in the children born under their protection; they are notified at subsequent rituals of transition such as circumcision and marriage, their continued protection is urged, and they are sent a portion of meat. Most important, people born under a condition of *trambungu* must themselves reinitiate such a condition when they wish to have children. They will turn either to the original guarantor or to the guarantor's successor. In the case of a spirit, this means discovering a medium in whose body the spirit now appears. Like the *rangginalu fady*, which is also most saliently associated with childbirth, the need for *trambungu* may be passed on bilaterally, yet its observance is most critical for the procreative partner of a susceptible male. In this manner, relationships initiated and constituted through the imposition and observance of taboos are reproduced from generation to generation.

The Temporal Dimension of Taboos

The rejection of food can dramatize acceptance of relationship; it may appear to do so less concretely than ingestion, but its results can be equally incorporative, profound, and even longer lasting. In the positive case, the rule of consumption becomes relevant in the context of the significant object; that is, as an act, it is episodic and context-specific. Food is rapidly consumed and digested. Unless the moment of exchange is defined as part of a longer cycle, as it is, for example, in those Melanesian societies in which feeding is the index of parenthood (e.g., Clay 1977), the message of the exchange and consumption may be quite transitory. But a taboo is relevant unless or until it is specifically dismantled. The principle of rejection requires a continuous stance: one must consistently stand on guard against the unwanted presence of the forbidden object and be ready to modify one's behavior accordingly. An adult in Mayotte takes care never to be left alone inside a house with a sibling of the opposite sex; a person who does not eat goat or chili pepper must inquire about the composition of every dish served outside the household or respond with nausea at the smell of the forbidden substance. The principle, relationship, or person that the objective rule of the taboo symbolizes in a relatively abstract fashion is simultaneously embodied in disposition. Daily practice and ordinary experience are shaped by taboo to a very fine degree.

My analysis presupposes a more performative than prescriptive view of society or "mode of symbolic production" (to turn Sahlins's terms [1985, xi, 29] to my own ends), in which action is as significant as rule. Moreover, the dialectic of objectification and embodiment is ongoing; Bourdieu's argument concerning the inherent temporality of exchange (1977) holds as well for taboo. There are moments at which specific rituals occur, including rituals that performatively initiate or terminate conditions of taboo, and hence one can speak of "before" and "after" states and periods. But I argue that a ritual dimension remains in effect for most, if not all, of the time, and hence that the boundaries and identities of bodies and persons (body-persons) are continuously vibrant. This is reminiscent of Leach's (1954) argument that ritual is the communicative dimension of activity and therefore omnipresent. The Leachian perspective on ritual was overshadowed by the power of Victor Turner's approach to rituals as transformative events and the focus upon the temporal and synesthetic aspects of ritual, but speech act theory allows us to return to Leach now that it is clear that acts and statements may be unified phenomena.[13] Performative rituals such as the utterance of marriage vows bring a new state of affairs into being through communication. If some rituals, such as the wedding vows, are temporally discrete events, I propose that others may operate continuously. Thus a man who dons a protective amulet is placing himself in a state of protection for as long as he wears it (Lambek 1990a) and not merely advertising that state to others, as in the Leachian paradigm. The words of the spell, written and enclosed in the amulet, function in the manner that the words of an oral spell do. The act of wearing the amulet replaces or extends the act of speaking the words; although in one case the performance is momentary and in the other continuous, the illocutionary effect is the same—namely, establishing and affirming a state of protection.[14]

To say this is not to attempt to weaken or trivialize Austin's notion of performative utterances (1962) but to use the insights developed from this approach in order to deepen our understanding of conventional acts. If

13. Speech act theory originates with Austin (1962); for innovative applications within anthropology, see Ahern 1979; Bloch 1989b; Brown 1985; Tambiah 1985; and, most relevant for the present argument, Rappaport 1979b.

14. The illocutionary effect is the same; the perlocutionary (persuasive) effect may be much stronger in a discrete, immediate performance.

Austin focused strictly on "cases . . . in which to *say* something is to *do* something; or in which *by* saying or *in* saying something we are doing something" (1962: 12), he also recognized a close affinity between such performative utterances and conventional acts or ritual in general (19, 69–70), and he concluded that some illocutionary acts could be accomplished by nonverbal means (118). One of the problems with which I am concerned is how to characterize the ongoing acts that I take the observance of taboos to be. Taboos are not merely imposed or lifted in discrete ritual acts and utterances, but are also observed over time. The observance of a taboo, when it is maintained under the sorts of conventionally prescribed procedures and conditions that Austin describes as prerequisite (appropriate time, place, agents, etc.), is a kind of continuous performative act in the sense that it brings into being and maintains—embodies—a particular (contextually defined) moral state. While not necessarily conforming to all features of Austin's definition of a performative act, the observance of a taboo is often considerably more than the indexical trace of such an act.[15] Abstention itself is an act and not simply the bodily inscription of one. For example, during the month of Ramadan, each day of fasting is preceded by a pledge. The pledge is a perfect example of a performative utterance in the pure sense described by Austin. Yet it is the fasting, not the pledging, that ultimately sanctifies. Hence it is insufficient to describe the fasting as merely the fulfillment of the pledge; moreover this would not correspond to the much higher saliency of the fasting than the pledging for participants. Hence the pledge might be described as a metaperformative condition for the felicitous enactment of the fast. There is not a great logical jump from this example of an annual fast to a lifelong abstention from pork or alcohol.

Appropriate adherence to socially legitimated taboos exemplifies Rappaport's (1979b) depiction of ritual as the union of the indexical with the canonical, together with the consequences of such conjunction that he elucidates. The canonical, in this case in the form of a "Thou shalt not . . .", is rendered present because of the act of commitment to the rule by the individual whose body demonstrates restraint. If we ask what is the practical difference between sacrificing an animal and holding it taboo, it lies precisely in the fact that the taboo is "pervasively performative," being inscribed into the continuous practice of everyday life.

15. Similarly, an ostensible index of the violation of taboo, such as breaking out in hives, might also be analyzed as a performative act that establishes a moral state of impurity.

Body, Personhood, and Society

One of my arguments here is that persons as moral entities are performatively constituted in part through the practice of their bodily taboos, that is, through living them. A similar position has been articulated by Gell. Beginning with the idea that the taboo is an emblem of the self, he quickly realizes that

> outside the specific acts, observances—and taboos—which specify a self as my self, there is nothing for an emblem of the self to be an emblem of.
>
> To observe a taboo is to establish an identifiable self by establishing a relationship (negative in this case—not eating) with an external reality such that the "self" only comes into existence in and through this relationship. In phenomenological language, the self only comes about in "intentional acts," and the observance of a taboo is such an "intentional act." It is nowhere except in what it accomplishes. (Gell 1979, 136)

The relevance of Gell's argument for Madagascar is reinforced by Ruud's observation (1960) that every positive intention is accompanied by its taboo. In a sense, the taboo is the embodied and inverted sign of the intention. But more than a sign, it is also an act, less direct but more concrete and continuous than the verbal intention itself. While Gell refers to the "self" here, I prefer the term *person* in order to emphasize that the practice of taboo is, as van Gennep argued, primarily a social act, directed, though not determined, by collective imposition. The emergence of the self is a significant issue, but it is complementary to the constitution of the person.[16] Taboos, as Gell argues, "establish and specify the individual at a number of levels" (1979, 136). In Mayotte taboos are distinctive at every level of social inclusion from humanity viewed as a whole down to the individual. Some taboos identify or differentiate relationships between men and women, young and old, members of a specific locality or particular line of descent, or people subject to a particular political authority. Taboos also

16. Another reason why I am reluctant to speak of the self here is that I am uncomfortably aware that the model elaborated in this article is essentially an external one, a "reading from without," rather than a "reading from within" (Boddy 1990). While the external argument is structuralist in that it provides for a relational constitution of the person or subject, a reading from within would doubtless be more substantive, taking into account the particular meaning and relative importance of each kind of act of restraint for the subject. I attempt this elsewhere (1990c). Fortes's work (1987b), while centered primarily on the person, remains an important attempt to bridge the Durkheimian and Freudian perspectives.

mark people undergoing specific rites of passage or curing rituals, or having particular relationships with spirits.

In general women bear a heavier burden of taboo observance than men, although not markedly so. It is not so much that women's taboos exceed those of men in number or content, but that women are expected to adhere to them more exactly. It is this adherence—again, practice more than symbolic content—that serves as a mark of gender. Thus, mothers rather than fathers are the focus of the birth taboos. And while everyone is tabooed tenrec (*trandraka*) meat, it is recognized (and tolerated) that young men hunt and eat the hedgehog-like animals in the bush. Similarly, while more men than women carry out the positive Islamic injunction of prayer five times daily, women generally observe the fast better than men. The gender bias of taboos raises a complex of issues related to the paradoxical relations between autonomy and value that I cannot address here (see Boddy 1989; and chapter 2).

Some taboos are individual. These may be established by means of astrology (Vérin and Rajaonarimanana, n.d.), but they are often discovered or allocated in a manner not dissimilar to the way Westerners talk about having allergies. Thus, a healer expressed the view that each person is different and must be treated accordingly. This was illustrated for me when I unsuccessfully attempted to treat a small boy's sore with antiseptic ointment. Some months later, the boy returned with another sore on his leg. When I offered the same ointment, the boy's mother flatly turned it down, asking for an alternative medicine. It was not that she rejected the healing powers of the ointment or that she thought it was not suitable for treating sores (indeed, she accepted some for her other children). But it was evident to her that it could not work on her son. The failure of my first attempt at cure had established a lack of fit between this particular kind of ointment and her son. The ointment was fady for him.

The totality of a person's taboos provide a summary of his or her current social status as well as a kind of retrospective account of that person's moral career, in much the way that, in Fortes's classic account (1983), individual Tallensi articulate particular constellations of ancestral guardians. Being both indices of present conditions and icons of past events, taboos may also be symbolic of intention, and therefore of the future—for example, the taboos engaged upon by a couple having trouble producing offspring. Thus, taboos provide both the grounds on which the person is distinguished from the wider context and hence comes to be a demarcated and coherent entity in the first place and, as signs of status, history, and intention, the means by which the person is constituted by selective incorporation and rejection of particular aspects of the context. As forms of negation, taboos provide the space within which individuality and personhood can be constructed at several levels of inclusion. The taboos at each level appear as choices within the more general level, even as they circumscribe the space within which further discrimination can take place.

Having argued that taboos are conventional acts, I must reemphasize that this constitution of the person or self—of present status, past history, and future intention—occurs by means of the body. Here we can observe a contrast with the Tallensi case in which taboos, though important, are less critical than the objectification of ancestral links in the spirit shrines. The body is not merely a handy set of signifying devices, a kind of alphabet, map, or forest of symbols used to encode a predetermined message, but a living, active, sensate, dynamic entity, a center. The experience of fasting cannot be reduced to the rule of abstention any more than the rule can be reduced to an expression of hunger or satiation. As Gell argues, the body helps to constitute the very things of which it speaks. Jackson (1989, 136) puts the point more strongly:

> My argument is against speaking of bodily behavior as symbolizing ideas conceived independently of it . . . it is misleading to see the body as simply a representation of a prior idea or implicit cultural pattern. Persons actively body forth the world; their bodies are not passively shaped by or made to fit the world's purposes. As Merleau-Ponty [from whose *Phenomenology of Perception* this position largely derives] puts it, "Consciousness is in the first place not a matter of 'I think that' but of 'I can.'" (1962, 137)

To the degree that this is so, we cannot speak of a mind/body or even a body/society distinction. It is insufficient to state, for example, that the categories of food and nonfood represent society, precisely because it is the acts of eating and refraining from eating that constitute society. There is no realm of pure or primary social relations existing apart from meaningful acts of refraining from, engaging in, passing on, sharing and withholding food, sex, labor, comfort, knowledge, and the like.

Indeed, what impresses me most about the Malagasy case is the degree to which body and society are understood to form a totality. The social nature of the body (or, conversely, the embodied nature of society) is quite explicit among Malagasy speakers in Mayotte. Before demonstrating this I need, at the risk of reintroducing dualism, albeit of a culturally contingent order, to describe briefly the concept of *rohu*, from which the body, or *nengin*, is chiefly distinguished. Rohu (from the Arabic *ruh*) shares features of the English words *soul*, *character*, and *consciousness*, though these words are partial and inadequate glosses. The rohu is the locus of the emotions; one's rohu may be temporarily happy (*rav'ravu*), sad (*malahelu*), or calm (*kutrulia*). But the rohu is connected to will, intentionality, as well as to emotion and may be described by others as essentially good (*tsara*: "kind, well-disposed to others") or bad (*ratsy*: "unkind, nasty, ill-disposed"). Attributions of rohu include reference to someone who keeps to him- or herself, doesn't raise children, or has no friends; someone so unselfish as to raise and care well for the children of a co-wife; someone who is lazy and cannot stick to cultivating, as opposed to someone who works hard but doesn't succeed.[17] As consciousness, the rohu is diffused throughout the body, hence insubstantial: no matter where you're cut, people explain, you feel it. Yet the rohu is also given a physical locus at the base of the neck just above the breastbone and is evident in the physical signs of the breath or pulse. It remains attached to the body when you faint or are in trance (when it is surpassed by the stronger rohu of the spirit), but unlike the flesh, which rots, it survives after death.

I have claimed that through taboos we can see the embodiment of society. By pursuing the distinction between nengin and rohu, we can add a political dimension to the argument. Embodiment is a primary means, perhaps *the* primary means, of legitimation. It achieves this by ostensibly naturalizing the social rule (or, conversely, naturalizing resistance to the rule).[18] This can be observed in the distinction that Malagasy speakers in Mayotte make between not doing something because one cannot and because one does not feel like it. The first of these is often phrased as *nengin tsy mety*, literally "the body does not allow it, does not grant it the possibility." The latter is *rohu tsy tia*, literally "the rohu does not like it." In other words, the former is grounded in inevitable bodily constraint or consequence, while the latter is a matter of individual will or freedom. The constraint of the nengin is social as well as physical. The phrase is used to explain not only something whose impossibility is given in the nature of its physical source, say the inability of a cripple to walk, but also a fady, something impossible because of its negative consequences. Moreover, in the latter case the constraint of the

17. Alternative and overlapping discourses of accountability make use of "destiny" (*nyora*) and "God's will" (*bok'an drangahary*).

18. Naturalization may be a general function of indexicality. Writing of the creative use of a linguistic index in order to bring an aspect of the context into cognitive relief, Silverstein remarks that "under these circumstances, the indexical token in speech performs its greatest apparent work, seeming to be the very medium through which the relevant aspect of the context is made to 'exist'"(1976, 34).

nengin is socially significant and becomes a recognized part of one's social identity, while the taste of the rohu is idiosyncratic. Hence the constraints of the nengin are intrinsic and unquestionable, while those of the rohu are subject to independent moral evaluation.

Given the bilateral basis of the kinship system in Mayotte, the inheritance of taboos, along with succession to mediumship (Lambek 1988b), provides a basis for articulating kinship connections in successive generations. Thus, the members of a particular descent line (*razanga*) may share a taboo against a particular food substance, say octopus, claiming that to eat it makes their teeth fall out. Each descendant must decide whether to follow the taboo of the relevant parent or to ignore it, following instead the practice of an alternate ascendant or of none.

> *Fieldnotes, October 1975.* Mdala remarks that his *razanga* is tabooed goat. He points out that this taboo originated in Madagascar. His mother's mother has it and so did her husband, his mother's father. When the latter ate goat, his wife, Mdala's grandmother, became sick. In fact, she won't go anywhere near where a goat is being slaughtered. When Mdala married, his grandmother warned him not to let goat meat into the house. Mdala's father does eat goat, although the spouse of someone who is *fady* goat really shouldn't. The husband of Mdala's mother's sister also eats goat, though his wife doesn't. Two of their children have reactions when they eat it, while the others seem able to consume it freely. All the children in Mdala's family tried goat, but Mdala stopped as soon as it made him sick. He spat blood when he tried it. His mouth itches when the plate he is eating from has previously held goat meat. But some of his siblings do eat it. "*Kula ulung ndraka nenginy* (each person according to his or her own body)," he says. The bodies (*nengin*) of some people follow the taboos of their *razanga;* the bodies of other people do not. The children of people who have stopped observing the taboo are no longer subject to it themselves. [Note that X, Mdala's mother's brother, can eat goat meat; indeed, he says he cannot think of anything better, that he comes running when he hears there is a platter of goat.]

Taboos can be activated or not in a myriad of ways, enabling (with some allowance for family politics and public opinion) individuals to cast their personhood for themselves, to have it emerge in the course of life and experience. If your body cannot tolerate goat meat—if you break out in a rash or become nauseated every time you taste it—this indexes a salient aspect of your identity, most probably linking you via the taboo to members of your mother's or father's or one of your grandparents' descent lines (cf. Lan

1985), whereas, if you just don't like the taste of something, it is socially insignificant. Maintaining the goat taboo or, conversely, ignoring it and suffering or not suffering the consequences legitimates your identity, both to others and, perhaps even more significantly, to yourself. Eating goat freely without negative consequences may index—and legitimate—your relative autonomy from the descent line (though it cannot erase or revoke the connection), just as abstention demonstrates and is an act of commitment to it. Your action is not an insignificant whim or antisocial refusal to participate in a collective practice, but an expression, through the nengin, of the way things are.[19] Persons are distinct entities, but they are fundamentally social. Or rather, in Mayotte, personhood is simultaneously social and natural, and socially acceptable because it is evidently natural, rather than individual and idiosyncratic.

In an interesting twist that serves to underline the basic point, there was a man who refused publicly to acknowledge his origins in a distant Malagasy group, yet continued to practice the food taboo characteristic of that group, thereby tacitly undermining his own conscious claims. The reverse process, where immigrants legitimate and naturalize their claims to a new identity by sickness cured through adherence to the relevant taboos, is discussed by Sharp (1989) for the Ambanja region of Madagascar.

Taboos function to legitimate spirit possession in a manner similar to the way in which they regulate descent. People who are possessed often attempt to disregard the taboos their spirits have imposed. They then suffer the consequences, anything from mild nausea to serious illness. The bodily reaction not only demonstrates the presence and power of the spirit, but also the host's ostensible lack of complicity in the process of possession. By demonstrating the distinctiveness of host and spirit, the attempt of the former to evade the latter, and the lack of success at resistance, the process contributes to the naturalization of possession in general (spirits exist "out there" and can enter and harm people) and its legitimation in this instance (the host is a victim of possession). Hence in legitimizing convention, embodiment simultaneously mystifies the human agency required for the ongoing production and reproduction of convention.

The following brief account gives a taste of the subtle and frequently humorous role of taboos in the negotiation of identity and relationship in

19. Nevertheless, it is evident from the brief description in my field notes that how the taboo is accepted or rejected—compare the claim by Mdala of a violent reaction if his utensils have ever even come into contact with goat, and the exaggerated statement by his uncle that nothing tastes better—suggests that a strong psychological dimension often underlies the social choices.

spirit possession. The occasion is one in which a woman named Mohedja has entered a trance in order that I may greet one of her senior (male) spirits upon my return to the field after an absence of four years. The spirit is speaking through Mohedja, contrasting its relationship with her and with me.

> *Fieldnotes, July 12 1980.* The spirit tells me it is glad that we are good friends, that I haven't abandoned the relationship once I received what I wanted. The spirit stresses it is pleased that I have returned, that it wishes me nothing but good, that it follows me wherever I go. It then goes on to remark that it is fady chili pepper (*pilipily*) and will fight with Mohedja [the host] if she doesn't stop eating it. The spirit says that it feels sorry for her and so is telling her gently first; it does not want to cause her any more illness. Mohedja's husband has always treated it well and Mohedja should too. The spirit adds that it has many fadys, such as that Mohedja cannot eat from a dish that the children have eaten from, nor from any dish previously started and mixed [i.e. the sauce with the rice in order to start eating] by anyone else. But it says it goes easy on these fadys since Mohedja is raising small children.
>
> Later, when Mohedja is out of the trance, she says she ate *pilipily* yesterday and it made her ill. She really likes hot pepper and every once in a while she cannot resist having some, but she is always sick afterwards. Mohedja insists that she cannot keep the spirit's taboos not to eat with the children. At first it made her very sick. She would drink a little cologne with white clay [spirit medicines] and feel a bit better. Now she is more used to it and does not get too ill. Chili pepper still always makes her sick, though it didn't before she was possessed by the spirit.

In this discussion I have had in mind Durkheim's distinction between the person and the individual, yet the nengin/rohu contrast provides a critical twist to Durkheim's argument. For Durkheim, "it is not at all true that we are more personal as we are more individualized. The two terms are in no way synonymous; in one sense, they oppose more than they imply one another. Passion individualizes, yet it also enslaves. Our sensations are essentially individual; yet we are more personal the more we are freed from our senses and able to think and act with concepts" (1965, 307–8). Following Kant, Durkheim associated the universal with reason and the individual with the body, and he argued that society provided the means to transcend the individual body in favor of reason. "There really is a part of ourselves which is not placed in immediate dependence upon the organic factor: this is all that which represents society in us. The general ideas which religion or science fix in our minds, the mental operations which these ideas suppose, the beliefs and sentiments which are at the basis of our moral life, and all these superior forms of psychical activity which society awakens in us, these do not follow in the trail of our bodily states" (1965, 307).

In contrast to this Western view, which associates the body pole of the mind/body dualism with the mute rather than the articulate, the natural rather than the cultural, the asocial and individual rather than the social and personal, the discourse of taboo in Mayotte grants the body greater social value. It is the body that substantiates what is socially significant, whereas individual preferences and passions are linked more closely to the mind (rohu). The indexical, embodied qualities of both taboo observances and the manifest consequences of their violation form a means of substantiating, simultaneously "naturalizing" and "socializing," and hence legitimating, both public rules and personal departures from them. Although it is the body rather than the mind that ostensibly constrains the passions here, my argument still supports and draws inspiration from Durkheim in its focus upon constraint and moral transcendence. Hence taboos in Mayotte personify rather than individuate.

This is true even where the taboo is observed by a single person. As we saw in the case of the boy who could not use the antiseptic ointment, when a medicine that has alleviated a particular set of symptoms in many individuals fails to do so in someone new, it is neither the medicine that is seen to be at fault nor the individual (rohu). Nor need it be the meaning of the symptoms that is questioned. Rather, it is claimed that the medicine simply doesn't work for a certain patient, that it is incompatible with him (*nengin tsy mety*), and he will not be offered it again. It is the cause-and-effect relationship between the person (body) and the medicine rather than between the disease and the medicine that is naturalized.

There is thus a strong political dimension to the body in Mayotte. In a sense we are talking about how society constrains the body, but in the local ideology this is nicely inverted so that it appears to be the body that asserts or denies social connection. By a process that is at least partially mystified, it is the body that sets demands and constraints on the person. Bodily experience, whether nausea or breaking out in hives, supersedes the conscious will of the individual, thereby grounding events in ostensibly inevitable processes. This is naturalization; as both an indexical center and the site of experience (emotion, pain, illness), the body clearly provides a "natural"—and highly salient—symbol for naturalization.

The political dimension is most explicit where a distinct authority figure imposes its will on and through the body. In northern Madagascar this was apparent in the taboos imposed by monarchs on their subjects. In Mayotte, the royalty are all dead, and external taboos come by means of dreams or spirits. Spirit possession is sometimes viewed in explicitly coercive terms. When I asked one man to describe what the experience of possession was like, he suddenly reached out and gripped my arm tightly. "*Coup d'état*!" he exclaimed.

Yet it is important to recognize that the source of the power is diffuse. In some Malagasy societies at certain historical periods, it has stemmed from coercive leaders (though only from those operating within the system), but the kinship example cited earlier locates the source within the person and the family. People who take on or ignore their descent-line taboos are ultimately the agents of their own decisions, even though the explicit recognition of their autonomy in this regard is denied them and others. The taboo may also be a vehicle of resistance to external power. Feeley-Harnik (1984) has shown how the power of deceased kings has been used successfully in a political struggle against the French over the imposition of demands of work, both as regards the nature of the tasks and the time required to perform them. *Nengin tsy mety* . . . it is not that I don't wish to work, to accept your demand or offer, but that my body cannot tolerate it; if I accept, I will get sick. (Of course, as we all know from experience, sickness is a widespread form of everyday resistance; the association with taboos in Madagascar makes it a legitimate one.) Sickness is also social punishment for reneging on one's moral commitments to a social identity, as son, subject, or whatever. Here the manifest effects of ignoring the taboo again naturalize the underlying connection and force. Conversely, to the degree that one accepts the authority of the taboo-imposing force, or simply its greater power, submission to the demands may be onerous but will not necessarily encroach on one's self-esteem or sense of justice.

Taboo and the Constitution of Moral Persons

People in Mayotte possess social identity and value not only because of what they do but also because of what they reject or refrain from doing (see chapter 2). Rather than following prescriptive rules and automatically taking on or stepping into previously determined social positions, they carve socially relevant space for themselves by establishing acceptable boundaries. They legitimate these boundaries by embodying their limits.

Boundary crossing has, of course, moral implications. The old statement that taboos are made to be violated need not be understood through the current fascination with transgression and the culture of infinite consumption. Rather, the violation of a taboo (a double negation) and its consequent effects are what legitimate it. Furthermore, the violation of taboo need not be viewed in terms of individual morality, according to a Judeo-Christian-Islamic logic of divine proscription, temptation, and sin. To the degree that the impositions and enactments of taboos form conventional acts, their violations are, in Austin's (1962) inimitable vocabulary, "infelicities," in the sense that they are interruptions of acts that by convention ought to be consistent and continuous. How given cultures interpret infelicitous acts is likely to depend on various contingent factors, including local, context-specific judgments. Broadly speaking, in the Malagasy system the taboos need not serve to protect a universal positive ideal, transgression of which would be an instance of defilement.[20] Rather, as I have argued earlier, the taboo carves out a space for the self-construction of identity more than it ascribes identity *per se*. Generally speaking, then, one is not identified as better or worse by the observance or neglect of Malagasy taboos, but as a more or less differentiated person. Some people simply have fewer taboos than others. Moreover, the incidental failure to observe a taboo that one does have may be more a matter of being unrealistic, inattentive, stubborn, defiant, skeptical, unserious, or out of context than of being immoral. Similarly, van Gennep argues that "in the last analysis the real meaning of *fady* is that of dangerous" (1904, 23) rather than prohibited or wrong. Individual moral evaluation is precisely a matter of rohu rather than nengin, of disposition rather than prohibition, of freedom rather than perceived necessity.

In Mayotte ignoring taboo is less immoral when it concerns one's own body than when it consists in failing to observe the taboos surrounding the bodies of others. Transgressions of the taboos of violence and sexual conduct (which are also, of course, among the most generalized) are attributed to the rohu, and individuals are held accountable. When this violation of others' bodies is carried out indirectly or secretly, it is *voriky* (sorcery, or witchcraft).[21] Sorcery is a surreptitious attack on another person, most vividly symbolized as an attack on and into the body, in part by means of impure bodily substances, hence as an act that is a kind of anti-observance of taboo. The desire to commit sorcery (i.e., to violate such taboos) comes not from the nengin, the body, but from the individual rohu. The intention is not naturalized or legitimated—no taboo is initiated, nor is there any attribution of Zande-like bodily witch substance—but remains a matter of

20. In this sense the Islamic and non-Islamic prohibitions found in Mayotte are not commensurable.

21. Van Gennep also notes that the most strictly prohibited things are referred to by the term *vorika* (1904, 87).

individual responsibility. The same is true for the violation of incest taboos and other sexual rules. In other words, the naturalization of choice does have its limits, and leaves a sphere of individual accountability.

The condition of sorcery as well as its removal are also expressed in concrete bodily idioms, indeed in graphic, visceral and often painful ways. Acceptance of an imposed taboo and rejection of imposed sorcery make similar use of the body. Again following Rappaport (1979b) on ritual, we can conclude that the formal and explicit extraction of sorcery from the body is a necessary component both of the recognition of its passage from the person and of the acceptance of the set of ideas that underlie its reality. In other words, reality—publicly, socially legitimated views of how the world *is*—is established not simply through thought but through bodily action and experience: through posture, movement, desire, pain—and, most basically and significantly of all, through presence.[22]

Hence, if intentionality is ascribed explicitly to the rohu, the moral qualities of the embodied taboo stem less from intentionality than from the manner, in a Durkheimian sense, in which taboo provides a legitimate and, indeed, an often-required means of self-transcendence, social commitment, and personhood. The ultimate antithesis of taboo is not evil but undifferentiated unity. Whether this is viewed as chaos, entropy, ecstasy, nirvana, or liminal creative flux depends on the context. In Mayotte, prior to the embodied marking that differentiates circumcised from uncircumcised boys and appropriately deflowered women from virginal girls, both boys and girls undergo what is generally agreed to be a more painful operation than either of these, in which their bodies are pervaded with a dense cloud of acrid smoke produced from the burning of a wide range of disparate ingredients. This, I think, is an antithesis of taboo. The body is opened out and suffused with the amorphous smoke. Initiates perspire, gag, and choke; their eyes and noses run; and they emerge black and stinking. The normal boundaries of the body are entirely transcended. What happens to the body indexes and constitutes what happens to the person. In classic liminal fashion, initiates

22. That the presence of the body signifies the acquiescence of the person is most graphically displayed to the people of Mayotte in its violation, when the body is present, but the person has been replaced by another, that is, by a spirit. But one could say too that the spirits only become real, social persons through their embodied presence. Having no visible bodies of their own, they need to take on the bodies of humans by *coup d'état*. And it is the bodily act of possession that signifies acceptance of the reality of spirits on the part of the temporarily absent host. Likewise, it is the interactions of other human persons with the spirit present in the body of a human host that constitute their own acceptance of the phenomenon.

are virtually stripped, enclosed and hidden away, and reduced to undifferentiated equality. Completely pervaded, lacking boundaries, they lose their identities. Although subsequent rituals will definitively engrave adult, gendered, and sexual status, during the smoking, young boys and girls may be taken together and are not distinguished from one another in any way. Taboos frame the liminal space (for example, one may not enter or leave the house during the smoking), but they do not compose it. Other taboos help to constitute, differentiate, and identify the persons who are created out of the amorphous mass of the liminal experience. Thus the imposition of taboos serves to create persons, while their breakdown reduces personhood.

In sum, my argument has been that one cannot have a theory of the human person without the body (and vice versa). The body is the primary seat, the ground and signifier of the person. As Rappaport (1979b) has argued, it is the presence of the body that renders ritual distinctive and powerful. Through their bodily presence, persons commit themselves to the religious and social order of which the ritual action or event is a part and thereby help to create not only themselves but the social order itself. Commitment, which is a social and moral relation, is enacted or performed; hence it is physical, embodied. If, following Durkheim, the person is a moral entity, and if moral commitment is established by presence, then bodies are necessary for persons; there can be no fully disembodied persons,[23] nor can there be a disembodied society. For Durkheim and Rappaport, ritual lies at the heart of society; for Lévi-Strauss and Freud, taboo does; I am merely pointing out that these are the same thing.

Whatever their generality, it is of course important to remember that these are ideal statements. In reality, not all societies are alike. From arguing that taboos are acts, it follows that they are not abstractions or timeless processes but are situated in concrete historical contexts and with respect to specific discourses and practices that articulate with one another and with wider forces and more powerful dialectics of encompassment and resistance (Comaroff 1985). Taboos are but one kind of practice in a wider field of intersecting discourses in Mayotte, discourses that exist in some opposition to

23. Bodiless persons (gods, ghosts, etc.) are always special cases. While spirits act and are conceptualized as persons in Mayotte, they only become persons to the degree that they invade and are manifested in human bodies. Indeed, it is precisely such embodiment that differentiates possession from myth or the indirect propitiation of spirits at shrines. Moreover, the morality of spirits is problematic and becomes an issue precisely to the degree that the spirits are embodied. Murphy (1987) provides a compelling account of the effects on personhood of partial disembodiment.

one another. As with totemism (Lévi-Strauss 1963), the validity of taboo as a general category must be kept in question. Not only may various taboos be more or less directly performative, but we need to keep asking in the name of whom or what, and at whose instigation, does renunciation take place, and whether the various instances are truly comparable with one another.

The picture of personhood and the body that I have drawn for Malagasy speakers shares certain features with the interpretation of the Kabyle house and, by extension, of precolonial North African society more generally, proposed in Timothy Mitchell's (1988) recent rereading of Bourdieu's account. Unlike the European "world as spectacle," in which order is understood as a framework,

> whose lines would bring into existence a neutral space in terms of which things were to be organised, [the North African] ordering does not work by determining a fixed boundary between an inner world and its outside. . . . It is not concerned with an order set up in terms of an isolated subject, who would confront the world as his or her object. Nor, finally, is it concerned with meaning as a problem for this individual subject of fixing the relation between the world and its plan or representation; or with truth as the certainty of such representation. . . . What we inhabitants of the world-as-exhibition would ordinarily take for granted as the elements of any order—framework, interior, subject, object, and an unambiguous meaning or truth—remain problematised and at play in the ordering of the Kabyle world. (50–51)

Thus, the Kabyle house has "a life made up not of inert objects to be ordered but of demands to be attended to and respected, according to the contradictory ways in which they touch and affect each other, or work in harmony and opposition, or resemble and oppose one another" (1988, 51). And, "rather than a fixed boundary dividing the city into two parts, public and private, outside and inside, there are degrees of accessibility and exclusion determined variously by the relations between the persons involved and by the time and the circumstance, . . . the dynamic relation between openness and closure, . . . [so there is] a city with no fixed exteriors . . . without facades" (1988, 56).

What Mitchell and Bourdieu describe so well for the North African house and city resembles my view of social life in Mayotte circa 1975. What exists is not a stable structure, a cast of discrete characters, but a play of forces and relations. The "person" is a continuously emergent product of these forces and relations; there are no "sovereign [essentialized] bodies" nor sovereign individuals.

And yet, of course, persons have agentive qualities that spatial structures do not. Taboos are not merely relations, but acts. Taboo is both the complement of exchange and its condition. Being a person entails the right and ability to refuse the total permeability of one's being, to reject the dissolution of identity in limitless exchange and interpenetration, and therefore, as Lévi-Strauss argued, the consequence of having nothing of value left to offer at the appropriate moment (chapter 2). Being a person also entails resisting a total inward collapse, that is, resisting the rejection of all material or social connection with the outer world. Thus, exchange and taboo, openness and closure, engagement and resistance, must be understood conjointly. Taboos help to regulate the fluid boundaries of inner and outer worlds. They provide a concrete and material means to carve out and connect personal and social spaces and to grant such spaces the legitimacy offered by both objectified public rules and immediate bodily experience.

FOUR

The Past Imperfect: Remembering as Moral Practice

This essay was written during a period of excited debates about memory and truth. It was the product of a joint project with Paul Antze in which we engaged an interdisciplinary group of writers to contribute to Tense Past *(Antze and Lambek 1996). This essay seeks common ground in approaches to collective and individual remembering, a point further developed in our introduction to the volume. The essay also convenes a broader range of theorists than I have managed since, from narrative theory to the philosophy of the self and its conjunction with psychoanalysis. In particular, I would like to draw attention to philosophers Casey, Gadamer, Taylor, and Tugendhat as relatively untapped resources for anthropological accounts of ethics.*

> The self we know in self-knowledge can't be construed as an object. Being a self is a matter of how things matter to us.
>
> —Ernst Tugendhat, *Selbsbewusstein und Selbstbestimmung,* as paraphrased in Taylor 1989

> It is time to rescue the phenomenon of memory from being regarded merely as a psychological faculty and to see it as an essential element of the finite historical being of man.
>
> —Hans-Georg Gadamer, *Truth and Method*

> To remember at all . . . is to become enmeshed in the thicket of the past.
>
> —Edward Casey, *Remembering*

This chapter first appeared in *Tense Past: Cultural Essays in Trauma and Memory,* edited by Paul Antze and Michael Lambek (New York: Routledge, 1996), 235–54.

Ian Hacking's critique of the prevalent assumption that memory is an appropriate object of scientific knowledge leaves us seeking a more appropriate way to approach the subject. I propose that one interesting way to understand memory is as a form of moral practice. The argument has two strands: that we think about memory as a human, cultural practice rather than a natural object or process, and that we understand the kind of practice it is as moral rather than simply technical, intellectual, or instrumental.

I build my case by alternating pieces of abstract argument with fragments of ethnography from fieldwork among Malagasy speakers on the island of Mayotte and in northwest Madagascar. The ethnography, which is suggestive rather than decisive in this form, draws particularly on my reflections on spirit possession, which is common in the area. In brief, possession refers to the relations that particular disembodied creatures ("spirits") engage in with particular human hosts, such that the host is periodically "absent" from her own body, replaced by the voice and persona of the spirit.[1] On the surface, spirits resemble the distinct alters of multiple personality disorder (MPD) described by Antze (1996), and there is a similar gender distribution and similar expressions of liveliness and sometimes of child personas (Hacking 1995, 76). But the possessed do not generally suffer the extreme anguish of at least some people with MPD: cases of possession are treated by means of a standardized ceremonial scenario and generally lead to a socially and psychologically positive outcome; the spirits are drawn from a public repertoire and legitimated as distinct from their hosts; and the spirits do not memorialize private suffering so much as they speak to the wider family and community. Their message is, in part, one of the prevalence of suffering (rather than its individuality) and also of the transcendence of suffering (rather than its fixation). Possession leads to greater rather than lesser connection to others. Spirit possession is in many ways a moral discourse, exploring the ambiguities of power (Lambek 1981). Here I speak only about the connection to issues of memory.

A few days following my return to Mayotte (Comoro Archipelago, Western Indian Ocean) in 1980, after a four-year absence, my mentor Tumbu took me aside, fixed me with a penetrating look, and asked whether I hadn't forgotten to greet anyone. I was delighted when he reminded me of my

1. For more comprehensive accounts of possession in Mayotte, see Lambek (1981, 1993b). For rich accounts of spirit possession elsewhere, see Boddy 1989 and Crapanzano and Garrison 1977.

social ties to the spirits that possessed his wife Mohedja. (I had not forgotten them, but was waiting to see what would progress.) I had to call them soon, he said, because they could not appear once Ramadan began.[2] When Mohedja's spirits rose in succession, we greeted each other as old friends; such affirmation was a fulfillment of moral obligations entered into some years earlier. During our conversation I was introduced to a new spirit of Mohedja's, Zaliata, who had not yet held her ceremony. Zaliata asked whether I would sponsor it. Although sponsorship is expensive, I took this as a positive overture. Sponsorship is usually taken by the spouse or close kin of a host and is an affirmation of ties and indeed a way of consolidating them. Moreover, Mohedja knew this would provide me with further opportunity to see a possession ceremony from the inside, as it were. I agreed, but cautiously. My visit in 1980 was only of several weeks' duration, and much of that was during Ramadan. I had no way of knowing whether I would ever return to Mayotte; indeed, at the time, I thought of the visit as possibly my last one, intended to close off unfinished business and say good-bye. I explained to Zaliata that I might not be in a position to hold the ceremony and that she must not exhibit impatience nor make Mohedja ill in the meantime, as spirits who have not held their ceremonies often do. The spirit agreed to this condition, and we parted.

The spirit's request meant that business in Mayotte was not finished (how could relations among friends ever be?), and I thought about it often in subsequent years. When I returned to Mayotte again in 1985, urged in part by the memory of Zaliata's outstanding request, I called up Zaliata and said I intended to keep my commitment. But at this, there arose unexpected difficulties. Mohedja's adult daughters objected. What disconcerted them most, I think, and what surprised me most, was that the situation was so unexpected. They had not even known of Zaliata's existence, they said, or at least they had not remembered that she possessed their mother. The simple fact of the matter was that Zaliata had never once risen in Mohedja during my five-year absence, nor had any illness or communication been laid to her door. Mohedja's other spirits had risen during this time. However, Zaliata arrived promptly at my request and remembered our agreement perfectly. Indeed, Zaliata's absence in the intervening years had been precisely an index of the retention of the memory of our contract. Her appearance in my absence would have been pointless, since only I could carry through with the next stage of the possession script.

2. Thus, incidentally, possession "remembers" Islam (cf. Lambek 1993b).

Mohedja's daughters attempted to dissuade their mother and her spirit from undergoing the new ceremony. I was embarrassed by the turn of events, apologized to the daughters, and told Mohedja I would be happy with either outcome. Mohedja agreed with her daughters' decision, but immediately thereafter fell sick, her symptoms testifying to the violation of the agreement. Zaliata remained stubborn and refused to accept the daughters' arguments. Mohedja's daughters became reconciled to the situation and helped me sponsor the ceremony. Mohedja herself danced blissfully in trance.[3]

Let us distinguish two broad conceptualizations of memory. One of these, dominant in America now, emphasizes the role of memory in the expression and validation of the discrete, private individual. Memory here is simultaneously objective and subjective; this conjunction may be what gives memory such discursive power. Memory is subjective in that it is uniquely ours, something that distinguishes each of us from others and defines who we are and how we see things. It is something that each of us "possesses" and that validates our unique presence as an independent witness, whether as bystander, agent, or victim. Yet this possession is objectified in a number of ways. Memory is pluralized and thus rendered discrete, transactable, and even commodifiable. Memories are objects, not acts. Advertising brochures tell us we can collect them on foreign beaches, produce them during candlelit dinners, and capture them on film, but when they are contested, they appear more like unshreddable bureaucratic files. To the degree that memory is conceptualized as an act, it is a passive one, analogous to a video camera left running in a corner of the room, recording or reviewing, but not shaping experience. But this means that memory is judged entirely according to objective criteria, how well it conforms with "the facts." Our memories may be depicted as complete or incomplete, but never as subtle, tactful, or reasonable, well or poorly crafted, elegantly or clumsily performed. They are accurate or inaccurate, but never justified or unjustified. Finally, memory is

3. Memory is a function of the person and the relationships and contexts to which she commits. Each of Mohedja's spirits retains its own memories; thus, memory is one of the means by which the distinctions between the spirits and between the spirit and host are legitimated. However spirits are no mere fragments of the individual self. A given spirit can have a relationship with more than one host. When spirits shift between hosts, ideally the memory goes along with them. Thus a spirit possessing Mohedja ought to remember clients who had approached it when it was active in Mohedja's mother. The demand for such continuity is an ideal, a function of the claim to identity.

evaluated objectively because, as Hacking has been at pains to show (1995 and 1996), it has become an object of professional knowledge about which experts can discover the timeless truth. Moreover, memory is understood as no mere human product but as constitutive in a causal sense of who we are as individuals and as societies or ethnic groups. In the extreme, the conflation of excessive subjectivity and objectivity leads people to identify with their hypostatized memories.

The analogies to the files and video camera are not, of course, arbitrary. Our reified, naturalized concept of memory is undoubtedly linked to our technological capacities, especially to reproduction by means of the camera.[4] The memory constructs of other societies are linked to *their* cultural means of inscription, storage, and access (such as spirit possession). My point is not that diverse cultural technologies provide more or less accurate and complete memory, but that they provide diverse ways of imagining memory and hence distinctive qualitative emphases. The objectifying devices of contemporary Western memory production have at least three significant qualities that distinguish them from the idea of memory as ongoing practice: they freeze words and images; they put frames around them; and they render remembering mechanical and impersonal (Casey 1987, 270, 298). This enables us to resituate memory ostensibly outside engaged experience and the give and take of social relations. An inherently and preeminently temporally constituted process like remembering is thus detemporalized. This is nonsense, but it is difficult to see it as such when authoritative discourses in psychiatry, law, and history so often attempt to validate it.[5]

Let us try to imagine memory in another way, one that resists the extremes of both excessive subjectivity and excessive objectivity—one that situates memory in time and sees it as a function of social relationships, in part a mutual affirmation of past interaction, in part the traces of our introjection of one another. There is a sense that, in the ordinary course of events, the memories of parties to a social relationship ought to be compatible with each other. People ought to maintain their relationships over time and be able to take up where they left off, to acknowledge the commitments they have made to one another. The intermittent quality of the appearance of spirits and hosts (not to mention anthropologists) and their respective

4. It is also linked, of course, to computer storage. Hacking points out that the memory "flashback" is derived from the movies (1995, 252).

5. Terdiman (1993, chap. 2) addresses the temporality of memory production by means of an insightful application of Marx.

consciousness serves to heighten these qualities of memory, but they are implicit in friendship, kinship relations, marriage alliances, and, indeed, any system of reciprocity.

Memory in this model is less a completely private yet potentially objective phenomenon stored *within* the mind and capable of remaining there than it is activated implicitly or explicitly *between* people, a confirmation of the sense of continuity (caring) and discontinuity (mourning) that people experience in their relations with others and that is likely acknowledged by additional parties.[6] Memory here is more intersubjective and dialogical than exclusively individual, more act (remembering) than object, and more ongoing engagement than passive absorption and playback. Applying this to contemporary psychotherapy, one could say that what occurs is not necessarily the replacement of amnesia by memory, false memories by true ones (or vice versa), so much as the alternation of social contracts—for example, in gross terms, the displacing of family relationships by those with the therapist; a reformulating of social ties and commitments. The value of articulating a particular version of the past would be explicitly connected to its moral ends and consequences for relations in the present.

Such an argument recognizes that how we view memory, and how we remember, have implications for how we view the person, and vice versa. It leads us away from understanding memory as purely "natural" or "automatic" activity (analogous, say, to digestion) and the product of unmediated gaze, and hence away from accuracy as the only criterion by which to evaluate memory. It leads us toward seeing memory as always and inevitably culturally and socially mediated and hence subject to evaluation along a number of dimensions whose relative importance is open for debate. This is not to deny the importance of accuracy, but to recognize *why* we consider accuracy important. The questions to ask of any given acts of memory are, what is affirmed, and what is denied?

Such an approach treats memory not as a neutral representation, more or less accurate, of the past, but as a claim or set of claims, more or less firm, more or less justified, more or less appropriate, about it. Both remembering and forgetting may be claims, motivated acts of some sort; this indeed is Freud's argument regarding forgetting. In this sense neither memories nor their gaps should be taken at face value, not even after therapy or inquisition and validation by other kinds of experts. Like speech, memory contains

6. Caring and mourning are drawn from Casey's remarkable discussion of what he calls "the thick autonomy of memory" (1987, 276), a phenomenologically derived depiction that has much in common with the one developed here.

both semantic and pragmatic dimensions, and involves both locutionary and illocutionary acts. As Antze argues (1996), to remember is never solely to report on the past so much as to establish one's relationship toward it. Memory is never out of time and never morally or pragmatically neutral.[7]

The same argument applies when we move from instances of remembering to formal discourses of memory. Any invocation of "memory," whether in psychology, psychotherapy, psychiatry, neurology, history, or anthropology, is "motivated" by claims regarding time, person, consciousness, reality, truth, and the like. Hence, to break through the theoretical circle of self-validating disciplinary analogies may require, short of sheer brilliance, borrowing ideas from the equally self-validating but substantively distinct analogies of other times and places.

The illustration from Mayotte draws upon the usual, doubtless exaggerated, comparison between the individualist West and the socially embedded Rest. Yet I use it less to provide a sense of difference than as a source for insight about Western experience. There are also plenty of Western models at hand, ranging from Halbwachs (1980) on collective memory or Mead (1934) on intersubjectivity to Janet on memory as an act (Leys 1996) and contemporary debates in psychoanalytic theory between proponents of the classical drive model and what Stephen Mitchell (1988) refers to as the "relational model." My argument may be faulted for resting on ideal types. But the public discussion we have now is largely restricted to understanding memory through the ideological, albeit implicit, lens of a possessive individualism. What happens if we reconstitute the discourse of memory in the key of object relations?

We have seen that spirits retain specific memories and thereby index the social relations to which they pertain. They provide, in effect, a sort of "parking" function between rounds of communication. This is, however, far from the whole story; spirits are memorable in and of themselves. Above all, they are memorable irruptions in the personal lives of their hosts. Mohedja and Tumbu can tell stories about the arrival of each of their spirits. Each is linked to a specific phase of their lives, particular problems, projects, and relationships at the time (such as Mohedja's relationship with me), often

7. For parallel arguments, see Schafer (1976) on agency in psychoanalysis; Fingarette (1963) on avowal and disavowal; and Felman and Laub (1992) on witnessing and testimony. Hacking (1995, chap. 17) turns to the way agency is attributed in memory to past actors and how the availability of new forms for describing actions can transform memory.

to serious illness and conflict. The spirit condenses these memories in its person. Each subsequent intervention on the part of the spirit draws out (rediscovers and extends) the narrative of which it is the central character and the relationship to the world of which it is the embodiment, and also provides the occasion for reinterpretation. Moreover, with the hindsight of having a spirit, one can reinterpret past events, knowing now, as one did not then, that they may have been caused or influenced by the spirit before it had chosen to make itself fully known to the host. Spirits thus aid in constructing and authorizing revisionary accounts of the personal past. At the same time, however, they are not, in Paul Antze's useful phrase (personal communication), memorials *to* the past. What counts is not only how they entered the hosts (pain, victimization), but their progress through the ceremonial scenario and the commitments engaged upon thereafter. Spirits provide their hosts both new channels of communication and internalized self-objects, enabling continuous adaptation to the present and engendering a working-through process.[8] Central to spirits are their narrative and performative functions. Spirits are vehicles *for* memory rather than the frozen remnants of memory.[9]

Higher order consciousness, consciousness of being conscious, requires the representation of a self. The self-representation of this self, its consciousness of temporal and spatial existence, is memory. Memory in this sense, argues Oliver Sacks (1993) in his review of the work of Gerald Edelman, is something neither deposited in the brain nor having a specific location within it. It is, rather, a symbolic practice.

What are the relations among memory, consciousness, and the symbolic vehicles, of which perhaps the most important is narrative?[10] Benedict Anderson (1991) argues that narrative enters precisely to replace

8. I cannot develop this here. Often a spirit has appeared in a close senior relative before moving to the current host. Social and psychological implications of communication and succession are variously addressed in Lambek 1981, 1988b, 1993b, and later work.

9. The contrast with the case of the Moroccan man, Tuhami (Crapanzano 1980), who was bothered by spirits but never engaged in full-blown possession, is instructive.

10. In the ensuing discussion *narrative* stands metonymically for any form or vehicle through which memory is expressed. Narrative is not the only vehicle of memory, but I take it to be prototypical, and for the purposes of my argument, I ignore most of the differences between inscriptive and embodied remembrance (De Boeck 1995), or between recalling and remembering (Bloch 1998). Nonsemantic vehicles, such as smells, may be highly evocative, but their source is external; to the degree that they remain meaningful, they quickly get woven into narratives or scenes. The smell of a certain disinfectant powerfully evokes images of the high, white interior

memory—that is, that the presence of a narrative is an index of having forgotten the original experience. Thus he takes memory as somehow continuous and literal as opposed to "imagined." I suggest that neither of these pictures of memory, whether as direct, literal, and subjective, or as narrated, imagined, and objectified, is sufficient. The literalist picture ignores the fact that our experience of memory is generally indirect, by means of recall, recollection, or reminiscence (Casey 1987).[11] At the same time, it would be a mistake to go to the opposite extreme and mistake the fluidity of memory for the detached objectifications of collective memorials (including here the overly coherent narratives produced in some forms of North American psychotherapy). It seems more interesting to take these ideal typical pictures of memory as poles and to focus on the movement between them, on how one goes from the one to the other and back, how private experience and public narrative mutually inform each other. In other words, whereas Anderson distinguishes memory from (fixed) narrative, we also need to distinguish it from the immediacy of direct experience. Memory, as suggested above, concerns the consciousness of being conscious. Hence, we need to retain for memory the idea of perspective or clearing of space, the view of there from over here, of situated distance (cf. Kirmayer's landscape [1996]).

It follows that we must understand memory as *essentially incomplete;* memory is perspectival, and the perspective is a continuously shifting one. The voicing of memory is transitional, no longer fully subjective and not yet fully objective before it is legitimated in collective constructions like history textbooks, ritual commemorations, or legal testimony (or vice versa). Active memory (like acts of spirit possession and talk about spirits) lies between primary experience and the routinized "forgetting" that Anderson describes.

Anderson's memory that we cannot recapture and hence must replace by narrative is analogous to Freud's understanding of dreams. The experience of dreaming is not based upon a concrete, bounded narrative or image that we can then repeat verbatim; instead, the telling replaces the dream. In other words, it is impossible to know where the images perceived or originating in sleep break off and those in waking life, elicited in what is ostensibly a reproduction but becomes its own creative process, begin. Once formulated in words, it is this version we remember, the representation, not the original

---

walls of my grandmother's house, and then of events that transpired within them, but an image of the walls never produces the smell for me.

11. For Anderson (and for those who subscribe to the romantic view of unspoiled, premodern communities) memory would be simply continuity or repetition. But once the repetition becomes conscious of itself as repetition, it is no longer an exact copy (Leys 1996).

experience. What we call the dream is actually the highly mediated retelling. Similarly, memory can be understood as acts of narrative, retellings, a point Freud grasped in his formulation of screen memories, that is, memories of memories.[12] Accessible memory has no unmediated essence, either as subjective experience or as objective fact, but is always in the act of being made.

These points help us reflect on the differences between history and memory as constituted in contemporary discourse. For many people, history is secondary to memory in not being based on direct continuous experience, on I-witnessing. This valuation implies a dangerously literalist view of memory, the kind one might find in a court of law. It neglects the fact that, as Terdiman puts it, representation can never be identical reproduction (1993, 59). If the first person account has a certain kind of legitimacy of the "I-was-there" sort, conversely documentation provides a counterweight of its own. Thus the opposite tack on the comparison of history and memory, as oral historians have learned to their chagrin, is to trust only what has been recorded in writing, since, as it is said, memory is notoriously "unreliable," whereas, presumably, the texts stick to their stories. Here we have, in a nutshell, one of the salient distinctions between texts and practice.[13]

In contrast to Anderson (but in his spirit) I refer to narratives as vehicles of memory but recognize that they can become more or less objectified, more or less detached from the process of remembering. This view of remembering as symbolic practice understands neither personal memory nor scholarly history as literal; to the degree that both are narrativized constructions, the categorical distinction between them begins to dissolve. The critical distinction is one of fluidity—the degree to which any particular narrative is open to continuous reformulation; any event or document, to reinterpretation—and how such changes are legitimated.

Spirits are memorable not only for what they evoke about the host's experience but because they are themselves historical or mythic figures. If in

12. The point applies as well to fantasies remembered as real. As Terdiman puts it, "Memory cannot distinguish between the register of facts and that of interpretations" (1993, 346).

13. Historians' attempts to legitimate their craft by insisting on the value of history over memory resemble the attempts of anthropologists and sociologists to distinguish their insights from "common sense" or "common knowledge." Such questionable delegitimation of lay knowledge is opposed by arguments that carry the opposite risk, namely, romanticization. Memory is a popular topic in social history and anthropology today precisely because it is seen as a privileged site of resistance to hegemonic narratives. For more nuanced approaches, see the essays in Sider and Smith 1997.

Western discourse it makes sense to distinguish memory from history (although I have begun to deconstruct the opposition), this is less obvious in places where history is less text-mediated than voiced and embodied. When the spirits are persons from the past, once-living figures who reemerge after death, the narratives they evoke include dimensions of broad collective interest. This is crucial in Madagascar, where the *trumba* spirits who possess people are the ancestors of living royalty; the spirits draw their collective import both from contemporary political circumstances and from past events in which they were live agents. Each spirit is the vehicle for a history that is preserved, in part, through relations between contemporary hosts and the figures from the past who possess them. Taken together, the roster of spirits and the ways they interact with each other provide a collective historical memory. Spirits wear the clothing of the time when they were alive, speak the languages of the past, embody past habits, customs, and comportment; they continue to enact the concerns, relationships, and perspectives of the past. They are thus "living history" in a strong sense; they bring forward and force people to acknowledge the commitments of and to the past. The past is never completely over; it continues to shape the present, even as it is distinct from it, and at the same time it is available to be addressed by the present. Conversely, remembering entails engagement with the past.

Memory of any kind implies a self or subject who perceives the memory or does the remembering. Today our understanding of the nature of this self is increasingly dependent upon reference to memory—I am the product of who I was and what I experienced—just as the nature of memory is implied and constituted by the theory of the self or subject—you should remember what your therapist or civics instructor thinks you can because that is the way people or nations are. I take memory to be an intrinsic part of selfhood (such that memory and identity serve to mutually validate each other), but I also take these to be culturally somewhat variable (Bloch 1996). Thus the contemporary North American invocation of memory tells us about the boundedness and singularity of a particular subject and relationship of self and others. The cultural variability in identity supports the argument for the sort of dialectical relationship between narrative and experience I have suggested.

The practice of memory operates in partly similar ways for individual and collective subjects. In each case we narrate and represent our identity, and then reproduce these representations, by means of the public idioms and tools at our disposal. We create imagined communities (in

Anderson's brilliant coinage) and imagined selves and then attempt to live accordingly. In neither case is it useful for the theoretician to start from a pre-given, primordial or essential identity existing apart from the ongoing construction of itself. As Anderson argues, it is out of oblivion that narratives spring. It is precisely because I *cannot* remember in direct, unmediated fashion the experience of my childhood (i.e., can no longer experience as a child), and because I cannot remember directly the events that lead from the infant to the man, that I rely upon a narrative construction to realize this continuity. Individual memory, like the narration of the collective we call history, is never literal reproduction, but an artifice to render the continuity in change realistic.

In addition to being a necessary response to oblivion, such artifice also works in part by means of selective oblivion, or censorship. Objectified narrative may be understood less as an inadequate replacement for direct experience than as a purification of it, a transformation of past experience, a *poiesis* (Terdiman 1993). As Gadamer puts it, "Only by forgetting does the mind have . . . the capacity to see everything with fresh eyes, so that what is long familiar combines with the new into a many levelled unity" (1985, 16). In the best of circumstances, this may be sublimation, but even neurotic or hysteric symptoms have a symbolic consistency, as Freud demonstrated.[14]

This argument needs to be supplemented by another explanation for oblivion that suggests that foundational experiences become constitutive *of* the self in such a manner that they are no longer accessible *to* it. To the degree that the subject is constituted through such assimilative *forgetting,* conscious memory might be conceived as the unresolved, the residual. In this sense, conscious memory is significant less as the trace of the past than as the kernel of the future (Kugelmass 1996). Such a model acknowledges the relevance of two senses of "memory," as suggested by Anderson's original argument; however it requires at least two senses of "forgetting" as well.

Not only does the constitution of the collective subject work analogously to the constitution of the individual one in general, but particular experiences of the self and discourses of the self provide idioms for narrating collective experience and identity. This is immediately evident in the application of a term like *collective memory* and is well-developed in arguments that the concept of the modern nation is modeled on the ideology of collective individualism (Handler 1988). It is found also in the iconic representation of history by "great men," including the *trumba* spirits. Likewise,

14. Unfortunately, when subject to excessive external influence, both collective and individual narrated memories may resemble kitsch more than art.

the discourses of collective identity offer a language for expressing selfhood via kinship, ethnicity, gender, race, and class, or newer conceptualizations like sexual orientation and postcolonial subject, or my own transposition of "imagined community" to "imagined self." In other words, images of individual identities constitute a totemic system, so to speak, of collectivities, and vice versa. In both the individual and the collective cases, we have today in the West the conceptualization of highly bounded entities distinguished from one another by their property (Handler 1988), property that includes inviolable, sacred memories belonging to their rightful owners.[15] However, while such explicit memories may be extremely salient, they are poetic rather than literal and not necessarily as foundational as their subjects claim.

The narratives most salient to the Antankaraña of northwestern Madagascar today refer to events that took place in the first half of the nineteenth century, specifically to the incursions of the Merina on their territory. At one point some members of the royal descent group were pressed against an inlet of the sea. Rather than submit to the enemy, they plunged into the water, where many of them drowned or were eaten by fish. Sometime thereafter, the martyrs began to reappear, possessing living Antankaraña as *trumba* spirits. Every year the Antankaraña monarch holds a bathing ritual at which hundreds of people gather at the beach, and the possessed plunge into the water. Royal bathing rituals have significance throughout Madagascar; the Antankaraña version reenacts the death of the martyrs while also celebrating the emergence, empowerment, and renewal of the spirits. The ceremony is a positive, revitalizing one, constituting an ongoing exchange among the king, the people, the ancestors, and the spirits, but it also memorializes the historical trauma. Merina are not allowed at the site.

The martyrs appear on many occasions. Their pathos is reinforced by the fact that, like all *trumba,* they portray themselves at the point of death, mimetically reproducing the manner of their dying in the way they contort the bodies of their hosts on entry (Andrew Walsh, personal communication) and smearing these bodies with white clay to indicate the extent of their wounds. Moreover while most spirits exemplify generational succession and continuity, this group of spirits stands out by being composed of

15. In extreme cases this connection is essentialized, envisioned as somehow biological. For critiques see, inter alia, James 1995 and Suleri 1992.

a core set of siblings, all of whom died at once. Gathered together in public spaces, the spirits provide a kind of snapshot of a traumatic moment in northern Malagasy history which is still significant today. However, these Sea Dwellers (*Antandrano*), as they are called, come not to grieve but to engage in the passions of life. They make music, sing, dance and drink, engage playfully with the living, and often assist them with their personal troubles.

Here, in contrast to the view propounded by Michelet at about the same time the martyrs were drowning (Anderson 1991, 198), history does not speak for the dead who cannot speak for themselves. Northwestern Malagasy not only speak to the dead, they speak as the dead; in other words, the dead do speak for themselves. The royal dead are not framed and frozen in objectified, textualized memory, but rendered active in the present. Reciprocally, contemporary Malagasy live not only in the present but in the past. *They do not possess memories; rather they are possessed by them.* Put another way, time is not fully consecutive; the past is not finished and done with, receding ever further into the distance, but (in grammatical terms) imperfect. In the daily interactions of spirits with living people and the many phases of the ritual cycle I cannot describe here, past and present interpenetrate.[16] Historical memory is not determined by a fixed representation that is to be judged entirely by its accuracy but is a mutual tuning constituted in well-crafted and elegantly performed symbolic and moral practice.

To speak of memory as symbolically mediated rather than literal is not to endorse the idea that anything goes, that we have no grounds on which to discriminate when memories conflict. Nor is it to suggest that the most coherent narrative is the most adequate. Indeed, if anything, the reverse is the case—the smoother the story, the more evident that it is the product of secondary reworking. What symbolic mediation suggests is that any account of the past is organized by means of certain cultural conventions (Kirmayer 1996). Central among these will be what Bakhtin (1981) has called the "chronotope"—that is, the particular space-time continuum in which the action of any narrative (whether inscribed in writing, embodied in ceremonies, or voiced and under continuous reconstruction) is construed. The chronotope provides a useful analytical device for comparing the worlds in which the subjects of memory, the heroes of the narratives, subsist and,

16. The cycle is addressed in the doctoral thesis of Andrew Walsh (1998) as well as by Lambek and Walsh 1997. See also Feeley-Harnik 1991.

moving up a level of abstraction, which link the events of the memories to the events of their recounting.[17] Malagasy historical chronotopes differ strikingly from European ones.

As the concept of the chronotope suggests, space and time are not abstracted from one another in northwest Madagascar. Remembering is carried forward via weekly and lunar cycles, the opening and shutting of gates, the crossing of thresholds, the raising and collapse of vertical posts. Travel between shrines and the annual transport of certain royal artifacts across the countryside reinscribe political relations of the Sakalava monarchy, indexing simultaneously both past constitutions and present lines of power.[18] And while spirit possession is open to virtually anyone (subject to the will of the spirits; hosts do not consciously seek possession), the bearing of memory is spatially and socially distributed.

During the eighteenth century the Sakalava in the region of present-day Mahajanga formed the most powerful kingdom on the island. They were weakened by competition from the British-supported Merina, the collapse of the slave trade, and the advent of French colonialism. The polity fragmented into a number of smaller kingdoms and royal factions that share a common historical tradition and idiom for articulating it. The Sakalava polity was supported by a subtle organic division of labor among its component descent groups that is still evident in the distribution of memory-bearing tasks. Doing fieldwork among Sakalava, it is extremely difficult to get a reasonably full account of the past from any single informant. This is not only for the common reason that different people present versions that support their own interests, but because the responsibility for remembering is itself divided up in complex ways, both by task and by subject. People often do not know the nature of their neighbors' contributions (or at least do not feel they have the right to represent them), but taken together, over many hundreds of square kilometers, there is a remarkable articulation. In

17. See also the extensive work of Hayden White (1973, 1987) on the narrative construction of historical texts.

18. Groupings in Madagascar, whether the macro ones we misconceptualize as ethnic or tribal, or the more restricted ones we call clans, are generally not firmly bounded, discrete entities. Affiliation is nonexclusive and is acquired primarily through bilateral descent but also through living in a particular place and subscribing to local customs, taboos, and the authority of local royalty. In trying to distinguish Antankaraña or Sakalava, it seems least misleading to characterize them as those people who subscribe to a respective narrative or repertoire of narratives about themselves (Lambek 1998b; Lambek and Walsh 1997).

particular, the role of each distinctive royal personage from the past is maintained somewhere.

Local mediums, shrine managers, and guardians each play their part without knowledge of the whole. Yet in the ensemble a tremendous amount of history is articulated. Not surprisingly, much of this history concerns trauma and its overcoming. The trauma is not only that of war, as in the case of the Water Dwelling spirits (who are also recalled by Sakalava), but emerges from the "family romance" of generations of royalty. I give a brief illustration, drawing upon a single excerpt from but one story. Returning from battle and being informed by one of his sons of infidelity in his absence, a king brutally murdered his wife. Although this event is purported to have taken place some ten generations ago (mid-eighteenth century), it continues to be reexperienced by generations of spirit mediums. The medium of the murdered wife is said to reside at the woman's tomb and may never enter the city of Mahajanga, which houses the shrine containing her husband's relics. Should she do so, she suffers terribly. So does the medium of the husband if he is reminded of his past actions. The memory is kept alive less in the words of the story, which by no means everyone knows or has the right to tell, than in the embodied comportment and pain of a few localized mediums and tomb guardians. In similar fashion, the memory of each former monarch is kept alive and orchestrated with the others. Succession to mediumship is not determined by objective, ascriptive criteria. For the individual host, possession by a particular spirit—bearing a particular identity and trauma—connects his or her personal life to the wider historical narrative in a complex manner, conjoining private suffering with public performance and individual quests with collective projects.

If memory is approached as claims, then it is understood to have addressees, interlocutors who can in turn support, confirm, cast doubt upon, or challenge them. Memory is constituted in such dialogical relations (Bakhtin 1981), even if as a form of internal resistance to the claims of others. In using a language of claims, I am on dangerous ground, possibly approaching the forensic approach I decried earlier. One difference is that the people who engage in litigating memory often view their claims as mere descriptions of fact. More significant, however, is that the view of practice I have been developing far exceeds the instrumental. If memory is motivated, it is by no means only for private, selfish, or confrontational ends; nor, as the Malagasy case suggests, need the subject be as discretely bounded as we imagine.

We tend to view knowledge as objective fact, true or false, whose accuracy can be judged in a court of law or a psychological experiment. But much of experience is not like that. Memories are eyewitness accounts (assuming sight is the privileged sense; often it is not) only if the emphasis is put on the witnessing, a moral act, rather than on the eye. Rather than treat memory as a discrete thing, stored and retrieved, or as the biologically innate processes of storage and retrieval waiting to be discovered by the experiments of the psychologist, I have been arguing that we understand it as a culturally mediated expression of the temporal dimension of experience, in particular of social commitments and identifications. Remembering comprises contextually situated assertions of continuity on the part of subjects and claims about the significance of past experience. Such tacit assertions and claims, based as much on cumulative wisdom and moral vision as on individual interest, form a kind of moral practice.

If, as Charles Taylor (1989) argues, our life narration and our sense of self are inextricably linked to our sense of the good, the chronotope of memory must be a moral space. Taylor posits three axes of moral thinking: respect for others, understanding of what makes a full life, and dignity—that is, "the characteristics by which we think of ourselves as commanding (or failing to command) the respect of those around us." These axes exist in every culture but differ in how they are conceived, how they relate to each other, and in their relative importance (15–16).

Taylor argues for "the essential link between identity and a kind of orientation. To know who you are is to be oriented in moral space, a space in which questions arise about what is good or bad, what is worth doing and what not, what has meaning and importance for you and what is trivial and secondary" (1989, 28). If the spatial analogy is explicit, there is surely also a temporal dimension and an orientation toward the past as well as toward the future. "To know who I am is a species of knowing where I stand. My identity is defined by the *commitments* and *identifications* which provide the frame or horizon within which I can try to determine from case to case what is good, or valuable, or what ought to be done, or what I endorse or oppose. In other words, it is the horizon within which I am capable of taking a stand" (27; my emphasis).

My argument throughout has been in line with Taylor's staunchly nonreductionist view:

> We are selves only in that certain issues matter for us. What I am as a self, my identity, is essentially defined by the way things have significance for me . . .

> these things have significance for me, and the issue of my identity is worked out, only through a language of interpretation which I have come to accept as a valid articulation of these issues. To ask what a person is, in abstraction from his or her self-interpretations, is to ask a fundamentally misguided question, one to which there couldn't in principle be an answer. (1989, 34)

If remembering is a moral and identity-building act, so, to be sure, is forgetting. Freud saw it as an act of "moral cowardice" (1974, 123) that hysterics could not remember those feelings or ideas that ran counter to the ego. At the same time, it was a sign of moral character that the incompatible idea was disposed of by conversion rather than acted upon (157). Central to Freud's later understanding of the genesis of the person is the idea that we must have a history that we get wrong. Similarly, two commentators on nationalism, Anderson (1991) and Hobsbawm (1992), draw on Renan's remarks of 1882—*"Or, l'essence d'une nation est que tous les individus aient beaucoup de choses en commun et aussi que tous aient oublié bien des choses,"*—recognizing that the ethical quandaries of the historian and psychoanalyst are similar. In telling the stories of their subjects, must both remember the very things those subjects are determined to forget? Is their responsibility to support current identity politics or to break through the defenses in order to reposition the subject for new self-interpretations or radical change?[19]

The picture I have been trying to draw of memory as moral practice is elegantly captured by the Aristotelian ideal of *phronesis.* Although, for Aristotle, "practical wisdom is a kind of awareness of order, the correct order of ends in my life, which integrates all my goals and desires into a unified whole in which each has proper weight," he rejects Plato's linkage of this to our awareness of the unchanging and eternal order of the cosmos.

> Our grasp of the right order and priority of ends in life cannot be of this kind. It is an understanding of the ever-changing, in which particular cases and predicaments are never exhaustively characterized in general rules. The practically wise man (*phronimos*) [or woman] has a knowledge of how to behave in each particular circumstance which can never be equated with or reduced

19. Smith 1997 provides a reflection on the historical issue with reference to class rather than nation.

> to a knowledge of general truths. Practical wisdom (*phronesis*) is a not fully articulable sense rather than a kind of science. (Taylor 1989, 125)[20]

Our relationship to the past is ever-changing. How we acknowledge this relationship—via memory—is a form of *phronesis.*

Taylor's last sentence returns us to Hacking. How we view the subject of memory, what we seek from it as intellectuals, depends on our moral orientation as much as on rational reflection and scientific inquiry. It depends, for example, on whether we are romantics, "yearning after a richer past, one fuller of meaning, from the standpoint of an empty or shallow present" (Taylor 1989, 464), or whether we seek to decenter present subjects. To recognize this is to recognize that memory can be invoked by theorists for various ends and that these choices are ultimately moral choices. As *phronesis* rather than *episteme,* they are not to be judged solely according to their conformity to an externally existing reality, but also as constituents of that social reality.

20. See also the extended discussion in Gadamer (1985, 278–89), whose application of Aristotelian ethics to the hermeneutic problem "that the same tradition must always be understood in a different way" is highly relevant to understanding memory.

FIVE

The Anthropology of Religion and the Quarrel between Poetry and Philosophy

The first draft of this chapter was commissioned by Roy Rappaport for a panel assessing the anthropology of religion at the annual meeting of the American Anthropological Association (AAA) in 1996; a later draft was presented as a lecture in commemoration of Rappaport at the University of Michigan, April 15, 1998. As is evident throughout this collection, Rappaport's later work, concluding in his posthumously published Ritual and Religion in the Making of Humanity *(1999) has had a tremendous influence on me. Rappaport himself felt that most readers had not grasped his main points, and it remains puzzling to me why his work has not been taken up more widely. This chapter was my first serious attempt to link Rappaport's argument for the performative establishment of morality with that of Aristotle on practical reason, and in a manner relevant beyond the explicitly or formally "religious." The article had broader theoretical ambitious as well—to balance the discipline's attention to power with what might lie beyond it, to provide an account of practice that was less instrumental and self-interested than the one found in Bourdieu, and to provide a theoretically more sophisticated groundwork for the anthropology of religion. As a result, the essay tries to do too much, and I am now apologetic for its density. I had hoped it would receive* Current Anthropology's *treatment of responses from specific readers, but the editor, Richard Fox, decided it would be more visible as a stand-alone Commentary.*

It is difficult to reflect on the history of the anthropology of religion without recognizing to what extent that history is precisely what has constituted the substance of the subject. Religion is probably the only "institution" for which instructors routinely still begin their introductory lectures with nineteenth-century evolutionist theories. It is apparent that we have

This chapter first appeared in *Current Anthropology* 41, no. 3 (2000): 309–20.

been unable to make a clean break with the past, either simply absorbing and building upon it or rejecting and letting it go. If disciplines that don't know their histories are condemned to repeat them, disciplines that repeat them may be suspected of containing something never fully worked through.

One begins to ask whether the ubiquitous presence in the textbooks of Tylor et al. exemplifies not so much universal features of religion as elementary oppositions within Western culture so fundamental to our everyday thought that it is hard for us to escape from their terms. As Evans-Pritchard famously argued of Zande belief in witchcraft, "We cannot reason outside, or against, [our] beliefs because [we] have no other idiom to express [our] thoughts" (1937, 338). To start with the evolutionists, then, is not to go back far enough. If we follow the advice of hermeneutics and interrogate our own tradition, we find that the rationality debate originates not with Tylor or Lévy-Bruhl but with Plato's categorical distinction between objective and mimetic relations to the world—that is, in the opposition he sets forth between rational contemplation, or philosophy, and sensuous engagement, or poetry. Plato's argument has had at least two deleterious consequences. It has driven us to distinguish, classify, and rank discrete modes of thought. And it has forced us to choose between keeping an objective distance from religion and jumping in and identifying with our subject, producing most recently a virtual epidemic of what I am tempted to label the culture-and-profession-bound syndrome of ethnomimesis.

One way ahead is to go back—to Aristotle. Aristotle provides the opportunity to take an alternate route, one that enables us to see the particular conjunction of contemplative thought, reasoned action (praxis), and creative production (*poiesis*) characteristic of *any* given social setting. Of particular interest is Aristotle's concept of *phronesis* (moral practice or judgment)—both as a corrective for still-dominant characterizations of rule-bound and mystified members of "traditional" societies and as a way of thinking about practice in the contemporary global dis/order. If religion is inevitably bound up with the naturalization of power and the legitimation or sanctification of the world it constructs or inherits, it also enables (and directs) meaningful agency. Contemporary discussions remain merely cynical if they do not delineate the capacity and means for virtuous action as well as the limitations placed upon it. Analyses of the knowledge/power nexus need to be supplemented with a consideration of the moral, just as discussions of morality need to be informed by a practice approach. On both counts, Aristotle is formative.

Two caveats about the terms used in this chapter: First, I am in broad sympathy with those scholars who are skeptical about essentializing definitions of *religion*. Yet even Asad (1993a) does not dispense with the term. Like Asad, I am concerned with understanding the ways in which Western history shapes present discourse; however, where he diagnoses an erasure of "power" in that discourse, I (writing some sixteen years after the original appearance of his essay) question the absence of "moral practice."[1] I am equally skeptical of the perpetuation of disciplinary subfields like the "anthropology of religion" and have tried in my ethnographic writing to break through them (Lambek 1993b). My use of the phrase here is both a reflection of current practice and the label for a particular space of discussion. The intention is to urge both that anthropological students of religion keep a broad critical perspective on their subject and that students of social theory and global transformation pay attention to issues that are too easily relegated to a somewhat marginalized subfield.

Second, I am neither a philosopher nor a classicist; the terms *Plato* and *Aristotle* function in this chapter more as vehicles for an argument about anthropology than as signs of the full complexity of their work or the traditions that they initiated. My first suggestion is simply that the Plato/Aristotle contrast provides an interesting model for conceptualizing the history of the field. Thus, for example, in *The Savage Mind* (1966), Lévi-Strauss provides a rather brilliant solution or mediation of Plato's opposition by showing precisely a philosophy pursued by means of a poetry of the concrete, whereas Bourdieu can be seen as an Aristotelian rejoinder to Lévi-Strauss's Platonism. Secondly, by going back to Aristotle, perhaps we can draw from his concepts without all their subsequent baggage. For example, his notion of the soul, which is pre-Christian and pre-Cartesian, may fit certain African ideas better than later European versions. Outside the increasingly narrow and specifically demarcated domain of religion, *soul* is hardly a word in our discourse at all. Indeed, Tylor and Co. were discovering its centrality in primitive thought at the very moment, as Ian Hacking has argued (1996), that it was being displaced in Western thought by the sciences of memory.

In this chapter I make several arguments of increasing specificity: (1) that certain aspects of Aristotle's thought are useful for configuring approaches to religion, (2) that we must acknowledge the significance of morality in

1. In a subsequent essay (1993b) Asad does concern himself with the disappearance of the inculcation of the virtues in European Christianity and the effects of this transformation on our understanding of religion, but he does not discuss whether or how anthropology ought to attend to virtue in the present. One reading of his essay would suggest that it would be simply anachronistic.

the anthropology of religion and for social theory, (3) that approaches to morality should include a practice perspective in which Aristotle and Rappaport's accounts are complementary, and (4), conversely, that accounts of practice should contain, if not highlight, the moral dimension. Practice theory needs to attend to more than power, habit, or competitions of honor or taste and should attend to reasoned judgment as developed in recent accounts of Aristotle's *Ethics*. Thus I am arguing that we have to move beyond Plato's characterization and unique valuation of abstract reason and that we must supplement contemporary concerns with power and the political with equal consideration of virtue and the moral.

From Plato to Aristotle

Havelock's *Preface to Plato* (1963) examines critically how Plato distinguished philosophy from the forms of thought that had appeared earlier, all of which were lumped together as poetry and regarded as inferior. The divide that Plato articulated has remained pervasive in Western thought and the anthropology of religion, underpinning distinctions between oral and literate societies and indeed the whole question of "primitive thought."

In brief, Plato distinguishes reason from mimesis, characterizing the latter by its absorption in particulars and its inability to separate subject from object. Mimesis, in effect, is a kind of surrender to the immediacy of sensations. It provides a "discourse of 'becoming,' that is of endless doings and of events," which Plato would replace by "a discourse of 'being,' that is, of statements which are in modern jargon 'analytic,' are free from time-conditioning" (Havelock 1963, 182). Only the latter is capable of dealing with logical universals, mathematical propositions, true generalizations. Plato thus distinguishes the study of abstractions—goodness, beauty, and so forth—from a concern with specific instances, the permanence or timelessness of the abstract from the fluctuating character of the concrete, and philosophy from poetry, narrative, and opinion. He opposes the concrete, pluralized, sensuous, various, and confused to the abstract, unified, intellectual, timeless, and exact.

Plato's thought has lent itself to a whole series of related and pervasive oppositions: the blindness of mimesis versus the clear vision of reason, connection versus detachment, and, more generally, body versus mind. Plato, as Bordo writes, "imagines the body as an epistemological deceiver, its unreliable senses and volatile passions continually tricking us into mistaking the transient and the illusory for the permanent and real" (1993, 3). Bordo illustrates as well how strongly gendered this mind/body opposition has been in the West.[2]

A common response to the dualism has been to invert the valuation placed on the terms. Most often this entails a suspicion of rationality, in Pnina Werbner's pithy phrase, "a realisation of the irrational consequences of rationality itself" (1996, S57). Commonly described as postmodern, the argument has been explored in thinkers ranging from Weber to Bateson, and it provides a very interesting tension in Rappaport's work. Rappaport is at once skeptical of pure reason and centrally concerned with the relationship between the timeless truths and historical contingencies that are opposed in Plato. Rationality is especially suspect when concepts of abstract reasoning, of economic rationalizing, and of bureaucratic rationalization are conflated. Tambiah describes the pathology of pervasive rationalization as follows: "Science invades the economy, the economy invades politics, and now politics is alleged to inform us on morality, choice and the values to live by. And there's the rub" (1990, 150). This is exactly why we need to rescue morality as a relatively autonomous practice, understanding that it falls into neither causality nor participation, neither philosophy nor poetry, viewed as discrete, alternate modes of orientation. Aristotle is interesting precisely because he sees morality in terms that transcend this dichotomy.

The complement to a poststructuralist rejection of rationalism is an unqualified acceptance of the other pole, subjective participation—a radical swing into some kind of experiential essentialism or fundamentalism, going native, and so on. In a recent work Taussig (1993) celebrates *mimesis*, which is precisely the derogatory word Plato applied to nonphilosophical thought, and succeeds in habilitating it while at the same time destabilizing the uses to which it has been put. There is a good deal of interest in mimesis, as is illustrated, for example, in the remark by Havelock that "as a manipulation of the resources of the unconscious in harmony with the conscious it was

2. It is worth remarking that the categories of "causality" and "participation" with which Tambiah orders his masterly account of the scope of rationality (1990) are essentially Plato's opposition between rational, distantiated thought—philosophy—and immersed participation—poetry. Tambiah implies that both are valid "orderings of reality" or "orientations to the world" (105–10) despite the fact that science and religion have come to be understood as incompatible. However, in his chapter on commensurability Tambiah focuses on cross-cultural comparison rather than addressing whether these orientations are commensurable within a given culture. In my view it is the very fact of the production of incommensurable concepts, words, and discourses as a fundamental characteristic of human language and culture that vitiates Plato's aim of a philosophy of permanent abstractions, and instead demands continual negotiation in the practice of conversation and debate (cf. Lambek 1993b, chap. 12).

unsurpassed" (1963, 90). Yet there is the very real risk in this sort of work, as in the highly suggestive recuperations of Maurice Leenhardt (1979) or in some recent phenomenology (e.g., Jackson 1989), that a kind of Lévy-Bruhlian view of the primitive that has been rejected at the level of mind is renewed at the level of the body.

Pure mimesis is a fantasy of our hyperreflexive age—the inversion of our self-consciousness and the true Other to reflection. We seek it in therapy, attempting not to remember emotions but to relive them (Leys 1996) with the innocence and receptivity of childhood. And sometimes we seek it in ethnography, where it is a particularly sophisticated contemporary form of primitivism.

In less sophisticated thinkers than Taussig or Jackson, it has another twist. Although the idea of identifying with the religion of one's subjects is something few of the turn-of-the-last-century theorists imagined, I believe this movement, of which North American anthropology is now in the throes—witness the anthropology of consciousness, books about reincarnation, being changed in the field, and so on—stems from the same Platonic framework. After all, if religion is to be characterized by its contrast with distantiated reason, how else can one understand it than through the mirror of mimesis, identifying with those others who are themselves carried away by their own identifications? Moreover, if primitive thought is to be characterized exclusively by mimesis, how else to invert the persistent hierarchical contrast with modernity than by celebrating the dissolution of the subject/object boundary?[3]

If we begin with Aristotle, a new map emerges and a new territory. As a natural historian Aristotle is more empirical in his approach, more descriptive than prescriptive. Rather than Plato's binary opposition, he offers a triad of contemplative, practical, and productive intellect, respectively *episteme*, praxis, and *poiesis*, characteristic of humankind in general, as a species. They are complementary rather than opposed and thus not apportioned to one kind of society in contrast to another. Aristotle validates both praxis and *poiesis* as well as contemplative knowledge; indeed, he argues in the *Poetics* that "poetry is something more philosophic and of graver import than history, since its statements are of the nature . . . of universals" (1947). By focusing exclusively on abstract thought, we distort the primitive/modern divide and

3. Of course, these moves are limited neither to North Americans nor to anthropology but are, as Peter Pels (personal communication) suggests, rendered possible by the particular historical transformations of European religion (Asad 1993a) and by complementary transformations in selfhood.

also our understanding of what thinking itself is insofar as it is viewed quite separately from *phronesis* and *poiesis*.

Religions are embodied and imagined worlds (not necessarily imaginary ones). If religions construct the worlds their adherents inhabit, then *poiesis*, in the sense of the structures, principles, and acts of creative production, is critical for understanding the chronotopic configurations and movement within them. Poiesis has figured most explicitly in work on metaphor, exemplified by Tambiah's important papers on magic (1985). Conversely, Hayden White (1973) shows the *poiesis* underlying Western historical and historiographical works. Anthropologists who explore how ritual shapes experience or elaborate the moral transformations enacted within religious performances (Fernandez 1982; Kapferer 1983, 1997; Lienhardt 1961; Ortner 1978; Turner 1969; Werbner 1989) tend to draw on literary critics and philologists—Jakobson, Burke, Frye, White, Bakhtin, Becker—whom one may loosely group together as Aristotelian in inspiration. More has been and could be done with *poiesis* (e.g., Lambek 1998b), but it is sufficient to indicate here how it undermines Plato's bias, showing the reason within ritual or myth and the art within works of reason. Wherever it has been applied, it has breathed fresh insight into our understanding of "primitive" religion and—to a lesser degree, because it has been less done (there is a larger bias to overcome)—our understanding of literate religion, including Christianity.

Poiesis is also of interest in that, in Aristotle's original sense of *making*, it combines what elsewhere have been distinguished as the material and the ideal. It implies the ideality that goes into all material production and the materiality that is necessary for objectifying ideas in social space. *Poiesis* entails the means, objects, and manner of production. While the goal is often one of imitation, and hence Aristotle too uses the word *mimesis*, means and manner are left open. In religion we need to look not only at the historical dialectic of the imagination as past myth models and present circumstances confront and transform one another. As Rappaport (1999) understood, religion works by *realizing* the imagined, rendering it even more real than appearance and, indeed, even inverting the ordinary relationship between representations and their objects such that the imagined may serve as the basis against which appearance is judged. Religion draws upon the senses while asserting that its truths are more profound than what can be grasped by their means alone.

The concept of praxis also transcends Plato's categories. This is especially true of that aspect of praxis distinguished as *phronesis*, practical judgment or deliberation. *Phronesis* has to do with the application of reason to particular circumstance. As situated thought, it thus denies the unilateral connection Plato makes between reason and the abstract grasp of timeless universals. Indeed, Aristotle says quite specifically that it refers to contemplation of things that are variable. In Bernstein's words, "Phronesis is a form of reasoning and knowledge that involves a distinctive mediation between the universal and the particular," such that knowledge is not detached from being or becoming but constitutive of them (1983, 146). Thus Aristotle shows how thought is an intrinsic part of practice and in so doing circumvents the rigid distinction between subjectivity and objectivity that Plato complains is confused in mimesis. The virtue of Aristotle here is to locate reason, or at least to highlight that component we can call judgment, with respect to concrete practices, contingent circumstances, specific problems, and styles of life. (We might say, with the ethnomethodologists and ethnographers of science, that abstract reasoning itself becomes another situated, concrete practice.)

In sum, in shifting from Plato to Aristotle we move from purely abstract reason severely distinguished from mimesis to the admission of creative and practical reason as universal dimensions of the human intellect.

From Power to Morality

If one of my arguments is for a reappraisal of Aristotle, another is for renewed interest in morality. Ethics is creeping back into fashion in high theory, despite the suspicion with which it has been viewed by the Nietzschean stream of postmodernists and deconstructionists (Harpham 1995). In political theory there is also a flourishing field of neo-Aristotelianism concerned with communitarian ethics. Anthropology can contribute to these discussions, but not if an anthropology of religion is restricted to narrow intellectualist or emotionalist issues, and not if power is approached in an entirely Nietzschean or Foucauldian vein.

It is obvious that religion must be understood as a regime of power. But what distinguishes the anthropology of religion from other fields of inquiry is that it cannot rest with power but must contextualize the very conception and production of power within a wider cultural order, one which will equally contain alternatives to power in its repertoire of ends and means. Bloch (1986), for example, has shown not only how Malagasy ritual mystifies power but how the symbolic order outstrips the uses to which it is put. Dumont (1970) and Rappaport (1979a, 1999), by quite distinct lines of reasoning, have elaborated Durkheim's insight that it is the location of the sacred at arm's length from profane power that enables it to sanctify or curse, purify or pollute. The sacred can serve thereby both as the ultimate source and arbiter of social order and sustainer of profane power and as the very locus from which to issue authoritative challenges to conventional order and domination (cf. Parry 1994; Turner 1969). Further, the anthropology of religion must reflect upon the imagination of power and the intense attraction of submission to it.

We need, in other words, to ask what the study of religion can contribute to contemporary social theory as much as what it can draw from it. If it draws from it a serious concern with the ubiquitous workings of power, perhaps it can contribute the pervasive significance of morality. It can serve to remind us, as the saying goes, that while everything may be political, politics isn't everything.

While power is often naturalized and concealed as the everyday, as in Bourdieu's notion of the habitus, where it goes without saying, or Foucault's discourses, where it is constitutive of its very subjects, there are contexts, as Durkheim argued, in which power is highlighted, distinguished, elaborated, set apart. To the degree that power is conceptualized, this is done symbolically, and such symbols lie at the heart of religion. The anthropology of religion asks, How is power imagined (Arens and Karp 1989)? How is such power informed and substantiated—for example, by playing with the communicational constraints of the ordinary speech situation (Bloch 1989c; Lambek 1993a)? How do people represent power to themselves, and how do they attempt to contain, evaluate, exploit, or come to terms with it? How do they knowingly engage with it, submit to it, or repotentiate themselves? What are the ends for which power is wielded? What are the ends for which resistance is practiced? When and how are means also ends in themselves? In other words, to the degree that religion contextualizes, objectifies, and personifies power, it thereby enables power to be reflected upon, to be addressed, to be harnessed or warded off, to be explicitly internalized. In the space of religion, power is confronted with human concerns; in being distinguished, power is counterposed to something other, and that other is morality.[4]

4. It is also the case that Rappaport demonstrates, as Yang puts it, that "power is intrinsic to ritual" (1994, 228). Despite his antipathy to Foucault, Rappaport's account of the way people become fused with the messages encoded in the rituals they perform demonstrates an equally pervasive process of subjectification. Yet in her very interesting comparison of Rappaport to Ruist (early Confucian) thought on ritual, Yang argues that this power from within the social order, a power that is "contained in the reproduction and conduct of social relations," is to be radically distinguished from an objectified power imposed from without by the state (Yang 1994, 229).

The construction of ostensibly autonomous manifestations of power is critical if only because addressing them provides a means for knowing power and hence a first step in reflecting upon its effects—a reflection which, while never free from some sort of practical, discursive, and disciplinary location and therefore from the webs of power, is nonetheless in its nature moral. It is not, as a vulgar Durkheimianism might have it, that power is equated with morality, that religion is the unambivalent worship of society.[5] Further, if in religious action individuals willingly subject themselves to power, the boundaries between subjects and objects do become blurred. In depending on power people also come to internalize its objects, thereby empowering (as well as disempowering) themselves. But this is never done without a space for reflection. Here the examples of taboo and spirit possession as intricate combinations of passion and action, of both submitting to power and addressing and appropriating it, may serve to illuminate religious practice more generally (see chapter 3; Boddy 1989; Lambek 1993b). Possession is a complex practice in which power and morality articulate with one another in multiple ways, in which persons are inhabited by gods or spirits but never fully identified with them. And in that gap or difference, that boundary that is crossed but never obliterated, is room for a world of reflective practice or practical reflection.

The argument so far is that it is the very *poiesis* of religion that enables the clearing of spaces for situated reflection and expanded agency, and that religion provides objects and occasions, no less than models, "of and for" (Geertz 1973f) meaningful, ethical practice. (However, note that ethics is not to be limited to the religious sphere and certainly not to a theistic one.)

The insufficiency of power as an explanatory principle has been noted even by its most articulate advocates. Dirks, Eley, and Ortner argue that "power is neither some universal 'drive' lodged in individuals nor some elementary force transcending society and history. If historical actors sometimes embody what appears to be a Nietzschean will to power, it is equally true that any historical actor will also embody a wide range of other feelings

---

Rappaport himself is reluctant to conflate order with power. Here the contrast between the assumptions of Bloch and Rappaport (Lambek 2001a) is quite instructive.

5. At the same time, in arguing for the recognition of the power that society has over us to transcend our individual selves for the better, Durkheim collectivizes Plato's argument that one should place oneself under the guidance of the tyrant or philosopher. "What is truly shameful is not, as most men suppose, to put one's person . . . into the keeping of another, but *not* to do so, when that other's soul is what is in the higher sense most truly one's own self" (Nussbaum 1980, 413). Thus "Plato has argued that in order to give men the conditions of self-respecting activity it is necessary to remove their autonomy" (415).

and desires, including desires precisely antithetical to power—for love, for tenderness, for communion—although nowadays such terms can hardly be spoken with innocence" (1994, 7). They go on to cite Dews: "What sustains or rebels against a given social structure cannot be simply an effect of that structure itself. Social systems are both imposed by force from above—they embody relations of power—and are adhered to or rejected from below—they are invested or disinvested with desire" (Dews 1988, 110–11).

I submit that morality is a significant third domain alongside power and desire; if not to be invoked with "innocence," neither is it reducible either to power or desire or to refereeing the struggles between them. Morality in the Aristotelian sense is the striving for human good. Charles Taylor usefully delineates three elements of moral thinking: "Our sense of respect for and obligations to others, . . . our understandings of what makes a full life, . . . [and] the range of notions concerned with dignity, . . . [i.e.] the characteristics by which we think of ourselves as commanding (or failing to command) the respect of those around us" (Taylor 1989, 15). Significant questions remain: How is morality put into practice, obligation assumed, respect for others acknowledged, dignity enabled, a full life lived? We must also ask how and where human flourishing is curtailed or undermined, but Nietzschean contempt for morality is inadequate. To be sure, conventional morality often conceals terrible abuse, and, to be sure, we must not give up a hermeneutics of suspicion. But there is more to morality than petty moralizing.

Religion stands against secular power in yet another, deeper way—as order. Rappaport (Rappaport 1979a, 1999) argues that a properly functioning religion is constitutive of truth, providing a unique and ultimate means of judgment and standard of discrimination, and establishing, by means of a hierarchy of sacred entailment, a unified and absolute authority capable of withstanding the multitude of particular interests and lies.[6] While rationalism cannot achieve the Archimedean point of perspective to which thinkers since Plato have aspired, religion, in Rappaport's argument, has provided the next best thing—or perhaps something even better—and has done so not by means of discursive elaboration, disembodied distance, and ethical and epistemological neutrality but precisely by means of highly condensed utterances, embodied performances, and acts of commitment. Religion for Rappaport provides not merely the basis for specific moral judgments or the space for thinking morally but the very foundations of morality itself. It is this guarantee, rather than any specific content, that is of ultimate

6. I say "properly functioning" because Rappaport describes contemporary religious order as seriously compromised by capitalism.

significance.[7] And indeed, in Rappaport's view, the most sacred utterances carry no specific directives.

By grounding truth in sanctity that is established in ritual, Rappaport evades Plato's opposition (or perhaps mediates it in a distinct fashion). Yet his account of morality is incomplete and can be supplemented by that of Aristotle. Their positions are complementary.

The Scope of the Moral: Aristotle and Rappaport

A central tension in anthropological studies of ritual has been between approaches that emphasize rituals as discrete performances and those that emphasize ritual as a dimension of all activity. Turner (1974) mediates this distinction by seeing rituals as phases in broader social dramas. Rappaport does so by elaborating a continuum of formality and a hierarchy of contingency, but in fact most of his attention is devoted to rituals as discrete acts, performances of a particular kind. It seems to me that one of the next steps has to be to continue to articulate the relationship between such performances and what takes place between them. Put more baldly, and dropping the word *ritual* entirely, we have to integrate elements of a theory of practice with a theory of performance. One way to begin is to examine how Aristotle's and Rappaport's accounts of morality may complement one another.

Where one emphasizes the order in linked but discrete performances, the other emphasizes the contingency in ongoing and unmarked practice. In neither case is morality understood as simple conformity to a set of rules. Rappaport is concerned with showing how the conditions for morality are established and how specific moral states are produced through the performance of rituals. Ritual creates the contexts with respect to which subsequent actions will be judged. Aristotle is concerned with the ongoing exercise of judgment in personal practice that constitutes virtue. Such

7. Despite the originality of Rappaport's argument, the similarity of his position to those of both Aristotle and Durkheim is patent. Comparing the latter two thinkers, Challenger has recently argued that, for both of them, the root of society is not contractual but the moral basis for contract, the "'noncontractual elements' in the contract." He elaborates that "the stability and, indeed, the survival of society depend on an institutionalized system of enforcing the principles of promise-keeping and good faith and the avoidance of force and fraud in contract. These are the principles of moral obligation and justice that regulate human relations and without which there could be no social or political life. The 'non-contractual elements' of contracts are those nonnegotiable elements . . . that are assumed by the very definition of a social being" (1994, 179).

judgment is always contingent on circumstance and on the weighing of multiple considerations. Thus courage, for example, cannot be established in absolute terms but must be understood as a suitable balance between caution on the one side and foolhardiness on the other. In moral practice, Aristotelian *phronesis*, we engage in a continuous fine-tuning of our actions to suit our understanding of the context and circumstances in order to achieve the general aim of human flourishing. As Nussbaum points out (1994, 15, n. 5), this aim, *eudaimonia*, while often translated as "happiness," connotes activity. Hence it is at once end and means, the goal of life and the carrying out of a good life. Performances of ritual are marked instances of such activity.

All rituals entail, in Rappaport's terms, the conjunction of the canonical and the indexical, but Rappaport is more concerned with the way the latter serves the former than with the reverse. Someone has to be there for the ritual to take place, and it is by this means that the canonical is accepted and reproduced. But who is actively present is contingent on many factors. Although he notes that persons must decide whether to participate in given rituals, he gives little attention to what factors may draw them toward or away from participating. It is noteworthy that in many myths the violation of the conditions of felicitous performance is highlighted and in fact provides the basis for a new order. The Old Testament, or Torah, provides some noteworthy examples. Jacob slips in ahead of his brother Esau to claim the father's blessing. Once uttered, the blessing holds and cannot be recalled. It creates the succession, but, as numerous commentators have noted, it serves not simply as the reproduction of order from generation to generation but as an act of intervention in history. In a similar story from South India, Daniel (1984) describes how members of a migrating group that challenged the locals for rights to land slipped in a clod of earth fetched from their original homeland when they were asked to swear their connection. Not only are rules of succession or inheritance violated, but officiants are deliberately misled concerning whom or what they are blessing. I would have liked to ask Rappaport how he would analyze these stories. For him ritual is a means to curtail lying and its effects, yet here the achievement of blessing is based on a ruse.

Be that as it may, if we expand our view of morality from formal ritual acts, perhaps an answer can emerge. The Jacob story suggests above all that the identities of the individual participants, constituting the indexical dimension of the performance, are by no means accidental or irrelevant. We see not that order is replaced by disorder so much as that the judgment of the parties, notably the good judgment of Rebekah, the mother, and the poor judgment of Esau, prevails over the simple reproduction of patriarchal tradition. Jacob was the more deserving of the two brothers in the sense of being the more self-respecting; after all, Esau sold his birthright for a mess of pottage. The ritual affirms the distinction between the practice of the two brothers and adjudicates decisively.[8]

The point is that blind adherence to ritual is not a sure sign of good any more than is operating without a past. Rappaport emphasizes the importance of adaptiveness alongside that of perdurance and shows how the one guarantees or enables the other. This means that decisions about fulfilling the felicity conditions are a significant part of the performance of any ritual. Just as the performance of a given ritual shapes the way subsequent moral judgments can be made, so too do moral judgments shape participation in the performance of particular rituals.

In addition, the stories suggest that we understand moral practice not simply as the acceptance of obligation, as the tradition of Kant and Durkheim might have it but, in an Aristotelian vein, as a striving for human good. In the stories at hand, good is configured as a scarce valuable, and hence the striving is agonistic, but virtue need not be articulated in this fashion, such that the honor of one person depends on the shaming of another.

Rappaport helps develop this point by recognizing ritual as a site of moral creation.[9] Ritual definitively links the *is* and the *ought* not by conflating them—not, as Turner argued (1967), by transforming the necessary into the desirable—but rather in such a way that the former is to be judged in terms of the latter instead of the reverse. Moreover, participants are subject to ritual acts, in part constituted by them. In formal settings they *commit* acts of worship, of supplication, of benediction, of sorcery.

In this argument moral states and distinctions are established and transformed performatively. The primary recipient or addressee of the act of sorcery is the sorcerer himself; committing sorcery is the act of accepting responsibility for subsequent misfortune that befalls the victim (Lambek 1993b). Similarly, in prayer worshippers commit themselves to accepting that their subsequent well-being is due to the agency of their ostensible addressee. In this way ritual projects moral intentions and relations, establishing conditions in terms of which, as Rappaport argues, events are to be

8. The story also affirms, in a manner that would accord with Rappaport's model, that human order is always contingent on divine will.

9. Durkheimians similarly enlarge their understanding of the social basis from which the moral universe is established, as well as their formal concern with rules, by seeing ritual as the site of moral creation.

judged instead of the reverse. As a consequence of ritual performance, events and actions are evaluated according to how they conform to the instituted state of affairs rather than left as brute facts to determine our judgment. Prior to ritual, we describe the weather according to whether or not the sun is shining, but once the rainmaker has correctly done his work it is the rain that is at fault for its absence.

Performatively established morality is not restricted to highly marked, decisive events, such as being blessed and giving blessings, getting married or marrying someone off, but manifest also in the following of practical routines, in continuous acts such as observing taboos or wearing amulets. Thus what Leach (1954) argued is that the communicative dimension of action frequently encompasses moral claims.[10]

And yet this whole structural line of explanation seems insufficient to describe morality. Morality cannot be simply an act of commission or an acceptance of obligation but includes the reasoning behind choosing to do so and the reasoning that determines how to balance one's multiple and possibly conflicting commitments. Aristotle's insight is that in practice we always run up against contingencies; circumstances force us to continuously exercise our judgment. Such judgments may be founded in the objectifications of religion or the various disciplines, but the acts themselves can never fully be accounted for by them. Moreover, virtue is not merely the property of adherence to the terms established through performative acts but, in pursuing excellence, something which initiates them in the right circumstances. Thus, where Rappaport emphasizes the public means for constituting and distinguishing moral acts, states, and judgments, Aristotle is more concerned with personal agency and moral reasoning.

From the perspectives of both Aristotle and Rappaport, morality is not a coherent, imposed system, a specific set of rules, an unequivocal code, or an uncompromising disciplinary order to which people are obliged to submit unqualifiedly—as, in effect, simply another form of power—but the forms and acts by which commitments are engaged and virtue accomplished. Morality involves the practical judgments people make about how to live their lives wisely and well, and how, in the course of making those judgments, they do live their lives, albeit in the face of numerous constraints. This is neither the hypocritical moral code to which Nietzsche took exception nor the naive freedom of liberal individualism; it is action that

10. Hence the argument here not only transcends older attempts to distinguish magic from religion but casts doubt on the categorical nature of Asad's distinction between discipline and formal manners (1993b, 77).

is informed by culturally dense understandings of the complexities of judgment, the social contexts of commitments, and the fine line between happy and unhappy actions. And lest I be labeled a hopelessly naive optimist, let me insist that virtuous action comes together with all the bad things we know about human practice and society. Not only is social conflict not thereby avoided, but from Aristotle to Nietzsche, the practice of nobility implies the simultaneous lesser practice of the enslaved or incontinent, wherever these latter are located. A quotation from a philosopher may be apposite here: "Spiritual meaning has to do with relationships which establish integrity, not reference" (Fingarette 1963, 281).

Finally, it should be noted that there has been a trajectory of concern with moral reasoning in the anthropology of religion. It is arguable that *Witchcraft, Oracles, and Magic* (Evans-Pritchard 1937) should be read in this light rather than in functionalist or purely intellectualist terms, as of course should *Oedipus and Job in West African Religion* (Fortes 1983), and a concern for it appears in the work of a number of other Africanists as different as Beidelman (1993) and the Comaroffs (1992). Weberians address questions of theodicy and, as Geertz (1973f) put it, "moods and motivations." In *Knowledge and Practice in Mayotte* (1993b), I tried to show the sustained moral practice of a number of people with respect to both Islam and spirit possession and in their negotiation of the territory between them, as well as how these people related to each of these incommensurable disciplines alternatively from the perspectives of the Schutzian expert, the well-informed citizen, and the man on the street.[11] Moral reasoning is found not only in the reflective practice of healers and religious experts who provide advice and compassion but also in the way ordinary individuals strike out on careers. The daily acts of kin and neighbors toward one another are morally configured, as are the ways people reflect on the acts and lives of those around them—and all this before we even get to the great moral adventures and flamboyant productions of sacrifice, pilgrimage, and vision quests that some religions make possible or demand, or the heroic attempts, in circumstances as varied as those reported by Burridge (1969, 1970) and Myerhoff (1978), to maintain or regain dignity or the conditions for it. (We do not need to put this in the Christian terms of redemption.)

11. An implication here is that integrity need not imply full personal consistency or unity, a point that takes us back to Havelock's discussion of Plato's ideal of the reflexive yet unitary ego. This is a particular issue with respect to spirit possession.

A Dieu, Bourdieu: Morality as Disposition and as Practice

The next stage of my argument delineates a shift from current accounts of practice to one that gives greater space to morality. My heading is not meant to dismiss a great thinker; I use the phrase in the positive and literal sense, "à Dieu, Bourdieu," directing him, or rather us, to ethical dimensions of practice that transcend routine, profane habit, or agonistic displays of honor or taste, and that supplement accounts of strategy with reasoned judgment. I recognize, of course, that Aristotle's approach is not theistic, but I would argue that it needs to be supplemented with Rappaport's account of how moral judgments are sanctified, guaranteed, and directed by ritual.[12]

Among recent theorists, it is Bourdieu (1977) who most clearly draws on an Aristotelian account of praxis. Bourdieu is in some ways Aristotle to Lévi-Strauss's Plato, emphasizing an understanding of and by means of the particular, habitual, and historical over the abstract, universal, and objectivized. But what does Bourdieu tell us of morality? In fact, what is most critically missing, or at least underplayed, in Bourdieu is precisely the ethical dimension that Aristotle ascribes to practice, Aristotle's concern with virtue and happiness, and especially his development of the concept of *phronesis*, or practical wisdom. What Bourdieu emphasizes about practice is habit and strategy, whereas, for Aristotle, *phronesis* is both *intellectual*, in that it entails reasoning, and *virtuous*, in that its end is human flourishing. *Phronesis* is not calculative, instrumental reason. The exercise of judgment implies the exercise of *good* judgment (and not merely cleverness).[13]

Bourdieu is not particularly interested in religion or morality. His view of practice turns largely on habit and on the deployment of symbolic capital, apparently following here the logic both of honor and shame and of bourgeois consumer capitalism, as well as the competition for prestige in the intellectual marketplace. Yet not only is practice not just a matter of

12. In advocating attention to the moral, I am not arguing that religion is to be distinguished from the rest of life by its high-mindedness. The magic/religion distinction is often phrased so as to imply that only in religion do we have the development of an ethical dimension and that magic (and primitive religion) are essentially just manipulative. If one way to break down this dichotomy is to show the instrumental or practical dimension in the world religions, the other surely is to show the moral dimension in the practices of smaller-scale societies. The work of Douglas (1966) is notable here, although her conception of morality as essentially the maintenance of social distinctions appears rather conservative.

13. Although Rappaport was personally a virtuoso at *phronesis*, he curiously omits it from his discussion of religion, preferring to remain at a structural level of analysis.

competition for prestige or power, whether with respect to Maghrebian honor, Parisian taste, or Trobriand *kula*, but, as Mauss (1966) understood, it is often composed of an inextricable combination of interest and disinterest. Moreover, interest need not imply a mutually exclusive choice between self and others; it is questionable whether actors are the monads that much recent writing implies. Persons are subjects not simply of powerful institutional discourses or disciplines but of social relations. Habitus ought to be construed not simply with reference to the external built and natural worlds or to class and status but with reference to the social worlds of kinship and amity, of dependency and responsibility, of autonomy and connection, and of the commitments established through ritual.

Examination of modern interpretations of Aristotle can help enlarge our understanding of practice. Morality is learned, says Aristotle. Yet it is transmitted not in an abstract form via rule or proposition but by means of habit; morality comes to be embedded as a disposition. Ethical knowledge in Aristotle's sense is a form of *connaissance* rather than *savoir*; that is, it is integral to who one is as a person rather than simply a matter of how one represents oneself to others. But if it is not objectified, neither is it unconscious or unreflective. A moral virtue is "an established disposition for free and deliberate conduct of the right sort" (Kosman 1980, 103), entailing "the reciprocal capacities . . . of being discriminatingly receptive and resistant" (107). Thus, "self-respect seems . . . less like a feeling identified subjectively than like a disposition to both act and feel in certain appropriate ways" (Nussbaum 1980, 404).

One cultivates dispositions but chooses acts. One can learn to reflect on ethical practice—and in fact, it extracts a reflective process out of us (Lear 1988). It does *not* "go without saying" but requires, as we have seen, judgment of particular circumstances, deliberation over correct means, and intentional initiation of actions. Yet practical wisdom is not to be reduced to calculation or technical deliberations concerning means (Sorabji 1980, 214).

Morality has an embodied quality to it, yet it is necessary to distinguish it from more technical forms of embodied or practical knowledge, whether riding a bicycle or sitting up straight at the dinner table. Following Gadamer's insightful discussion, *phronesis* is to be distinguished from *techne* in several ways: ethical knowledge is a necessary part of the general human life situation rather than simply learned as needed; its end is no particular thing or product but "complete ethical rectitude for a lifetime"; it entails a continuous evaluation of the suitability of the means to meet each particular situation; and it requires an understanding and sense of connection with other human beings (Gadamer 1979 and 1985, 281–89; summarized in Bernstein 1983, 147). Means and end are inextricably connected; "The exercise of the virtues is a necessary and central part of [the good] life, not merely a preparatory exercise to secure such a life" (MacIntyre 1984, 149).

Ethics in Aristotle is not something you apply but how you act. And it is not a matter of *what* you do—its specific content—but a matter of acting well. Since moral knowledge is practical, it is indefinite, and therefore, since it cannot be finitely grasped, there is no science of it (Nussbaum 1980, 422). As MacIntyre argues, since each Aristotelian virtue is the mean between two corresponding vices (courage between rashness and timidity, justice between doing injustice and suffering injustice, etc.), any given action might in different contexts fall in different places on the continuum. Culture is undoubtedly a necessary part of the context, insofar as it suggests (for example) that what might be foolhardy for a woman might be courageous for a man, but does not exhaust it, nor can it determine the right course of action for any given person. Specific judgment is critical, and it distinguishes the virtuous person from the rule-bound or law-abiding one (1984, 154). Hence Aristotle's is a descriptive rather than a prescriptive ethics, and practical wisdom is always superior to opinion.[14]

While some authors emphasize that Aristotelian virtue includes habits of feeling (Burnyeat 1980; Kosman 1980), others argue that it concerns excellence at doing something. As Lear points out, it is unlike a Christian inner quality; virtues are free of conflicting desires and hence of neurotic conflict (1988, 167). Since virtue is based on disposition, it cannot be a matter of acting against inclination (MacIntyre 1984, 149). For Lear, "Someone who is able to realize his nature will lead a rich, full, happy life, and he will experience a certain unity and harmony among his desires" (1988, 168). Whatever interventions in such arguments anthropologists might wish to make, it is important to emphasize that the Aristotelians are neither positing the idea of a unique inner essence, nor are they quite as innocent as they sound. For one thing, Aristotle recognizes the prevalence of incontinence. The incontinent is someone who has heard certain ethical principles expressed and learned them rationally but has not inculcated them through

14. But see Hampshire (1983) on some problems with this view. If *phronesis* emerges from disposition instilled by habit, it is also relative to a specific cultural tradition. The question arises whether loyalty to custom constitutes a reasonable justification for particular acts. This is a dilemma that anthropologists know well!

habit so that they become disposition; his actions do not conform to the judgments he thinks he holds (Lear 1988). Conflict, then, is located between disposition and rationalization.[15]

A tension in Aristotle exists between his understanding of virtue as a matter of disposition and his recognition that any instance of virtuous practice is engaged in knowingly. I argued earlier that Rappaport's discussion of the ritual constitution of morality needs to be supplemented by an account of practice. In a complementary fashion I would now say that if responsibility must be individually *assumed*, one of the functions of ritual in Rappaport's argument is precisely to clarify and publicly articulate that assumption and its social consequences.[16] While questions of personal agency may never be fully resolved, ritual provides occasions for the unreserved assumption of responsibility and obligation in which agents, without distinction between the virtuous and the incontinent, acknowledge their agency and commit themselves to bearing responsibility for their actions. For Rappaport, ritual informs the inchoate, defines the indefinite, and punctuates the continuous (1999). Spirit possession and psychoanalysis likewise provide examples of local technologies that work specifically to clarify recognition of personal agency, accountability, and its limits (cf. Schafer 1976).

Conclusion

Practice is always in relation to structure and power. The anthropologist's job in part is to explore the possibilities for moral action and the means for cultivating the virtues in any given social context—say, in that of a certain class and postcolonial position under late capitalism—as well as the constraints and limiting factors on "human flourishing." Religion at its best attempts to provide space and direction for moral practice, to enlarge opportunity and access; at its most limited, it aims to make a virtue out of the constraints. All this may be mystifying, but it is generally hopeful, and at least it moves people or, rather, gets people moving in some direction off

15. As MacIntyre points out (1984, 157), "Aristotle cannot come near the Homeric insight that tragic conflict is the essential human condition—the tragic hero on Aristotle's view fails because of his own flaw, not because the human situation is sometimes irremediably tragic." These questions of happiness and conflict have led at least one Aristotelian scholar to turn his attentions to Freud (Lear 1990). For Nietzsche, virtue is the product of happiness rather than the reverse.

16. Such an assumption may be understood as a manifestation of the workings of power; yet equally, of course, the truly powerful may be able to evade public knowledge of their agency.

the couch of habit and beyond the official discourses and the competitive search for symbolic and material capital.

Aristotle's categories no doubt have found their way into many anthropological arguments. Marx and Freud owe a good deal to Aristotle, as do Durkheim and Weber.[17] However, it appears that philosophical commentators on Aristotle, such as Ackrill (1980) on responsibility, Nussbaum (1980) on self-respect, or MacIntyre on the history of the virtues (1984), might help us deepen our ethnographic and theoretical accounts. Arguments of this sort provide as yet relatively untapped resources for anthropology, both for enlarging and becoming more aware of its own tradition and for developing more nuanced understandings of its subjects.[18]

Conversely, anthropology can illuminate the philosophical issues, not least by supplying sustained accounts of moral practice in a variety of social and cultural contexts. One final point that needs to be made is that, while I have privileged Aristotle over Plato, it may well be that Plato's model is closer to the way some religions themselves operate, setting off a transcendent or ideal unchanging order from the mundane flux of everyday life. Indeed, this process may be intrinsic to what many anthropologists have taken to be religion (Bloch 1986, 1992). However, to argue this is not to obviate the remarks I have made about practice but merely to insist on the old distinction between listening to what people claim and observing what they do. Jean Comaroff's sophisticated attempt to work between contemplative and practical consciousness, "between ideology as explicit discourse and as lived experience" (1985, 5), illustrates the possibilities. This is territory where no purely deconstructive or genealogical analysis can go.

One of the virtues of practicing ethnographic fieldwork is that you see how people act in good faith, how they try to do what they think is right in

17. On Durkheim, see Challenger (1994). He points out that the title page of the French edition of *The Division of Labor in Society* has a quotation from Aristotle's *Politics*: "A real unity, such as a polis, must be made up of elements which differ in kind" (1.1261a.24). Both Durkheim and Aristotle, he suggests, believe that people find their full actualization only as members of society and that we need a social environment that inclines people to act virtuously. "The creation of such a social environment, each argues, is bound up with the formation of laws and educational systems that will help develop habits of virtue in the members of a society and in the creation of social and economic practices that are fair and just" (1994, 5). At the same time, there are aspects of Durkheim's dualism that show a greater affinity to Plato.

18. The dialectic of anthropological understanding is inherently reflexive. That is to say, we must deepen our understanding of concepts and debates in our own tradition in order to illuminate what we find elsewhere. What we find elsewhere forces us to seek an adequate vocabulary and framework in which to place it; conversely, new or newly and critically understood vocabularies and frameworks from our own tradition invite insights into our ethnographic material.

the face of conflict and try to maintain self-respect in conditions that work to undermine it. My reflections in this chapter draw from my entire experience in the field but especially my work with spirit mediums and other healers and religious practitioners whose moral locations and practices I have begun to document elsewhere (Lambek 1993b, 1996, 1998a, 2000c, 2002b). The recent literature on exchange and especially on money also helps demonstrate the significance of moral action and its impediments. Parry (1989) shows the great discrepancy between the Hindu case and that described by Taussig (1980) for the Cauca Valley, Colombia, which links market exchange or capitalist production with witchcraft. While suspicious of any extreme distinction between gifts and commodities, Parry shows how gifts (specifically religious gifts of a certain kind akin to sacrifice) are morally more problematic in Hindu North India than making money through trade. For one thing, the value placed on living on the fruits of one's own labor, prevalent in Western thought from at least Aristotle to Marx, is quite different from the ethical underpinnings of caste. Moreover, even the encouraged forms of religious exchange raise moral quandaries for participants that in the end are not unilaterally resolvable. Here it is not capitalism per se that produces contradiction, ambiguity, or disquiet—or, rather, that is the unique source of these negative conditions. In this case not only does "religion" not provide a clear and unproblematic scenario for moral action, it actually contributes to the shape and possibly the sum total of dysphoria. The model sets up a golden age that is literally impossible to emulate. There is perhaps a parallel to be drawn here with the North American and northern European disquiet—in some quarters fear and obsession—over child abuse, a problematic generated in part by a cultural and economic system of possessive individualism in which one's children and ultimately one's own childhood come to be seen as fundamental property or capital and are subject almost inevitably to devaluation (Lambek and Antze 1996). The general point here was established by Weber (1958)—namely, that particular cultural models or discursive and disciplinary orders set up specific anxieties or give particular weight to anxieties in certain directions. Practice must respond accordingly. All this serves to offset the easy optimism found in Aristotle.

In sum, I have argued that we should supplement rule-bound structural accounts of morality with attention to moral *practice* and supplement Bourdieu's account of practice with attention to *morality*. The writer who most clearly conceptualizes moral practice is Aristotle. And it is Aristotle's concept of reasoned moral practice, *phronesis*, that brings us back to our starting point, providing one strand of a path for an anthropology (of religion) that wishes to avoid the oppositions of Plato's quarrel between poetry and philosophy and instead locate thought in the thick of immediate circumstances, in historicity, and in the constraints and opportunities of life.

Reconstituted as neither the study of faulty beliefs about supernatural realms nor as an idealized mimetic identification with (and appropriation of) the knowledge and practices of our subjects, but as an investigation of the historically situated, socially constituted imagination and realization of meaningful ends, practical means, authoritative voice, dignified and virtuous agency, and reasoned as well as passionate submission (albeit in the midst of, and often by means of, exclusion, oppression, suppression, repression, discipline, denigration, hypocrisy, rationalization, etc.), the anthropology of religion ought to regain a central space in the arena in which the politics of sub/disciplinary knowledge are currently enacted.

SIX

Just Anger: Scenarios of Indignation in Botswana and Madagascar

COAUTHORED BY JACQUELINE SOLWAY

It could be argued that one of the weaknesses of my general approach to ethics has been its relative inattention to emotion (feeling, affect). This chapter is one attempt to address the lapse, although it is fair to say that Solway and I start from emotion and discover its ethical dimension rather than the reverse. More exactly, the inspiration for the essay was the remarkable Tswana concept and institution of dikgaba. *A relatively implicit concern of the essay is that we felt it important to contextualize the concept of "witchcraft," since it appears so frequently in the Africanist literature, and to show its place within a broader network of moral concepts and experiences like* dikgaba. *The Botswana material was collected largely by Solway and the Malagasy material by Lambek, but we conducted some joint research in both places and discussed the ethnographic material at length. The essay had its origins in an AAA panel organized, if I remember correctly, by Petra Rethmann and discussed by Ellen Corin.*

> At any particular stage in the historical development of any particular culture the established patterns of emotion . . . will only be adequately understood if they are understood as giving expression to some distinctive moral and evaluative position. Psychologies thus understood express and presuppose moralities.
>
> —MacIntyre 1988, 76–77

This chapter compares particular cultural scenarios concerning anger in two African societies in order to elucidate some of the complex ways in which emotion is related to cultural context and social practice. We do not try to take into account all manifestations of anger in these societies, nor to

This chapter first appeared in *Ethnos* 66, no. 1 (2001): 1–23.

generalize about anger in either of them; rather, we focus on specific cultural modes in which anger is highlighted as a problem to be resolved and in which the social meanings attributed to, and contributive of, anger are made explicit relative to its everyday, unmarked, or contingent occurrence in these societies. Although the modalities of each case do not correspond precisely to a description of anger in North America (nor to each other), we feel confident in translating the central concept as anger, both because this corresponds with usages by bilingual informants and because of the general features characteristic of each case. At the same time we wish to preserve a sense of the refinements and uniqueness of each scenario, both with respect to other societies, such as our own, and relative to other manifestations of anger outside these cultural scenarios in the societies concerned. We are not interested in producing either blanket statements about anger or the emotions in general, or individuated, homogenous cultural portraits in the fashion of the culture-and-personality school or more recent forms of cultural relativism.

Our two ethnographic contexts include Kgalagadi and Tswana of Botswana and Sakalava of northwest Madagascar. The choice is fortuitous insofar as these happen to be the societies in which we have conducted fieldwork. However, although the modes highlighted in the two societies differ from each other in many respects, we are able to point to certain similarities that underscore the point made by MacIntyre in our epigraph with respect to the significance of moral evaluation in the articulation of emotion. With respect to the scenarios at hand, there is a double evaluation at work: not only does the discovery of any given incidence (not necessarily an explicit exhibition) of anger suggest inspection of its appropriateness, but appropriate anger is in turn a sign of moral concern, of an underlying fault to be discovered and addressed. The allocation of responsibility is a central issue, and our analysis becomes one of ethnographic analogs of the ethnopsychological concept of "guilt."

Guilt inevitably turns the analysis in a functional direction: it is not only that patterns of anger are symptoms of particular forms of social hierarchy, but the ways in which anger is addressed may serve to support that hierarchy. Conversely, social hierarchy—in the lineal, generational forms that are ultimately realized in ancestors—may provide the means to contain anger and its consequences. More deeply, forms of anger and its resolution may be understood as salient dimensions of relationally constituted subjectivity and sociality. Here the two ethnographic cases both provide a useful contrast with the West, where, in popular ideology, emotion and its containment are understood in highly individuated terms.[1] We will show how, in both Botswana and Madagascar, the allocation of responsibility with respect to anger has been less closely linked to individual rights and responsibilities (autonomy) than in North American middle-class structures of feeling. This further illustrates how persons are embedded in larger systems of social relations necessary to their well-being. Nevertheless, in all three ethnographic contexts anger is interpreted with reference to local ideas of moral persons and correct, just, and justifiable behavior. We preface our ethnography with some general points and follow it with a brief contrast regarding the expression of anger in contexts where the moral order appears to be collapsing.

On the Study of Emotion and the Social Phenomenology of Anger

An anthropology of the emotions is characterized by a number of related oppositions between which it has proved difficult to strike a balance. First are the insights of a constructionist, cultural account as opposed to a naturalist position that acknowledges some essential, biopsychological core that can be recognized universally. Second is the question of whether emotion can be explained according to an instrumental logic that can be learned and perhaps brought under some kind of control, or whether it is fundamentally irrational or nonrational, a "wild card" in personal and social life. Third is the question of whether emotion can be brought within the realm of the discursive (as most attempts to investigate the deployment of emotion words would seem to imply) or whether it remains evanescent and emergent, its presence induced persuasively and realized indirectly through social interaction, cultural symbols, and ritual performance.[2] These questions in part

1. On the containment and release metaphor of anger in English, see Lakoff and Johnson 1980; Lakoff and Kövecses 1987. People are said to "bottle it up," "let off steam," "burst" with anger, and so forth.

2. The fullest cultural account of anger is that of Michelle Rosaldo (1980), but it was Renato Rosaldo (1984) who reflected on the universality of rage in grief. Myers 1988 and Leavitt 1996 represent notable attempts to transcend the dichotomy between cultural and biological accounts of the emotions, while Lutz 1988 offers a profound contribution toward relativizing Western views of emotion. Van de Port (1998) offers a powerful and provocative attempt to take the irrational, eruptive, and disruptive qualities of emotion seriously, while Fernandez (1986) and others have attempted to show the orchestrated emergence of emotion in ritual, particularly insofar as metaphor and other tropes are deployed to impose predications on the "inchoate" and even produce a sense of grace or emergent wholeness. Accounts that subtly locate emotional expression within the flow of social life include Besnier 1995 and Cannell 1999. Most of these authors omit reference to psychoanalytic perspectives.

reflect methodological dilemmas; where psychoanalysts can attempt to read between the lines or anticipate emotion through its ostensible absence in analysands' resistance, anthropologists, rather like anyone engaged in social relationships, necessarily depend upon discursive or embodied expression.

These issues may be intrinsic to the subject matter. Insofar as we cannot distinguish the communication of emotion from some essence that lies behind it, so we may never be able to separate the natural from the cultural.[3] In any case, we do not attempt or pretend to resolve them here. Instead, we inspect two dense ethnographic cases in which specific emotions are articulated: simultaneously reported and described in referential language; signaled through bodily comportment and events; and addressed and redressed by means of interpersonal communication and collective ritual. The aim is not to describe or account for anger "in general" but to elucidate more precisely particular modes of emotional expression in their social and cultural contexts. This is not dissimilar to the standard ideographic method applied to kinship, literature, or other cultural institutions, yet it appears to run counter to the expectation of many readers. Given the contemporary cultural formulations of emotion in Western society as simultaneously the epitome of the "natural," the sign par excellence of the "beast within" (Mitchell 1988), and the domain of rarefied private experience, it is often assumed either that any social scientific discussion of emotion must be generalizing from the start or that attempts to produce generalizations are impossible. Our position is neither objectivist nor relativist (Bernstein 1983); rather, we hold that it is only possible to grasp the general through an interpretation of the particular. In order to understand situated emotional expressions and performances, the ways in which our ethnographic subjects perceive and conceive, or "mean and feel" (Leavitt 1996), we think it useful to bring together psychoanalytic, phenomenological, and cultural modes of interpretation, but not according to any general formula established in advance.

With respect to anger, we make several general observations (or working hypotheses) regarding the social formation, announcement, and communication of what is undoubtedly a universal propensity. First, anger is manifestly interpersonal in expression. Anger is directed *toward* someone. More specifically, we must distinguish the person (or institution) who is the object of anger from the person who is the recipient of the anger. We could continue in this vein to distinguish generalized and specific others, original

3. Following Geertz's incisive account of human evolution (1973b), the continuity between emotion and its cultural expression may be an ontological as well as an epistemological issue.

and displaced objects, direct and indirect recipients, and so forth, but the point is plain that anger involves others. When it is directed toward the self as object or recipient, it is the self viewed "as another" (Ricoeur 1992); we may refer to this as guilt. One of the ways that we recognize anger in contrast to certain other emotions (e.g., sadness, resignation) is the force with which it addresses others and demands recognition: angry people seek others to recognize, confirm, or assuage their anger. However, the nature of the dialogical space here opened up is, as our cases will show, variably construed.[4]

The second observation is that anger is understood to occur for reasons. It is a (potentially) meaningful response to a particular social or existential context (Myers 1988) and is interpreted with respect to social context. At the very least, people distinguish justifiable from unjustifiable anger (Lutz 1988), again both with respect to its objects (who made us mad) and its recipients—(who is made to feel the force of our anger). Put another way, anger occurs with respect to a moral framework (Tavris 1982)—that is, relative to general convictions about respect for others, about self-respect or personal dignity, and about understandings of the good life, right action, and justice (to roughly summarize Taylor 1989). Moreover, anger occurs with respect to specific understandings about established commitments and the violation or betrayal of legitimate expectations. We believe you have the right to be angry with someone who has lied to you, broken a promise, and so on.

Anger, in this sense, has roots in indignation; it is produced or incited by judgments we make about our rightful place in the world and our treatment at the hands of others, judgments that are grounded both in general social principles and values, and in the histories of specific engagements we have entered upon. Moreover, anger itself is judged according to the rightness of its cause, expression, direction, degree, and so forth. We can summarize this by saying that anger occurs with respect to interpretations and expectations of entitlement. These interpretations are a matter of ongoing practical judgment. Similarly, the ability to stop being angry will be related to (among other things) our understanding of the moral agency of the objects of our anger as well as our understanding of ourselves as moral persons bearing a certain form of dignity.

4. On the pragmatics of the expression and invocation of the emotions, as well as the issue of how they are to be discriminated from one another, see Lutz 1988 and Lutz and Abu-Lughod 1990. Hochschild 1983 and Wikan 1990 describe the management of emotions. Reddy 1999 appears to conflate semantic and pragmatic accounts as "constructionist." Yet the implications of saying that the category is constructed are quite different from arguing that any particular emotional experience or any given presentation of self is constructed.

All these factors are, of course, mediated by the kind of society in which we live and our place within it. Our third observation, then, is that structural factors inhibit the realization and resolution of anger in certain social relations while enabling it in others; the directions in which anger can be manifest are constituted largely with respect to hierarchy and relative power. We do not enter here into the thorny question of the ways in which moral conceptions are informed by power, but we would point out that anger is one of the responses to what is perceived as an abuse of power.[5] Here Thompson's conception of the moral economy (1971) is a useful attempt to understand the process of moral violation and response as it occurs in settings of social inequality. As an aside, we note that while the literature on the emotions almost always follows the dominant ideology in focusing on the individual, work like Thompson's serves to remind us that we should also pay attention to collective expressions and to the ways in which moral outrage and individual anger can be channeled into political action. Moreover, as our ethnography will show, anger can be experienced and expressed on behalf of others as well as oneself.

Our fourth observation is that the previous features we have mentioned, the interpersonal, moral, and structural dimensions of anger, become positioned within as well as outside the self. The paradigm for this is the Freudian account of the capacity for—and pervasiveness of—guilt, understood as introjection of parental anger and judgment. Simply put, humans have the capacity to get angry with themselves for what they think they have done to others or to themselves. Humans often become their own severest critics. Yet at the same time, humans wish to present themselves to themselves (as to others) in the best light and so strive to conceal from themselves both what they consider to be their worst failings and their own responses to them, possibly by relocating the failings and responses in others. Phrased in a more abstract fashion, anger *circulates* in a dialectic of introjection and projection.[6]

For Freud, the source of self-punishment is located internally in or as the superego. Whatever one's adherence to Freudian theory, it may be admitted that the reification or personification of this locus appears somewhat arbitrary. In other cultural settings where, no doubt, the general points we have made about the expression and circulation of anger are well understood,

5. For a compelling account of the phenomenology of anger, and especially envy, in working-class experience, see Steedman 1986.

6. Clearly, much anger (e.g., in labor protests) may be far more direct than this Freudian model implies.

the path will be conceptualized somewhat differently and it may be the interpersonal or transpersonal rather than the intrapersonal phase that is highlighted. This is certainly true of the two cases that follow.[7]

Fifth, then, as our ethnography will illustrate, anger is an emotion that people are frequently quicker to recognize in others than in themselves. As often as not, the social exploration of anger begins with the experience not of feeling angry but of suffering or fearing the anger of others. The central issue concerns addressing, perhaps trying to appease, those whose anger is imagined to be at the source of one's own troubles. But if others are angry, it must be for a reason, so anger rebounds as defilement, sin, or guilt and, more generally, as heightened attention to one's own condition or practice, which is thereby rescued from "going without saying."

Finally, we recognize that this portrait of anger is undoubtedly "oversocialized" (Wrong 1961). No doubt anger threatens the social constraints and evaluative procedures we have pointed to and frequently escapes them. Anger is powerful and frequently seemingly irrational and unpredictable; as such it has both destructive and creative force.[8] In many African societies anger of the sort we are describing is precisely distinguished from witchcraft or sorcery with respect to matters of the legitimacy of its source, means, and ends; the kind of social channel or hierarchy at issue; the recognition of its objects as moral persons; and with respect to its overall unpredictability and destructiveness.[9] Partly because of the wide press given to African witchcraft, we think it important to document the equally pervasive understandings of and scenarios for justifiable anger and the socially responsible means to offset its effects.

Although we do not pursue the contrast with cultural constructions of witchcraft, we do wish to make a heuristic distinction between anger and rage as two ideal types on a phenomenological continuum. We speak of anger as a relatively legitimate response to provocation that contains or invites the possibility of an unfolding toward a meaningful conclusion. Anger entails a sense of finitude. By contrast, rage is particularly disturbing because there is little sense of its unfolding in any way other than increasing violence; rage escapes the bounds of personal and social circumspection

7. In the version of Freudian theory espoused here, note that human sociality rather than human (biological) individuality is primary (S. Mitchell 1988).

8. We thank Ellen Corin for making this point to us.

9. The connections formulated between witchcraft and the anger or protection of elders and of ancestors are variable across African societies and cannot be reviewed here.

and containment, and there is no immediate individual or mutual understanding of what might constitute a satisfactory conclusion. Rage is anger without expectation. Anger occurs in a context in which the parent or other respondent, actual or symbolic, responsive or responsible, is understood as ultimately available; in rage the parent is experienced as irrevocably absent, dead, hostile, or unreachable. We hasten to repeat that these are ideal types. What follows concerns anger rather than rage. That is, it concerns scenarios that contain the possibility of their own resolution. We return to the contrast at the end of the chapter.

Sekgalagadi Dikgaba: Anger as Disappointment in Botswana

Dikgaba, found among Tswana and Kgalagadi in Botswana, was succinctly described by Schapera as follows: "If someone fell ill soon after a family quarrel, the diviner would often attribute the illness to the anger of a senior relative. This illness, known as *dikgaba*, was believed to have been sent by the ancestral spirits as the punishment for the breach of respect to one's elder. It could not be cured until the anger of the offended person had been appeased. He would then wash the patient with certain medicines, saying at the same time, 'If it was I who caused the illness, may he recover' " (1971, 228).

In fact, there need be no particular family quarrel; Schapera adds that the diviner could always diagnose it in the knowledge that strained family relations were common (1971, 229). Moreover, dikgaba refers to both the condition of the junior person and the emotion of the senior (as well as to the ceremony and the plant used within it) and hence implicitly to the experiential and existential nexus between them and to a quality of ambivalence pertaining to kinship generally. However, what is critical about dikgaba is that it never goes from junior to senior relations. Moreover, although the central parties are often only one generation apart, or even siblings, it is the entire line of descent that is invoked. Thus, the illness is brought by the ancestors on account of their unresolved anger, or that of one of their descendants, at one of his or her (and their) descendants. Furthermore, dikgaba often strikes the most vulnerable person, often a child or the yet unborn of the original object of anger. Thus, as Schapera points out (1971, 228), miscarriage is often attributed to dikgaba. The substitutability of the generations is evident also in the fact that when a person dies while still bearing unplacated (and possibly hitherto undiagnosed) dikgaba, the condition may be resolved using a lineal descendant to stand in as a substitute for the offended deceased.

Dikgaba, Schapera noted, supported the social structure. Its moral valence is positive, and thus it forms a direct contrast with witchcraft, which concerns illegitimate intervention in the affairs of others. Moreover, where witchcraft connotes illicit consumption and personal gain, dikgaba connotes the need for harmony, connection, and positive affect. Not only is dikgaba legitimate, it is almost naturalized; that is, the disappointment or angering of one's senior relatives, often through simple neglect or disobedience, is expected almost inevitably to bring about dikgaba. And it may happen without the senior relative even being conscious of her own anger; certainly she does nothing specific to initiate its consequences and, as Schapera noted, the cure requires her to say, "If I was the cause" (a phrase strikingly similar to the response expected from the accused Zande witch, as described by Evans-Pritchard 1937). Her statement also dissipates the effects of the anger, providing, in essence, absolution for the ill person, the ostensible object of her anger. Intentional personal agency is both invoked and underplayed.

It needs to be emphasized that although Schapera was writing about the 1930s, dikgaba remains pervasive and central in Botswana, without respect for the significant urban-rural, class, and educational divisions. While not sensational or spectacular like witchcraft, it is part of everyone's experience, implicit in all interaction among kin. No one avoids the suffering of dikgaba; no one can go without questioning whether their acts are producing dikgaba (anger) in a senior relative or their feelings producing dikgaba (misfortune) in a junior relative. No elder should remain with *bothloko ba pelo* (pain in the heart) for fear of provoking dikgaba.

Despite what may appear, among Kgalagadi of Western Kweneng, dikgaba has not been directly about the validation of patriarchy or patrilineal relations. Indeed, it is not found primarily where relations of lineal-based authority have been violated but where expectations of intergenerational love and care have been disappointed. Dikgaba occurs most commonly matrilaterally, between mothers and their offspring or between sisters and their brothers or their brothers' children, and between mother's brother and sister's children, especially sons (the relationship that, like mother/child, is believed to be especially prone to dikgaba).

Both Klaits (1999) and Durham (1999) point out that Tswana conceptualize moral dispositions according to the qualities of love (*lerato*) and jealousy (*lefufa*). Jealousy tends to be associated with patrilineal kin. As one young Kgalagadi man put it, "There is more jealousy with one's father's kin because of inheritance. They see each other as threats to their property, especially cattle. My father's relatives see my cattle as theirs. You can trust your mother's relatives more."[10] Strongest in matrilateral relations, love is a powerful and volatile emotion. Relations of love carry implicit dangers. Therefore they require management. This is the reason Kgalagadi go so far as to say the law prevents one from living with *Malome* (mother's brother) once one is no longer a child. To do so, in the context of a relationship where affect and expectations run high, is to invite quarrel or disappointment. Worries about the production or accusation of dikgaba thus reveal the ambivalence inherent in close relations and the dialectical nature of emotional dispositions. They do so not only to external observers like anthropologists; they also provide a mirror to local people themselves. If dikgaba is sometimes provoked by jealousy, it is only jealousy that emerges in a context of love. Love is sought and expected, but its fragility is acknowledged; when love between close matrilateral kin appears to be betrayed, their relationship takes on the characteristics of jealousy associated with agnates.

Dikgaba thus follows the pattern of privileging within restricted contexts the structurally weaker component of the agnatically dominant system that Turner (1969, 125), drawing on Fortes (1949), identifies as "the structurally inferior as the morally and ritually superior" and as evocative of communitas rather than structure. Dikgaba also grants recognition and voice to women as sisters, mothers, and aunts; it is critical for a person's well-being not to disappoint them. Yet, at the same time, as the following case shows, satisfying matrilateral kin is secondary to meeting the demands of patrilateral (or affinal) ones, and dikgaba can be a way of rationalizing the choice that is entailed and thereby indirectly supporting the patrilineal order.

Unlike witchcraft, which is believed to occur as the result of direct and purposeful human action, dikgaba can occur without the knowledge and against the wishes of the party from whom it emanates. This is one reason Kgalagadi argue it is important to maintain residence patterns that minimize contact between persons most likely to provoke and receive dikgaba. The following case illustrates the point.

Moitsupi had suffered a vehicle accident the previous winter; the truck rolled on a desert road and he suffered a broken arm. He was immediately

10. Cattle, as noted, are a source of much intra-lineal feud. This is connected to the fact that property rights concerning cattle are simultaneously individuated and dispersed. All cattle are perceived as deriving from patri-ancestors, and the family herd is believed to exist as a result of the labors of past male family members—the ancestors of all patrilaterally related kin. The herd is shared patrimony to which all have some legitimate claim or entitlement (Solway 1994) but, at the same time, individuals "own" the animals. This competitive quality of agnatic kin, which Tswana express metaphorically by saying agnates want "to eat each other," is also emphasized by Comaroff and Comaroff (1991).

taken to hospital, and his arm was put in a cast; he saw a local healer (*ngaka*), who gave him a number of medicines. He then went to another *ngaka* who performed a divination ritual to determine the underlying cause of his misfortune. Strife between him and his *mmangwane* (mother's younger sister) that eventuated in dikgaba was identified as the problem. Mmamodisaitsane, his *mmangwane*, was a young widow; she had been the third wife in a polygynous union. When her husband died, she believed his brothers were making inappropriate claims on her household's cattle, and she feared witchcraft against herself and her children. She "escaped" her husband's village and returned to her natal village to settle in the area of her elder sister's household (close but not in the same ward as her brother). Knowing that building next to her brother and beloved mother would be too provocative and might place her mother in the untenable situation of having to choose to support a daughter over a daughter-in-law, she felt safer near her sister. But this posed problems as well.

Mmamodisaitsane was a relatively wealthy woman with a moderately large herd of cattle who assumed enormous responsibilities. She had children ranging in age from infancy to the early twenties; she plowed large fields and managed the herd with the help of a herdboy (her elder sons helped on school breaks but otherwise were away); and she was active in civic affairs. Despite her normal cheerful demeanor, the strain was great, and I (Solway) once found her crying near the kraal, saying she couldn't manage. She hoped her sister's son would help her, and occasionally she would ask him to. On one occasion she remembered well, she asked if he would help water her cattle. He refused. She felt the hurt in her heart, and she felt it growing and getting hotter. As she told me, "I love my nephew and I don't want to hurt him, but I can't help how I feel. I can't stop my dikgaba."

Mmamodisaitsane was not surprised when she was asked to participate in a ritual to "cool" the dikgaba in her. For his part, Moitsupi said he recalled a day that Mmamodisaitsane had asked him to help with a kraal fence she was building. He was helping his father-in-law water cattle that day and could not help her. He too said he felt badly, but one's father-in-law takes priority in almost all instances. In this case, the circumstances that led to the dikgaba might have been avoided had Mmamodisaitsane not located near her sister. But the rules and realities of social life repeatedly place people in compromising positions in which it is not the fact but the degree of disappointment and its consequences that must be managed. In this instance all parties easily agreed to participate in the dikgaba ceremony for fear that if not cooled, Mmamodisaitsane's dikgaba might affect Moitsupi's more vulnerable children.

The theory of dikgaba can be compared to the Western model of guilt. In both it is the perpetrators of offenses who experience the negative effects of their act. In dikgaba the mechanism is conceptualized interpersonally rather than intrapersonally; the source of harm is understood to be the person whom one has disappointed. Moreover, insofar as children of the guilty party may be the actual victims of the anger, dikgaba can be understood as transpersonal rather than simply interpersonal. At the dikgaba ceremony, the entire family is "cooled" by the aspersion of the medicated water.

It is striking as well that, although anger is stated as the central emotion in dikgaba, anger is nowhere directly expressed. No one actually acts angrily. In fact, direct displays of anger make Kgalagadi extremely uncomfortable. Anger is not deployed directly as a discursive strategy, and Kgalagadi go to some lengths to avoid its appearance.[11] For example, requests are rarely refused with a direct "no." Rather, one says no "sideways," by listing all the reasons one cannot meet the request (such as Moitsupi's claim that he was assisting his father-in-law and thus could not help Mmamodisaitsane).[12] In doing so, one mutes the stimulus to anger, thereby frustrating the possibility of developing an overt response. It is for this reason that dikgaba may also be identified within the realm of sadness (as Klaits observed in his fieldwork in the capital). Ill feelings may eventuate in dikgaba if they remain "in the heart" and are subject to periodic recollection. An original feeling of affront or disappointment is understood to build over time; sadness and anger are in this context understood as a continuum of emotional dispositions rather than as discrete categories of feeling.

Dikgaba thus exemplifies a broader underlying anxiety among Kgalagadi at the direct expression of anger. As noted above, patrivirilocal residence is justified in part as a means to minimize the possible eruption of anger. Parents who wish to punish their young children are admonished to pick up a light stick or wand and use that rather than applying their hands directly to their offspring. Just as the stick mediates corporal punishment, so too does the dikgaba ceremony mediate the display of parental anger. Instead

11. This may be why some visitors to Botswana have noted the prevalence of a kind of passive-aggressive quality in some interactions, especially on the part of junior parties.

12. It is not that Moitsupi was disingenuous; sons-in-law are compelled to assist their fathers-in-law, and it is likely that the scenario he described did indeed transpire. However, there were countless other occasions at which Moitsupi could have aided his needy aunt but chose not to do so. In general, Moitsupi was not noted for his industriousness.

of parents communicating their anger, for example by shouting or hitting, or even simply by announcing it, they calmly remove the effects of what they say might have been anger. The very fact that they are or were angry is revealed by the diviner rather than expressed in their own conversation or behavior.[13] The infusion and dispersion of the dikgaba plant in water during the ceremony "cools" rather than displays anger and, again, mediates the physical contact.

The administration of dikgaba medicine is not merely a recalling of the anger, it is also a form of benediction. Those whose parents die before they have performed such a ceremony may become victims of a more permanent ancestral dikgaba. The more a person is believed to have a sense of *go siame* (satisfaction) as they enter the status of *badimo* (ancestor), the less likely they are to be a source of dikgaba. This is one of the reasons that a proper death and funeral are very important for the living and the dead, and it contributes to the elaborateness of funerals in Botswana. Ancestral displeasure is, in effect, a kind of curse, a withdrawal of protection that may leave the descendant vulnerable to misfortune from external causes, natural mishaps, witchcraft, and the like. In addition to illness, crops can fail and animals die, lorries can break down, children can do badly at school, and their luck can always be bad. People whose dikgaba has not been resolved simply fail to prosper.

Sakalava Spirit Possession: Violent Others in Madagascar

We turn now to an ethnographic context in which the construction of anger merges more with intransigence than sadness but in which other features of the Kgalagadi scenario can be found. In northwest Madagascar many people are possessed by the spirits of deceased royalty. These spirits are powerful figures who are most often described by their mediums and others in the possession milieu as *mashiaka*. *Mashiaka* is an attribute of disposition rather than an emotion, and it refers to a violent temperament. Someone who is *mashiaka* is quick to anger, *malaiky meloko*, and retaliates without hesitation. A person who loudly or caustically berates her spouse or children is described as *mashiaka*. *Mashiaka* is not an entirely negative concept, however, and it is met with respect as well as fear.[14] It is an attribute of power

13. Thus, although dikgaba supports authority, it is unlike the case in Ifaluk, where simply to state that someone is justifiably angry "can constitute both an ideological ploy and a subversive move" (Lutz 1988,174).

14. But see Lambek 1992a on negative attitudes toward intra-familial violence in closely related Mayotte. Bloch has written a good deal on the value of ritually located violence among other Malagasy groups; see especially Bloch 1986, 1999.

that may be viewed ambivalently, but is not without a certain legitimacy; in precolonial times monarchs were *mashiaka* with respect to their subjects and violent in their relations with one another. Although less naturalized than dikgaba, it is equally clear that the appropriate direction runs from senior to junior.[15] However, unlike dikgaba, or anger more generally in Botswana, it is (by definition) freely expressed and can be itself a source and expression of pride, evidence of a kind of "no one messes with me" quality. It may thus disregard the expectations of kinship.[16] Those who are described as *mashiaka* (and they remain in the minority) may be granted the sort of grudging admiration that we might associate with the epithet "hot-tempered." *Mashiaka* connotes fierceness, impatience, and intransigence.[17] Perhaps the best translation is "terrible," as in Ivan the Terrible.

Mediums are at once proud and rueful in describing their spirits as *mashiaka*. They bear the brunt of their spirits' harshness and are afraid of it; at the same time, the depiction of spirits as mean, punitive, and remorseless only increases both their power and the value of getting along with them. Violence is also one of the means by which the presence of a spirit is signified. For example, when asked whether the spirit who had possessed her for most of her adult life was *mashiaka*, an elderly woman responded as follows:

> Is Ndramahatindry *mashiaka*? He is very *mashiaka* when he comes across something he doesn't like or when someone offends him! The spirit first rose in me in town but we planned to hold his ceremony at my mother's, in the bush. So we were storing the rum to take to the ceremony. But the bottles broke where they were stacked, smelling up the whole house. It turned out the spirit had been tabooed liquor, but he hadn't announced his taboos yet, so we didn't know. That's why all the rum was lost.[18]

15. Closer to dikgaba would be the Malagasy practice of *tsipirano* (or *tsodrano*), ancestral benediction that also includes the aspersion of medicated water. Among Sakalava it is not defined by specific reference to anger or disappointment (cf. Cole 1999).

16. Thus of one male spirit it is said that when he is angry, he won't even listen to his father or grandfather. And often he simply ignores the request of humans to come when he is needed.

17. Abinal and Malzac (1987) translate *siaka* as *violence, rudesse, séverité, méchanceté, cruauté, férocité, sauvagerie,* and figuratively as *causticité, violence de langage*. *Mashiaka* is *cruel, violent, méchant; caustique, violent dans son langage*.

18. The same woman a year earlier began our conversation by saying how *mashiaka* her spirit was. She told a story from his past life that exemplified his ruthlessness. Now when he rises, he says, "I am *mashiaka*! I can kill my descendants (*zafy*)!" One approaches him humbly (*mandady*), and he calms down. This medium is of royal ancestry herself.

More often, the violation of a spirit's taboos makes a medium sick. Thus the same medium continued to say that at first, before she knew she had the spirit, she would feel nauseous and vomit after eating eggs. Later she learned that one of his taboos was chicken.

This account is a little disingenuous, since some of the taboos are widely known. A person who becomes nauseous on eating chicken or eggs is in fact announcing to the world that she is becoming possessed, even if she may not consciously recognize the fact. Practiced mediums are extremely conscious of the potential for anger of their spirits, negotiating a fine line in their daily lives between doing what they please and avoiding the spirits' anger. Mediums who have several spirits, each with their own demands, must live in a manner that takes them all into account.[19] Illnesses are often diagnosed as caused by the anger of their spirits and mediums regularly medicate themselves with a plant known as *fangala heloko*, the removal of anger, that is, the removal of any inadvertent offense. This same medicine comprises the first bath of the initiation ceremony of a new spirit, said to remove any anger the spirit might have because it had been neglected for so long. This bath "clears the air" (*manazava*) and is thus somewhat akin to the dikgaba ritual.

What spirits generally get angry about is the violation of their personal taboos, which serve as signifiers of their identities and memories of their lives. These taboos thus do not draw their symbolic import directly from the lives of the mediums, but rather from the lives of the historical personages who are incarnated in the mediums. They are thus of collective rather than merely personal significance.[20] The more ancient and senior, and hence more powerful, spirits are the ones that guard their taboos most stringently.[21] In addition to personal taboos, there are those that are relevant to the entire system. No one with a senior spirit would dare visit the house where a corpse is laid out, and no one returning from visiting the bereaved or attending a funeral ought to drop in at the home of a senior medium

19. This entails observing their taboos with respect to work, diet, and dress even when the medium is not in active trance. Space precludes an account of the daily practice of mediumship. See Lambek 1981, 1993b, and 2000c for neighboring Mayotte, and see Lambek 1998b and 2003a for Mahajanga.

20. On the significance of taboos more generally, see chapter 3, as well as the various essays in Middleton 1999a. The taboos also have personal resonance that we cannot discuss here.

21. Of one ancient figure, Mbabilahy's elder sister, one consultant said: "*Mashiaka io*! That one's *mashiaka*! Her tomb guardians always die quickly. Her discipline is too severe. One small mistake and she kills!" Likewise her mediums are said to live only two to three years before succumbing.

before bathing and changing into fresh clothing. A taboo of this sort carries forward customs that were once more broadly practiced, leaving mediums solely responsible for carrying the burden of tradition. If a visitor were to pollute the medium's abode, it is the medium who would suffer the anger of the spirit. Hence, if we are to speak of anger and punishment in terms of conscience, we can say that what the mediums maintain is the conscience—and not simply consciousness—of history (Lambek 1998b, 2000c). (Here the French word *conscience* perhaps serves us better.)

That the anger inflicted on mediums is not simply of individual or subjective import is illustrated by the following case. When I (Lambek) arrived in Mahajanga in June 1996, the first thing my friend and mentor, the senior (female) medium of one of the most important (male) spirits, known as Mbabilahy, said was that she had been very sick, with a pain in her lower left side that pulsed like *pulmonaire,* a sore right ear, and a visibly swollen right cheek. The spirit was very angry and had caused it. She explained that the local living ruler (*ampanjaka be*), who is a descendant some eight generations from Mbabilahy, together with the custodians of the main shrine in the region were planning major renovations to the temple and, as was proper, had asked the permission and advice of the senior spirits before proceeding. Because the construction materials departed from tradition, and because, in fact, the whole project was highly controversial, the spirits at first refused the request. Eventually Mbabilahy established a compromise between the other spirits and the living managers, and instructed the custodians to carry out expensive ritual procedures. When they disregarded the spirit's instructions and began the construction without even informing the spirits, Mbabilahy was furious but said nothing.

A few days later, when Mbabilahy was called upon at the shrine to start up the annual festival, he didn't rise. Both the shrine manager (*fahatelo*) and the Big Woman (*bemanangy*) tried to coax him. The medium could feel her skin burning; she felt on fire. Finally, after a long time, Mbabilahy appeared briefly and said, "I'm no longer involved!" Then he left again. After that, the medium became sick with her swollen cheek. The Big Woman also fell very sick and "nearly died." Then the spirit's clothing disappeared from his locked box in the shrine.

The medium herself said that her physical condition was the result of the spirit's fury. But what of the missing clothes? The community of spirit mediums collected the funds to purchase a new outfit and called up the spirit in order to inform him that his clothes had been stolen and that they had purchased replacements. The medium explained that Mbabilahy rose very angry but that his "father" (i.e., Mbabilahy's father, risen in a charismatic male medium), calmed him down and said that things (i.e., the behavior of the shrine managers) were like this now and that Mbabilahy should accept the circumstances and not be upset. He also said to everyone, "I gave my son the kingdom (*fanjakana*) and you must show him the respect (*vonahitry*) he is due." So she began to get well.

According to the representative of the living ruler, Big Woman Honorine, who was also present, Mbabilahy surprised the large gathering by announcing, "Since you never do what I ask, I've gone home to my mother. I took the clothes myself!"[22] The medium herself maintained that she had no idea what had happened to the spirit's clothing. She shared in the expense of purchasing the new material and went to a good deal of trouble in preparing the outfit. In the end, a night-long ceremony was held at the shrine, at which virtually the entire royal descent line, stretching back to 1700 (but with the exception of the living ruler), as well as many other people witnessed Mbabilahy's acceptance of his new clothing (Lambek 1998b).[23]

This is not the place to enter into the complex politics of this case. It shows the weakness of the spirits *vis-à-vis* the living ruler and shrine managers at the time. In effect, the only direct outlet the spirit had for his anger at the insult he (and the other closely related ancestral spirits he represented) had received was against the medium herself, who appears here rather as the battleground of the whole affair. Yet the spirit's destruction of his clothing was, in addition to being a vivid sign of his withdrawal from the shrine, a ploy successfully calculated to invite and demonstrate the community's support for the medium. The violence of the spirit is here an expression of righteous indignation which, while exacted on and by means of the body of the medium, has political and collective significance for those to whom it is addressed. In sum, the anger that spirits display toward their mediums signifies both their transhistorical power and the limitations of that power in the present-day political domain.

Despite the public significance of the episode, it is clear that the wrath is introjected rather than projected. As with dikgaba, the process works like guilt (although in this case it is the "innocent party," the medium, who is hurt). Is this the anger of the powerless? Or is it anger that has been in some

22. This convocation took place a few days before Lambek's arrival. He heard about it from an excellent source, the medium who was in trance as Mbabilahy's father at the time and was subsequently told what had been witnessed. Mbabilahy's medium herself never admitted this.

23. Some 30–35 distinct spirits were present as witnesses. Another active participant was Ampanjaka Tsialaña, a living member of the royal descent group who is more rooted in tradition than his distant cousin, the current ruler, and who serves as the royal representative at the shrine.

sense sublimated? The medium is personally subjected, yet she never forgets that she is acting with respect to, and as an agent of, a wide regime of power. Here it is worthwhile to observe that the deceased rulers, who are individuated incarnations of historical figures, specific as to gender, age, generation, and historical period, are understood both politically, as taking over the ancestral role from the personal ascendants of commoners, and personally, as parental figures for their mediums. A medium may have first encountered her spirits while they were in possession of her parent or grandparent, and in many instances a medium succeeds a parent or grandparent in bearing a particular spirit (Lambek 1993b). Although irascible, uncompromising, and quick to anger, spirits are understood as caring for their hosts, protecting and empowering them and looking out for their welfare so long as the hosts respect them and observe their taboos. Often they intercede in a medium's life long before she is first possessed by them. To the degree that hosts come to identify with the spirits that already have parental identification, we may speak of introjection of the parent.

In bearing the brunt of the spirit's wrath, Mbabilahy's medium is identifying with the spirit. She is acting as the embodied conscience of history, bearing witness, quite literally, to what has transpired against him. The injury she received—a swollen face—is as public a sign of the spirit's indignation (a "slap in the face") as his missing clothing.

Finally, it is worth pointing out that, despite the intransigence of the living monarch and shrine managers, sources of acknowledgment and appeasement were available. Mbabilahy's anger was removed by the calming words of his father and then by the collective support shown him by his entire family (and, in effect, shown the medium by the community of mediums).

Conclusion

The anger we have described is remarkable for its displacement, diagnosed by means of its effects. In both dikgaba and Sakalava spirit possession, the angry person strikes at someone who may not have been the original transgressor or source of their anger—in the former case, often a child. But whoever the object, it is their suffering or symptom that serves as the sign of affront; the anger of the senior person is inferred from the circumstances of the junior. The locus of the experience lies primarily in the recipient rather than in the angry person herself, less in being angry than being the subject of someone else's anger. In dikgaba, the angry person must even be informed that she is angry, and only then is she legitimately allowed to acknowledge her anger. Yet the displacement is one that invites resolution and perhaps absolution.

This displacement may be described in the terms we used earlier as the circulation of anger in a dialectic of introjection and projection. In Botswana a junior sufferer of dikgaba understands his position by projecting his guilt onto the parental figure, whose anger (transferred further onto the ancestors and back) is then discovered to be the source of his problem. But it is the previous introjection of the parental figure that both provokes and renders possible the guilt that seeks resolution. Juniors need not even seek the source of the anger in any particular act on their part since, in the Kgalagadi view, parents are (at some moment) inevitably disappointed in or hurt by their children; guilt is a condition of social existence. But this recognition is compensated for by a clear avenue for forgiveness and benediction. In Sakalava spirit possession, the host is made the victim of the spirit's anger at events taking place in the external world. Here we might say that what has been projected from the medium onto the spirit (or the medium's parents) becomes re-introjected. Spirit mediums become, in effect, the living conscience of history. For both Sakalava and Kgalagadi, ancestors uphold the moral order and do so insofar as they are introjected by their descendants.

Spirits, parents, and ancestors show compassion, but periodically that state of compassion has to be performatively reinstated. Compassion and love are not simple habit, and whatever their "natural" source, they need to be socially marked. In the dikgaba ritual, compassion is not merely shown, it is performatively brought into effect, instantiating a condition of blessing or love. Rather than diagnoses of anger or disappointment contributing to the breakdown of interpersonal relations, the performance of the dikgaba ritual actually helps to reinforce such relations and, more importantly, to reproduce the moral order of which they are a part. Similarly, the anger of the Sakalava spirits helps both to constitute them as persons distinct from the mediums who are the recipients of their anger and to initiate conditions by which they can be appeased and social relations with them (re)established. In each case, authority figures who have the potential to be justifiably angry, but also compassionate, with their successors and subjects are reconstituted, as is the moral order that they represent.

Both of our ethnographic cases thus move us far from the common Western cultural stereotype of the lone individual declaiming his *own* anger into an anonymous world. Anger, in that picture, is a sign and instance of possessive individualism, precisely as described in Hobbes. As explicated by

Macpherson, and later elaborated by Sahlins as the dominant ideology of Western capitalist society, this is

> a conception of the individual as essentially the proprietor of his own person or capacities, owing nothing to society for them. The individual was seen neither as a moral whole, nor as part of a larger social whole, but as owner of himself. The relation of ownership, having become for more and more men, the critically important relation in determining their actual freedom and actual prospect of realizing their full potentialities, was read back into the nature of the individual. . . . Society becomes a lot of free individuals related to each other as proprietors of their own capacities. (Macpherson 1962, 3; quoted in Sahlins 1976b, 98)

Despite active participation in the relations of a capitalist economy, certain social ideas and practices of both Kgalagadi and Sakalava remain far removed from possessive individualism. Ethnographic particulars and local social formations aside, we believe they illustrate something far more general about the moral and relational qualities of anger.[24] At base, they demonstrate the importance of the Other in the construction of the self. This is possibly a trivial observation for anthropologists, but we think it bears repeating, especially when we consider debates both within psychoanalysis (Kohut 1977; S. Mitchell 1988) and between psychoanalytic and ascendant neuropharmacological psychiatric models (Luhrmann 2000). In brief, the ethnographic data continue to demonstrate that possessive individualism is more ideology than transparent description of reality (cf. Sahlins 1996). But this formulation also raises the question, What happens when potentially angry yet fundamentally empathic parental Others are absent (in reality or from the social imaginary)? What happens when access to the relational "means of self-production" is restricted? Here we turn briefly to some deliberately provocative remarks.

In contrasting situations of anger with those of sheer violent rage, such as the "necklacing" of suspected witches described by the Comaroffs (1999) or the refusal of empathy that must underlie the epidemic of child witches in Kinshasa reported by Filip de Boeck (personal communication), we would note the following. Although the situations in South Africa and the

24. As Lutz puts it, summarizing her analysis of anger on the Micronesian atoll of Ifaluk, "In perhaps too simple outline, offenses threaten relationships on Ifaluk, rights in the United States" (1988,178).

Democratic Republic of Congo/ Zaire include both alienation and anomie (not to mention simple frustration), we question whether the problems are not deeper than what is generally conveyed by these terms. Where in one context people are turning on their elders and in another on their children, we can only concur with Ashforth that the situation is one of deep anxiety, in which "very real fears . . . spring from, relate to, and are located in realms of being that are both ineffable and open to transcendence—that are not subject to forms of knowledge adequately represented by clear and distinct ideas" (1998, 62). However we would not see this sense of exposure to unseen harmful forces as a product of "the proliferation of interpretive authorities" (65). On the contrary, the latter is equally a symptom of the problem, which is a moral, not an epistemological one.

Society must offer both a moral framework and the material and social means and conditions for achieving personal dignity. Among Sakalava and Kgalagadi, we have spoken of just anger. We have seen that rights to specific forms of anger are the product of relationships and are connected primarily to the parental position and to seniority more generally. Anger expressed in the other direction, from juniors or subordinates to seniors or superordinates, is less easily recognized. Elders are understood to have the love, wisdom, and practical judgment to engage in the performance of the rituals that can curtail their anger. Less explicitly, elders may also be able to contain some of the anger of juniors and transmute its danger. Furthermore, parental anger is a form of moral education; the objects of anger are expected to respond, and to respond responsibly, as responsibly as the parents themselves when they are informed that they are sources of dikgaba. Both those who are angry and those who are the objects of their anger are respected as moral, self-respecting agents.

The situation is much less clear when the subjects and objects of anger do not participate in a system of seniority, do not agree on their relative positions within it, or, more critically, when they are unable to recognize each other as moral persons or are not in sight at all. For example, it may be easier to express anger toward colonial authorities who flaunt their power in ceremonial displays than against the faceless and unlocatable directors of postcolonial, neoliberal policy. Anger may be less accessible, and less useful, against diffuse discursive power than against its more direct forms. Anger and its resolution require the presence of parents, ancestors, or disinterested parties who can be addressed and who respond, who can enable displacement, guarantee containment, grant absolution, and repotentiate or restore a level of self-respect, dignity, and moral worth to those who have found fault with others and especially with themselves. We have presented two ethnographic instances of such ambivalent and conflictual yet functioning social worlds. However, not all current situations are as enabling. When parents and ancestors are no longer considered worthy predecessors or are understood, for whatever reasons, to have permanently abandoned their descendants and their charges; when, that is, the capacity for indignation collapses into a condition of apparently permanent indignity, the successors may be left with nothing but rage.

SEVEN

Rheumatic Irony: Questions of Agency and Self-Deception as Refracted Through the Art of Living with Spirits

This chapter was originally submitted to American Ethnologist, *but when I received what I considered an anomalous "revise and resubmit" message from the editor, I decided to build a book around it instead. This was* Illness and Irony, *edited with Paul Antze. We became aware of Jonathan Lear's work on irony only as we were going to press. Lear's discussion could enrich the argument I make, though where I describe spirit mediums as living their irony and hysterics as embodying it, Lear identifies the recognition of irony with therapeutic action and suggests that "the hysteric is the ideal candidate for irony" (2003, 153).*

> . . . unresolved—that is life and humanity, and it would betray a dreary lack of subtlety to worry about it.
>
> —Thomas Mann, *The Magic Mountain*; quoted in Nehamas (1998, 19)

Something that anthropology can be and is about, though it is almost never phrased as such, is the art of living. I borrow this phrase (along with much else) from a recent book of that title by Alexander Nehamas (1998). Nehamas's subject is philosophy—in particular certain heroic philosophers who have seen the artful, and at times agonizing, creation of their own lives as exemplary (his subtitle is *Socratic Reflections from Plato to Foucault*). Anthropologists sometimes discover characters among their subjects who stand out for their genius or the style or emphasis with which they lead their lives, cutting a swath through convention. But perhaps we learn most

This chapter first appeared in M. Lambek and P. Antze, eds., *Illness and Irony* (New York: Berghahn, 2003), 40–59. It was published concurrently in *Social Analysis* 47, no. 2 (2003): 40–59.

by exploring how ordinary people draw on local conventions and idioms in the living of their individual and interrelated lives. Their actions can prove exemplary or edifying when they illustrate the potential of local idioms for generating or articulating insight and movement of general relevance.

I have gradually come to see that one of the things that I have been exploring over the years is the art of living as practiced and demonstrated by spirit mediums in the Malagasy-speaking world of northwestern Madagascar, Mayotte, and, increasingly, France. What has intrigued me is less the ritual of spirit possession or the temporary state of trance than the integration of other voices, other persons, with the self in the construction of a life for oneself and with others—a life (as we say) for better and for worse, in sickness and in health, in good times and bad. That is to say, I have been intrigued with tracing the place of spirits in the lives of mediums over time; with the ways in which spirits are entwined with the biographies of people and families (and sometimes whole communities); with the ways they figure in informal autobiography and memory as people construct and reflect on their lives in narrative and practice, in retrospection and in prospect; and thus with the art of living with spirits, or rather, with spirit possession *as* an art of living.[1]

Here I do not wish to individualize my subjects too strongly, both because spirits can be shared among people and form a vehicle of connection between them, and because possession cannot help but draw attention to itself, becoming a display that draws, engages, and provokes an audience, much as Socrates did (Nehamas 1998) and much as a written text does. Insofar as the events of lives lived with possession become public, so they become objects of contemplation, interrogation, identification, and edification for those around them. Possession thus becomes a vehicle with respect to which the nonpossessed or soon-to-be-possessed also reflect on and live their lives, if only by resisting its form, messages, or imprecations.[2] The salience of other lives is heightened through spirit possession, not only because possession is simply noisy and disruptive but because virtually everything about possession calls attention to itself as an artifact.

1. See Lambek (1988a, 1996, 2000c, 2002a, and 2003a).

2. It is true, in any case, that the lives of our friends and contemporaries, insofar as we know them, become the objects of our contemplation—John falling sick when and as he did, Mary having a child, John and Mary raising their children as they do. The ways in which the lives of our friends, colleagues, and consociates become available to us as objects of moral contemplation and the questions they raise for us are intensified in "life-term" communities (Moore 1978).

I see the accomplished spirit medium somewhat as a Western artist or craftsman. An acclaimed violinist needs her instrument in order to create beautiful music; a great philosopher needs the texts of his predecessors. The analogy is rough, but in the Malagasy world the spirits are likewise vehicles, instruments in a technology for creative expression and building, for that dimension of human activity Aristotle referred to as *poiesis*. But much more clearly than the violin, spirit possession is also a vehicle or instrument for a second dimension of human activity, what Aristotle called *phronesis*, practical wisdom—that is, the exercise of situated moral judgment, being a decent, dignified, virtuous person, acting on behalf of what is considered right and good. Here there appears a stubborn paradox, or at least a place of resistance, with respect to dominant contemporary Western notions of personhood and of direct, unmediated consciousness in moral judgment. How can the evidently impassioned spirit medium be simultaneously a moral agent? How can she be acting virtuously when she is evidently temporarily displaced by another voice, another person? And in speaking about her agency, do I thereby risk importing an ethnocentric Western concept into a situation of non-Western personhood? Or conversely, by declining to speak of agency in this context, would I collude in a picture of disempowered, less than fully realized moral selves?

I would rather turn the question around and ask what an account of spirit possession can contribute to revising dominant Western views of autonomous selfhood and agency. To speak convincingly, such an account must engage with Western theory, especially by drawing upon those streams of thought that have challenged extreme individualism. I begin with brief reference to one of the strongest of these, the object-relational—or now simply relational—school of psychoanalysis, which recognizes, as Joan Rivière put it, that "Each personality is . . . a company of many. . . . We are members of one another" (as quoted in Chodorow 1989, 158). Such mutual membership is the product of a dialectic of introjection and projection that begins in infancy. Our psychic reality is thus relational as well as individuated. An excessive weighting or overreliance on either pole creates a problematic personality, and each pole may be seen as a kind of defense against the other.[3]

3. Unlike ego psychology, the focus of object-relations is not primarily on individual autonomy so much as on growth through relationships and on the necessary permeability of selves. I believe this psychic basis to be universal—and to be universally recognized—insofar as I can easily empathize with Malagasy friends and they with me, and we can agree about our descriptions and our likes and dislikes of other persons or our interpretations of motivation (even when we are mistaken). I assume this to be true, with a little mutual effort and good will, anywhere in the world. With sufficient acquaintance of cultural frames and forms of personal expression,

For Stephen Mitchell, who was a major spokesman for relational psychoanalysis, "Being a self with others entails a constant dialectic between attachment and self-definition, between connection and differentiation, a continual negotiation between one's wishes and will and the wishes and will of others, between one's own subjective reality and a consensual reality of others with whom one lives" (1988: 149).

Likewise, Nancy Chodorow states, "If a person is to develop at all, the self must come to include what were originally aspects of the other and the relation to the other. . . . We become a person, then, in internal relation with the social world. . . . People inevitably incorporate one another; our sociality is built into our psychic structure, and there is no easy separation of individual and society or possibility of the individual apart from society" (1989, 149).

It may be, then, that Marilyn Strathern's Melanesian "dividual" (1988), or something quite like it, is universal at the level of psychic structure. The question is whether cultural idioms and social practices recognize, articulate, and enable—or disclaim, constrain, and mystify—these processes and where, in a given social world and with respect to given social statuses, the balance between autonomy and connection lies or is expected to lie. The following discussion of spirit possession demonstrates the point.

Among Malagasy speakers, to gain (most kinds of) spirits is also to become increasingly connected to others. Relative to their hosts, spirits are in one sense originally alien beings, nonselves, but they are also social persons, and as such they carry with them the prior histories of their relations with humans. To become impassioned by a spirit is to introject aspects of this history. A woman who becomes possessed by a spirit who previously possessed and spoke through her mother or grandmother is identifying deeply with them, not only acknowledging her prior identification but introjecting another aspect of their persons (Lambek 1993b). A break in the unity of the conscious self is thus at the same time a bridge to the identities of others. In this respect, I think, spirit possession is radically different from multiple personality disorder, in which dissociation is generally private, alienating, disruptive, fragmenting, and socially distancing.

Spirit possession is thus not entirely beyond the range of at least one Western conception of selfhood. Concomitantly, possession is markedly resilient in the face of social change, accommodating itself to Western contexts and accommodating those contexts to itself. The story I now tell

---

one can discriminate among people who appear overly dependent, assertive, aggressive, and so forth—and people whose quiet autonomy is impressive.

exemplifies these points while raising the question of how a relational perspective can address agency and accountability. The central figure, both narrator and character, is not a spirit medium. He is, nevertheless, someone in whose life a spirit has intervened, sharply and strikingly, and in a manner relevant to and for others, at least for the kind of moral tale anthropologists like me like to tell.

Ali's Brief Military Career

This is a story about a friend of mine, a young man of the once-remote village in Mayotte that I have studied since 1975, who was in the very first cohort to receive a full French education and subsequently to become a member of what his cousin referred to as the small set of village intellectuals. "We were the ones," said Ali, "who discovered school."[4]

Ali is a very sweet guy and is attempting to make a difference in his community. In August 2000 he was the director of the new elementary school and was very concerned to keep it running well. He was proud that, unlike a cousin who directed the school in a neighboring village, he did not allow his relatives to deplete his supplies. He showed me a cupboard filled with notebooks, pens, and other implements ready for the new school year. He had plans to seek subsidies in order to start a school snack program of bread and cheese that would minimize the hardship of poorer families. Ali was also very involved in music. Not only was he the conductor of a local young people's choir, but as a board member of the island-wide Association des Jeunes, he tried to enable participation for talented youngsters in music competitions in the metropole. However, he said he preferred teaching to administration and was hoping to return to school for a specialist degree in music education.

Ali thus took his civic responsibilities very seriously. We could, if we wanted to use the term, consider Ali one of the most "modern" people in the village. While his wife is away working on a higher degree in La Réunion, Ali, unlike almost everyone else in his community, eats dinner alone and late. He explains he is usually too busy to eat with his in-laws and children.

4. His name and some of the incidental details have been changed. Since my original fieldwork, Mayotte has been increasingly integrated into the French state and has become the object of rapid development. In 2000 a referendum was held to change its status from that of *collectivité territoriale* to that of *collectivité départementale*. An African island in the Comoro Archipelago of the Western Indian Ocean, it is now using the euro. While most citizens of Mayotte speak Shimaore, a Bantu language, the members of Ali's village are Malagasy speakers. Their ancestors arrived before the French conquest in 1841 or during the early colonial period.

For similar reasons, he rarely gets to the mosque. Time has become a scarce resource and more precious than informal sociality or religious practice.[5]

In the last decade an ever-increasing number of people, most of them youths, have begun to move from Mayotte to La Réunion and metropolitan France. In many instances these moves are temporary, but they can last several years. One of the first people from the village to do so was Ali. After completing his *3ième*,[6] Ali first went to continue his studies in La Réunion, but his older sister, who was married to a navigator in the French navy, asked him to join her in France to keep her company during her husband's long absences. So Ali moved to Nantes in 1987, when he was around twenty years old. He finished *2ième* in France and then began to work as an electrician. From photos, I could see that his sister's family lived in a tall apartment building. They were dressed in French clothing, and in one picture there is an elaborate Christmas tree set up for the children.

In retrospect, Ali says he prefers life in Mayotte to that in France, especially now that he has a family. The only way France would be better than Mayotte would be if he had a really good job. In Mayotte, the vast majority of people older than Ali had been subsistence cultivators who supplemented cash-cropping when the market made it worthwhile and who are now largely unemployed. In contrast, Ali earned a salary of more than 10,000 FF per month when living in Nantes. As he says, money counts.

In fact, Ali was able to save a good deal of money in France. He returned home in 1992 with a car, a lot of luggage, and the cash for a splashy wedding. The wedding, which cost several thousand francs and which he paid for himself, included what he called a *sirop d'honneur* and a *dîner-dansant,* in conscious and expensive mimesis of French affairs. The bride wore a white dress. Before this, while he was in France, his mother had been busy setting up the engagement. On a visit to France, Ali's mother had found him in a relationship with a Malagasy woman. She wanted him to marry in Mayotte and preferably within the village. She brought videos of eligible girls from

5. Ali says that since his stay in France, he no longer has the patience to sit through night-long religious recitations of the kind frequently performed in the village. However, like others of his social status and education, Ali is by no means opposed to Islam. He willingly joined in rebuilding the village mosque, and he helped pay for his father's participation in a pilgrimage circuit in Madagascar. He assures me he will pray consistently when he gets older.

6. According to the French system of calculating high school education, completion of *3ième* is three years prior to the *bac* degree, which is the prerequisite for university. La Réunion is a French *département d'outre-mer* in the Indian Ocean east of Madagascar and some 1,700 kilometers from Mayotte. The two islands were connected in 2000 by numerous direct flights. Metropolitan France is some 9,000 kilometers from Mayotte and was reached via La Réunion.

which he made a selection agreeable to his mother, began correspondence, received a photo with the reply, and knew it was on. Ali's fiancée was in any case a close cousin (*mushemwananya*) through both her parents, and her father was a good friend, though with nowhere near the education of Ali. She was nine years Ali's junior, and he wanted to wait until she had finished high school and was "up to his intellectual level" before marrying. But the wedding was held in 1995 after his fiancée found him with another woman. She said if he was going to sleep with someone, it should be her. It was still important for a bride to be a virgin at marriage, and Ali and his wife ensured this was the case. During the dance celebrating her virginity, his mother's (male) trumba spirit rose briefly to express his joy.[7]

Ali's wife soon surpassed him in education by earning her *bac* and equaled him in modern outlook. In a community where most people have between eight and a dozen children, they planned to have three because, as his wife put it to Ali, "If we have four we won't be able to rent a car on family vacations!" (The French have strongly enforced their driving code, including seat belt regulations.) In sum, then, we can say that Ali appears successfully and self-consciously "modern" (bourgeois?) in outlook and practice.

Although physically and mentally very active, Ali has not been free of illness. He says he was a victim of sorcery from his father's other wife, with whom he was sent to live as a child because at the time his home village was without a school. He had a short, acute illness, and something remained, bothering his stomach for years so that he became very thin. When his mother visited him in France, her trumba spirit rose and said he would need to have sorcery removed when he returned to Mayotte. This eventually took place, and he has felt better since, though he has never regained his weight. In secondary school he suffered from headaches, and he gave this as a reason he withdrew before achieving the *bac*.

Ali's life might have turned out very differently were it not for another experience of ill health. During his stay in France, Ali eagerly embarked on a military career. He enrolled in the army and was happily in training at the base in Nantes when his mother arrived on a visit in order to help his sister, who had just given birth. She was not happy with Ali's new direction, and, more to the point, neither was the trumba spirit that had long inhabited

7. In fact, not all new brides are virgins (see chapter 2). Trumbas (*tromba* in Malagasy spelling) are Malagasy spirits, usually members of the royal Sakalava descent group, whose genealogy stretches back to before 1700 and who rise in and speak through specific mediums (Lambek 1981, 1993b, 2002a; Sharp 1993).

her and recently had become quite active. To begin with, the trumba made her stay in the apartment difficult. Being very sensitive to bad smells, it took offense at the indoor toilet, and at first Ali's mother refused to use it. They placed her bed as far from the lavatory as they could, but the trumba would rise crying "*Mantsing! Mantsing!* [Stinky]." In fact, said Ali, it rose much more often in France than since her return home.

But the worst thing was that Ali began to feel sick every time he put on his uniform or set foot on the military base. He suffered terribly. He couldn't bend his legs and could barely walk. "It was rheumatism," said Ali. "It took me five minutes to pull on my socks." And it took him some thirty minutes just to get over to the canteen for meals.

To add insult to injury, he was persecuted by his commanding officer, who accused him of malingering and deception. This was not altogether an unreasonable deduction, because on weekend leaves Ali felt fine. The moment he reached the bus stop he was well; he walked normally. As he said, "As soon as I left the base, my symptoms disappeared." But each time he returned to base, he was sick and could barely move.

Ali's condition lasted for some three months. Finally, he requested a medical discharge because he was suffering from both the illness and the anger of his commanding officer. He was placed in the hospital for three days and given X-rays over his whole body, but they showed nothing.

So, much to his disappointment, Ali was forced to quit the army. Ali's mother, who, remember, was visiting at the time, had explained to him that it was the family spirit, the *trumba ny razaña*, who sent the symptoms. It was said (*ary*) that the spirit didn't like him in the army. "Military clothes are dirty; spirits don't like them [*tsy tian' trumba*]." His mother said she too was upset and couldn't accept his career decision; she was afraid for him.

I was not able to put two and two together when Ali spoke to me in 1995, but the second time Ali told me the story (in 2000), he made the point explicit. His mother's visit to France had coincided with the beginning of the Gulf War. She confirmed this. Not only was she frightened he would be sent to the Gulf, she said, but from watching the televised reportage, she realized that he would be placed at high risk: "And I could see they were putting black people [*ulu mainting*] in the front lines."

At the time, Ali got angry with the trumba (not with his mother). He said he was a man and wanted to take risks. He was even hoping to train as a submarine diver. On base it was part of Ali's duties to call the ambulance whenever a recruit was injured during training exercises. The trumba said to him, "So can't you see that people in the military get hurt?"

Ali's Agency

Ali's story provides the gist of the issue that anyone interested in understanding personhood across cultures must face. If our own concepts and idioms of personhood come with moral entailments, as they must, how are we to evaluate the conduct of persons whose identity is construed somewhat differently? How are we to understand agency, avowal, and accountability in a universe in which the relational quality of personhood is granted value alongside individual autonomy?

There is perhaps not much in the actions of Ali's mother or the trumba that needs direct explanation. Their interests and arguments are perfectly rational, their agency and observations only too clear, and their fears realistic. Whereas many of my previous analyses of instances of spirit possession entail interpreting the double and ostensibly conflicting voices (messages and desires) of spirit and host, this is a case in which not only their underlying interests but also their stated motives coincide. But the case is more complex with respect to Ali, who, several years later, still felt regret that he was coerced by the spirit into giving up something dear to him.

Although Ali is adamant that he himself has never been possessed by the trumba spirit, and never will be, when Ali was on the base, his actions were formally like those of possession. He acted, or rather his body acted, contrary to his conscious intentions; it was as though his body spoke with one voice, and Ali with another. His body, if not his mind, was evidently in the grip of the spirit.

Ali's situation thus nicely illustrates a point I have long made—namely, that in thinking about the incidence of possession (at least, in Mayotte), one cannot take account of only the mediums themselves (Lambek 1981, 1989). While it is true that the majority of mediums in Mayotte are women, the spirits nevertheless interact with men as well. Spirits engage with those around them, and neither their presence nor their significance can be explained reductively in terms of trance or the intentions and personalities of the mediums alone.

Ali's mother is, of course, an interesting and powerful woman in her own right. She had the courage and foresight to send away her children for the sake of their education and later followed them intrepidly to France. I remember her pride and her enthusiasm for what she had seen after one of her returns to Mayotte. She has handled the experience of rapid social change with grace, her first encounter with indoor plumbing notwithstanding, but she also sees herself as representative of an older way of life. She has appointed herself my primary raconteur of folk-tales. She is what I would describe as a classy lady in terms of comportment and self-esteem, but also because of an implicit elitism, the assurance of coming from one of the "best" local families.

Yet this is not simply a kind of mother-son story either. As a trumba, the spirit has a personal identity as an individual member of the Sakalava royal descent line. Moreover, the spirit is identified not specifically with the mother but as a *trumba ny razaña,* a trumba of Ali's family, ancestry, or descent line. It is a trumba that has long possessed members of this family, a family that has a sense of its own importance. For many years the trumba was particularly associated with Ali's mother's mother's brother (the same man who happens to be the grandfather of Ali's wife), who himself spent part of World War II in the French army, but stationed in Madagascar.[8] Before any important event, such as a circumcision or a journey, the spirit would be informed, and its assistance requested. It has since gone on to inhabit several younger members of the family—including not only Ali's mother and his wife's father's older brother, but several of Ali's older sisters—and it thus serves, in part, as a sign of the unity, distinctiveness, and continuity of the family (Lambek 1988b). It speaks with the voice of someone who has an enduring association with the family and has long been concerned with its welfare. What Ali hears, therefore, is not simply a transformation of his mother's voice, but a voice that condenses the weight of several generations of ancestors and collateral kin. The spirit acts with the authority of a Sakalava king, but equally with the force of ancestrality and the established commitment to intergenerational continuity and reproduction.[9]

The distinction, then, between the voice of Ali's mother (the host) and the voice of the spirit here lies less in the content of what each is saying in this instance than in the rhetorical force of their respective presence. As the mother tells the story, she and the spirit were in complete agreement. But where her remonstrances might have been ineffective, the trumba's intentions were realized in their effects. In the face of the urgency of the spirit's

8. The trumba never fully rose in this man (he never went into full trance), but he would shake when the spirit was manifest and had purchased all of its clothing. The military connection may hold significance for the recurrence and knowledge of the individual spirit, but I have not been able to discover it.

9. The situation is a bit more complex than this, in that the expensive ceremony in which the spirit announces its name has not yet been held for Ali's mother, nor was it ever held for her mother's brother. The name of the spirit should thus not be uttered (Lambek 1981), and its common identity among family members remains latent. There is also some conflict and competition over the production of the ceremonies. Succession to specific spirits marks segmentation no less than family unity (Lambek 1988b).

concern, Ali could scarcely remain impassive. And he did not. He acquired the symptoms of acute rheumatism.

The next question is whether Ali's mother and the trumba were able to enunciate a wish that Ali is unable to acknowledge is also his own. Did he want, on his own account, to retract his decision to enter the army, and should we therefore see Ali's action (or inaction) as a product of his own fear or instinct for self-preservation? Is it a kind of pre-traumatic stress disorder? Or should we take a different approach and see it, in Stephen Mitchell's terms, as part of the "constant dialectic between attachment and self-definition" (1988, 149), or as representative of the psychic internalization of sociality described by Chodorow (1989, 149)? Did Ali come, to a degree, to internalize the family's wishes as his own? Did he come to take their part? We could let the psychoanalysts fight this out among themselves,[10] but I think that I have already given enough evidence to make the relational argument highly plausible. At least I have shown how spirit possession as a practical idiom exemplifies, articulates, and enables the processes of which the relational theorists speak. But let us move from the murky realm of the psyche to the more sociological concept of agency. In what sense is Ali responsible for his rheumatism?

Here we have something of a double task: how to understand spirit possession as a form of human agency and how, in turn, to rethink agency so that it can take account of possession. In what follows I omit from discussion Marxist conceptions of agency, with their emphasis on grasping hegemonic social relations, so as to gain a purchase on radical change. I am concerned with action on a less grand scale, as it functions in the day-to-day tasks of taking control of events concerning work, family, and the living of one's life in some meaningful, dignified, and authentic fashion.

In the general social sciences literature, *agency* is sometimes applied in a rather idealized fashion, ignoring much of what philosophers, psychoanalysts, and anthropologists have taught us about human intentionality and mind. Agency is a naive or romanticized concept insofar as it implies (*a*) that acts are transparent to their agents, that they are always the products of deliberate plans with specific ends in mind or of calculation among means and ends in a rational-choice model; (*b*) that agents fully understand the consequences of their acts or the relationships between acts and

10. As Donald Tuzin noted (personal communication), Freudian ego psychologists might speak of the "secondary gains" of Ali's illness and the way his "somatic conversion" provided a face-saving way of submitting to his mother's will. Mel Spiro (personal communication) has suggested simply that part of Ali wanted one outcome, and part wanted the other.

consequences; (*c*) that agents' intentions are not often dense, complex, and possibly even contradictory; that agents do not routinely suffer from ambivalence and possibly from self-deception; (*d*) that agents—or we as observers—can fully and objectively recognize what constitutes their interests; (*e*) that agency is a capacity of fully autonomous individuals rather than relationally constituted social persons; and (*f*) that action occurs without respect to convention and commitment—that is, as if agents were not specifically located social persons operating within moral universes, with respect to prior and binding commitments both to specific liturgical orders (Rappaport 1999) and to specific other persons. For example, a person's sexual agency may be informed by prior commitment both to a certain form of marriage that he or she has undergone and to a specific partner.

While all these points are relevant for interpreting Ali's situation, I focus in particular on the issue of deception. Is his rheumatism a case of simple, outright, knowing deception? If we disagree with his commanding officer on this question, which I think we must, we are faced with a second question: Is it a case of self-deception? If so, how are we to understand and evaluate such self-deception?

I want to argue that, although Ali does not avow his agency in the immediate acts of getting sick or choosing to get discharged, in fact he acts responsibly and in terms of an acceptance of responsibility within a wider frame of reference—as a son, as a member of an ancestry, and as a member of a community. His withdrawal from the military is ultimately not very different from his acquiescence to marrying in the direction and manner that his parents wish. In both cases his agency is evident; in neither case is it autonomous. In getting sick, he accedes to the will of the trumba. The difference is that in this case he does so apparently self-deceptively, that is, without acknowledging to himself that this is what he has done.

Self-deception often implies denying what is authentic and thus in some sense harming oneself or living a less than fully realized life. But arguably in this case, the consequences for Ali have been a more fully realized life than he could have held in the military, and probably a longer one. Moreover, at exactly which phase can we assert that Ali was more fully self-deceived? Perhaps the brunt of Ali's self-deception lay in his idealization of a military career with dreams of heroic underwater feats rather than the brute realities of the battlefield. As the trumba spirit said to Ali, "Can't you see that soldiers get hurt?"

In an insightful discussion, Fingarette analyzes self-deception as "the disavowal of a continuing engagement" (2000, 137). He distinguishes avowal of personal agency (identity) from acceptance of moral agency (responsibility). A sociopath can acknowledge his act (avowing that it was he who committed it) while refusing to take responsibility for it, that is, without any moral concern about it. The self-deceiver, however, does not avow his act, and this may be precisely because

> What is threatened is some aspect of integrity rooted in moral concern. The less integrity, the less is there motive to enter into self-deception. The greater the integrity of the person, and the more powerful the contrary individual inclinations, the greater is the temptation to self-deception. . . . It is because the movement into self-deception is rooted in a concern for integrity of spirit that we temper our condemnation of the self-deceiver. We feel he is not a mere cheat. We are moved to a certain compassion in which there is awareness of the self-deceiver's authentic inner dignity as the motive of his self-betrayal. (Fingarette 2000, 139)

Ali's case is virtually the complete inverse of the sociopathic personality. He does not avow his agency, but he does accept responsibility insofar as he is the victim. He is very concerned about the illness and its implications, and he realizes that as a result he must request a discharge. He understands that his responsibility is inevitably bound up in his relationship to his mother and to the family trumba.[11]

Another strand of Fingarette's approach is the argument that self-deception occurs all the time, that it is "as ordinary and familiar a kind of mental activity as one can imagine" (2000, 162), if only because our attention cannot be focused everywhere at once. In this view, self-deception is frequently morally neutral, such as when we walk home without being able to recall the route we took, but even in stronger cases Fingarette's inclination is to follow Freud and be nonjudgmental. This is obviously not the case for Sartre's analysis of the specific form of self-deception he termed "bad faith." Can Ali be said to have acted in bad faith?

Bad faith as described by Sartre (here quoted by Audi), is an "'inauthentic and self-deceptive refusal to admit to ourselves and others our full freedom, thereby avoiding anxiety in making decisions and evading

11. For Fingarette "avowal is a necessary condition of responsibility" (2000, 147), yet this does not appear to hold for Ali's case. However, Fingarette also acknowledges that "the issue [of acceptance of responsibility] is complicated by the fact that a person is responsible, in spite of unconcern with respect to a specific engagement, if there are other concerns of the person's by virtue of which he has indirectly committed himself to be concerned for the engagement at issue" (146).

responsibility for actions and attitudes' (Sartre 1956). One self-deceiving strategy identified by Sartre is to embrace other people's views in order to avoid having to form one's own; another is to disregard options so that one's life appears pre-determined to move in a fixed direction" (Audi 1999, 70).

In sum, bad faith is the dishonest and cowardly refusal to take responsibility for one's choices and actions. Is Ali's disavowal a matter of cowardice or dishonesty? It may be true that Ali has refused to accept his full freedom. But this is not necessarily out of a refusal to confront an unpleasant truth that he cannot admit to himself. What is difficult for him to reconcile is the discrepancy between his courage, enthusiasm, and skill as a man, an adventurer, and a soldier (as far as he understands what being a soldier entails) and his obligations to his family and to himself as a family man. Choice in favor of the latter is seen by the military as cowardice, laziness, or retreat, attributions that are simply not acceptable to Ali. Indeed, there is no reason to assume that he is either cowardly or lazy, and much evidence to the contrary. However, Ali is left with the dilemma of finding a face-saving way of making his choice, of withdrawing from the military, a decision in which, for reasons of moral integrity, as described by Fingarette, he will not reveal to himself his abrogation of the commitment he engaged in by signing up.

It seems apparent that the existential emphasis on the freedom of the individual self is very different from the moral questions facing the relationally embedded person. There is a difference between exercising one's judgment and claiming absolute freedom of choice.[12] Moreover, Ali's case differs from most discussions of self-deception precisely because he is not the sole agent of his deception, and, in a sense, his way out of the dilemma is imposed upon him. The suggestion of the trumba plays a large role, and the explanation for the illness is reinforced by the family. The means are there at hand for disavowal, for letting the rheumatism take over. From the standpoint of the family, as opposed to that of the military, it is the socially correct thing to do.

We could reconstruct the whole story as one of resistance to French hegemony, or we could say that, following his mother's intervention, Ali made the choice to fall under the spirit's influence. Not to have fallen sick would have been to reject his mother's and the elders' persuasion as well as the force of culture, tradition, and the ends to which he had been raised and

12. However, Sartre's argument was an important ethical and political intervention in postwar France.

had already committed himself.[13] Ali knows that the spirit is tricking the commanding officer; the latter is right, after all, to be suspicious, though what he can never suspect is precisely whom he is dealing with.

Finally, whether or not we call this self-deception or bad faith depends, of course, on how we understand spirits and spirit possession, how we understand their social reality for people from Mayotte, and how people themselves attribute agency to spirits. Ali was subject to the spirit's grip, and he suffered for it. Suffering may be a sign of truth (Lambek 1998b). At least it is self-evident; you cannot argue with it. Thus, an attribution of Sartrean bad faith has to be relative to how compelling we take the social reality of spirit possession to be for people of Mayotte in general and for Ali in particular.[14] The fact that Ali's illness is precipitated by the cultural institution of spirit possession, however, enables us to take the analysis to another level.

Rheumatic Irony

So far I have been pushing the case for Ali's sincerity. But Ali's personal sincerity has to be counterposed to the inherently poietic and ironic qualities of spirit possession. Let me begin with irony. In a well-known statement, Becker (1979) argues that spirit possession transforms the ordinary communicative event so that the presupposition of the identity of the speaker is challenged.

> Trance speaking can be defined as communication in which one of the variables of the speech act (I am speaking to you about *x* at time *y* in place *z* with intent *a*) is denied, most frequently the variable *I* is paradoxically both speaking and not speaking, or speaking involuntarily or nonintentionally. Trance is a kind of incongruence between statement and intent (I/not I am speaking to you/not you . . .), and covers a wide spectrum of linguistic experiences, from

13. The argument here is essentially the same as that used to describe the role of suggestion and illocutionary acts in therapy.

14. We might also ask whether spirits are portrayed as acting individualistically or relationally, exercising free choice or social judgment. One of the themes of *Human Spirits* (Lambek 1981) is that the possession "cure" entails socializing the spirit and thus moving it from the former position to the latter. The drama of the cure, including vociferous interchanges between the spirit and the healers, provides instruction for everyone. But equally, the socialization of the spirits remains inconclusive and ambiguous; spirits can always utilize means, such as sending rheumatism, that would be illegitimate were they applied by humans. This contrast between humans and spirits is itself one of the edifying features of possession.

> the minor trance of singing the national anthem—or any song you *believe*—to the major trance of hypnosis and schizophrenia. (Becker 1979, 232–33)

Disregarding Becker's provocative examples, his analysis clearly holds for the institution of spirit possession as found in Mayotte and many other parts of Africa. What is striking is how close this picture comes to the analysis by certain literary theorists and philosophers of irony.

In a brilliant discussion of Socratic irony, Nehamas quotes Lionel Trilling to the effect that "irony implies 'a disconnection between a speaker and his interlocutor, or between the speaker and that which is spoken about, or even between the speaker and himself'" (Nehamas 1998, 57, citing Trilling 1971, 120). "Irony," Nehamas writes, "is acknowledged concealment" (1998, 67); it "allows you simply to refuse to let your audience know what you think and to suggest simply that it is not what you say" (55). And so "irony allows us to pretend we are something other than our words suggest. It enables us to play at being someone, without forcing us to decide what we really are or, indeed, whether we really are anyone. . . . Irony always and necessarily postulates a double speaker and a double audience" (59–60). Finally, to bring home the connection I am making, Nehamas says that "through his irony, Socrates *dissociates* himself from his words" (61; my emphasis).

If Ali has not deceived his commanding officer, he suspects that the spirit has. But where does the agency of Ali leave off and that of the spirit begin? Whose agency is at issue? Who is communicating through the signs and symptoms of Ali's body? Ali is ostensibly speaking sincerely, but he is speaking about, with, and through an idiom that is intrinsically ironic. For Nehamas, irony understood as concealment moves interpretation away from the question of truth versus deceit. "Like truthfulness, concealment does not distort the truth; like lying, it does not reveal it" (Nehamas 1998, 62). But in addition, "[i]rony often insinuates that something is taking place inside you that your audience is not allowed to see, but it does not always entail that you see it yourself. Irony often communicates that only part of a picture is visible to an audience, but it does not always entail that the speaker sees the whole. Sometimes, it does not even imply that a whole picture exists. Uncertainty is intrinsic, of the essence" (67).

Once we accept the irony intrinsic to any invocation of spirit possession, the question of self-deception becomes more complex, murkier. There is always in possession a hint that things are not what they seem. Possession is asserted and established as real, but at the same time there is a knowing glint in the spirit's eye (though not in that of the host or, as in Ali's case, in that of the object of the spirit's attention), as though to say, "After all, *I* am not deceived." At some level, Ali, too, is not deceived. His self-deception lies only in the sincerity with which he protects himself from his knowledge. But "not deceived" about *what*? It is we who deceive ourselves if we mistake the essential uncertainty, or ambivalence, of human selfhood for some substantial core or definitive choice.

Thus, I have been asked how I can call Ali ironic in the absence of conscious intentionality. My response is twofold. First, the irony lies in the recognition of the very ambiguity of intentionality. Second, how can one help but be ironic when one takes up, or is taken up by, a discursive form that is itself intrinsically ironic?

I hope you will now not find me unduly ironic if I refer to Ali's condition as one of an *ironic illness*. I do not mean that it is ironic that Ali fell sick, or ironic that his illness was rheumatism, but that the very illness is constituted through irony. Ali was sick in an ironic mode. Much better to speak of rheumatic irony than of rheumatic hysteria.

Indeed, embodied irony might prove a fruitful redescription of the condition suffered by the women recorded by Freud and Breuer (1955). The tension between Freud's diagnoses and his consistently positive descriptions of his patients' high moral character and lively intelligence could be reread in this light. This would also fit Susan Bordo's (1989) interpretation and comparison of hysteria with agoraphobia and anorexia as caricatures of dominant modes of femininity. In referring to the illness or mode of illness as irony, I am suggesting that the irony is embodied and intrinsic and precisely *not* that it is conscious or reflective. I am not denying the authenticity of the suffering. Rather, I am suggesting that, however real the symptoms, they cannot be reduced to a single, clear-cut cause or that, if there were such a cause, we could never know it with complete certainty. The irony of the illness is precisely an expression of its evasion of being pinned down by sufferer, observer, or therapist.

Self-textualizing Acts

The final part of my argument concerns acknowledging spirit possession not only as something done, but as something made—that is, not only as a practice or as an idiom of practice, but as *poiesis*, as artful creation. Specifically, I attend to the way in which such creation draws attention to itself. What I am suggesting is that if Ali's condition is one of self-deception, insofar as it involves a spirit, it is self-deception that subtly but inevitably draws attention to itself as concealing something. And insofar as it does this, can it be self-deception after all?

That spirit possession is an aesthetic artifact to be engaged with should come as no surprise; it is the point at which analysis of possession rituals could start (Boddy 1989; Kapferer 1983; Lambek 1981). Spirit possession is simultaneously a part of life—something that really happens, that hurts, harms, or heals and establishes relationships—and an artistic production and performance, a lens or drama through which life is inspected, highlighted, reshaped, reflected upon, and responded to (often with explicit, theatrical irony or satire, as with the spirit's complaints about the smell of the toilet). It is serious business and aesthetic commentary, simultaneously part of the texture of life, the portrait of that life, and the gazing over the shoulder at the portrait. This kind of space for spectatorship, for theorizing (to draw on the original meaning of the word) is available not only for us or for Ali's friends and family, but for Ali himself (cf. Boddy 1988). This is true not only of full-blown possession ceremonies with their costumes and music, but of every appearance of possession in daily life.

What happened to Ali was not something that simply happened and was over, but action that contained the seeds of its own textualization (see Barber 1999; Ricoeur 1971; Silverstein and Urban 1996). Indeed, perhaps possession can be described more broadly as composed of *self-textualizing* acts. I cannot pursue this here except to suggest that through the framing and marking qualities of possession, ordinary people simultaneously become *characters* in dramas that are immediate and social but are also at arm's length from their immediate context, having historical associations or allegorical qualities, and that always contain the leavening of irony.[15]

Although Ali is never directly possessed by a spirit, both what happened to him and his narrative of the events have a heightened, created quality. Ali tells a good story. His symptoms have a kind of extravagance, and he describes his condition with verve. There is a dramatic tension as he doggedly hangs in at the military base, suffering and yet trying to convince his superiors of his will to work and stay on, determined to have his condition medically diagnosed and treated. When the X-rays came back negative, he says he was "disappointed" (*déçu*). He wanted his condition medicalized, even though presumably that would have been harder to cure than the effects of the spirit. And yet there are signs—the way the illness started and stopped each time he entered or left the precinct—that he knew all along this was no ordinary illness.

15. Such textualizing is incomplete insofar as the indexical qualities never completely disappear. Were they to do so, the intrinsically ironic quality of possession would be lost.

Ali's self-narrative is itself ironic. At one level, the story is about whether Ali suffered from ordinary rheumatism or was in the hands of the spirit. But there are multiple levels of ambiguity. One suggests that Ali was self-deceived to hope he could be free of the spirit. Another asks if he was not after all in some agreement with the spirit. Was not his ostensible resistance the space of his self-deception? Can we not hear Ali saying: "If I had only had sufficient critical distance, I might have recognized my own collusion." Or is he saying: "What difference would it have made? The ending was inevitable from the start."

Ali tells a story in which he appears doubly self-deceived. Relatively explicit is his deception in thinking his condition might be ordinary rheumatism. Relatively implicit is his deception in attempting to resist the spirit and his illness. But in thinking he is self-deceived, he may be deceiving himself, and we, too, may be deceiving ourselves. Would we have remained healthy in Ali's situation? Would we have asked for an immediate discharge? Would we have gone to the front? Could we have exercised some Sartrean existential ideal of freedom? Would to claim that we (or Ali) could have done so not be evidence of our own bad faith?

Whatever we would have done in his place, the point is that Ali's story is there before his eyes, but also before ours—to enable us to be presumptuous about our own ostensibly more sovereign agency, to ask the question of ourselves, and, very possibly, to recognize the limits of autonomy in the face of an exigent mother, a determined spirit, and a relationally constituted self. Those people in or from Mayotte who hear about what happened to Ali must reflect on their own knowledge of the force of other persons in their lives—and of course on the delicious fact that their spirits are able to overcome the lure of French military heroism and even the power of military discipline.

The textualization of acts of possession also enables us to expand our appreciation of irony from the playful, rhetorical, and dialogical Socratic version to the tragic Sophoclean one. Ali and others can observe the effects of human agency against or with the tide that fate (structure, determinism) plays in their lives.[16]

My account owes not a little to Nehamas's reflections on *The Magic Mountain*, in which Thomas Mann "shows that the attribution of self-deception to others is one of the surest paths to the deception of oneself"

16. Marxian structure (via Hegel) and the Freudian unconscious both derive from the Sophoclean version of irony. I am indebted to Paul Antze for these points (cf. Fortes 1983).

(Nehamas 1998, 32). In a fashion similar to Mann's narrative, possession "relentlessly undermines our ability to make unconditional judgments in the same process that it tempts us to keep doing so" (30).[17]

As they become textualized, the events in which spirits intervene in people's lives become objects of contemplation, much as literature can move in the opposite direction to intervene in people's lives. We can read *The Magic Mountain* and be deceived by Mann, much as the hero of the novel deceives himself; so, too, with possession. I am all too well aware that to posit the intrinsic irony of possession and its textualization makes it an object of interpretation and moral pleasure for *me* (I have made my living from it) and that literary theory offers familiar instruction in the appreciation of texts. I have also begun to wonder whether the relationship of anthropologists to their subjects is not intrinsically ironic in much the same way that I have described spirit possession.[18] In sum, if irony is to be attributed like illness, it may be contagious! But I think that through irony and textualization, spirit possession also becomes an object of edification and pleasure for those who engage with it on a more intimate and regular basis. Ali's encounter with the spirit was immediate, painful, and deeply embodied. But it was also distanced and objectified sufficiently to be available to Ali and others in the form of a narrative. The nature of his illness, as artfully enshrouded in ambiguity as that of the hero of *The Magic Mountain,* invites all who encounter it to contemplate agency and its limits, dignity and its vicissitudes, individuality and its relational entailments, hope and contingency, the essential uncertainty of life.

Earlier in the essay I asked what spirit possession might teach us about agency. The answer I propose is akin to Mann's depiction of the ironic saturation of his characters' situation. Any invocation of "agency" must itself be tinged with irony. Agency is to be taken seriously, but not always literally.

17. I have been criticized for undertaking to judge Ali's motives and for shifting to an experience-distant mode of understanding, but my aim has been neither to judge nor to criticize Ali, but rather to expose, as Nehamas says of Plato's dialogues, "our ignorance of our own ignorance" (1998, 44).

18. I owe this idea to Andrew Walsh's suggestion (personal communication) that when Ali was reciting the story to me, he, too, was doing so ironically—not lying, but not revealing everything either. The anthropologist's stance is also at issue. I am ironic insofar as I hold two sets of beliefs or hold one of them back. "Is it possible," asks Walsh, "that any invocation of an ethnographic encounter (like that between you and Ali) is ironic in the way that any invocation of possession is?" Crapanzano (1980) provides sustained reflection on these issues. See also Fernandez and Huber 2001.

Looking Forward

Let us remember the relational quality of personhood in Mayotte that is exemplified by spirit possession. We have seen how Ali's agency is harnessed to realize the intentions of another. That Other, as his mother, is also a part of himself. And his mother's own Other, her self-object, the spirit, is in part a refraction of her parents, in turn, and beyond them, of a deeper ancestry for which she is just a contemporary vehicle or trustee.

Earlier I mentioned Ali's comfortable assertion that he would never become host to the spirit himself. I do not know whether to interpret this as a refusal to extend the relational boundaries of the self, as a limit on his ironic self-recognition, or to interpret it as a sign of strength or realism, or as undecidable.

Near the end of my stay in Mayotte in 2000, Ali and I were talking about the return of his wife from her year at university and her choice of a career; she had chosen education over medicine. He mentioned that while they were enjoying a drive in the countryside, his wife became rigid in the seat beside him, her arms and legs outstretched so that he had to lift her out of the car. In some concern, I asked whether she had seen a doctor. I should have known better. "Oh," he laughed, "It's not worth going to a doctor. We know already that it is trumbas." He added, "And that's why she didn't want to study medicine. The trumbas can't stand dirty things like blood."

Of course, one of the trumbas who has entered his wife and wants to establish a permanent relationship with her is the very spirit who is to be found in Ali's mother and who accompanied her on her fateful visit to France. As his cross-cousin, Ali's wife, too, is in line to succeed to the spirit, and in her case the marital and affinal connections are probably equally compelling. As for Ali, he will find that the spirit is never too far away.

EIGHT

On Catching Up with Oneself: Learning to Know That One Means What One Does

This chapter was originally written for a conference on learning religion organized by Ramon Sarró and David Berliner in Lisbon in 2005. It is probably the first time I drew on Cavell. I would not change what I have written here, except to state clearly that I do not think ritual language is parasitic on "ordinary" language. What does it mean that the performance of an act or the utterance of a statement is an iteration (reiteration)? What is the relation of the performer to the performed? How do we come to acquire the conviction necessary to carry off our performances? I agree with Cavell, whose remark that the issues addressed are "immeasurably complex" I cite. I certainly do not think I have got to the bottom of the matter.

> What is education? I should suppose that education was the curriculum one had to run through in order to catch up with oneself, and he who will not pass through this curriculum is helped very little by the fact that he was born in the most enlightened age.
>
> —Kierkegaard (1968, 57)

> Whatever the one generation may learn from the other, that which is genuinely human no generation learns from the foregoing. In this respect every generation begins primitively, has no different task from that of every previous generation, nor does it get further, except in so far as the previous generation shirked its task and deluded itself. The authentically human factor is passion.
>
> —Kierkegaard (1968, 130)

This chapter was first published in David Berliner and Ramon Sarró, eds., *Learning Religion* (Oxford: Berghahn, 2007), 65–81.

> Shamanism is like acting or playing music—received knowledge and training combined with originality, skill, and performance. To know what you are saying and doing, you must learn from others, but to be any good, you must add something of yourself.
>
> —Stephen Hugh-Jones (1994, 35)

Nothing is simple in the kingdom of analysis. The topic of "learning religion" requires us first of all to consider what we mean by *learning* and what we mean by *religion* and how the answer we give to each will shape the answer we give to the other. There are, of course, no absolute or definitive answers to these questions, and in this chapter I formulate them pragmatically, with respect to the body of ethnographic material I wish to address. This is not to say that I stick to local formulations of *learning* and *religion* or that I am advocating an extreme nominalism; rather, I develop a mode of analysis or interpretation that seems pertinent for grasping a particular set of practices and elaborate a more general point that they seem to illuminate. I argue that to learn religion entails learning to take one's acts seriously and thus to acknowledge one's share of responsibility for their felicitous outcome.

Knowledge, Practice and Wisdom

In an earlier work (Lambek 1993b), I observed side by side and in some detail three traditions—Islam, astrology, and spirit possession—as they were engaged in by Malagasy-speaking villagers on Mayotte, a French-controlled island in the Comoro Archipelago of the Western Indian Ocean. I argued that the respective means by which learning took place in each was related to the ideas within each tradition regarding what constituted knowledge and how widely it should circulate. Drawing upon Schutz's (1964) distinction among experts, well-informed citizens, and "the man on the street," I showed how in practice people alternated among these different orientations toward knowledge and also how they respectively articulated the three traditions in their own practice. This included comparing how well invested in particular bodies of deliberative or procedural knowledge members of a community are; how deeply they are committed to them; and how adept they are at drawing upon them. With respect to inquiring how people acquire depth, one might shift from the Schutzian categories to the five levels of practical knowledge described by Flyvbjerg (2001, borrowed from Dreyfus and Dreyfus 1986), ranging from novice through competent performer to expert.

In studying more specifically the lives of spirit mediums on the island of Mayotte (and subsequently in northwest Madagascar [Lambek 2002a]) I have also found it useful to disentangle three levels of engagement, from learning to host a spirit or perform in character as that spirit, to working actively as a spirit medium, and then to becoming a strong or mature member of society in a manner that incorporates having spirits and working as a medium (Lambek 1988a). In the abstract, these are successive levels of appropriation, maturity, and judgment, but in practice advancing at each level contributes to the next, cultivating an art of living (see chapter 7 and Nehamas 1998). In the end, learning religion could mean becoming wiser, exercising ethical judgment more soundly, balancing deep passion with equanimity, and living a better life.

Performance

In this chapter I strive toward the same goals but from a somewhat different angle of analysis, akin to practice but not identical with it—namely, performance. Learning to perform means learning to imitate or iterate.[1] I approach this through a discussion of the philosophy of speech acts. Speech acts, and more specifically the category that Austin (1962) termed "illocutionary," can be taken as a kind of kernel or elementary structure of what I mean by performance, or ritual performance, more generally. They are formally iterated acts that produce a marked difference in a state of affairs or bring a new state of affairs into existence. Performing an introduction or making a promise has this in common with uttering a prayer or carrying out a sacrifice, an act of purification, blessing or worship, with establishing the social identity of an infant or disposing of a corpse, and with committing an act of sorcery or an act of sorcery removal.

However we wish to locate religion, it is possibly useful to consider it as something different from ordinary utterances and everyday acts, whether for practitioners or from the perspective of arm's-length observers like ourselves. But these acts and utterances do not need to be extraordinary either; they may entail nothing more than slight shifts and reframing of ordinary speech and ordinary acts, no more than the difference between not eating

1. See also Taussig (1993). I have preferred to avoid the word *mimesis* because of its Platonic connotations (see chapter 5).

a certain food because you don't like it or because it is declared taboo (see chapter 3). A question then is whether such non-ordinary acts and utterances are parasitic on ordinary ones, "etiolations of language" in Austin's terms.

Of course, to take such an approach requires us also to look at the mystery and marvelousness of the ordinary and even perhaps to conclude with Wittgenstein that what is authentically religious *is* part of the ordinary and that all the *talk* of religion—the metaphysics, as opposed to the *acts* of religion—is rationalization and misleading. But that is an issue I cannot address here.

The iterative performance of the priest, shaman, or spirit medium can be usefully compared to that of the stage actor or the musician, but it is not the same as either of these (just as performing a character on stage or in film is not the same as performing a piece of music). Most obviously, performance on stage is less illocutionary than perlocutionary (rhetorical, persuasive), but religious performances include a perlocutionary dimension as well. Secondly, stage and film acting maintain certain boundaries—victims of gunfire do not really get shot, and lovers (with the exception of porn) are not supposed to get sexually aroused—and even then, not emotionally aroused. In certain forms of mysticism, quite the opposite is true. In general, one can argue that what we call religious performance is comprised of a variety of genres or kinds of acts that can be distinguished precisely according to whether and how the performance is understood in relation to the performed (the signifier to the signified) and—precisely because this is not simply a matter of an abstracted text, but of an embodied performance—according to the relationship of the performer to the performance, the actors to their acts. These approximate more or less what Rappaport refers to as the "canonical" and "indexical" aspects of ritual.

Thus, where Austin can give a precise description of what English speakers intend when they say that they "pretend" to do something, so too, if I were up to the task, could I describe what Malagasy speakers intend when they recite passages from the Qur'an (*midzor*), when they call spirits to enter them and then speak as spirits, or when they fall ill because they have violated a taboo particular to the spirit said to possess them. Malagasy spirit possession works hard to deny certain boundaries that Western stage actors maintain, but it is not without boundaries of its own (which are most evident when people enter or leave active states of possession). Both stage actors and spirit mediums must sustain characterizations, must have the skill to carry off their performances successfully, and must, as Hugh-Jones

(1994) notes, add something of themselves to the performance. Both must also balance what they reveal and what they conceal, and must strive, in particular, for specific and very delicate balances between irony and sincerity (see chapter 7; Taussig 2003). However, as noted, while spirit possession is like performing on the stage in many respects, they are not the same kinds of acts.

From this perspective, learning religion includes learning to perform specific genres and acts of iteration (and possibly of unlearning the ordinary or everyday) to which are intrinsic certain kinds of intention. It is a question of framing, of adding sanctifying brackets to certain acts or utterances, of speaking and acting under quotation, in italics, or *sous rature.* Competence in the performance of iteration includes learning how and when to move among these stances, to remove the brackets around iteration or raise them to a higher rather than a lower power from ordinary life. By higher power, I intend to underline the seriousness with which an act is performed; by lower power, I mean such forms of iteration as "pretending." The deployment of iteration thereby has an ethical dimension, and competence in such deployment could be part of what is meant by ethics. This can include learning when and how to perform with irony, to suppress it, or even, as Kierkegaard propounds, to transcend it.

While for Kierkegaard religion is defined by absurdity and faith and is the product of passion, in the philosophical tradition I am describing it is a matter, in the first instance, of the structure, cultivation and performance of possibly non-ordinary, but generally not extraordinary, iterative acts and utterances. Habitual usage may make them come to seem very ordinary indeed.

Seriousness

At the heart of any theory or practice of iteration there is the question of what I obliquely referred to above as the iteration taken to a certain power: of the relation of the performance to the intention of the performer. As Laurence Hérault (2007) notes for contemporary catechists in Switzerland, "the faithful do not mimic what Jesus did, they re-enact it." But how does one make, recognize, or learn the difference? In Christian thought and in Western philosophy, this is often phrased as the question of sincerity. As Stanley Cavell, on whose discussion of iteration I have been drawing, puts it, the fact that human utterances and acts can be imitated "betokens, roughly that [they] are essentially vulnerable to insincerity (you may say false consciousness)"

(1995, 58). Augustine's anxiety as to the difference between a sincere and a theatrical confession haunts this tradition, yet I think this is but one cultural refraction—others might be stage fright (Geertz 1973e) or grace (Bateson 1972)—of a widespread feature of the human condition, a vulnerability to the ruptures inherent in (self-) consciousness, not an exclusively Christian problem. Indeed, what is phrased as the problem of insincerity with respect to action is analogous to the problem of skepticism with respect to knowledge. In the absence of a better term, I refer to the general quality of action and the relationship of performers to their acts that is at issue here as one of *seriousness*.

How do we know when we are being serious? How do we come to acquire the conviction that an act of iteration is not simply one of mimicry but real and consequential on its own terms, and how are we able to recognize seriousness in others and in ourselves? One could add, Is it possible to be serious (or sincere, or have conviction) without knowing that one is (or does)? Is it necessary to intend or profess seriousness in order to *be* serious or to act seriously?[2] There is also the matter of whether sincerity and conviction are important in local ideology, and whether they are made evident through introspection or by means of the outward success of the performance itself. Finally, how can or does religion, when fully "learned," overcome or quash the anxiety of knowing whether we are serious? How can learning religion address learning to know that we do indeed mean what we say and intend what we do?

I follow certain of Cavell's reflections on what he rightly calls these "immeasurably complex" issues (1995, 55) concerning the seriousness and sincerity of acts and utterances. Austin asks whether performative utterances (e.g., a promise) must be spoken "seriously" in order to be taken "seriously" and whether

> their being serious consists in their being uttered as (merely) the outward and visible sign, for convenience or other record or for information, of an inward and spiritual act; from which it is but a short step to go on to believe or to assume [without realizing] that for many purposes, the outward utterance is a description, *true or false,* of the occurrence of the inward performance. The classic expression of this idea is to be found in the *Hippolytus* ([Euripides] 612), where Hippolytus says, "My tongue swore to, but my heart (or mind or other back-stage artiste) did not." Thus "I promise to . . ." obliges me—puts

2. On self-deception, see chapter 7. On the multivalence of the verb *to act,* see Turner 1982.

> on my record my spiritual assumption of a spiritual shackle. (Cavell ibid., quoting Austin 1962, 9–10)[3]

Austin suggests that distinguishing an inner from an outer voice provides people with illegitimate excuses, and he continues to argue himself that, "Accuracy and morality alike are on the side of the plain saying that *our word is our bond*" (Cavell 1995, 56, quoting Austin 1965, 10). For Austin, the performative utterance is what counts; inner doubt is a mere infelicity in an otherwise successful performance. In other words, I would say, (outer) seriousness is not to be confused with, seen as a mere expression of, reduced to, made dependent on, or viewed as lesser than (inner) sincerity.

A question is whether such a promise is an "ordinary" use of language or some kind of iteration, a non-ordinary usage, in non-ordinary circumstances. Cavell writes (in parenthesis) as follows:[4]

> (When Hippolytus says, "My tongue swore to, but my heart did not," is he an actor on a stage? Does he think he is, that is, take himself to be on some inner stage? Does Austin imagine one or other of these possibilities to be in effect? Does Austin think we, or anyone at any time, may not be able to tell these differences? Or not tell them in the case of Hippolytus because we cannot tell them in ourselves? Is there something in the figure of Hippolytus that would confuse Austin about all this? [His slam at the 'back-stage artiste' suggests that there is.] I am trying not to let such questions take over.) (1995, 56–57)

Rappaport—who cites the same passage from Austin (Rappaport 1999, 121) but does not cite Cavell—is beset by a somewhat analogous problem—namely, the potential that human language offers us for deceit and alternatives, and he accepts Austin's analysis as a way to provide a solution for the problem of ambiguous communication. Rappaport (1999) demonstrates (by means of a lengthy argument that, unfortunately, I must reduce here to mere assertion) how ritual addresses the problem by affirming the social relevance and priority of the exteriority of the tongue's "doing" over the interiority of the heart's "saying." Ritual makes certain acts and utterances definitive and renders internal feeling irrelevant to their effects. In other

3. Cavell goes on to show that Austin himself has been unfair to Hippolytus, who did not utter this phrase as an excuse and did not break his word.

4. Cavell is extremely fond of both parenthesis and quotation; of course, the problem of how to interpret their contents is formally similar to the problems of seriousness and iteration that he is addressing.

words, ritual effects the production of a specific class or genre of performative acts in which seriousness is established from the outset. It doesn't matter what performers think to themselves; the act of participating in a ritual commits them to accepting both the public message and the metaperformative means by which such communicative acts are enabled and specific messages are established. (An easy illustration is the person who gets married while being uncertain of the wisdom of the act or cynical about the authority of the ceremony.)

Rappaport, like Geertz before him (1973d), thus draws upon the philosophical critique of private language. It is as though the public advocation of seriousness, established through ritual, trumps any private concerns with sincerity. For Geertz, this enables the anthropologist to interpret culture without recourse either to inaccessible layers of subjectivity or dubious theories of mind. For Rappaport, it is important because ritual insulates social order from the vagaries of human ambivalence and passion.

Rappaport's argument builds upon Austin's and also strengthens it by emphasizing the way ritual reinforces the performative effects of otherwise ordinary utterances. But Cavell would not be entirely convinced. He continues to wriggle over the issue, in large measure because he worries that dismissing ostensibly nonserious forms of language as merely parasitic on ordinary language is politically dangerous (insofar as it targets the arts, parody, etc., and "takes non-seriousness to be a declaration of self-exclusion" [1995, 58]), and because (if I have understood him correctly) taking the transparency of ordinary language at face value obviates a position of personal responsibility and philosophical skepticism. Cavell continues to ask, "*Must* we mean what we say?" (1976; my emphasis).[5]

Conviction

I accept Austin's point that seriousness is not a matter of an outer performance corresponding to a prior inner intention and that the outer performance is therefore not to be judged as true or false with respect to some hypothetical inner one. Arguments concerning public versus private language are enormously helpful. Austin (and other philosophers of language) demonstrate the consequences of public utterances, and Rappaport adds

5. "Cavell is seeking to draw us into a position where we are denied both the possibility of an epistemological guarantee for our beliefs and the possibility of a skeptical escape from those beliefs. Of course, this is hard for us to bear, but it is here that we must learn to, as Putnam [1992, 177] puts it, 'wriggle'" (Critchley 2005, 48).

the way that ritual both reinforces or enhances illocutionary force and commits performers to accept the liturgical orders in which they are participating. But they omit a good deal when it comes to learning religion; that is to say, they omit a good deal if learning religion is to mean more than acquiring deliberative and procedural knowledge, and if we recognize that participation in ritual acts can have a significance for participants or raise concerns that exceed (or otherwise depart from) their public acceptance of the liturgical order of which their own acts are a part. One does not need to posit an independent "inner artiste" in order to ask what the acquisition of religious knowledge or competence comes to mean for those acquiring it; what the performing of specific acts comes to mean to the specific individuals who carry them out; and what kinds of performance anxieties attend the specific liturgical regimes. It remains valid to consider the passion with which certain religious adepts pursue their goals or accede eagerly, happily, or with equanimity to the challenges religion places before them, or conversely, to consider their concerns over whether they have things right, are as virtuous, powerful, or effective as they are supposed to be, and so forth. In sum, a central problem in learning religion—and not just Protestantism, though it may be found most acutely there, in the form of sincerity—is acquiring conviction. Kierkegaard summarizes the problem succinctly when he writes (in the first epigraph of the chapter) of learning "to catch up with oneself."

Even when one has learned to smoothly inhabit a way of life and a set of practices that comprise it, these practices and this way of life will continue to throw up challenges—and indeed must do so (within reason) if they are to retain our interest. Intrinsic to the idea of a challenge is discovering whether we have been up to it. Learning then entails both meeting specific challenges and recognizing that they are meetable, that in general we are up to meeting the challenges that this way of life, this set of practices, throws our way. In the case of ritual this includes learning that the certainty of acceptance entailed in performance does trump the vagaries of belief and skepticism. Seriousness entails a commitment to ensuring that the performative acts in which one participates are carried out felicitously; conviction (here) can be understood as the knowledge that they can be. These can only be realized after the fact.

What can go wrong in the performance of ritual? Austin elaborates a typology of infelicities. In his inimitable language, or rather, in his inimitable capacity to draw upon and to finely discriminate among the resources of ordinary language, Austin distinguishes two broad kinds of infelicities. There are *misfires,* which are acts purported but void, and *abuses,* acts professed but hollow. *Insincerities* are a category of abuses in which the thoughts, feelings, and intentions for subsequent conduct are inappropriate. They are what exercised Austin about Hippolytus and have exercised many since. Austin points out that it won't do to call upon insincerity to rescue oneself from a poorly judged act, as though to say, "But I didn't mean it" could serve as a valid excuse; nevertheless, the recognition of one's own insincerity can cause considerable anguish.

In the arguments propounded by Austin and Rappaport, insincerities are not sufficient to produce misfires, that is, to void the act itself. But in the case of spirit possession I am about to discuss, the problem of knowing or trusting one's own intentions—of knowing whether one is serious, or how serious one is—is relevant precisely because of such a threat to the outcome. That is to say, the uncertainty of knowing what one wants or what one is capable of is salient not as a form of insincerity but because it risks the disallowance or vitiation of the act itself. The performance anxiety here is that if one doesn't "really" have a spirit or the right spirit, the possession ritual will be a misfire, either a *misapplication,* in which (following Austin's definitions) the persons and circumstances are inappropriate for the act, or worse, a *misexecution,* characterized by the flaw that the procedures cannot be executed by the participants correctly. While this is not a matter of insincerity, it shares with insincerity a tension between knowing the correct convention and doubting one's ability to carry it through. That is to say, it suggests a want of conviction and a threat to the seriousness of the act and occasion.

Acquiring Conviction

The problem of sincerity faced by speech act theorists is somewhat artificial so long as it is phrased in terms of the analysis of single utterances. This has been a weakness of the philosophy of language. Indeed, there is a certain irony, in that, while speech act theory turns the study of language from semantics to pragmatics, it has tended to do so abstractly, by means of artificial examples analogous to the way Chomsky illustrates transformations in sentence structure or, in Cavell's case, by means of quotations from written texts. Even when speech act theory draws upon conversational analysis (or rather, when conversational analysts draw upon speech acts), the study is likely to remain closely bound to specific instances and narrow, immediate contexts, as manifest in the transcriptions. Yet seriousness (conviction, confidence, sincerity) is not something that one "has" or starts with, or that is self-evident in any individual segment of discourse (that is, not a property of any backstage artiste), but something that one learns—or grows into. Anthropologists know this: Rappaport sees it as a consequence of participation in ritual; Geertz (1973f) writes of the acquisition of specific moods and motivations; and Asad (1993a) emphasizes the role of disciplinary power in inculcating specific dispositions. Further, if learning is something that, as Kierkegaard argues, one must do for oneself, it occurs in the context of supportive (and coercive) relations with others and it may in fact entail internalizing or introjecting others. Conviction is not unconnected to what one could call a growth in confidence or self-confidence in the language of Western psychology (or ethnopsychology); faith, in the language of Christian theology; or disposition, in the language of Aristotle or Bourdieu.

Conviction, then, does not take place instantaneously, nor is it evident in (or "behind") a given utterance; it is not the matter of a single speech act. Nor is conviction a direct object or objective of learning (but rather an indirect object of deutero-learning; see Rappaport 1999, 304–5). It is less an active endeavor than a kind of passion; one becomes surprised or overtaken by one's own conviction. It is thus analogous to what Aristotelians describe as the cultivation of character; indeed, in proper measure, perhaps it can be seen as a virtue. If conviction is not necessary to produce a given speech act, it may be necessary for the happy (I do not say "felicitous") living of an ethical or religious life. It can inform speech acts but it is also informed by them. It builds gradually. Nor is it a prior or private matter, the fancy of some "inner artiste," but the product of public ritual and of interpersonal relations, albeit relationships that take place both in the outer, social world, and inwardly by means of identification, introjection, and individuation (see Harding 1987 for a striking illustration). In a slogan, conviction is *confiction*, the product or metaproduct of a project of world-making engaged in with others. Of course, conviction is rarely unassailable. What we are after might be qualified as "working conviction." Learning religion entails acquiring conviction in the course of acknowledging skepticism.

These points are well argued and illustrated in Lévi-Strauss's famous essay on the Kwakiutl shaman (1963) who first practices what he considers to be pretence and in the course of doing so and observing the effects of his actions and the response of others comes to understand them as truthful and his work as serious. We could go on to say that thenceforward his acts are performed with conviction, that the irony entailed in understanding his deception gets reframed or transcended. In learning the techniques of the shaman and in performing *as if* one were a shaman—thus insincerely or without conviction—one eventually surprises oneself by *becoming* a shaman, by realizing oneself as one, by discovering that one *is* a shaman.[6] Shamanistic performance becomes serious. Taussig's acute recent reinterpretation (2003; cf. Whitehead 2000) makes the point that the dialectic between conviction and skepticism, between the word or symbol and the body, or between revealing hidden mysteries and exposing the trick, remains open rather than closed. The mystification of performativeness remains vulnerable.

Alongside public certainty is performance anxiety. This is a world "backstage," as it were. But it is not the "backstage artiste" of Austin's scorn or the ghost in the machine, but merely backstage to public ritual—the practical, informal, and sometimes unconscious, sometimes public ways in which religious adepts convince themselves of what they know, of the seriousness of their enterprise and the sincerity and strength of their own engagement. The point here is not to establish or rely upon a distinction between inner and outer, evident though that may be in tragedy, but to describe a space that is neither specifically inner nor outer. Skepticism is no more—or less—private or internal than is conviction.

Spirit Possession

Spirit possession raises squarely the question of the parasitic nature of certain kinds of iterations and the problem of seriousness and conviction. If it provides a good entrée into questions of learning religion, such learning, conversely, offers a productive way to think about possession. When I began studying possession, the reigning paradigm was epidemiological, and the arguments concerned who got possessed and why. It was a matter either of risk or instrumentality, and very mechanical. Changing the register to "learning" from "infection" or "strategy" enables one to think more broadly about the circumstances of possession, the complexities of taking on a character, the growth of insight, the intrinsic irony of possession as a cultural form, and the value that adepts find in engaging in such practices.

Possession has no explicit pedagogy. The ideology in Mayotte states that possession is not deliberate; it cannot be learned and should not be sought out. It is spirits who decide to possess humans, not the reverse, and spirits who then must be educated, and so its eventuality and course are unpredictable. Thus, how people learn possession and their reflections on that

6. See also my discussion of the way in which the healer of sorcery works his technique upon himself (Lambek 1993b, chap. 9).

process are best grasped retroactively. In fact, its development is intimately tied to biographical features.

The following material is based on discussions I have had with the main protagonist, Mohedja Salim (all names are pseudonyms), during 1975–76 and again in 1980, 1985, and subsequently, as she reminisced about her first experiences with spirits. Had space permitted, I would not only have presented a much more extended account but would also have included the perspective of her husband Tumbu, whose own acquisition of knowledge, spirits, and conviction was closely tied to that of Mohedja. Indeed, the two play off and reinforce each other so deeply that presenting only a portion of Mohedja's side offers a partial and overly simplified picture. Sometimes Mohedja and Tumbu gave me identical accounts of events, and sometimes they differed; they differed too over time, but each conversation supplemented the others and was consistent with them in its general thrust. While the discussions purport to report on events, they also help realize or consolidate what they describe, like memory work more generally, both forming a narrative and assimilating its content to the self of the narrator.

When I first met Tumbu and Mohedja in 1975, they had been married some twenty-five years, a mutually satisfactory union of unusual durability for Mayotte. They lived in the village of Lombeni Kely, where they cultivated dry rice and cash crops, and where they were each consulted as healers. They were each possessed by several spirits of different types and ages. Here I discuss only the onset of Mohedja's senior (elder) *patros* spirit. Patros is a category of spirit said to be indigenous to Mayotte, but the names of individual patros are recorded in Arabic books consulted by astrologers. In some mediums the patros spirits become healers. They make use of a variety of medicines and techniques, including local medicinal plants and astrology, and in some mediums they also extract sorcery from the bodies of clients. Patros display themselves publicly at ceremonies known as "drums" (*azulahy*), at which they congregate, dance, and eat strange foods. A feast is held when a patros announces its name and thus legitimates its presence in a new medium (Lambek 1981; cf. Janzen 1992).

Tumbu and Mohedja drew on their patros spirits not only to heal and advise others but also to address their own concerns and those of their immediate family. The spirits spoke with a degree of confidence or certainty not readily or directly available to Mohedja and Tumbu themselves, and helped them to make decisions and to act with determination.

Mohedja was raised in the village of Chirongue. Her father died when she was quite young, and she had two older male siblings. When she was in her teens, she moved with her mother to Lombeni Kely. Tumbu had just returned there after several years working on the island of Anjouan. Although their backgrounds were quite different, a marriage between them was quickly arranged. They married around 1948–49. Within two years, Mohedja gave birth to their first child, Nuriaty.

The Arrival of Mze Bunu

Mohedja said she was only the second person in Lombeni Kely to get a patros. There were already plenty of patros in Chirongue, and Mohedja used to go to the ceremonies and watch the dancing. But she was afraid to eat the cakes served there because she had been told that if she did so, she too would get a patros.

Mze Bunu rose shortly after Nuriaty was born. Mohedja recalled that she was very sick for six months after giving birth and that no one could cure her. She was bedridden and so ill that often she did not know the time of day or who was talking to her. They tried all sorts of cures, blessing rituals (*shijabu*) and sacrifices (*swadaka*) but to no avail. People feared for her life, as did Mohedja herself.[7]

Finally, her older half-brother Samba arrived from Chirongue. His patros spirit rose and said the stars were against him being the curer, that he was not compatible (*mwafaka*) with her case. At this Mohedja became even more despondent and was sure she was going to die, since Samba was already a very successful and well-known healer. But Samba said that he would try anyway, lest it be said that he had refused to help his little sister. He made her an amulet and fed her medicine composed of a handwritten Koranic verse dissolved in water (*singa*). Mohedja—actually, the spirit that was now manifest—tore off the amulet. But for the first time in six months she was able to get up. However, two days later she was sick as before.

Samba's spirit then advised them to seek Samba's (classificatory) elder brother, Kasimu Juma (no direct kin relation to Mohedja herself), as the healer (*fundi*). Kasimu's spirit, Mze Bunu, rose and announced that a spirit was bothering Mohedja. Mohedja laughed over this as she told me, since it turned out that it was Mze Bunu himself who was troubling her, though he did not say so at the time.

On his first visit Kasimu extracted a *sairy* and gave her medicine to drink. The *sairy* is the material manifestation of sorcery and its removal (Lambek

7. Postpartum delirium was a part of many women's experience. In one case I observed in 1976, a woman became psychotic shortly after giving birth and died soon after. Mohedja has often been ill upon giving birth, but this is the only birth accompanied by spirits.

1993b), but Mohedja is certain there was no sorcery in this case.[8] The *sairy* was simply a product of the arrival of the spirit. "Big" spirits, especially those intending to manifest themselves as *fundis* (knowledgeable healers) in their hosts, often enter people of their own accord (rather than being sent by sorcerers), making them sick. Patros require the removal of a *sairy* before they will stop making the host sick and rise to her head.

In the distinction between spirits sent by sorcerers and those coming of their own accord, Mohedja is suggesting that the spirit is ego-syntonic—that its arrival is acceptable and even desirable, that the spirit is there for her. It is not clear whether she knew at the time that it would become a *fundi,* but it appears that she and her *fundis* were attempting to transform her illness into something positive. It is interesting that right from the start of her marriage, she is tacitly setting the course for a possession career.

Kasimu said he would return and that in the meantime they were to cook a red chicken, setting aside the blood, and also provide a red cloth. Gradually during that week she improved until she was able to get out of bed and even walk about a little—after six months! At the end of the week Kasimu returned with the other leading patros *fundi* from neighboring Lombeni Be. Together they asked her spirit to rise. A patros rose in her right away and even drank blood that first night. This event was sufficient to constitute the *ishima* (courtesy), the first ceremony of a possession cure (normally it is a large public event, but this was not generally a part of Kasimu's practice). Kasimu asked the spirit what it wanted for the *azulahy be,* the big ceremony (that would serve to fully and publicly establish the spirit's relationship to Mohedja and to cure her), and the spirit requested a red goat. Kasimu gave Mohedja more medicine, and she became well and was soon going out to the fields again.

The spirit said that Mohedja should hold the big ceremony. But Tumbu, who did not yet have a spirit himself and was not interested in them, refused. And so, after a year, Mohedja became sick again, though not as gravely as before. Tumbu continued to refuse to sponsor the ceremony. Finally, Mohedja lit some incense and spoke directly to the spirit, saying that if he wanted his ceremony, he was bothering the wrong person, since she did not have the means. He had better do something about Tumbu, since it was he rather than she herself who was the obstacle. Two days later (in another version, "That very night . . .") Tumbu himself fell very ill. Without informing Mohedja, he sought a diviner. The diviner told him that his wife's spirit

8. Mze Bunu was accompanied by another spirit on whom the sorcery was displaced (Lambek 2002b).

lay behind his illness; he had broken his promise to the spirit and should hold its ceremony. Immediately he rushed off to seek a large red goat. When Mohedja saw it, she asked what it was for; she was truly astonished. Tumbu replied it was for her ceremony, and she knew that her trick had worked. But to this day [Jan. 5, 1976, some twenty-three years after the event] she has never told him what she did, for fear of having him accuse her of trying to commit sorcery against him.

The two of them went to Kasimu Juma's to schedule the ceremony. By this time Kasimu had married some distance away. When Kasimu's spirit rose, Tumbu also asked what medicine he needed to cure himself. The spirit replied that holding the ceremony for Mohedja would be sufficient, nothing else was necessary. Tumbu asked a second time to be very sure he didn't need any medicine of his own. [This remark is characteristic of Mohedja's precision in reporting such matters.] Then they amassed the goods they needed for her ceremony and set aside rice to make cakes.

Before her ceremony, Mohedja went to Lombeni Be to invite people there who had patros spirits. But they laughed at her and said they wouldn't come, since she didn't really have a patros. The reason they thought this was that throughout the past year, whenever they had held patros ceremonies in Lombeni Be, Mohedja had never participated as people with spirits are wont to do. She heard the drums from afar but never felt moved to follow them, nor did her patros rise at the sound. Both she and they didn't know that on his first appearance Kasimu Juma had specifically told the spirit that he didn't want him going and dancing at other people's ceremonies.

Mohedja grew discouraged and she thought to herself that maybe people were right and she didn't really have a patros after all. On the day of her ceremony, very few people attended. The people in Lombeni Kely came to watch but none of them had patros yet. They urged and urged her patros to rise, singing and clapping, but nothing happened, and Mohedja kept thinking that maybe the Lombeni Be people were right. Finally, she heard a guest from another village say the whole thing was a waste of time and there was no patros. They had never heard of a patros that asked for a ceremony and then refused to rise to celebrate it! Mohedja felt very upset and embarrassed. People were getting tired and wanted to go off to sleep.

All this time Kasimu Juma had been in trance, and his spirit had been chatting with Tumbu and others. Now the spirit announced that he was leaving, and the people said that if the spirit did so, that would be the end of the matter. But the moment Kasimu Juma left trance Mohedja entered it! People danced until, at the appointed hour, the spirit was bathed and reemerged to announce his name. He was Mze Bunu, the same spirit as that of her *fundi* Kasimu.

Then the others understood why her patros had not risen earlier. He was already up in Kasimu, and a spirit cannot be in two places at once. The reason they had not thought of this before was that they were all still quite inexperienced at dealing with patros. Nowadays people can often tell the identity of a spirit from the first time it rises in a new host, although it has often puzzled Mohedja how they do this, since, she says, she herself generally cannot.

Learning to Mean It

I have used this story elsewhere, under other names, in order to illustrate the suspense of an emerging identity and the rule-bound nature of the dramatic process. What is striking for the present discussion is the way in which Mohedja is determining who her spirit will be, even while this knowledge is denied to her conscious mind. It is she, with the assistance of Kasimu, who has given direction to her emerging identity, who has, in a sense, taken control even while in apparent subjection. Not only has she demonstrated autonomy in selecting the identity of her spirit, but (as I cannot go on to demonstrate here) the particular identity she has selected is also salient for her own self-construction. Nevertheless, she has not yet realized her own conviction and is uncertain whether she has a spirit or who it is (i.e., whether she can carry through). The felicitous public performance, including the tense moments of ostensible misfire, confirms her judgment and manifests her competence. What she describes is the course and means of her own conviction, learning to "mean it," and coming to recognize where she stands.[9]

In recounting these events Mohedja also demonstrates another side of what we might mean by "learning religion." That is, not the learning equivalent to enculturation, but that comparable to acculturation. Mohedja portrays the entire community as ignorant of the way patros work. She is learning what it means that she is not in trance while her *fundi* is, even if we surmise that subconsciously she already knew this. At the same time, she is

9. Mohedja's ostensible ignorance of her spirit's identity, all the while acting in such a manner as to make it a certainty, is only one way a possession cure can play out. Often the host and her healers know the name, but to mention it before the spirit introduces itself at the correct moment during the ceremony would produce a misexecution.

taking something of a risk; the ceremony could have failed. But the risk and its upshot only add to her own growing confidence as a medium and *fundi* herself. The events are not only illocutionary in their effects, but perlocutionary. They establish with certainty the identity of the spirit, the intimate connection (tacit collusion) with Kasimu, and Mohedja's competence as a medium. They indicate also (to us) that possession is not a mechanical process, nor is it a matter of simply responding to social expectation.

This account of Mohedja's development of conviction is incomplete. For example, in 1985 Mohedja told me that Mze Bunu had started healing people through her before she held his *azulahy* or he had given his name. I have not addressed the profound importance of this spirit for the remainder of her life, or the ways in which conviction and seriousness continued to build. What the account begins to illustrate is the fact that to "learn spirit possession" is not only to learn how to enter and exit trance or to perform competently as specific spirits or with their help, but to take their presence seriously and to practice with conviction. Someone like Mohedja learns to fully accept the reality of spirits, to live with them and, more fully, as herself. Moreover, this reality happens through public performance and is collectively realized. Speaking through Mohedja (18 Oct. 1975), Mze Bunu told me that he does not like to rise in many people and would possess no one else in Lombeni. For the next thirty years this proved to be the case.[10]

Conclusion

In the field we distinguish as "religion," conviction derives not only from facility *with* iterative performances or the objective vehicles or instruments of larger powers, but from agility *as* their vehicle, instrument, or subject. Subjects are not prior to or independent of the iterative performances on which they draw and from which they learn to trust their knowledge, inspiration, and judgment (while balancing this with reasonable skepticism).

The problem, named "insincerity" with respect to Protestantism, is a locally (ideologically) informed refraction of a property intrinsic to, but also potentially resolved by, iteration. We only "catch up with ourselves," come to realize that we do indeed mean what we say (or intend what we do), after the fact, in light of felicitous performances. This is surely part of what it means to "learn religion."

10. For what happened to Mze Bunu as Mohedja approached death, see Lambek 2011.

NINE

Sacrifice and the Problem of Beginning: Reflections from Sakalava Mythopraxis

This chapter was delivered as the Presidential Address to the Society for the Anthropology of Religion annual meeting in Vancouver in 2005 and as a public lecture at the London School of Economics (as well as at Berkeley and Oxford). As an essay on "religion," it tries to offer an original approach to sacrifice and a corrective to the impact of Victor Turner's (extremely rich and important) emphasis on the liminal phase of ritual. I would now clarify my argument to acknowledge that Turner's liminal period is one of intransitivity, much as I speak of beginnings, but the point remains that the essence of ritual for Turner is its transitivity. Taking sacrifice as a discrete act, the essay conversely ignores the ways sacrifice can be understood as a form of continuous submissive practice (e.g., Mayblin 2013; Shohet 2013). However, the chapter is not only about sacrifice or ritual per se but also uses sacrifice to say something about the nature or problem of human action and passion.

Imagine you are standing at the podium about to deliver a public lecture. Your voice cuts into the silence and you begin. No moment is so sheer, so existentially chilling. Having begun, the lecture will run its course; practice follows its routines, speakers their texts. This is not a metaphor of cast dice. Inadvertent circumstance may disrupt the speaking; practice reshapes itself to meet contingency; writing itself takes turns the author does not expect at the outset. But no event is so autonomous, so simply itself as beginning.

Of course, a paradox about beginnings is that when we stop in the middle of things to think about them, they are always already in the past. So, whether by means of myth or by memory, we are often trying to understand a present open to the future that is itself already located imaginatively in the past.

This chapter was first published in *Journal of the Royal Anthropological Institute* 13, no. 1 (2007): 19–38.

"The problem of beginning" wrote Edward Said, "is the beginning of the problem" (1975, 42).[1] Nowhere in theory is this problem fully resolved. If beginning was unrecognizable to structuralism, it has fared little better in practice theory's revisions of that doctrine. Beginning is an embarrassment for social theory—and yet it is a regular part of our experience as we gird our loins, face the day, start our computers, embark on a journey, a book, or a love affair; or as we collectively set our sights, step forward to battle or toward a new world—or imagine our predecessors having done so.

Beginning is a problem not only for theory, but for practice itself. This essay addresses the problem of beginning in Sakalava practice and the enactment of beginning in Sakalava historical consciousness; how descendants of the polity of Boina in northwest Madagascar have imagined the beginning of their monarchy (events that took place around 1700 CE) and how that beginning forms a kind of prototype for other beginnings; how beginning again is always a beginning *from* the beginning. Following the Sakalava lead, this chapter is also about sacrifice. That is to say, it is about sacrifice as a kind of beginning—at once a means, an act, and a sign of beginning—and possibly about beginning as a kind of sacrifice.

Sakalava Beginnings

Scene One: The Curation of the Knife

The village of Bemilolo sits in a pastoral setting of oxbow lakes along the Betsiboka River, a place of abundant rice fields, waterfowl, and fish, about a half day's travel by bush taxi from the port of Mahajanga. Among the houses is a fenced-off enclosure containing a small building. This belongs to Ndramandikavavy, the founding queen of Boina. Her name means "Noble-lady-who-surpasses-all-women." The shrine contains her material artifacts, notably a knife (*viarara*). The shrine is cared for by local inhabitants who claim descent from the queen. They form a clan, the Tsiarana (Peerless), whose duty it is to attend to their ancestress as well as to matters of cattle sacrifice in royal ritual. On the occasion of the annual ceremony honoring the queen, many other Tsiarana gather in the village, along with members of

1. Here is the larger context of the phrase: "'Beginning' alternates in the mind's discriminations between thought that is beginning and thought about beginning—that is, between the status of subject and object. Paraphrasing both Hegel and Vico, we can say that formally the problem of beginning is the beginning of the problem. A beginning is a moment when the mind can start to allude to itself and to its products as a formal doctrine" (Said 1975, 42). I am indebted to Aram Yengoyan for long ago having directed my attention to this book.

the royal family (*mpanjaka*), who also descend from her (through a different offspring than the Tsiarana). Ndramandikavavy herself speaks through one of her spirit mediums seated on a raised platform outside the enclosure. The knife is deployed whenever there is a burial service at the royal cemetery nearby (at Betsioko). Cattle sacrificed at a royal burial must have their throats cut with Ndramandikavavy's knife.

Sakalava are concerned with the enactment of *fanompoa,* a word that means "service to royalty" and, specifically, "care of royal ancestors"—named personages in the royal genealogy. While care is ongoing, especially *taking care* not to offend them, specific ceremonies are directed to the curation of the ancestors and their property—their bones and relics, tombs, houses, and artifacts (Lambek 2002a). Some of the ceremonies, like the queen's, are annual events. The largest one, the Great Service (*Fanompoa Be*), held in a temple on the outskirts of Mahajanga, is a new year's ritual. And yet, as different shrines across the countryside hold their own annual services, each serves in part as a necessary beginning, a prelude, for successive ones at other locations. Thus the Great Service cannot itself begin until other services have taken place. It is as if the problem of beginning is itself continuously displaced, pushed back into a kind of infinite regress. But such deferral cannot be infinite; if there is to be a conceptualization of beginning, there must be a first beginning—or a first step in the act of beginning. How that is indicated—the problem of beginning—is the problematic of this chapter.

The queen's knife also figures prominently in the Great Service, although it is not literally the same object as the one in Bemilolo but a different materialization of the same conception. It is carried at the head of the annual procession that marks the climax of the new year's festival, during which the four male ancestors whose relics reside at Mahajanga are paraded around their shrine immediately after their annual bath. Each year the queen's knife is purified along with the relics of her menfolk; each year Sakalava begin their historical journey.

Why is the knife of sacrifice such a critical element? And why does it belong to the queen? The queen herself is markedly absent from the main shrine, which is commonly known as the Shrine of the Four Men (*Doany Efadahy*). These include the queen's husband and their son.[2] The queen can never appear on the shrine precincts, and yet the annual service cannot take

2. Strictly, it is *Doany Ndramisara Efadahy,* Ndramisara's Shrine of the Four Men; Ndramisara was a diviner and architect of the polity (Lambek 2002a, 93–94, 97), and sometimes identified with the queen's brother.

place without her permission. More than that, the Great Service begins with a sacrifice of cattle in her name.

I do not want to treat either myth or sacrifice as discrete things that can be isolated and inspected in and of themselves. Rather, I look at sacrifice as it appears in Sakalava narrative about the past, in characters instantiated in the present, and as enacted in performance. Our idea of myth—sacred narrative abstracted from its context—is itself secular (Asad 2003a) and therefore cannot give us much sense of what it might be like in a more holistic universe. For Sakalava, myth is living or lived, quite literally. Ancestral personages are invoked in prayer, accounted for in the observance of taboos (and manifest in symptoms of their violation), and encountered in embodied performances of spirit mediums. Narrative has no intrinsic priority. Conversely, "sacrifice" is not only an act carried out, but an idea or image explored in narrative and other kinds of performance. My narrative, now well begun, is therefore about neither sacrifice nor myth per se, but rather about a set of Sakalava images and practices from which both sacrifice and myth could be precipitated as analytic constructs—by an earlier generation of anthropologists, perhaps. It is better to say succinctly that my article is about beginnings.

In *The Weight of the Past: Living with History in Mahajanga, Madagascar* (Lambek 2002a), I portray the texture of historical experience among present-day Sakalava, considering how the past structures and sanctifies the reception of new events in the present (cf. Sahlins 1985) as well as how the past is continuously realized—made real—by the work of the present. But it could be said that I took beginnings for granted, colluding in the common anthropological wisdom that the explanation of beginnings lies beyond our reach of competence. Yet if we cannot say *why* things begin, perhaps we can still say *how* they begin, or *what* beginnings are, what it *means* to begin. This is not an offer to replace one myth with another, as Freud (1958) does in *Totem and Taboo*, for example. The question is less about origins, or the problem of discovering *what* happened, than it is about understanding beginning *as* a problem.

I distinguish between beginning and origin. We often think of myths as stories of creation; myths of origin are about the emergence of something from nothing, of order from chaos, of absence replaced by presence. In contrast, beginnings occur in the midst of life, rarely as a very first beginning, but each time a *new* beginning. Beginnings emerge against what precedes them.

Beginnings are located in time and in society, whereas origins may be situated on a pretemporal or prehistorical horizon. Evans-Pritchard, for example, distinguishes Nuer accounts of past events that "have therefore a position in structure" from "the horizon of pure myth. . . . One mythological event did not precede another, for myths explain customs of general social significance rather than the interrelations of particular segments and are, therefore, not structurally stratified" (1940, 108). Beginnings are acts and therefore require specific actors or agents. Origins are events and imply extrahuman forces. Beginnings entail human intention. Beginnings also imply a narrative that leads forward from their present. An origin is the culmination of its narrative.

The acts of Sakalava narrative belong to a human age. Indeed, in northwest Madagascar there are no prominent first acts of creation, and it is said that people came to the island rather than originating there. Key acts are ones of planting, burying, and setting down roots rather than of coming up autochthonously through the soil.

Edward Said, to whom I am much indebted, argues that "beginning is . . . an activity which ultimately implies return and repetition rather than simple linear accomplishment; . . . beginning and beginning-again are historical whereas, origins are divine" (1975, xiii). He says further that "the designation of a beginning generally involves also the designation of a consequent *intention*; . . . when we point to the beginning of a novel, for example, we mean that from *that* beginning in principle follows *this* novel. . . . *The beginning, then, is the first step in the intentional production of meaning*" (5; his emphasis). Thus, beginnings are active, humanly made, not naturally or divinely given.[3] Along the path through the forest, they are the first step into a clearing, the first stroke of the axe to mark the trail.

Scene Two: From the Schwartzwald to Bourg la Reine and Thence to Ithaca—The Rites, Wrongs, and Rings of Passage[4]

The ring of the axe is no idle metaphor. Chopping, cutting, spilling, killing—in a word, sacrifice—is one of the ways that we mark time, one of the clearest acts of beginning. In beginnings, the flux of homogenous time is overcome, the stream is parted into a before, a now, and a henceforward—into a past, present, and future. Beginnings signal the self-conscious insertion

3. Said writes, "As consistently as possible, I use *beginning* as having the more active meaning, and *origin* the more passive one: thus 'X *is the origin of* Y,' while 'The beginning A *leads to* B' " (1975, 6).

4. References here are to dwelling places associated, respectively, with Heidegger, van Gennep, and Turner (Ithaca, NY, as well as the prototypic end of the voyage). This section owes a good deal to a conversation with Joshua Barker.

or intervention of the human act and the recognition of time's place in human experience. Simultaneously, they make spatial discriminations as beginning is materialized—in the chopping of a tree or the spilling of blood—and localized, marking a place in the extension of space, a point, a path, and a direction.

In *The Rites of Passage*, cutting is described as a symbolic act of separation. Arnold van Gennep (1960) understands ritual as both temporally constituted and temporally constitutive, enacted and enacting, moving its subjects along trajectories of successive social statuses. He pictures the life cycle as the successive habitation of a series of rooms. The passage between them is enacted through ritual, as though one paused at each threshold to rearrange one's habit and demeanor—and took a deep breath before stepping through.

Victor Turner developed the model in a series of brilliant analyses (e.g., 1967, 1969), but with hindsight it may be fair to say that this elaboration became a kind of appropriation. Where van Gennep distinguishes three phases of ritually produced movement—separation, transition, and incorporation—Turner famously focuses on the middle, liminal phase. Turner's exploration of transition is certainly true to an aspect of ritual and temporality, but as a result we have come to think of the liminal phase as primary, and the other phases as mere brackets or containers of the precious liminal cargo. The power of this model of transition entails two emphases that I wish to counter. First, the action of separation, the bracing of the shoulders and decisive first step, is displaced by the passion characteristic of liminal beings and their rebirth. Second, the intransitive quality of the act is overshadowed by the transitive.

Consider the term *initiation*. Whereas initiation as the prototypic rite of passage has come to connote some kind of drawn-out process, the verb *to initiate* more fundamentally means simply "to begin" or "set going."[5] Think also of the meanings of *initial* and *initiative*.

Furthermore, in the sense of "beginning", the verb *to initiate* does not have the strong transitive sense of initiating *someone*, but only a weaker transitive sense of initiating a course of action. The verb *to begin* can also be used in the intransitive sense of simply *beginning*. Here the end or object is intrinsic to the means, and thus the action is understood as valuable in itself rather than instrumental.

5. "Initiate *v.t.* 1. Begin, set going, originate. 2. Admit (person), esp. with introductory rites or forms (*into* society, office, secret, *in* mysteries, science, etc.)" (*Oxford Illustrated Dictionary* 1975, s.v. "initiate").

In other words, the model of ritual as transition (and essentially transitive) is ready for another look. Viewed as wholes, *rites de passage* might sometimes be better characterized by a shift of emphasis as rites of beginning. Indeed, the first phase, the new departure, is critical insofar as it anticipates the point of the entire ritual sequence. As a codification and realization of intention and commitment, it subsumes what follows. Enactment of the remaining phases of the ritual is but fulfillment of what is established in setting forth. Initiation means literally "beginning," and then "admission." "Transformation" and "induction" are secondary meanings, reinforced by the tripartite van Gennep-Turner model.[6] Turner's elaboration of the middle phase obviates understandings of sheer beginning or final end.[7]

Liminality is a spatial metaphor of waiting and passivity; I would supplement it with a temporal phenomenology of action. Rituals are frequently culminations of what is past and anticipations of what will follow. Often they are both simultaneously. Sacrifice is both a passionate culmination for the victim and a significant initiative by the person who offers it. It draws a line in blood between "before" and "after." Once you have killed something, there is literally "no going back" for either victim or killer. Sacrifice is thus a materialization of intention and a consummation of resolution. Consider how much more powerful all this is when victim and sacrificer are one and the same person.

Scene Three: The Shrine of the Four Men

The Great Service sets the Sakalava community on a fresh start every year. But critical to the success of the ceremony of new beginning is its own beginning. In Sakalava fashion, the key acts happen backstage. Each year, ancestral approval for the service must be sought and confirmed; rising in the bodies of spirit mediums, royal ancestors "open the gate" or "clear the path" to move ahead. Thus intentionality is marked from the outset—in both the intention of the living producers of the ritual, who state their aims very clearly in addressing the ancestors, and the intention of the ancestors, who explicitly acquiesce and join in the wish to see the ceremony successfully completed (*vita tsara*).

6. They are further reinforced by the ubiquitous practices of fraternities and sororities on American campuses that served as undergraduate essay topics.

7. The relevance of *both* modes is amply discussed by Rappaport, to whose analysis I am much indebted. Following Rappaport (1999, 95), any ritual qua event takes the preceding (analogic) flux of uncertainty and indecision and, in a clear (digital) act, definitively transcends it.

A week before the public beginning of the new year's festival, and consequent to her acquiescence, descendants of the queen gather at the shrine to make a bovine sacrifice on her behalf.[8] They signify their commitment by offering the beast—and the animal itself, like all Sakalava sacrificial beasts, must indicate acquiescence by not bellowing or struggling when it is thrown.

The skin of the dead beast is then stretched to dry and used to refurbish the shrine's two sacred drums (*mañandria be*, "great ennoblers"). The vitality inherent in the life of the beast and the intentionality of the offering are transposed into the vibrancy of the drums (compare Ruel 1990). There is a literature associating percussion with transition (Knauft 1979; Needham 1967), but I emphasize here its significance as beginning and enactment. Drumming is both energetic and unambiguous. The drummer beats the drum; each movement of the arm is specific and deliberate. The energy of the arm is transferred to and enlarged by the vibrations of the drumskin. The rhythm of the drum continues to emit the intention of the sacrifice. The passivity of the beast silently submitting to the knife is transcended by dynamism, noise, and vitality. The drums are a medium for the active force of the victim.

In contemporary Sakalava sacrifice, "value" moves from the labor of raising the animal through its market price; but it also moves from the intention of the donor through the acquiescence of the beast; and from the throb of life through the spilled red blood to the pulsing of the drums made from the victim's skin; then from the drums that excite and incite to the acts of those who respond to its rhythm, in anticipation, in attention, in dance, and in labor and loyalty, in virtuous acts of commitment to the monarchy, obeisance to the ancestors, and acknowledgment of hierarchy, hence in granting power to Ndramandikavavy. This is a version of the process of the "dissolution of death . . . into authority" analyzed by Maurice Bloch (1989d) for the neighboring Merina, which combines mystification with morality.

The initial sacrifice is described as an offering on behalf of the queen, but it is also a repetition of her original sacrifice. Those who perform the offering stand in for their ancestor who made the first sacrifice. Just as Ndramandikavavy's original act began the polity, so does it begin the new year, which is also a celebration and reenactment of the polity and includes offerings to the original monarchs by their subjects. Because many of the

8. I observed this event in July 1994. That year the Tsiarana pooled their resources to purchase the animal. There are no rules regarding the sex or age of the bovine offering. Compare the killing of a bull to initiate Merina rituals of blessing, an act Bloch "hesitates" to call a sacrifice (1986, 59, 98).

offerings end up in the hands of the living monarch, and because acts of work, offering, and obeisance form the substance of the polity, the celebration is a literal as well as symbolic enactment. But my point here is simply that both the historical polity and the annual enactment begin with the queen's sacrifice. Indeed, just as the liturgical cycle enacts the beginning of the polity, so the beginning of the polity is equally the initiation of the liturgical order. However, the queen's original offering was not composed of cattle. This is a point to which we shall return.

Sakalava emphasize and elaborate the beginning of their Great Service with various deliberate steps before the public display, putting the weight, one could say, more on the intention than on the accomplishment (which is a kind of anticlimax, or at least it was to me). The sacrifice of the queen's beast forms a preface to the ensuing festival. It is relatively private (concerning only her own direct descendants, mediums, and shrine workers), whereas the festival is public, incorporating thousands of people through numerous forms of attachment. The sacrifice is also quite discreet; most people do not know the connection between the queen and the drums. But it is absolutely critical. The festival cannot take place without the queen's acquiescence, as provided in her speech through a medium and performatively accomplished in the sacrifice. Moreover, the drums are one of the most important heirlooms and signs of royal legitimacy; they must be renewed each year, their skins must be those of the queen's cattle, and their rhythm must punctuate the ensuing events.

More than the rehearsal of a genealogical charter, these acts are also conditions that enable the felicitous performance and the performative effects of the subsequent main ritual events. But they are also performative events in their own right. The Great Service is front-loaded with a series of such events that establish the intention and willingness to proceed. It is as though Sakalava are preoccupied with the sort of infinite regress of intentionality—the ghost in the machine—described by Gilbert Ryle (1949), albeit in the Sakalava case this is located in the external, interpersonal world of the polity, rather than the internal, private one of the mind. Ryle, of course, saw regress as the product of a category mistake. But it may well be that this category mistake is not so easy for humans to avoid, that mind and body and the mind/body problem are part of the human condition, that the Durkheimian problem of social solidarity and moral commitment is formally similar, and that the problem of beginning is one of its manifestations. The series of ritual acts productive and demonstrative of intention and commitment—each a necessary condition for the succeeding one—are Sakalava expressions of the problem.

Scene Four: Morningside Heights (Manhattan)

Some years before he became famous as the author of *Orientalism*, Edward Said wrote *Beginnings*, subtitled *Intention and Method*, from which I have already quoted. Here Said is interested in creative production. Every work of art has its beginning—its conception and the way that conception is activated or materialized in a first sentence, note, or brushstroke.

Said does not explicitly consider beginnings to be characteristic of social practice, and hence he ignores the field of ritual. And yet his account is extremely relevant for social practice. "What sort of action," he asks, "transpires at the beginning? How can we, while necessarily submitting to the incessant flux of experience, insert (as we do) our reflections on beginning(s) into that flux? Is the beginning simply an artifice, a disguise that defies the perpetual trap of forced continuity? Or does it admit of a meaning and a possibility that are genuinely capable of realization?" (1975, 43).

Said speaks of the necessity "to acknowledge the mind as providing self-concerned glosses on itself over time, the mind as comprising its own philosophical anthropology" (1975, 43); surely these glosses are found in ritual no less than in literature. Indeed, Said argues that beginnings are necessary. "Without at least a sense of a beginning, nothing can really be done, much less ended . . . A beginning gives us the chance to do work that compensates us for the tumbling disorder of brute reality that will not settle down" (49–50).[9]

Said makes a careful distinction between transitive and intransitive beginnings. These are "really two sides of the same coin. One, which I call temporal and transitive, foresees a continuity that flows from it. This kind of beginning is suited for work, for polemic, for discovery." However, "In attempting to push oneself further and further back to what is only a beginning, a point that is stripped of every use but its categorization in the mind as beginning, one is caught in a tautological circuit of beginnings about to begin. This is the other kind of beginning, the one I called intransitive and conceptual. It is very much a creature of the mind, very much a bristling paradox, yet also very much a figure of thought that draws special attention to itself" (1975, 76–77).

9. For example, while weddings are commonly seen, in accordance with alliance or descent theory, as acts of exchange or affinity or as the transmission of rights in offspring, property, and services, a characteristic of the weddings I have observed or participated in, both in North America and among Malagasy speakers in Mayotte, is the sort of optimistic refocusing ascribed by Said to beginnings. Indeed, I would say that "beginning" forms both a central function and a self-interpretation or theme of weddings (chapter 2; Lambek 2004).

In sum,

> The point of departure . . . has two aspects that animate one another. One leads to the project being realized: this is the transitive aspect of the beginning—that is, beginning with (or for) an anticipated end, or at least expected continuity. The other aspect retains for the beginning its identity as *radical* starting point: the intransitive and conceptual aspect, that which has no object but its own constant clarification. . . . These two sides of the starting point entail two styles of thought, and of imagination, one projective and descriptive, the other tautological and endlessly self-mimetic. The transitive mode is always hungering . . . for an object it can never fully catch up with in either space or time. The intransitive . . . can never have enough of itself. (Said 1975, 72–73)

Scene Five: The Countryside West of Mahajanga, Circa 1700

The Sakalava have reached the country of Boina, where they would like to settle and rule. An oracle advises the king, "In order to succeed, you must sacrifice what is dearest to you (*raha tsifoinao*)." The king offers the best cattle from his herds, but they are not acceptable. He offers gold, and then fine Chinese porcelain, but they too are insufficient. Finally his wife announces, "I am what is dearest to you." And so she sacrifices herself. This is an extreme distillation of more elaborated and divergent narratives of the founding of the Sakalava polity,[10] but it is sufficient for my purpose here.

We can see now that if Ndramandikavavy is absent from the main shrine, it is precisely because its very existence is predicated on her death. Moreover, it is not merely the sacrificers who take the queen's place in the annual ceremony, but the cattle themselves. They are killed not only on the queen's behalf, or in her honor, but with her knife and in her stead. The throat that this knife first cut was the queen's. Each sacrifice is a repetition and recognition of her original act; each victim is identified with her. It is her skin and her life that animate and empower the drums. It is her intentionality that produces and permeates the ensuing ceremony and that infuses the resolution of the celebrants as loyal subjects.

As a character in the Sakalava *poiesis* of history (Lambek 2002a), Ndramandikavavy symbolizes *determination*. It is her determination that is harnessed to ensure and energize the enactment of the Great Service. It is her determination that is diffused to her descendants and her subjects—the

10. The king is Ndramandisoarivo. The identity of the oracle varies from version to version, as does the method by which the queen dies.

general population (*vahoaka*) who have produced and renewed the polity through their own acts of sacrifice, service, and celebration over the course of three hundred years. Her resolve is evoked in her every appearance and lends itself to every act carried out with her knife and in her name.

Determination is an interesting word, seemingly pulled between free agency and inevitable coercion. Ndramandikavavy's sacrifice is deeply intentional, yet to call it choice trivializes it, as though Abraham or Isaac had a choice. To draw upon Said again, it is "a necessary certainty, a genetic optimism, that continuity is possible *as intended by* the act of beginning. . . . Consciousness of a starting point, from the vantage point of the continuity that succeeds it, is seen to be consciousness of a direction in which it is humanly possible to move (as well as a trust in continuity)" (1975, 47–48; his emphasis).

In fact, Ndramandikavavy extracted a promise from her husband as a condition of her sacrifice—namely, that only their joint descendants would rule; his continuity would be equally hers. In its transitive aspect the beginning thus conforms to Malinowski's notion of a charter in that it establishes legitimacy to rule and both specifies and restricts succession to office. Yet it differs from many genealogical charter myths in validating an ancestral *couple*. The queen effectively cuts off all the king's collaterals and other descendants. The king's and queen's respective children by other partners form two separate clans, closely associated with royalty but distinct from it. Descendants from the queen alone are Tsiarana—the Peerless—who maintain and wield the sacrificial knife.[11]

In comparison with the Judeo-Christian-Islamic tradition, especially the story of Abraham and Isaac, the following points are salient: (*a*) the victim is a woman; (*b*) the victim is said to "kill herself " (*mamon teña*); (*c*) the victim is not an offspring but a spouse and parent; (*d*) the sacrifice is fully carried out—there is a human death; and (*e*) there is no direct recipient, no divine being to whom or on whose demand or behalf the sacrifice is given. There is much to say about gender and about mothers and sons, but having begun an essay on beginnings, I must stay on track.[12] Germane to the present analysis is the determined yet voluntary quality of the sacrifice, the completion and finality of the act, and the absence of a divine arbiter or recipient. Thus, whereas biblical sacrifice seals God's promise to look

11. The clan descended solely from the king holds authority over royal burial grounds.
12. For exposition of the gender of sacrifice, see Lambek 2007b, 2008a.

after His people, Sakalava sacrifice seals the people's promise to care for Ndramandikavavy, her son, and his descendants.[13]

Sacrifice as Exemplary Beginning

There are many theories of sacrifice. I do not intend to review them or to adjudicate among them. Nor do I propose to add another theory; I merely provide a redescription. I want to show that sacrifice is an exemplary mode of beginning and hence that beginning affords one way to interpret sacrifice.[14] This is certainly not the most intuitive interpretation, since—for the person, animal, or object destroyed—sacrifice would appear to form most saliently an ending. In a sense, each new beginning signals simultaneously the end of what it departs from and perhaps the death of alternatives not taken. But I suggest more strongly that endings form and substantiate beginnings. I do not suggest that this is the only way to understand sacrifice, but I admit that one way to read my argument is that no *theory* of sacrifice—no explanation that draws upon forces external to the act itself—is necessary.[15]

Sacrifice as a Literal Act

By *literal*, I mean here "univocal, exact, unmediated," and "unambiguous"—hence, a context in which certainty can be distinguished from uncertainty. The body is often the ground for the literal.[16] The body is literally grounded in burial, and authors such as Astuti (1995), Bloch (1971), and Middleton (1999b) have noted how in Madagascar this—finally—establishes exclusive

13. The queen's act draws on symbolism that stretches back earlier, to the kingdom of Menabe, as does the royal genealogy.

14. A precursor of this view is found in Hubert and Mauss's classic *Sacrifice* (1964). They highlight the presence and destruction of a victim as well as the Vedic model of the creation of the universe as a sacrifice. Indeed, Malamoud observes both that Vedic creation presupposes a sacrificer, oblation, and model (hence that it is a beginning rather than an origin) (1990, 188) and that the rites themselves elaborate the process of beginning and begin with an act of violence, a "first slice" (*une entame*) (190). I am very grateful to Anne de Sales for providing the relevant text. Parry (1994) offers an exemplary ethnographic exposition of Hindu death as sacrifice and creation.

15. This is akin perhaps to Lévi-Strauss's argument with respect to totemism (1963) or Franz Steiner's with respect to taboo (1956).

16. This is the case despite the fact that the body itself is often grasped by means of metaphor.

social identity. Sacrifice is one of the most literal acts possible, both as an action and in terms of its end product, that is, a dead body.[17]

To be sure, the sacrifice of an ox for a human, or a cucumber for an ox, can be understood metaphorically. But these are merely replacements of one object of sacrifice for another, not metaphors for other, more consequential kinds of acts; at bottom, they are still sacrifice. For the ox, his life is no metaphor. Cut flowers die; liquid cannot be put back into its container; like Humpty Dumpty, a sliced cucumber cannot be put back together again. There may be some ambiguity as to whether a given act of killing is sacrificial or what that might mean (Ruel 1990), but killing in and of itself is always a literal act. For the victim, there is no return, nor can the killer withdraw her act.

In this sense, killing is like ritual. One of the things about rituals is that you cannot take them back in protest that you did not mean it. Once done they cannot be undone, at least not without going to the trouble of holding another ritual of a different kind. Sacrifice ensures and epitomizes this quality of ritual action. Cutting throats and spilling blood are literal acts. The object can be metaphorically displaced—from royal self to human subject, from animal to vegetable—but the act of sacrifice is no metaphor.

The Gift and Its Limits

It is often argued, following Mauss, that there can be no "pure" gift, since the obligation to give is always met with the obligations to receive and to return a gift. The recipient who does not offer a return is beholden to the donor, and the donor achieves a higher moral status in that respect. Hence no gift can be said to be characterized by pure disinterest.

What of sacrifice? In Ndramandikavavy's case, while her sacrifice was noble and courageous, no Sakalava would suggest it was undertaken without self-interest. The queen struck a bargain; she asked for something in return. However, what her sacrifice shares with the idea of the pure gift is the impossibility of a full return. Here lies the source of her power. Why can there be no equivalent return? To answer that, I must address the question of who her recipients are and how I know her gift was not disinterested.

There is no third party, no deity to receive or be honored by Ndramandikavavy's sacrifice. The instigator is a diviner, and he is responding to the workings of a neutral, amoral destiny. The immediate beneficiary

17. However, Sakalava leave the death of royalty ambiguous and unspoken. Rotting flesh is separated from enduring bones, and the royal ancestors perdure as *tromba* (possessing spirits).

is posited as the king, her husband, but her death is simultaneously his loss. Indeed, it is phrased explicitly as that with which he could not bear to part, *raha tsifoinao*. Yet Ndramandikavavy's quick response actually turns things in a more interesting way; in sacrificing herself, she seizes his role as the offerer of sacrifice and achieves the perdurance of her own name and rule. What the king loses is not just his wife but his agency (what is dearest to him indeed).

By establishing his exclusive right to succession, the queen makes their son the direct beneficiary. It is only toward him that her sacrifice might be said to be disinterested, and yet it is precisely because of her identification with her son that it is most self-interested. It is his—and therefore her—descendants who succeed him. The king's offspring by other women are specifically excluded and disinherited.

More generally, the beneficiaries are all of the subsequent members of the kingdom of Boina. This has a sharp ideological angle: the queen's subjects are expected to honor her for effecting the conditions under which her descendants rule over them, as well as identifying with her as an ideal subject.

When Ndramandikavavy rises in the bodies of her mediums, it is evident that she went willingly but not selflessly. She retains great attachment to the things of this world, especially to her son. And she is especially rude to her husband. He shows his wife great affection and puts his arm around her, but she soon gets impatient. After a few minutes, she says brusquely, "What are you still doing around here? No one needs you any longer!" And so the conqueror and first king of Boina slips meekly away from his shrill wife and out of the body of his medium. He is, in her eyes, irrelevant. He is eternally beholden. He cannot return her gift.

If the queen gave up her life on behalf of her husband, it is clear that he in turn has given over his authority to her. In response to supplicants, the king speaks in platitudes and is generally amenable to whatever is proposed; the queen is forthright, assertive, and tough, expecting people to uphold the standards of the polity for which she gave her life. She inspires respect and fear not only in her husband but also in her human subjects. She is known to be harsh (*mashiaka*), and her devotees are afraid of her wrath.

Ndramandikavavy's sacrifice is a gift that must be received, yet cannot be returned in full and hence canceled. The debt to her is in a sense what keeps the polity running. Generation after generation must bow to her authority, respond to the interpellation of the drum; each royal succession must ensure that the promise to her remains fulfilled. Acknowledgment is mandated, but no return could ever be sufficient to cancel the debt.

The queen's gift cannot be canceled not only because she courageously gave her own life—and no larger gift could be imagined—or because the existence and persistence of the political community are the outcomes of her act, and not only for the obvious reason that she is no longer fully present to benefit from a return gift, but also because what she offered was manifestly a *first* gift. Any and all returns—even were they to be equivalent—are quite literally secondary. Only one act in a sequence can be first.

Insofar as her act is original, Ndramandikavavy points to a problematic of the gift literature left largely unaddressed by Mauss and his successors. These are the questions: What constitutes a first gift? Which donor stands out as the original source of the *hau* to which the gift must return? Moreover, if every gift engenders a return, how do we know that any given gift is not always already a return? How is a gift marked as first? Where and how does the chain of reciprocity begin? How can one break it and start anew?[18] We are back to the question of beginnings.

My point is that sacrifice is one way to mark a gift as "first." Indeed, this may be implicit in our understanding of the distinction between sacrifice and gift. Blood sacrifice or self-sacrifice makes an especially good beginning, a first gift, because it is a gift that does not—indeed, cannot—return to its origins. It is the gift that cannot be returned, or canceled, or withdrawn. The only thing to do with it is to honor it.

Words and Deeds

Ndramandikavavy's sacrifice is not a gift to a transcendental being, but one dictated by fate. It is in this respect unmotivated and unreceived. Thus I do not wish to place undue emphasis on sociality, communion, commensality, appeasement, or supplication. A sacrifice is purely what it is and not something else.[19]

18. See Schwimmer (1973) on the "starting mechanisms" of exchange and on exchange as sacrifice; Graeber (2001, 176–88) on the *hau* and the meaning of Maori initial gifts; and Caillé (2000) for a lively discussion of sacrifice as utilitarian exchange. Like that of Caillé, my discussion of sacrifice does not include the sense of abnegation.

19. For this reason also, I do not emphasize the feast. In this I follow Sakalava practice—the meat of animals sacrificed at the shrine is divided up and, for the most part, taken to individual households to be cooked and eaten separately. In contrast to commensality, the act of killing is a salient aspect of animal sacrifice virtually everywhere. As an indirect piece of evidence, I note that depiction of animal slaughter is practically *de rigueur* in ethnographic film. Of course, consuming the sacrificial object could be seen as the final, incorporative phase of the rite; and, like cutting and spilling, eating and digestion are irreversible acts and processes that cannot be taken back.

Goethe's Faust rewrites the New Testament to begin, "First was the act!"[20] Sacrifice (cutting, killing) is manifestly neither word, nor object, but act. What distinguishes sacrifice from simple giving or killing is that it is explicitly performative, bringing into being a new conventional or moral state.

Performative acts—in Austin's sense—are frequently beginnings, and they are spoken in the first person. They can be understood as public expressions and objectifications of resolution. Austin provides examples such as "I . . . take this woman to be my lawful wedded wife; I name this ship the *Queen Elizabeth*; I give and bequeath my watch; I bet you sixpence" (1962, 5). Each of these casts intentionality forward—as vow, promise, contract—most generally, as commitment. Henceforward, the state of affairs, the name, the relationship, the expectation, shall be understood in the terms established in the performative act. Thus, the state of marriage is brought into being in the enactment of the wedding service. As Rappaport notes (1999, 133), acts subsequently committed by persons subject to the conditions initiated by means of the performative act are to be judged with respect to those conditions.

In Muslim societies a simple and ubiquitous act of beginning is found in the utterance of *"b'ismillah."* Trobriand spells are also beginnings and performative acts in this sense. As Malinowski portrays it, Trobrianders utter a spell at each new phase of the *kula*, from felling the tree to make a canoe (1922, 126–27) to meeting the *kula* partners (334–49). The utterance of each spell *is* the beginning of each new phase. The spell can be understood to mark a reorientation in the stream of practice and to begin what lies ahead. The *kula* expedition as an ethical enterprise is thereby constituted as a series of marked intentions, each initiated by a performative utterance that constitutes the quality of the time/space and action of what is to follow (cf. Munn 1986; Tambiah 1973).

Austin's insight is that such utterances are simultaneously acts. Rappaport describes ritual as comprised of both acts and utterances, but it could be said that he also privileges utterances. Thus he singles out ultimate, sacred postulates, phrases like *b'ismillah*,which are unquestionable and invariant, and which sanctify the acts and more specific utterances they accompany, as when a political pronouncement includes the phrase "in the name of God." Yet if utterances are acts, certain highly conventionalized acts may be considered simultaneously utterances (chapter 3).[21] We can speak of sacred

20. *Faust* (Goethe 1992, 39).

21. Acts of lime-cutting in Sri Lanka (Obeyesekere 1981) or sharing kola nuts in Nigeria are examples; both entail cutting.

acts no less than sacred postulates, and sacrifice is surely among them. Of course, sacrifice is an act generally composed of both word and deed, but it is one in which the deed speaks more powerfully than the word.

Just as Rappaport describes a hierarchy of postulates with respect to their sanctity (1999, 314), so, I suggest tentatively, we may think of acts.[22] This hierarchy is one of unquestionableness, invariance, precedence, and inclusiveness; one could add irreversibility. As a pure beginning, the first sacrifice sanctifies and establishes the condition for the acts that follow. Indeed, it sanctifies the entire subsequent history of the kingdom, for so long as it is respected. It also establishes the grounds of value or meaning, providing the standard against which other acts can be understood. Subsequent sacrifices of lesser value—ranging from human subjects, through cattle, down to a few coins or drops of rum—can only approximate, rehearse, and evoke the ultimate sacrifice. But like it, they are performative acts that sanctify the conventional and moral states they initiate. My point is not that in the beginning lies the deed, or lies the deed alone, but rather that in the performative deed lies a beginning.

Execution

Heidegger has written that "to the anticipation which goes with resoluteness, there belongs a present in accordance with which a resolution discloses the situation" (quoted in Steiner 1978, 110). The question is, How is resolve disclosed or realized—made real—both for actors and for their public? The irreversibility of blood sacrifice is certainly one way.

A blood sacrifice is an execution. The meaning of *to execute* is as follows:

> 1. Carry (plan, command, law, will, judicial sentence) into effect; perform (action, operation, etc.); make (legal instrument) valid by signing, sealing, etc.; discharge (office, function). 2. Carry out design for (product of art or skill); perform (musical composition). 3. Inflict capital punishment on. (*Oxford Illustrated Dictionary* 1975, s.v. "execute")

22. Indeed, utterances *are* acts, a point made not only by Austin but also, from an alternative philosophical tradition, by Arendt (1998). Systematic analysis would show similarities and differences between sacred postulations, in Rappaport's sense, and other kinds of acts. In any case, alongside Rappaport's ultimate sacred postulates (1999, 263–76), one could add ultimate sacred acts, of which sacrifice may be a prototypic example.

To execute a living being in sacrifice is simultaneously to execute a plan or course of action.[23] In both Malagasy (where the relevant verb is *manapaka*) and English, we see how central killing is to the idea of carrying out a definitive and irreversible social act.[24]

Outright killing is not the only form of executive blood-letting. Scarification is one example; defloration another. In Mayotte a woman's relinquishment of her virginity is marked. Done in the wrong context, it is simply an ending and thus destructive. Done in the right context, it is a beginning, the first moment of adult sexuality and the consummation—as we say—of marriage. The act of submitting to defloration is sacrifice in this sense, a formal, decisive, and irreversible execution and a gift that can never be fully returned. It is no coincidence that it is likened to the act of male circumcision (see chapter 2).[25]

Action and Passion

Rituals are decisive deeds, yet they are acts in which people submit to something larger than themselves. In this respect, as Heidegger would put it, "man is not the opener of truth . . . but the 'opening for it'" (Steiner 1978,

23. The executive significance of sacrifice can also be gleaned from its refusal. Evans-Pritchard describes the Nuer leopard-skin chief threatening a curse against those reluctant to accept mediation.

> He would take an ox and rub its back with ashes and begin to address it, saying that if the injured party were to insist on revenge many of them would be killed in the endeavour. . . . He would then raise his spear to slaughter the animal, but this would be as far as people would care to let him go. Having asserted their pride of kin, one of the dead man's family would seize his upraised arm to prevent him from stabbing the ox, saying, "No! Do not kill your ox. It is finished. We will accept compensation." (1940, 175)

24. This might be linked to Heidegger's formulation of the violence of being in his *Introduction to Metaphysics*, and is described by Nelson (2009, 195) as "an originary strife . . . that contests the reification of identity."

25. Ideally, defloration is followed by a liminal period and final incorporation in van Gennep's sense. Nevertheless, it is evident in the manner in which the defloration is immediately celebrated (with congratulations, ululations and sexy dancing) that a new beginning for the bride has been achieved. As for circumcision, insofar as cutting the foreskin is a repetition of Abraham's sacrifice of Isaac, it is itself a sacrifice. Circumcision is a mark not only of difference or singularity but also of intentionality, a performative act establishing the kind of person one (or one's child) is intended to be and in respect to which one accepts subsequent conduct to be evaluated. Among Dogon, sacrifice introduces differentiation, "the birth of a discontinuous world" (De Heusch 1985, 134); circumcision as sacrifice is linked to menstruation, periodicity, and alternation, but compare Bloch (1986) on non-Muslim Malagasy circumcision.

115). Rituals thereby combine action and passion in a heightened manner. These two dimensions correspond respectively to Said's transitive and intransitive modes of beginning.

Whenever I mention Heidegger, I am skating on very thin ice, and you may already have concluded that I have fallen in. But I cannot resist allusion to Heidegger's concept of *Gelassenheit*, "releasement" or "letting go," which is not simple "inaction or passivity." As Dallmayr notes, "An engagement in being . . . challenges or decenters the customary focus of action theory on desire, will, or deliberate intentionality; . . . instead, the accent is shifted to ontological participation in which the actor is released at least partially from the dictates of an instrumental pursuit of objectives. This shift . . . does not . . . remove moral-political responsibility" (1993, 58).

Sacrifice, especially self-sacrifice, exhibits this inextricable connection of action and passion, or "resoluteness of released engagement" (Dallmayr 1993, 58–59). It is not dying in a simple, passive sense, or killing in a simple, active sense; not accepting the inevitability of death but, as Lienhardt (1961, 296) emphasizes for Dinka, converting it into life. Sacrifice is a negation of the act of giving birth and yet strangely like it. It is "giving death," submitting to it, yet bearing it forth; like birth, an act at once transitive and intransitive. And it can provide a sharper sense of beginning even than birth.[26] A birth can be undone—through death. But a death cannot be undone.

As Rappaport argues, in lending themselves to a ritual, performers inevitably accept its terms and effects (1999, 117–24). There is no more complete mode of participation in this sense than allowing oneself to be sacrificed. Self-sacrifice is the limit act of committing oneself to the liturgical order and hence of confirming, establishing, and realizing it through one's very being. This is equally a form of identification with it. Others then realize their own commitment through their attachment to, or identification with, the sacrificial victim or sacrificer. Instances of exemplary acceptance of this kind include Jesus on the cross, Dinka spear masters buried alive (Lienhardt 1961), and dying Hindu pilgrims who prepare their bodies as offerings to the gods on the model of Vishnu's act of creation (Parry 1994, 30–32, 188–90). As the sacrificer is identified with the sacrifice, so is the ending coextensive with the beginning and the transitive with the intransitive.

26. In a companion essay (Lambek 2007b) I interpret giving birth as a form of sacrifice. Conversely, Ndramandikavavy's sacrifice is a form of birth—a claim to being mother of her son and an act that gives birth to the polity of Boina. On Sakalava birth, see Feeley-Harnik (2000); on action as natality, see Arendt (1998, 9).

The sacrificer conjoins in her act the indexical and canonical aspects of ritual and does so more completely than can be imagined through any other means. We see in this fusion a deeper significance for sacrifice than that presupposed by communication or communion with a deity. In submitting to the liturgical order, it becomes a part of her being, and she too becomes an intrinsic part of that order (Rappaport 1999, 119). Actors and action can then only be described, interpreted, and evaluated with respect to prior commitments—with respect to what has been begun.

Ndramandikavavy simultaneously acts and submits. Such action by means of submission, or subjection through action, is the hegemonic form of belonging in the tributary Sakalava polity; in this sense Ndramandikavavy is an exemplary subject and, like all Sakalava rulers, expected to be simultaneously more powerful than the average citizen but also more bound by taboo and obligation to the ancestral order, more intimately part of it. Equally, we can see in sacrifice an epitomization of the Durkheimian understanding of society in which each member must give up some individuality in order to be transformed, at a higher level, into a moral person.

Social being more generally entails a dialectic of action and passion, of taking in, doing, and becoming what is expected of us (or what is unexpected), as well as taking a purchase on what we are becoming and have become, and making it ours. The idea of beginning captures this double edge of social subject and agent. In beginning a new project—even as one is the agent of its production or enactment—one throws oneself into it, one subsumes oneself in the practice that it entails, and one is thereby partially consumed by it. *And so, if beginning is signified or realized in sacrifice, that is in part because beginning is, in a way, itself an act of sacrifice.*[27]

Time and Intention

"We do not live 'in time,' as if the latter were some independent, abstract flow external to our being. We 'live time'; the two terms are inseparable." So says George Steiner in his explication of Heidegger's *Sein und Zeit* (1978a, 78). If so, what other way to punctuate time than by means of death? Sacrifice executes a beginning and, in producing a present, realizes both the past that

27. I am certainly not attempting to romanticize sacrifice or intending to allude to contemporary acts of violence. The suicide bomber is not beginning anything nor transforming death into life. While the act is surely decisive and irreversible, it is neither part of a liturgical order nor explicitly performative, and its aim is purely instrumental. [Rereading this in 2014, I am less sure of the last points.] On the dangers of applying the religious language of martyrdom to politics, see Hasan-Rokem (2003).

it displaces and rehearses and the future that it anticipates. Sacrifice founds beginnings; it is foundational.[28]

My argument here is less functionalist than poietic or rhetorical. Functionalism assumes the prior existence of the whole, whereas I am describing how certain kinds of wholes are brought into being. Having learned about rites of passage in school, Simon Lambek (my son) asked insightfully how sacrifice could be a ritual if it had no closure. This is exactly the crux of the problem and the basis of my critique.

Both van Gennep and Turner understand rites of passage as transitions. I have been interested more in sheer beginnings, in beginning as an existential problem and also in how people conceptualize, announce, and enact beginning—how they in fact *begin*. In Said's terms, this is to shift the emphasis from transitive to intransitive acts. Understood in its intransitive aspect, beginning, in the form of sacrifice, is neither a gift, nor an instrumental act, nor a referential statement; it is simply itself. Here we approach Wittgenstein's critique of Frazer: it does not make sense to see ritual as an expression of something other than itself; it simply is what it is, a necessary part of the life of a ceremonial animal (1979; cf. James 2003).

Many rituals have both transitive and intransitive aspects. For example, if a wedding ritual entails marrying in the transitive sense, something one does to or with a partner or to one's growing children as subjects of a ritual performed on their behalf, there are nevertheless moments in marriage festivities when the intransitive mode prevails, where the act of marrying is experienced or understood as just that, "getting" married. Here is a sense of "the blossom breaking from the bud" (Steiner 1978a, 137), sheer potentiality without any object. This constitutes a ripeness, a sense of capacity rather than utility (Macpherson 1973, 4–5). Such a state of being (*Dasein*) shares features with Turner's compelling depiction of "liminality," but, understood as intransitivity, it is a different way of conceptualizing the ritual act.

Writing as a professor of literature, Said is naturally most interested in beginning as *poiesis*, the "bringing into being" (Agamben 1999, 69) of a new cultural artifact, a work of literature or art. I have emphasized less *poiesis* than practice, seeing beginning as the intentional engagement in social endeavors, commitments, or games. This is partly a matter of anticipation of outcome, partly of submission to the rules, craft, or ethics that the practice entails. Aristotle distinguishes *poiesis* and practice, making and doing,

28. Sakalava make blood sacrifices beneath the corner posts of new temples, at doorways, and along paths that people must step over.

but in beginning—in authoring a book, performing a ritual, or founding a polity—the distinction may be negligible.[29]

Following the Sakalava cue, I have argued that the resolution entailed in beginning is well signified in the act of sacrifice. Problems of uncertainty and alternatives come into focus most clearly at beginnings. Sacrifice can—and with a stroke—end them. Sacrifice combines the ethical consequentiality of judgment with the decisiveness of choice. It thereby forms not merely a kind of "natural symbol" (Douglas 1970) of beginnings but a natural means to execute them.

I argue both that the story of Ndramandikavavy addresses the problem of regress in Sakalava historicity, providing—retroactively—a founding moment and a coalescence of intention, and that the continuation of sacrifice—henceforward figured in her name, by means of her knife—continues to make this available in the ongoing life of the polity.

Rites de passage belong to long cycles of generational repetition, and that is an important part of the experience for participants. But Ndramandikavavy's act is portrayed retroactively as original, a "first" act of beginning, an initiation in the literal sense of the term, a particular and deliberate intervention in history. The sacrifices that punctuate ordinary life realize, focus, and display resolution and add weight, direction, and significance to specific acts and utterances and to the projects and states of affairs they initiate, introduce, and inform. Their force is greater insofar as they draw upon the paradigmatic act of intervention, firstness, and resolve, the perduring sacred prototype or ultimate sacred act of Sakalava beginning.

Ethics and Ending

Without beginnings, it is hard to see how action could be conceived in ethical terms. Beginnings cast intention forward; in drawing from the past, they render valuable what follows from them, and, as performative acts, they set the terms of reference against which actors, events, and practices are to be judged. Who we are as moral persons is in large part a consequence of the beginnings we have enacted or participated in. Some of these happen before we reach adult consciousness, as we are named, baptized, circumcised,

29. Compare Arendt (1998), for whom the difference between making ("work") and doing ("action") is highly consequential. Arendt emphasizes the radical unpredictability and irreversibility of action in contrast to the routines of practice. A full theory of action would bring together the philosophical literature on intentionality and ethics (e.g., Cavell 1976) with sociological discussions of "social creativity" and social action (Graeber 2005; Joas 1996).

and so forth. Later in life we take up charges with fuller consciousness and resolve, and we indicate this to ourselves and to others, just as we realize it *for* ourselves—sometimes retroactively—in beginning. It is through such explicit engagements and undertakings that our specific ethical lives and characters are formed; they provide the basis for both the cultivated dispositions and the ends and means that constitute us as ethical persons. As a powerful and definitive mode of beginning, sacrifice exemplifies these ethical functions.

Once committed and remembered, sacrifice can be intrinsic to who one is, as a person or a society. Who one *is* is thereby understood existentially rather than essentially, through the sheer initiation of being. And yet, despite the emphasis on intention and resolution, this is hardly the continuous "freedom" that Sartre advocates. That is because each act of sacrifice is simultaneously a passion; each turns us irrevocably in a certain direction, locates us on a certain path; and each invites identification and repetition. Each undertaking we initiate must be made with respect to commitments always already engaged, subject positions already assumed, each new beginning with respect to beginnings already begun.

I am describing regulation or channeling in the flow of social and existential value, the mastering of creative and ethical potential—that is, setting its direction and establishing and accepting its consequences. Of course, this does not happen equally effectively everywhere and not without considerable debate. We might contrast an ostensibly relatively orderly tradition, like that of Sakalava, with more chaotic scenes in which society appears to have lost its way. These may be characterized by epidemics of witchcraft which, by inverting or perverting the logic of sacrifice, both demonstrate and effect the collapse of ethical order (de Boeck and Plissart 2003). The rhythm of regular beginning is displaced by rupture and increasingly frantic attempts at establishing new beginnings. The place of ethics and the formation of ethical persons will be distinctive in these circumstances.

I have been using beginnings as a means to read across the tradition/modernity divide, but I should add that Said himself worked with a distinction between tradition and modernity that has quite different implications. Indeed, he sees beginnings as distinctive of modernity. He argues that contemporary writers and critics can no longer easily imagine themselves within a tradition, "a place in a continuity that formerly stretched forward and backward in time" (1975, 9). After Nietzsche, a text has become "an invitation to unforeseen estrangements from the habitual" (9). In a masculine idiom quite foreign to Sakalava, Said distinguishes father-son succession, which is "dynastic, bound to sources and origins, mimetic," from that of brotherly displacements, which involve "complementarity and adjacency; instead of a source we have the intentional beginning" (66). He contrasts these in Viconian language as "sacred" and "gentile," respectively (13).

This distinction doubtless owes its formulation to the structuralist contrast between the syntagmatic and paradigmatic no less than to Vico. I find it overdrawn and indeed something of a rehearsal of modernity's own ideology; an ideology—dare I say it—of "traditionalism" comparable to that of "orientalism." I have demonstrated the relevance of Said's analysis of beginnings precisely for the succession characteristic of tradition, which is not nearly so uninformed by intention, reflection, uncertainty, contestation, or women's agency as Said would appear to imply.

Tradition is neither timeless nor mindless; that is to say, it is not without beginnings. Beginnings are not routine; at least, in Sakalava "service" every effort is made not to take them for granted. Each beginning actively solicits intention and explicitly demands it. Such intentionality, as Rappaport underscores, is transformed through ritual action into commitment. A difference from the situation of the modern writer described by Said is that commitment is not simply to the work at hand, hence fragmentary and fragmenting, but to a wider order within which specific works and beginnings are construed and authorized.

If beginnings per se do not serve to distinguish between tradition and modernity, perhaps the gentiles can no longer encode them as sacrifice. Marshall Berman (1988) finds modernity's myth of beginning in Goethe's *Faust*. Faust's pact with Mephisto is a precise inversion of sacrifice: you reap the material benefits and postpone the ethical reckoning. It is life lived on credit, or capital.[30] Yet even Faust must sign his contract with a drop of blood. "Blood's a very special ink, you know," says Mephisto.[31]

If endings are beginnings, so too, I have indicated, are beginnings endings of a sort. And so I end this somewhat recursive discussion with a final word from Said: "Beginning is a consciously intentional . . . activity . . . whose circumstances include a sense of loss" (1975, 372).

30. Goethe also works with a contrast between inward activism and outward worldliness (Berman 1988, 46–47), a theme of German culture that entailed additional contrasts between Christians and Jews as well as between Kantian idealist and Aristotelian practical ethics. Berman argues (ibid.) that Faust's inversion of "In the Beginning was the Word" was understood as replacing Christ with the Old Testament God who makes the world. It was part of Weber's brilliance to complexify and transform these oppositions.

31. *Faust* (Goethe 1992, 54).

TEN

Value and Virtue

This chapter continues the discussion of sacrifice, but from a different angle, less as a specific kind of act than in terms of the way it grounds or produces and signifies value. I begin to think about ethics by means of the concept of value more generally, here understood in both its moral and economic senses, and, indeed, at their interface. I also develop a distinction between choice and judgment and explore the significance of incommensurability to complement more structural accounts. The first draft was prepared at the unexpected invitation by Paul Eiss and David Pedersen to participate in an AAA panel on value of Marxist or Marxian inspiration; later drafts received helpful responses from audiences at Toronto and at the Scottish Training in Anthropological Research workshop convened by Jonathan Spencer in 2007 in Crieff. Some of the ideas broached here are followed up in chapter 13.

> To go to the slaughter is always the same sacrifice for the ox; this is no reason for beef to have a constant value.
>
> —Marx 1971, 127

As this chapter is going to be rather abstract, I begin close to the ground. In a recent article, Andrew Walsh (2004) discusses the puzzlement of Malagasy sapphire traders concerning the value of the uncut and ugly stones they extract from the earth. Perhaps nothing better than gem stones illustrates the arbitrariness of value and the curious effects (and machinations) of supply and demand crossed with ideas of display and concealment. Although without much ostensible use value—and certainly none for the Malagasy miners and petty traders—sapphires are part of the world of goods. In economics,

This chapter was first published in *Anthropological Theory* 8, no. 2 (2008): 133–57.

goods get compared with one another, but why should goods be accorded the primary site of tokens of value in the first place? What about deeds, practices, powers, or human capacities? What values exist to contextualize the value of goods?

This chapter attempts to face theories of value with insights drawn from the field of ethics, articulated here as the relationship of value to virtue. I make two, possibly contradictory arguments. First, it does not make sense to talk about value without virtue, or vice versa, especially if one understands value as a function of acts rather than simply of objects.[1] Second, it is dangerous to conflate value and virtue. I leave open a definition of *value*. By *virtue* I wish to signal that the chapter concerns ethical value as much as it does material or economic value, and that my approach to ethics is drawn largely from an Aristotelian version of moral philosophy. In particular, if attention to the ethical component or dimension of value moves us from a consideration of objects to acts, virtue ethics moves beyond acts (making choices, following rules) to persons or character; it shifts the focus from having to doing, to being. Virtue ethics asks not how we can acquire objects of value nor how we can do what is absolutely right, but how we should live and what kind of persons we want to *be*. I take the latter to be significant human questions, if not specifically anthropological ones, even though I do not necessarily go along with the assumption of Aristotelian virtue ethics that a good life must be a single or unified one. In sum, this chapter attempts to contribute to the anthropological discussion of value by showing how it is, and asking how it might be further, informed by ethical theory.

I want to make clear from the outset that there is nothing in this argument to support a simple form of ethical relativism. We do not have to agree on the moral value of any particular practice to understand that it is constituted *as* a moral practice, that it is virtuous from someone's perspective or relative to someone's world. In other words, we ought to be able to locate something in the sphere or domain of the moral as having an ethical quality, without ourselves thereby necessarily either placing a value judgment on it or, conversely, cautiously refusing to do so.

Ethical and Economic Value: Absolute and Relative

In contemporary society there is seen to be a great rift between ethical value and economic value, the former increasingly subjectivized (at least in some

1. This is the approach of David Graeber (2001), taking his cue from Nancy Munn (1986).

quarters), and the latter by now virtually completely objectivized. One of the great merits of David Graeber's book *Toward an Anthropological Theory of Value* is that it shows that value in the economic sense can be—and has always been—linked to value in both the ethical and the semiotic senses, and it brings together Marx and Mauss in this exercise. Indeed, both Marx and Mauss—and one should add Weber, Simmel, and Macpherson—have each in their own way supplied an ethical context and critique to conceptions of economic value and rationality as developed under capitalism. At the same time, as each of these thinkers implies, it would be dangerous to produce a model of value that was overly unified; such a theoretical move would (now) risk participating in the neoliberal inclination to subsume ethical value in economic terms. We must preserve another set of values or ideas about value with which to critically appraise the production and expansion of capitalist value.

Whereas the best recent work in the anthropology of value (a Maussian/Marxist tradition developed by Munn and Turner and extended by Graeber [2001] and others) operates with an ostensibly holistic theory of value (but see Eiss [2007]), I begin by attempting to contextualize values with respect to one another. That is, I emphasize the heterogeneity and incommensurability among distinct values rather than explore the production and circulation of abstract value per se. I begin my inspection of "value" not as an objective entity or mysterious force, nor as an abstract or universal anthropological construct, but by considering the divide between the idea of "ethical values" and "value" in the sense of liberal economics, that is, as "market value" or "price." I hasten to acknowledge that contemporary economics as well as human practices with money as documented by anthropologists (Maurer 2006) comprehend more sophisticated and heterogeneous conceptualizations of value than my schematic depiction here.

To argue that there is good reason to keep discussion of ethics, morality, or virtue at arm's length from, or in some tension with, politics and economics is hardly original, but I think it is worth articulating some of the theoretical and empirical rather than specifically moralistic reasons behind it. The first concerns the relationship between ostensibly absolute and relative value. Ethical values, at least in Western thought, are generally posited with respect to some absolute standard (the life of the ox for the ox) that, unlike fluctuating economic values (the cost of beef) cannot be negotiated. Economic value, as viewed by liberal economists, is intrinsically negotiable and relative; value is a matter of market price. More than this, absolute values cannot be simply substituted for one another. Kant put it this way: "In the kingdom of ends everything has either a *price* or a *dignity*. If it has a price, something else can be put in its place as an *equivalent*; if it is exalted above all price and so admits of no equivalent, then it has a dignity" (Kant 1964; quoted in Asad 2003b, 137, n. 21; italics in original).

As Simmel, in particular, showed, money transforms quality into quantity (1978). Ostensibly constant, absolute standards are thereby increasingly at risk of being undermined by regimes of fluctuating and relative value. This is what is understood to happen when the range of commodities is expanded—to include, for example, votes, sex, parenthood, genetic information, or the writing of grants and even ethical protocols by consulting agencies. Commodities, in turn, are reimagined as quality. As the editor of *Le Monde Diplomatique* put it, US global hegemony and marketing are "all based on the principle that *having is being*" (Ramonet 2000; quoted in Asad 2003b, 152; my emphasis).

In liberal economics value can be measured, and its authority has risen since the nineteenth century, when measurement imposed itself as the basis for scientific validity—value—and the means for knowing or expressing things about truth (Menand 2001). Value thus becomes probabilistic, informed by statistics (Hacking 1990).[2] The rise of information technology has also supported a conception of knowledge or truth as comprised of decomposable but commensurable bits. Ethical value, perhaps partly in a defensive reaction, has been understood as immeasurable, certain, and integral.

Discrete, relative, fluctuating, substitutable, measurable, divisible, and probabilistic economic values imply—even, demand—choice; concomitantly, economics is a science built largely on assumptions about choice. Both Marx and Mauss, each in their own way, challenged the foregrounding of choice, showing that it is never as simple or as "free" as Western ideology suggests. Mauss wrote rather in terms of *obligation*, a word that connotes ethics, as practiced by those in the lineage of Kant and Durkheim. The Maussian gift (1990), with its *obligations* to be given, received, and returned, is a precise exemplification of Durkheim's understanding of society as a moral system. However, Bourdieu's subsequent interventions helpfully bring out the underlying strain in Mauss of a very different moral philosophy from either the Kantianism of his uncle or the utilitarianism to which he is most clearly opposed. The latter, of course, is the ethical philosophical position most closely linked to liberal economics.

2. Interestingly, monetarization may spread with the rise of gambling (Geertz 1973a, 432, n. 18). Whether gambling is viewed as immoral or, as Geertz suggests of Balinese cock-fighting, of moral import, is also of considerable interest.

As Bourdieu (1977) was at pains to point out, the "obligations" to give, receive, and return entail neither mechanical acts of rule-following nor simple or maximizing choices. They are neither categorical nor strictly calculative. Practitioners of the gift economy must bring together many considerations. They have to exercise judgment about *how* to fulfill their obligations—how generous to be, how quickly to act, in what manner, and so forth. In addition (a point perhaps less recognized by Bourdieu), blanket obligation needs to be broken down with respect to the various kinds of commitments that people have made or that have been made for them (as well as to their capacities for fulfilling them). People have to consider how deep the obligation is in any given instance and how to balance it with overlapping or competing obligations. How they act in any given circumstance is in part shaped by their cultivated dispositions and their particular character as social persons. This is an Aristotelian depiction of the situation.

This is also the conclusion of Knut Myhre (1998), who argues for the Aristotelian substrate in Mauss on the basis of the relationship between means and ends. "As a practice where the end is inseparable from the activity, [Mauss's account of] gift exchange resembles Aristotle's concept of virtuous action, where the end is immanent in the practice" (130). Myhre even conjectures that "Mauss's account of gift exchange is influenced by, if not modeled on, Aristotle's investigation of virtuous action in the *Nichomachaean Ethics*" (133).[3]

Obligation, Choice and Judgment

Key words in Kantian, utilitarian, and Aristotelian traditions of moral philosophy are, respectively, *obligation*, *choice*, and *judgment*. In contrast to the way most anthropologists have seen it, I set up as counterpoint to the concept of choice in economics not obligation, but judgment. I believe it is a good idea to try to keep these concepts—choice and judgment—reasonably distinct, or at least to be very clear when and how they are being articulated.[4] However, it is not immediately evident how to do so. Where they are not clearly distinguished, as perhaps in Bourdieu they are not, ethical practice appears to get subsumed within an agonistics of honor or taste (chapter 5) and an ethical disposition—to do the right thing, to be a good person, or

3. The same could be said of Weber's discussion of the Protestant ethic (Weber 1958).

4. What I call *judgment* is often referred to as *practical reasoning;* I avoid that term here, as its use by Marshall Sahlins (1976a) is almost exactly the inverse of what I mean by it. He uses it to refer to the utilitarian position. My meaning derives from Aristotle's *phronesis*.

to lead a good life—is replaced by narrower instrumental and competitive calculations—to get what one wants and to do so ahead of, or at the expense of others.

Thus, although Bourdieu draws upon Aristotelian practice as opposed to Kantian rule, he presents an analysis that in the end looks more like economics than like either of these ethical traditions. This is because he does not fully absorb the Aristotelian relation of means to ends, nor the relative weight placed on "purposeful activity" as opposed to "the consumption of satisfactions" (Macpherson 1973, 5), nor the embedding of virtue in character and practice. For Bourdieu, value is located primarily in the ends rather than the means and continues to be understood as a measure primarily of objects—epitomized in the very term *symbolic capital*—rather than as a quality of acts (virtue) or of actors and lives (character).

When value is understood as inhering in means rather than simply in ends (i.e., in acts and practices rather than simply in goals or objects), the problem of scarcity, and hence of competition, becomes less acute. Macpherson argues this point well in his distinction between the maximization of utilities and the maximization of human powers—

> that is, [people's] potential for using and developing their uniquely human capacities. This claim is based on a view of man's essence not as a consumer of utilities but as a doer, a creator, an enjoyer of his human attributes. These attributes may be variously listed and assessed; they may be taken to include the capacity for rational understanding, for moral judgment and action, for aesthetic creation and contemplation, for the emotional activities of friendship and love, and, sometimes, for religious experience. Whatever the uniquely human attributes are taken to be, in this view of man their exertion and deployment are seen as ends in themselves, a satisfaction in themselves, not simply a means to consumer satisfactions. It is better to travel than to arrive. Man is not a bundle of appetites seeking satisfaction but a bundle of conscious energies seeking to be exerted. (1973, 4–5)

I will return to means and ends later.[5]

While the invocation of judgment serves to begin to distinguish an approach that attends to ethical value from one concerned with economic value, it also complicates or undermines making that distinction, as I seemed to do at the beginning of the article, on the grounds that the former

5. For further discussion of Macpherson, see Lambek (2007c). Sahlins also draws heavily on Macpherson.

is absolute, and the latter is relative. Or rather, it qualifies what is meant by absolute value or how absolute value appears in practice. Understood as judgment rather than obligation, ethics itself relativizes or at least contextualizes value. Practice emerges through evaluation, the sizing up and fitting of action to circumstance. Yet judgment selects among alternatives not by means of a binary logic of exclusive acceptance or rejection but by balancing among qualities. Such evaluation or judgment is grounded in more general, culturally mediated, understandings of the human condition and the ends of human life as well as those internal to the practice at hand. Contingency solicits what I would call a measured rather than a measurable response.

My point here can be illustrated from another direction. A recent popular expositor of pragmatism (Menand 2001, 351) asks, "What makes us decide to do one thing when we might do another thing instead?" The issue is one of judgment, and he continues as follows:

> "Do the right thing" and "Tell the truth" are only suggestions about criteria, not answers to actual dilemmas. The actual dilemma is what, in the particular case staring you in the face, the right thing to do or the honest thing to say really is. And making those kinds of decisions—about what is right or what is truthful—is like deciding what to order in a restaurant, in the sense that getting the handle on tastiness is no harder or easier (even though it is generally less important) than getting a handle on justice or truth. (351)[6]

Menand continues, "When we are happy with a decision, it doesn't feel arbitrary; it feels like the decision we *had* to reach. And this is because its inevitability is a function of its 'fit' with the whole inchoate set of assumptions of our self-understanding and of the social world we inhabit, the assumptions that give the moral weight—much greater moral weight than logic or taste could ever give—to every judgment we make. This is why, so often, we know we're right before we know *why* we're right" (353).

I am suggesting that any adherence to or advocacy of an absolute value like truth or justice must be qualified in and through lived practice, and this will entail the acknowledgment of additional values among which a balance appropriate to any given situation is sought. Ethical practice thereby

6. Menand adds, "In the end you will do what you believe is 'right,' but 'rightness' will be, in effect, the compliment you give to the outcome of your deliberations. Though it is always in view while you are thinking, 'what is right' is something that appears in its complete form at the end, not the beginning, of your deliberation" (Menand 2001, 352). If this is self-serving, it doesn't appear this way.

inevitably begins to relativize ostensibly absolute values. Conversely, however, the highly relative and contingent values of the market often seem to call up in reaction the need for absolute value—whether to legitimate and uphold the system or in direct opposition and resistance to it. Phrased by its proponents as an exclusive and a priori obligation that appears to preclude situational judgment and that often categorically refuses certain consumer choices, this idiom can be called, by those who disagree with it, religious fundamentalism. (I have something more positive to say about religion later.) Between them, trivial choice and absolute obligation appear to squeeze out any room for practical judgment.

The historical conjunction of highly relative but ultimately trivial values, such as those expressed in consumer choice, or ones with uncertain outcomes, such as investment, with values that claim to be absolute, certain, and obligatory (like the sanctity of marriage, the truth of God's scriptures, and so on) may be no accident. It follows that we need to examine the claims made for relative and absolute values and the efforts taken to construct, maintain, or reduce the distance between them in any given period or argument. Additionally, and irrespective of the specific contents attributed to them, we can inquire about the articulation, dynamics, and dialectics of relative and absolute value—the forces that pry them apart as well as pull them together or transform one into the other—in any given sociohistorical context and practical circumstance.

Commensurability and Incommensurability

I began by considering whether relativity is a useful way to distinguish economic from ethical value. I have suggested that comparing choice and judgment weakens the distinction between relative and absolute value. However, the same comparison suggests an alternative way to think about the problem—namely, in terms of commensurability. My argument has two strands. I suggest that—at least under capitalism—ethical and economic articulations of value are incommensurable with one another. After exploring various dimensions of incommensurability, I suggest that the primary reason for the incommensurability of ethical and economic value is precisely their distinctive constitutions with respect to commensurability.

As noted earlier, Graeber articulates three ways of thinking about or using the concept of value—the economic, ethical, and semiotic. While Graeber is certainly correct to set his three kinds of value or "ways of talking about value" at work together, and correct to imply that they interact or overlap differently in specific cultural and historical contexts and conjunctures, we need to attend to whether, where, and how economic and ethical value are not actually commensurable, how they do not map directly onto one another, a point suggested implicitly by making the distinction in the first place. We live at a time when economic value is striving mightily to subsume ethical value, but despite the vast waves of corporate corruption or the tides of commoditization that seem to rise ever higher on the shore, like the hurricanes they indirectly produce, such subsumption cannot be completely successful. As Marx indicates, the sacrifice of the ox is simply not commensurable with the value of its flesh.

I am not discerning or proposing a utopian alternative—vegetarian or otherwise—in which everyone puts the welfare of others first. (I leave that to certain late or post-Judeo-Christian philosophers.) Nor am I suggesting that all ethical and economic values are inherently contradictory or in opposition to one another. The Protestant ethic, as interpreted by Weber, in which, for example, time is money and money is a possible sign of divine election, certainly shows at the least an elective affinity. Nor am I, obviously, taking the utilitarian line that ethical and economic value are commensurable, that, as Bentham postulates, "1st. *Each portion of wealth has a corresponding portion of happiness*. 2nd. *Of each two individuals with unequal fortunes, he who has the most wealth has the most happiness*" (Bentham 1931, 120; quoted in Macpherson 1973, 27; his italics). I am arguing that perspectives based on ethical and on economic concepts and principles, on judgment and choice, respectively, are incommensurable; that is to say, following Kuhn, they "must fail to make complete contact with each other's viewpoints" (Kuhn 1970, 148; see also Bernstein 1983, 79–87). Each provides us with a transection of social life, but they are not isomorphous, and each leaves a remainder.

Individual regimes or structures of value imply commensurability among their components (at least within a given "rank" or "sphere" of exchange). I think, however, that incommensurability is as fundamental to culture, society, and human experience as commensurable value is to the functioning of the market. Like the Lévi-Straussian "itch" produced by the grain of sand in the oyster around which the pearl of myth forms (a metaphor I first heard from Sherry Ortner), the incommensurability of meanings and values provides a significant basis for imaginative creation, speculative thought, and innovative practice, as well as for ambiguity and undecidability (Lambek 1993b, 400–403). Incommensurability is the basis of much conversation and is central both to understanding the world and to misunderstanding other people; in short, it is a basis for cultural thickness and richness. (It is certainly an implicit source of much debate—both productive and unproductive—within anthropology itself.) A theory of value must show the limits and limitations of any internally unified regime or structure with respect to commensurability, both in theory and in practice.

This discussion has led us to the third of Graeber's kinds of value: semiotic value. As I use the term, *incommensurability* does not imply a complete absence or blockage of communication or translation but a partial barrier, a lack of clear or complete equivalence that must lead to distortion, juggling, compromise, or working misunderstanding. In the best case scenario, it leads to productive dialogue and a breakthrough to commensurability at a new level of abstraction or to poetry, and perhaps the former is where the anthropological discussion of value is heading. However, my assumption is that between words and objects, language and the material world, there is some incommensurability, and that hence, to the degree that this is so in any given domain, any two languages or language games are likely to be incommensurable with one another with respect to those objects (Lambek 1993b). Obvious examples would be color or kin terminologies or, following Needham and Schneider, the very nature of "kinship" itself; religious cosmology provides an even more complex field.[7]

Translation is never perfect, but it is always interesting. I cannot take concepts that I weakly translate from Malagasy as "spirits" and fully match them up with whatever that word means or has meant in English. French anthropologists have translated the words for these same spirits as "*diables*," which is hardly the same. Malagasy speakers on Mayotte themselves juggle the original Malagasy terms with the Bantu *patros* and the Muslim *djin* and *shetwan*, and now with the French and English glosses. The issue becomes even more complicated when a noun like *God* is used to translate religious concepts like *Kwoth*, whose designators may well be shifters (deictic) in their original languages (Lambek 2008a). It is difficult for the semantic value of words or the paradigm sets to which they may once have belonged and from which they drew semantic value to remain stable under the circumstances.

The problem is not simply one of comparing synchronic structures or integrating words derived from one discrete structure into that of another structure or language, but the fact that words and structures themselves are in motion. As Adam Ashforth reflects as he struggles with representing the discrepancies between what he and his South African subject, Madumo, understand by "witchcraft," the problem is also increasingly that

7. I am side-stepping both social constructionism and Whorfian linguistic relativism here, although obviously the various arguments have relevance for one another.

> the terms we use are already translated from one language and culture to another and back again, over and over through generations. There is no pristine vocabulary of difference available to Madumo to describe his experiences with witchcraft that I could translate and then present to the world in terms familiar to the West; no language to make the words seem unique, or the effort of translation worthwhile. The words, like the worlds, are already pretranslated. And yet, there remains something radically and irreducibly different in his experience of these matters from mine. (Ashforth 2000)

The basic point, as professional translators know, is that there is always a residue. However, as Ashforth's statement implies, commensurability is not only an issue between different languages but also within them. In a sense, this is also Alasdair MacIntyre's complaint in *After Virtue* (1984) about the confused state of ethics in modernity, although MacIntyre may mistake a general feature of the human condition for a historical effect. As John Austin noted, "There is no necessity whatsoever that the various models used in creating our vocabulary, primitive or recent, should all fit together neatly as parts into one single, total model or scheme of, for instance, the doing of actions. It is possible, and indeed highly likely, that our assortment of models will include some, or many that are overlapping, conflicting, or more generally simply *disparate*" (1970, 203; his emphasis).[8]

Austin continues in a footnote:

> This is by way of a general warning in philosophy. It seems to be too readily assumed that if we can only discover the true meanings of each of a cluster of key terms, usually historic terms, that we use in some particular field (as, for example, "right," "good" and the rest in morals), then it must without question transpire that each will fit into place in some single, interlocking, consistent, conceptual scheme. Not only is there no reason to assume this, but all historical probability is against it, especially in the case of a language derived from such various civilizations as ours is. We may cheerfully use, and with weight, terms which are not so much head-on incompatible as simply disparate, which just do not fit in or even on. Just as we cheerfully subscribe to, or have the grace to be torn between, simply disparate ideals—why *must* there be a conceivable amalgam, the Good Life for Man? (Austin 1970, 203, n. 1)

8. Compare also Raymond Williams' *Keywords* (1976) and various recent genealogical accounts.

Phrased another way, it is remarkable that Saussure was correct about the commensurability of the set of phonemes in any given language. Lévi-Strauss and the ethnoscientists notwithstanding (and leaving aside entirely the arguments from pragmatics), the Saussurean model is of limited value to semantics. It works for small islands of related words or concepts, isolated paradigm sets, but hardly for the vast sea of language. If it did, we wouldn't need philosophy.

Although culture is riven with incommensurables and, indeed, incommensurability is necessary and inevitable, various discursive schemes and systems of practice strive mightily to deny or do away with it, to open up spaces of commensurability. Bounded language games and domains of commensurable value are constructed and defended, and they are often reasonably—that is, provisionally—successful. This is one way to understand Weber's notion of rationalization or Foucault's of discursive regimes. The capitalist market, disembedded from the social whole (Polanyi 2001), offers commensurability and transvaluation across a different transection of social life.

Metavalues

When I was a child we played a board game called Careers. As I recall it now, the object of the game was to collect a total of sixty points in three categories, wealth, fame, and happiness—represented, not surprisingly, by dollar signs, stars, and hearts, respectively. At the start of the game, players would each record how many points they aimed to accumulate in each category. The first person to acquire sixty points in the proportions he had established at the beginning was the winner. Given the way the game was set up, the soundest strategy was to go for twenty points in each category. My mother inevitably placed her entire sixty points in the happiness category. Her reasoning was that happiness is all one needs or wants in life; if one were happy one would, by definition, be satisfied with whatever wealth or fame came one's way. Conversely, wealth or fame without happiness would be worth nothing.[9] She was a very literal-minded person, and it was never much fun playing with her.

9. It is tempting to give happiness a specific content, but that is not my intention. Roger Crisp suggests that, "happiness is not sex, wealth and power, but partly at least, justice itself" (1996, 9). May and Abraham Edel remark that there may be alternative conceptions or kinds of happiness, and it may not be always consciously sought. The American conception of happiness

This vignette illustrates a number of points central to my argument. Let us treat economic, political, and ethical value as corresponding to the game's categories of wealth, fame, and happiness, respectively. In the game, they are commensurable insofar as they are each measured in equivalent points. The points—the frame of the game itself—thus provide a metavalue or absolute standard of value—winning or losing—against which these other values are relative. However, once you had placed your bets you couldn't convert one to the other. Money, as they used to say, cannot buy happiness (though there is by now a superfluity of oxymoronically labeled reality television shows that run counter to this proverbial piece of wisdom).

Are wealth, fame, and happiness—in real life now—commensurable, as the framework of the game proposes; are they incommensurable, as the game transpires; or are they arranged hierarchically (possibly in a Dumontian sense) so that one is actually not in competition with but encompasses the others (Dumont 1981)? The answer to this might be historically contingent, as the ethnographic literature, the current state of the world, and the arguments supplied by Mauss, Weber, Simmel, Dumont, and Graeber appear to imply. Or rather, historical contingency might show the range of possibility within certain human constraints.

My mother's argument was essentially that in life happiness has—or ought to have—the function that winning does in the game. It is the aim or end of life, the *telos* that encompasses other values, with respect to which other ends can be evaluated and in whose absence all other ends are actually devoid of value. Within the game, however, happiness was merely equivalent to fame and fortune.

One can debate whether in real life, outside the game, and in this view, outside all games, happiness holds the position of ultimate or metavalue. The most famous argument that it does so is Aristotle's, as presented in the *Nichomachaean Ethics* (1976). Aristotle's position has recently been subject to deconstruction by Jonathan Lear (2000), who argues on the basis of psychoanalytic insight against all teleological arguments (including Freud's).[10] Lear suggests that it is of the nature of mind always to find another goal outside the prevailing system, to fantasize something beyond current values.

---

is "an extremely local view which heavily weights physical comforts, individual achievement, successful mastery of obstacles; which gives a central place to an ideal of forward movement or progress; and which tends to thrust aside such other candidates as 'contentment,' contemplation, and any suggestion of spiritual insight through suffering" (Edel and Edel 2000, 234). This is certainly not what my mother meant.

10. An additional Freudian criticism of Aristotle is that Aristotle underestimates the sources of human unhappiness, in particular those of contradiction, ambivalence, and guilt.

Lear writes, "It is constitutive of human life—life influenced by fantasy, life in society, ethical life—that there is an experience that there is something more to life, something left out. There is an inchoate sense that there is a remainder to life, something that is not captured in life as it is so far experienced. Thus there is pressure to construct an image of what lies outside" (Lear 2000, 163).

In other words, there *is* no "real" life entirely outside of games; the "outside" is always and can only be relative to some frame. But equally, life is a lot more complex than the frame of a single game, even a very large and important one like the cultivation of happiness or the pursuit of *kula*, or capital. The frame is never very solid; there is always something visible or imaginable outside it. Even the Azande, who, Evans-Pritchard famously reported, "reason excellently in the idiom of their beliefs, but . . . cannot reason outside, or against, their beliefs because they have no other idiom in which to express their thoughts" (1937, 338), ought eventually to discover, invent, or imagine alternatives to witchcraft. For Lear, mind is inherently self-disruptive. Whether he is correct that thinking outside the box is the product of either sheer perversity or happenstance, like genetic mutation, or whether we can provide a nobler or more objective source or intention, the general point is well taken and complements my argument that sets of commensurable values always encounter signs, concepts, practices, or values with respect to which they are incommensurable. Lear's point, in sum, is not only that happiness cannot hold the position of ultimate value, but also that nothing can.

However, alongside Lear and the evidence for cultural incommensurability, one could equally argue that it is the nature of society, culture, or mind to posit or require some absolute standard of value or a metavalue that could provide a sound and universal measure of things, and for certain strong thinkers to seek one out—truth for Plato, happiness for Aristotle, God for the Judeo-Christian-Islamic tradition, meaning for Weber, justice for political liberals, profit for capitalism, possibly creative labor for Marx. But such aims are never finally successful. There is a dialectic in human history between establishing absolute values against which everything else is relative and to be measured—hence rendered commensurable to one another—and discovering things that render those absolutes relative in turn. (I think we can agree that Hegel was right about dialectics and wrong about totality.) Commoditization is only one, albeit very powerful and comprehensive, means by which values get relativized. This dialectic operates both at the rhythm of the historical *longue durée* and within the scope of the individual human life. It is, in a sense, Weber's problem of meaning.

We weave the fabric according to a pattern, but inevitably it stretches thin in some places, or the style changes.[11] Webs are flimsy; spiders, assiduous.

A key point here is that, while values are commensurable with respect to a given metavalue, metavalues themselves are incommensurable with one another.[12] Among other things, this complicates the reconstruction of theory; it is thus quite misleading to make a list of truth, happiness, God, and labor as I have just done. Happiness is posited by Aristotle as itself a final value, the end of life; the Judeo-Christian-Islamic God is the arbiter, guarantor, and, in Christianity at least, redeemer of value; in capitalism, money is reckoned ostensibly as a measure and store of value rather than as its substance; for Marx, creative labor is the source of value; and so on. Truth, justice, happiness, faith, labor, and wealth simply do not map perfectly onto one another, not even in the abstract.

Exceptions to and Expansions of the Concept of Metavalue

Incommensurability evokes the anthropological problems of translation and comparison in a nutshell, but it does not render them impossible (Lambek 1991b) nor vitiate theorizing. As noted, many theories would argue or assume that relative value be defined with respect to some kind of logically higher standard or metavalue, which is itself, in this context, claimed not to be relative. Such claims may be logically necessary, but no individual claim of this order is sustainable in the long run. Absolutes are impossible, either because of the nature of the world or, as Lear would have it, the nature of our minds, or (doubtless) both. More immediately, in no two societies, interest groups, or social positions will people continue to agree on the relevant metavalue or on how to apply it. Thus the absolute or metavalue is at risk of becoming relativized or of having its relativity revealed and hence of being displaced, after some confusion, by another standard.

An interesting exception to arguments that values are set respective to metavalues lies with structuralism (and perhaps the various poststructuralisms). At least, this is one of structuralism's most interesting claims. Saussurean value is always and only relative, in the sense of being

11. The allusion here is not only to Weber, which as a German common noun means "weaver," but, as students of Sahlins will know, to Benedict on patterns and Lowie on shreds and patches of culture, no less than to Kroeber on cycles of dress style.

12. Along with MacIntyre and others, I reject the utilitarian idea that human goals can be measured against each other like commodities against a standard of money.

the product of relations to other terms. The explicit metavalue is replaced or its function taken by the structure understood as a whole.[13] In the *Mythologiques* (1970–81) Lévi-Strauss explodes the notion of the whole, following instead chains, loops, and spirals of signifying relations. But because of the absence of a hierarchy of value, the more he does so, the more arbitrary and pointless signification appears to become, until the value of "meaningful difference" itself approaches nil, that is to say, until semiotic value itself appears to have no value.

In sharp contrast to structuralism, Rappaport (1999) is concerned precisely with hierarchies of meaning or value and metavalue, phrased in his language as sacred postulates. It is part of the genius of his work on ritual and sanctity to show how what I have described as the dialectic of constructing and destroying standards of value gets slowed down or, rather, moves at different rates at different levels of the hierarchy, so that stability, trust, and meaning are possible. (He also shows how this process has been damaged under capitalism.) Rappaport thus provides a framework for understanding the articulation of relative and absolute values within any specific social system and religious tradition.

In one respect Rappaport's argument approaches that of Lévi-Strauss: Rappaport argues that metavalues do their work best when they are stripped of informational content and specificity. Ultimate sacred postulates like "God is one" may be deeply meaningful to their adherents, but they are effective and enduring because they are referentially empty and unfalsifiable. This, in turn, affords an interesting comparison with Lear. Lear speaks of the human predilection to be seduced by enigmatic signifiers: "oracular utterances, . . . which we can recognize as having a meaning—indeed as having a special meaning *for us*—but whose content we do not understand. [He is thinking not of mysticism but of "happiness" in Aristotle and "death" in Freud.] But the latent content of seduction is the idea that there is an explanatory end-of-the-line, an Archimedean point of explanation" (Lear 2000, 21).

For Rappaport, the lack of content of what he calls ultimate sacred postulates is significant not for its seductive, oracular quality but for the way it serves to bind and insulate sets of values from untoward forces—including the very activity of the mind in producing seductive fantasies—and especially from corruption by values of greater specificity that operate in favor of

13. Or perhaps one could say that the ground of value for one level of a hierarchy is established by another; thus the value of phonemics would be set by morphology. Dumont's hierarchies of encompassment may be something of this order.

narrower and more immediate interests. Ultimate sacred postulates are not Archimedean points of explanation; rather, as final sources of authority at arm's length from particular political or social arrangements, they exercise a critical social, regulative, or, as Rappaport might have it, ecological function. When socially specific values move up the regulative hierarchy, a phenomenon Rappaport refers to as "idolatry," the result is socially and ethically chaotic and harmful. As philosopher and psychoanalyst, Lear's analysis and critique concerns abstract or personal systems of thought, whereas, as anthropologist, Rappaport's concerns functioning social systems and human ways of life.

Finally, I note that Kantians may have a very different view of metavalue. Thomas Hill writes of what he calls "deep deliberation," which entails rational review of one's ends and commitments as well as one's means in order to justify one's choices not just to others but to oneself.

> The "preferences" or "ends" that I have attributed to deep deliberations are not highly variable first-order values like a love of chocolate or philosophy; nor are they the substantive controversial values that philosophers have debated since ancient times, like fame, power, wealth, pleasure, and peace of mind. The alleged "end" or "value" I presume deep deliberators to have, as implicit in the questions they raise, is just the procedural, second-order concern that one's choices, whatever their content, be capable of surviving a kind of deeply reflective scrutiny of and by oneself. (Hill 1991, 177–78)

The nonsubstantive metavalue here is that one's choices survive self-scrutiny and "the commitment to make my choices justifiable to myself later" (186).

Choice : Judgment :: Commensurability : Incommensurability

I argued earlier that it is important to distinguish choice and judgment. Admittedly, it is also difficult to say precisely how they differ from one another. I suggested that this is because they are incommensurable, but that doesn't help a lot. At this point I should acknowledge that I have not read the philosophical literature that is presumably addressed to the issue. I want to suggest, however, that *choice* is the operative term among a set of items commensurable among themselves, or with respect to a given metavalue. In these contexts relative values are readily distinguished according to the axis of comparison—price or utility in the case of commodities—that makes them commensurable with one another. Choice in this sense is relatively easy; the alternatives are discrete and measurable, and sometimes not a lot is at stake. Advertising to the contrary, most brands of laundry detergent or antacids—and possibly even injury-claims lawyers—are equally effective.[14] To be sure, calculations of profit can become quite complex. Equally, in the absence of a clear axis of difference, choice can be difficult and merges into judgment.[15] Choosing between the purchase of apples and oranges is straightforward when price is the only consideration; deciding what to order from a menu when price is not a consideration, as we have seen, is another matter altogether.[16] This raises the complex matter of aesthetic judgment or taste, which I briefly address below.

In contrast to choice, judgment applies to incommensurables—that is, in contexts where there is no standard of measurement or the alternatives cannot be clearly compared along a single axis. Here, judgment has at least the following overlapping dimensions or qualities. Following Aristotle, it entails first establishing a balance between extremes, finding the golden mean between, for example, selfishness and self-sacrifice, where the mean is the virtue situated between two opposing vices. Second, it entails the Aristotelian virtue of *phronesis*, or practical judgment—that is, fitting one's conduct to meet the particular context and circumstances, and also discerning between alternative interpretations of the context. Third, judgment entails balancing among alternate human goals or virtues that are incommensurable to one another (for example, justice and compassion).[17] Fourth, here implicitly following Rappaport, judgment entails discernment with respect to a hierarchy of values and metavalues running from the more relative and situational to the more absolute and encompassing, with respect to which there can be less compromise or alternative. One must know when to invoke the higher-order values, which thereby risk compromise by the contingent circumstances, and when to leave them behind the scenes.

In sum, *ethical and market value are incommensurable with one another precisely because economics chooses between commensurable values operative under a single metavalue, while ethics judges among incommensurable values or metavalues.*

14. However, the very act of seeking to make a choice (a purchase, for instance) may entail judgment. This is the sort of issue addressed in Miller's work on consumption (1998). Moreover some financial choices may be very consequential.

15. This is captured in the old joke about the Jewish mother who buys her son two neckties. He puts one on, and she says, "So what's the matter, you don't like the other one?"

16. Recall the menus without prices that were once handed to women in the company of men in expensive restaurants.

17. However, some virtue theorists argue that the virtues are harmonious and complementary rather than competing.

Choice and judgment in my usage are of course ideal types, and the distinction may be inappropriate or impossible to sustain in all cultural contexts or domains of human activity. After all, we speak about choosing from a menu rather than exercising judgment about what to eat. In fact, I don't know how to express the distinction between choice and judgment with respect to aesthetics.[18] Perhaps coming to grips with that very discernment is one of the prime objectives of aesthetic theory. Here too the crux may concern whether and how metavalues are brought into play, and whether comparison is understood as taking place between commensurable or incommensurable criteria. One might say that choice becomes judgment when the ethical dimensions of practice are realized, and the incommensurability of ostensible alternatives is recognized; judgment is reduced to choice when they are elided.

Is Competition Ubiquitous?

It is obvious that the pursuit of value is not always undertaken virtuously and that even virtuous acts do not always rule out competition. It is not only that virtue ethics includes attention to vice and that therefore to assess the ethical value of particular acts is not necessarily to judge them positively. Certain games or practices require that value be exhibited in material tokens that more ascetic regimes, such as some forms of Protestant and Kantian ethics, would decry. This produces the ubiquitous phenomenon of "tournaments of value" (Appadurai 1986; Meneley 1996)—for example, which suburban house has the neatest lawn?—and the tension between display and the potency of concealment (Graeber 2001). Such tournaments embrace conspicuous consumption, exhibitions of taste, and competitive hospitality or generosity, but also the striving for excellence (and the risk of failing) in a variety of domains and arenas from "lifestyle" to sport and academic papers—even to competitive modesty. Such endeavors are by no means specific to capitalist societies. They can be analyzed along lines of "economic" value and sheer competition when they entail a clear axis of measurement or discrimination.

Taste is obviously no more a matter of unique and autonomous sensibility than choice is ever "free." Bourdieu has shown the degree to which it is constrained or cultivated by such forces as class and hence can be viewed as objectified rather than subjective (1984). Yet objectification does not rule

18. Certainly, many writers would not wish to equate judgment with taste.

out incommensurability, and the appellation of tournaments of value can be too simple and may overlook what I would consider the ethical rather than the purely "economic" dimensions of value. Here I mention a few cautions that serve to illustrate that competition need hardly be the only or central thing at issue.

First, the lens of competition is inappropriate when means and ends are not fully distinguished, as for example, in sportsmanship or in the pleasure of listening to or making music, or indeed in the enjoyment of giving and receiving gifts and hospitality. These are values that MacIntyre (1984) refers to as "internal" to a given practice and might include particular kinds of skill, grace, or beauty. Tournaments transform the values internal to a practice into a commensurable medium that extends "externally" between practices, as when amateur players turn professional. When the competition remains internal to the practice, it is incommensurable with things outside of it.[19]

Values internal to a practice may also be said to be operative more with respect to expanding what Macpherson (1973) terms the human capacities, whereas the external relations are more readily described as ones of utility. It is only with the shift from capacity to utility that the question of scarcity becomes relevant and hence that we can speak of competition.

Second, there is often no single axis of measurement for virtuosity in a given "tournament"; incommensurables are at issue, and judgment is critical. This is not to say that there are no axes of discrimination. Scoring by judges of Olympic gymnasts or ranking students for fellowships are possible yet also uncomfortable insofar as one realizes that judgment spills over choice or measurement.

Third, Friedman rightly critiques Bourdieu's account of taste insofar as it is based entirely on establishing class or other specific status distinctions.[20] Consumption in modernity, he argues, is not merely a definition of one's social position but "a material realization, or attempted realization, of the image of the good life" (1990, 105). In the case of the *sapeurs*—the competitive dressers of Brazzaville—appearances are deceiving. Elegance is a moral practice and not to be reduced to a mere quest for distinction. Rather, the relative value of the clothes and their labels subsists in a wider context of

19. The question of how broad the scope of any given practice is remains open—for example, the practice of the spirit medium in a specific performance as a spirit, the practice of mediumship as a career, or the practice of a unified life of which mediumship is a part (Lambek 1988a). This is a large issue that I cannot address here.

20. My thanks to Jackie Solway for directing me to this essay.

value that is not that of the market but of Congolese understandings about catching and maintaining power. Friedman argues that the clothes come to be constitutive of who their wearers are; in this respect the *sapeur* is quite distinct from the European "dandy" (at least as Friedman understands the latter). Congolese ideas of power constitute a higher value—absolute with respect to the game of dressing well—and one that changes much more slowly.

A similar lesson can be drawn from Meneley's elegant discussion of Yemeni hospitality (1996) and other interpretive accounts of what might sometimes better be called spectacles of value. The more general point is that insofar as values are relative, they enable and may even entail competition or a sense of mutual evaluation among people who embrace them. But insofar as they are subsumed under a metavalue that is not itself understood as commensurable or scarce, the relevance of competition as the axis of interpretation has its limits. This point is recognized in the frequently observed paradox in many ethical systems that drawing attention to one's virtuous acts (overt display, or possibly even any self-consciousness) undermines the value of what is being indicated. Here the virtue of dignity trumps generosity, fame, and so on. As the Sakalava say, "Full containers don't rattle."[21]

Finally, the ubiquity of competition gleaned from the ethnographic literature may be exaggerated. The virtuous path, to follow Aristotle once again, is a path of moderation. Acts of moderation tend to get overlooked in accounts and reanalyses of societies such as the Trobriands, Kwakiutl, and Maori—or, for that matter, of capitalism. This may be because it is the selfish, aggressive pursuit of value by some that sets the conditions of life for others. It may also be because description of extreme acts and obsessive practices makes for more interesting reception or serves a more potent ideological function (witness Donald Trump on the reality TV show *The Apprentice*) than judicious ones that by their very nature do not call attention to themselves. It may be a product of the ethnographic practice of abstracting particular local practices from the matrix of alternate and incommensurable ones. A Trobriand player of *kula* is also a husband, a brother and brother-in-law, a maternal uncle, a resident of a locality, and a chief or a follower—each of these relationships providing obligations, rewards, and arenas for virtuous practice that must in fact impinge on his judgment of how much *kula* to play, how to play it, and so forth. The value of *kula* must ultimately

21. See Lambek (2002a), and compare Graeber (2001) on display more generally.

be understood relative to other, possibly incommensurate values as well as to the more encompassing metavalues concerning the kind of person one is or aspires to be and the kind of life one lives or aspires to live. The situation is similar for a scholar, an athlete, a stockbroker, and so forth. Persons and lives are unlikely to be fully understandable in competitive terms. It may be also that the societies selected by Mauss (1990) are precisely those in which, for particular structural or historical reasons, competition was encouraged or required (cf. MacIntyre on the virtues characteristic of "heroic" societies). If so, and following in the spirit of Mauss himself, we should not see such tournaments of value as ideological mirrors of capitalism.

In sum, the significance of tournaments of value depends in part on whether they are construed as internal or external to specific practices and thus, in part, on whether the emphasis is placed on means or ends—and on how these are linked up to, or embedded within, other practices and values.

Any healthy society enables the "exercise of the capacities." This is something quite distinct from the logic of capitalist accumulation (Macpherson 1973), and it will necessarily involve practices that seek to discern, produce, or enhance value through the overcoming of some kind of obstacle. However such "labor" is not to be understood as external to its ends.

Religion

I began this chapter with the concern that in capitalism virtue appears to be converted into value. There is a domain, however, in which the reverse may observed—namely, religion. To begin with, it is evident that certain kinds of rituals transform value into virtue. They do this by means of the money and labor that goes into their performance and that is displayed and consumed during that performance. Rappaport's discussion of rituals of display, such as the potlatch, makes more or less this point (1999). Here we could acknowledge that what has appeared to outsiders as tournaments of value can have profound moral significance for participants. The accumulated wealth or number of followers gathered may be counted and marked, but ultimately what they display is force or *mana*, or some equivalent concept. More generally, Burridge (1969) writes of religions as forms of redemption and notes the frequent concern over money in millenarian movements. Even in a middle-class church service, when the collection plate is passed or when congregants donate to charity, this kind of transformation takes place. It is as though one of the functions of religion were "money-laundering," turning "ill-gotten" gains, or at least the profits and earnings of the everyday world, into such virtues as largesse, generosity, charity, or honor. The transformation of wealth into sanctity is central to Bloch's analysis of ritual in highland Madagascar (1989c), and it forms a highly salient part of the annual ritual at the Sakalava shrine on the west coast (Lambek 2002a). One of the means by which ritual achieves this feat is through the use of a digital code that, as Rappaport explains, permits what communications engineers call the transduction of information between incommensurable systems. This is achieved by reducing complex information down to a binary signal (Rappaport 1999, 97–98). This function of religion may provide one kind of explanation for its popularity, which is expanding alongside the penetration and expansion of the capitalist economy. Indeed, it may provide the only way not just to siphon off capital, but to transcend capitalist regimes of value.

The Ox and the Beef (*Le Boeuf et Du Boeuf*)

I close with some remarks on my epigraph that, I fear, I have abused, using it to illustrate points that were not those of its author. Marx draws upon the image of the passive ox in order to criticize Adam Smith for supposing that the value in labor is constituted in simple sacrifice, understood as the forsaking of rest (Marx 1971, 126). For Marx, the source of value cannot lie in pure negation, in the ox's passive sacrifice. Labor is to be understood as a positive, creative engagement with and upon the world. Among other things, labor is not to be measured quantitatively, as pure time spent; its nature is to be discerned in the quality of the act, hence, in my terms, with respect to ethical rather than simply economic value. Thus the foundation of value is not passive sacrifice of time but active productive labor. Famously, of course, Marx also argued that in capitalism the connection between this ultimate source of value and the currency of circulating values is occluded and mystified. The heart of the problem lies in the transvaluation of acts into objects, epitomized in the commodification of labor (and often referred to as alienation), on the one side, and the re-transvaluation epitomized in the fetishism of commodities (objects into agents), on the other.

Marx's theory of the production of value is of course highly relevant to the present discussion and forms a whole field of scholarship in itself (see Eiss and Pedersen 2002). One of the distinctive strengths of Marx's analysis is that it transcends the rather static quality of value portrayed in formal models. In Marx, value is active and always in systemic and historical motion. Value is continuously being produced, congealed, circulated, expropriated, hidden, displayed, contested, fetishized—subject to transformation as it moves from one sphere to another. It is like a current of electricity but with its source always in human activity. It is the understanding of value as a quality or product in the first instance of intentional acts rather than arbitrary objects (like sapphires) that informs the best anthropological work on value.[22]

Here I wish to speak not of the beef but of the ox. I think there is more to the ox than Marx allows. It is striking how many societies posit blood sacrifice at the root or grounds of value.[23] Sacrifice lies at the heart of many foundational myths, and it may serve as an act of ultimate or metavalue against which other acts come to have value with respect to one another. It is as if the fluctuating economic value of beef *is* somehow established or contextualized with respect to the constant and absolute value of the life of the ox. This is true of sacrifice in the Abrahamic (Judeo-Christian-Islamic) tradition but also in many others. We might think not only of Homeric Greek myth but also of the death of Socrates at the origin of Western philosophy. My own insights derive from the place of sacrifice in the Sakalava polity of northwest Madagascar.

In each of these cases, this base is at once temporal—posited as a historical precedent—and structural. For Freud, sacrifice—aggressive and then renunciative—is the source of kinship, the family, religion, and psychological maturity. For Durkheim, more abstractly, it is the means of social self-transcendence, and for Lévi-Strauss, it is the basis of the gift and hence of society. Recounted and enacted in a cycle of love and violence that rivals in saliency the myths of Abraham and Oedipus, Sakalava sacrifice is the source of political legitimacy, determined agency, sacred power and truth, and the meaning of history (see chapter 9 and Lambek 2001b, 2002a, 2007b, 2008a).[24] Sakalava sacrifice is neither as passive as Marx understood it nor as aggressive or forced as Freud saw it, but ideally a virtuous act of will on the part of the victim. A cow or ox that complains is spared; it is evidently not giving itself willingly and signals that neither is its owner offering it willingly.[25]

22. On transvaluation, see the beautiful discussion by Eiss of the transformation of value among meat, money, and grace in Mexico (2002). On the containment and fetishization of value by Sakalava, see Lambek (2001b). On the opacity and currents of value associated with sapphires, see Walsh (2004); conversely, on the impact of circulating ideas of virtue on the value of diamonds, see Solway (2007, 2009). On questions of the semiotics of materiality more generally, see Graeber (2001) and Keane (2007).

23. Or, as in the case of the Jains, the explicit rejection of blood sacrifice (Babb 2003).

24. Research among Sakalava of Mahajanga throughout the 1990s and subsequently has been supported by the Social Science and Humanities Research Council of Canada.

25. I disregard here additional cultural specificity—notably, the fact that among Sakalava, the prototypical hero/victim is a woman rather than a man (Lambek 2007b).

Marx's proverb is thus extremely apt, but his own interpretation of it is wrong. Sacrifice is not a passive act,[26] and it is hardly without consequence for the production of value. Sacrifice, especially self-sacrifice, is a virtuous act, an exemplary instance of judgment rather than choice. If anything, it situates economic value narrowly conceived (market value) with respect to political, religious, and ethical value—the value of objects with respect to the value of acts. Sacrifice is a site for the production of metavalue, for the transformation of value into metavalue, and of relative value into absolute value. Indeed, sacrifice may come to index and iconically represent transvaluation itself.

Marx is correct insofar as his conception fits the passivity of the bourgeoisie, understood not as the sacrificed ox but as the complacent consumers of beef. Beef is simply on sale at the butcher's, or better, the restaurant; the slaughter of the ox is invisible (except in ethnographic film, where animal sacrifice is ubiquitous) and the labor of raising it is not the consumer's. Under capitalism, perhaps we have lost the connection between positive acts of sacrifice and the secular values by which we run our lives or choose what to consume. In the post-Puritan world it is assumed that value is something to be gained at no cost to the self—as interest, dividends, or other forms of exchange value. Perhaps that is also part of the explanation for why we are never really satisfied.[27]

Nevertheless, there remains in the West, as elsewhere, also the conception that blood sacrifice—the active, even positive, renunciation (or threat of renunciation) of life, whether that of Abraham or Jesus, Socrates or Wilhelm Tell, or even the valiant unknown soldier or humble cancer victim—lies at the heart (the bloody, beating heart) of human value.[28] This need have nothing to do with asceticism as we commonly understand it. At least, the systems of value it has shored up include those exemplifying dubious forms of display, power, hierarchy, military aggression, and exploitation.

Sacrifice is frequently analyzed with respect to exchange rather than production, yet exchange is but one sort of value transaction, one kind of act that needs to be grounded in metavalue. Taking a cue again from Sakalava, blood sacrifice itself need not be primarily a matter of exchange. Sacrifice,

26. See also Asad (2003b) on the agency that adheres in suffering.

27. I owe the idea of no-cost value to a lecture long ago by Aram Yengoyan. As both Macpherson (1973) and Sahlins (1996) demonstrate, there is a long tradition of neediness in which Western philosophy can be seen almost as a complaint discourse in search of a fix.

28. The wars that lie at the heart of so many national mythologies, the tombs of unknown soldiers, statues of leaders who died under fire, and the like, are all evocations of sacrifice (cf. Verdery 1999).

as a *productive* act, often initiates a state of affairs (see chapter 9), opening moral vectors, introducing specific commitments, establishing the seriousness of the ensuing values and acts—the ends and means—that are at stake. These are among the performative effects of ritual in Rappaport's analysis, in which commitment to the liturgical order is intrinsic to its enactment. Blood sacrifice is not part of his analysis, but it seems to provide a vivid iconic as well as indexical instantiation of what is at issue. It is certainly something that, once conducted, is not retractable. Hence it epitomizes absolute rather than negotiable value, an incommensurable act, or Kantian dignity, rather than a commensurable object, or Kantian price.

Sacrifice also exemplifies the power of transvaluation, in which the act of destroying something of one kind of value is actually productive of some other kind of value.[29] When it is marked, it emphasizes not the transformation of ethical into material value, of life into meat, but rather the reverse; frequently it is a transvaluation of the material to the ideal, of "bare" life to ethical, human life, of commensurable value (one ox or another) to indexically established, incommensurable metavalue (*this* ox, *my* act).

One might speculate that if, after Aristotle, the virtuous path is one of moderation, metavalue is created by acts of immoderation, acts of metavirtue. I take the prime instance of such acts of metavirtue to be what we conventionally call sacrifice, the life of the ox for the ox. The sacrifice of life marks or determines life as valuable. Sacrifice suggests that the ground of human value is *life*, that life itself is the absolute or primary metavalue (cf. Bloch 1992; Ruel 1997; Agamben 1998). In this respect, Aristotle's conception of *eudaimonia*—happiness, human flourishing—as an ultimate end may not be so far off the mark.

Conclusion: Virtue and Value

Alliteration aside, what is virtue doing in this chapter alongside value? Perhaps we should reserve *virtue* to the ascription of acts and "value" to objects. Moreover, virtue could be understood as internal to acts or practices, whereas value is generally external to objects (but see Weiner 1992). Value is something we attribute to practice viewed from outside, as though the practice were an object (as in the commoditization of labor); virtue expresses the qualities needed to excel in the practice viewed from the inside. Yet value has also been used to acknowledge both the productive qualities

29. This may be explicit in some systems of thought, for example, among the Kwakiutl (Goldman 1975).

and the intentional orientations of acts, and many of the most interesting discussions in the field have transcended easy distinctions between acts and objects. Virtue also marks a shift in anthropological discussions of ethics away from the dominant Durkheimian view of rule and obligation toward practice and character. I offer two alternative conclusions. Take your pick. Or use your judgment.

Conclusion One

By using the word *virtue,* I have been drawing attention to a universal ethical dimension of human practice. I have also been expressing a judgment concerning which ethical theory among utilitarianism, Kantianism, and virtue ethics I find most valuable. Even if MacIntyre is right to suggest that virtue theory cannot be applied coherently or consistently today, it remains true that it corresponds better than the other two theories to what is empirically the case, not only in a vast range of pre- or extra-modern societies, but among ourselves. We do strive much of the time to do what is right and to do so with respect to standards of excellence. Such an endeavor, understood as situated judgment with respect to articulating a variety of incommensurable practices, may be understood as itself a kind of practice of practice, or metapractice. To bring this close to home, we strive to write the best papers we can while balancing our work on them with our other commitments. We do this because we have learned to care about both the practice and the outcome, not in rational calculation of the greatest good—a theory which, in effect, would have us reduce judgment to choice; not because we feel rationally bound, against our inner desires, to follow the rules; and not exclusively in a tournament of value, in a game of Careers or in a career understood as a game, in aspiring to gain greater prestige, power, or income. We do it because (on whatever neurotic basis) that is who we are or who we have come to be. *Who we are* is something larger than can be described or circumscribed by any single hierarchy of value or set of commensurable values.

Conclusion Two

In a holistic universe, maybe there was no clear separation between quality and quantity, nor between acts and objects, means and ends, or perspectives located inside and outside practice. Following Mauss, maybe there was no clear distinction between public and private; person and individual; society, religion, and economy; gift and commodity; virtue and value.

I only partly believe in the historical existence of this holistic universe, although I do value it as an ideal type (in both senses of "ideal"). Our immediate experience should not limit our ability to imagine qualitatively distinct alternatives to capitalism. But I am afraid that pictures of the holistic universe are sometimes influenced a bit too strongly by what we would like to see. In addition, insofar as these alternate social worlds are pictured simply as mirror images of capitalist modernity, that is, binary distinctions of quality versus quantity and so forth, they become measurable against the present, commensurable along an axis of comparison. Everything I have said here leads me to think, to the contrary, that the alternatives—why limit them to just one?—are incommensurable rather than commensurable with capitalist modernity, and hence—and this may sound paradoxical—that these alternate social worlds are in some ways more different but less easily distinguishable from our own than we imagine.

ELEVEN

Toward an Ethics of the Act

This is the chapter in which the ideas about practice and performance raised in chapter 1 are most fully developed. The essay was originally much longer and was rather arbitrarily severed from what became the introduction to Ordinary Ethics. Ordinary Ethics *itself was the product of an intense conversation that took place at a workshop I convened in Toronto in 2008 following a graduate seminar organized with Paul Antze and Jack Sidnell in 2006. Some respondents to the essay have taken the first sentence too literally, as though they had not continued to read the following two sentences.*

Where is the ethical located? I shall argue that it is intrinsic to action. I look at action in two related ways—as specific acts (performance) and ongoing judgment (practice)—and show that ethics is a function of each. Criteria for practical judgment are established and acknowledged in performative acts, while acts emerge from the stream of practice. Performance draws on previously established criteria, or felicity conditions, in order to produce its effects. These effects can be understood as committing performers to one particular alternative or set of alternatives out of many, and these commitments in turn inform subsequent evaluations of practice, and thus practical judgment itself, but they do not determine practice. A simple illustration follows. Insofar as the performance of a wedding instantiates the state of marriage, it provides criteria for evaluating the actors' subsequent practice as spouses. The act of marriage does not determine whether people remain "faithful" or practice "adultery," but it entails that their actions fall under

This chapter first appeared in *Ordinary Ethics: Anthropology, Language, and Action* (New York: Fordham University Press, 2010), 39–63.

such descriptions. If practice is rendered possible and meaningful through performative acts, practice also inevitably reveals the inadequacy of such acts and the limits of criteria and descriptions, especially their vulnerability to skepticism, and hence the need to start anew. Ethics, then, is not only about executing acts, establishing criteria, and practicing judgment, but also about confronting their limits, and ours.

A Personal Prolegomenon

The ethical has come to seem central and even necessary for my work along at least three overlapping routes. First, there has been my experience in the field, experiences (*Erlebnis*) that, across different sites and over many decades, have in this respect not changed in the slightest, except insofar as it is *my* experience (*Erfahrung*) that has grown or ripened.[1] Very simply, the people I encountered have attempted, routinely—but also anything but routinely—to do what they think right or good, sometimes as a matter of course, sometimes in a struggle to know what the right path was, and sometimes ineffectively, infelicitously, inconsistently, incontinently, or not at all, but always with respect to what they or others think or have established as right or good. They also interpreted the actions and characters of others by criteria similar to those they applied to themselves. Put another way, they have acted largely from a sense of their own dignity; they have refused positions or attributions of indignity, and they have treated, or understood that they ought to treat, others as bearing dignity of their own. I do not think the Malagasy speakers I have met are exceptional in this regard, yet social theory has focused almost exclusively on rules, power, interest, and desire as forces or motivations for action.[2]

Second, and to move up a level of abstraction, in trying to interpret and account for the acts and practices I encountered, I discovered the inadequacy or limited nature of previous theoretical models that attempt to explain a rich cultural tradition and set of practices with respect to the needs and immediate intentions of its participants and that reduce intention to interest, compulsion, obligation, competition, or imitation, hence to a kind

1. The German distinction between Erfahrung and Erlebnis captures something not directly available in English experience; see Martin Jay's (2005) comprehensive account.

2. I do recognize that the attempt to do right or good is often distorted by rationalization, self-deception, or denying the humanity of others. As Jackie Solway (personal communication) has pointed out, particular distortions may be characteristic of specific regimes of power, such as capitalism, slavery, and so forth.

of social or psychobiological mechanics, or, in the least mechanical of cases, to deception or game playing, thus formulating action either too automatically, too strategically, too self-consciously, or too self-interestedly, but never seriously, complexly, judiciously, passionately, or even ambivalently.[3] Spirit possession, for example, became an epiphenomenon rather than a practice, genre, tradition, or form of life that exists in its own right and that enables human creativity and skill in no less a fashion than any artistic or religious tradition that scholars of the humanities hold dear.[4] Moreover, as I have come to understand it, in its combination of passion and action, playfulness and seriousness, spirit possession itself is replete with moral insight.[5] Indeed, no less than Islam, Christianity, or Hinduism, spirit possession offers the means (for those who accept it) to cultivate an ethical disposition or sensibility.

Third, and moving to a yet higher level of abstraction, I have been deeply influenced by the later work of Roy Rappaport on the illocutionary function of ritual and hence from ritual back to ordinary language as formulated in J. L. Austin. From my other teacher, Aram Yengoyan, I was directed to *Must We Mean What We Say?* by Austin's student, Stanley Cavell, though twenty-five years were to pass before I took Yengoyan's advice, or perhaps was only then able to begin to understand what Cavell meant by what he wrote. Whereas Rappaport informed me of his own impatience with the hair-splitting of philosophers, I was taken by Cavell's complex style (evident in a lesser key in Clifford Geertz). Such a style adds to the locutionary, illocutionary, and perlocutionary means of language what I have the conceit to think of as the circumlocutionary. In the right hands, the fineness of insight expressed

3. Weber, of course, is a partial exception, but most Weberian-inspired anthropologists have been impatient with Geertz's attention to meaning and ambiguity, and have searched for more muscular kinds of explanation (Ortner 2006).

4. It seems odd to keep making the point. This is, in a nutshell, the critique of Lewis 1971 as set forth in Lambek 1981 and Boddy 1989, as well as by a number of other scholars. The argument can be found at a more abstract level (with no reference to spirit possession per se) in Sahlins 1976, but structural or cultural mediation says nothing about the forces underlying or stemming from specific actions.

5. Again, see Lambek 1981. On the ethical practice of spirit mediums, see Lambek 1993, 2002a, 2002c; on various other ethical dimensions of possession, see chapters 4, 7, and 8 as well as Lambek 1988a, 2002b, 2003a, 2007a, and 2010a. When I say "spirit possession," I refer in the first instance to the traditions and sets of practices I have encountered and described on the island of Mayotte and in northwest Madagascar in fieldwork since 1975. I leave open to what degree this might be exemplary of some broader category or family of traditions and practices of "spirit possession" that are not culturally specific, thus embracing forms of life found in West Africa, Brazil, Malaysia, and so forth (Boddy 1994; Johnson 2014).

through circumlocution is no less than that to be found in the directness and clarity of Austin; Cavell speaks truth to the consequentiality of speaking and the recursiveness of human experience.[6]

Rather than providing specific lessons that could be summarized from their texts, writers like Cavell and Derrida offer their readers, as Cavell puts it, the opportunity of being read by their texts (somewhat as attentive participants are "read" by their observation of spirit possession or students of traditional Qur'anic recitation come to embody the text). This is reading as ethical experience. Immersion in ethnographic fieldwork is similar, as the fieldworker is "read" or tested in multiple ways. But irrespective of any insight or wisdom forged in this manner, the interpretation of ethnographic phenomena should contribute to the expansion and refinement of philosophy's attempts to reformulate and address classic problems.

Having criticized reductionist arguments, I am equally uneasy about jumping to a position directly in opposition to them, namely, to seeing the human condition as essentially one of freedom (or reason) and, as a corollary, where this primary freedom is constrained, as inevitably one of resistance (ending, thereby, exactly back in a reductionist position). That is to forget all we know about structure, cultural mediation, social interpellation, violence, subjectivity, and psychic conflict. Recognizing that people want to do good and that attending to intention or motivation is critical for understanding human life is necessary but insufficient. Such insights cannot account for all the contexts in which good intention is derailed or misguided. Nor can they displace the analysis of particular cultural models and social practices, or the general ways in which speech and action work. I argue that ethics is an intrinsic dimension of human activity and interpretation, irrespective of whether people are acting in ways that they or we consider specifically "ethical" or ethically positive at any given moment. One can neither reduce human motivation to the ethical nor, as James Laidlaw argues (2010), reduce the ethical to human psychology.

6. One might distinguish between two ideologies (or ethics) of writing—Austinian plain speaking, in which one's word is one's bond, and therefore clarity is of the essence (though Austin himself is also deeply ironic), and the circumlocutionary or otherwise indirect forms characteristic of Socrates (Plato), Derrida, or Cavell, in which wisdom is to recognize what (or that) one does not know or cannot put into direct words. However, the work of the reader includes avoiding "an act of pious merger with Cavell's . . . all-but-inimitable sensitivity" (Gould 2003, 54).

How to Recognize and Produce Ethical Criteria and Judgment through Ritual Performance

Ethics entails judgment (evaluation) with respect to situations, actions, and, cumulatively, actors, persons, or character.[7] The exercise of judgment is prospective (evaluating what to do, how to live), immediate (doing the right thing, drawing on what is at hand, jumping in), and retrospective (acknowledging what has been done for what it was and is). Articulated more strongly as forms of action, these can be epitomized, respectively, as promising, beginning, and forgiving (Arendt 1998, 237–46). Judgment is both of others, thus social and conventional, and for oneself, thus linked to freedom and self-fashioning but also to responsibility, care, guilt, forgiveness, and insight, and to recognizing the limits of what one can know or do or understand.

In order to exercise judgment, there must be criteria. Whence come criteria? I assume some come from mind and some from experience. But criteria are also instantiated through human speech and action. Ethics is intrinsic because there are always criteria already in place, because speaking entails and generates criteria, and because there are always places where disagreement over criteria or their absence is troubling. Criteria serve as the basis for judging how to conduct oneself—whether to commit or exercise specific acts, to what ends and in what manner—but also for deciding what constitutes a given act or kind of act; where specific acts begin and end; whether acts have in fact been committed correctly, completely, and legitimately (Austin's felicity conditions); and how to evaluate one's own and others' actions. In the ordinary course of events, criteria are implicit, internal to judgment itself, but they are also available for conscious discernment and deliberation. It should be evident that criteria are not rules for using words that can guarantee the correctness or success of our claims but "rather, criteria bring out what we claim by using the words we do . . . in making claims to knowledge, undertaking actions, and forming interpersonal relationships" (Guyer 1999, 128).

As Cavell notes (1979, 30), if in ordinary usage (as in prize juries or admissions committees) agreement over criteria makes possible agreement

7. I use *judgment* for similar ends but in virtually the opposite sense from Veena Das (2010), for whom "the crucial requirement is that we should be able to take an abstract, nonsubjective vantage position from which we can orient ourselves to the world." My usage is thus not that of the definitive attributive actions of the courts. Thanks to Carolyn Hamilton for urging the clarification.

over judgments, for Wittgenstein it appears that the ability to establish criteria is based on prior agreement in judgment. Wittgenstein's "appeal to criteria is meant, one might say, exactly to call to consciousness the astonishing fact of the astonishing extent to which we *do* agree in judgment; eliciting criteria goes to show therefore that our judgments *are* public, that is, shared" (31). However, for that reason, criteria do not often need to be publicly enunciated; we appeal to criteria only when the sense of mutual attunement is threatened (34). As Shiner helpfully explicates, for Cavell, Wittgenstein's criteria are in the nature of things, not a matter of imposed convention. "Criterial rules . . . are not external to, but *internal to* the human form of life" (1986, 364; his italics). To call them conventional, "alienates us from them, and thus from ourselves, for our form of life and our criteria are one" (ibid).[8]

I take this to indicate the fundamental givenness of ethics. Nevertheless, while certain criteria are continuous or perduring, others are contingent. If criteria define contexts of action, there must be the means to transform the context and hence the relevant criteria. There are times when new criteria must be brought into effect or applied to new persons or new contexts and hence when they must be made relatively explicit. Rappaport (1999) shows how ritual operates as a central means through which this happens. Among Tsembaga Maring of highland Papua New Guinea, rituals effect—bring into being—particular states of war and peace. These can be considered ethical states, since any aggressive or nonaggressive act is interpreted and evaluated as such in their light (that is, differently according to whether the current state is one of peace or war). Likewise, acts may be discerned as cooperative or uncooperative among those constituted as allies by having undergone the ritual together. More generally, rituals effect states of ethical personhood and relation, transforming a biological infant into a named social person, a man and woman into a married couple, a novice into a monk, a profane condition into one of blessing, a breach into a reconciliation, and so forth. To each of these persons, relationships, and states, criteria departing or renewed from or additional to what has hitherto been the case apply.

Whereas Austin argued that criteria of truth and falsity do not apply to illocutionary statements, Rappaport showed that in a sense they do, but in an inverted fashion. A locutionary statement is judged true or false according to whether it is in conformity with the state of affairs that it purports to describe or refer to (it is raining; Sarah Palin is president). However, following

8. The depth of human agreement is acknowledged in Cavell's phrase "the conventionality of human nature itself" (1979, 111; quoted in Hammer 2002, 28).

a felicitously enacted illocutionary utterance, it is the state of affairs or the subsequent actions that are to be judged as true or false according to whether they are in conformity with the utterance (you are false not to keep your promise or the peace; the drought is false once the rain magic has been performed). These are faults (falsehoods, lies, errors, sins, etc.) insofar as they are not in conformity with the moral condition that has been brought into effect. When the state of affairs is in conformity with the performative act, then the state can be said to be "true" (or correct, right, or good). Once I am inaugurated as president, my conduct is judged with respect to my status as an office holder and no longer as a contender. It is my conduct that is in question, not the act of inauguration or the office. If I serve as witness to a marriage, I cannot henceforward deny that the couple are married, nor act toward them or evaluate their actions as if they were not. To undergo a ritual is to commit, says Rappaport, both to the specific effects or conditions it produces (thereby agreeing to apply to them the relevant criteria) and, more generally, to the relevance of the criteria that the ritual underwrites or reproduces, as well as to the means of producing them (the nature of marriage, the legitimacy of weddings). Thus, the performance of a ritual initiates or transforms a specific moral state or condition relative to the participants, while also reproducing the felicity conditions or criteria that apply to such a transformation. Hence Rappaport says that ritual is simultaneously performative and metaperformative.[9]

The performance of a ritual, argues Rappaport, is characterized by the conjunction of indexical and canonical dimensions—that it is me undergoing it here and now (indexical), and that it is these previously inscribed and relatively unchangeable (canonical) utterances and acts, part of a perduring liturgical order, that I hereby repeat. Rappaport argues that, by their submission to its bodily demands (of presence, posture, endurance, etc.), the participants performing or undergoing a ritual demonstrate to others and to themselves their acceptance of both its message and its form. They do so whether or not they "believe" in any specific propositions associated with it; hence the outward, public consequences prevail irrespective of the inner states of the participants. This evades the problem of recursiveness inherent to theories of intentionality, as well as the instability of subjectivity. In these respects Rappaport is very close to Austin and somewhat akin to what Derrida means by "tethering," or avowal, or what Cavell means by

9. Here and below I severely condense what is actually a highly elaborated and systematic argument (Rappaport 1999).

acknowledgment, and quite distinct from what is commonly meant by sincerity. I can pray effectively, for example, without being certain that I believe in God, that I want to do so, or that prayer is the means to address God; I can successfully ask for forgiveness without feeling particularly contrite.[10] Indeed, in Rappaport's view, I am *likely* to be uncertain; the point of ritual is to substitute public clarity for private obscurity or ambiguity, that is, to establish beyond question the relevant criteria. The central criterion—being accountable for what one says and does—is virtually universal, in contrast to the substantive criteria put into effect by specific rituals. Definitive ethical commitments and criteria are thus produced publicly and irrespective of personal doubt.

Rappaport begins his book not by acknowledging the universality of acknowledgment but by asserting that recognizing lies is a human problem. Insofar as symbols form the basis for human language and culture, hence for creativity, speculation, and so forth, and hence, following Kant, for freedom from immediate sensations and circumstance, thought and communication by means of symbols raise two enormous problems. These are the problem of the lie and the problem of the alternative. The problem of the alternative can be seen as the flip side to Geertz's observation that culture always manifests itself as particular (1973a); it is always in some specific form and thereby in contrast to alternative forms. This raises the following questions. On what basis should I follow one alternative rather than another? Is the choice mutually exclusive? (Does the acceptance of one entail the rejection of all others?)[11] How do I indicate which alternative I have chosen? How do I come to accept that I have made the (right) choice and hence stick to it? Rappaport attends more explicitly in his subsequent

10. The matter of sincerity has been the subject of considerable debate, especially over the interpretation of Austin's citation of the words Euripides gives to Hippolytus, "My tongue swore to, but my heart did not" (Austin 1962, 9–10; Cavell 1995, 1996). Presumably its salience as a felicity condition depends on the "semiotic ideology" in place (Keane 2007; cf. Lambek 2007a). Mahmood (2005) and Hirschkind (2006) have pointed interestingly to an ideology in which the "inside" of a person is part of the context that is expected to be transformed by performative acts and utterances. Here, then, is the reverse of the idea that a "good" or "true" utterance corresponds to an existing interior state. Rather, a person becomes better insofar as his interior state becomes appropriately shaped by the right acts and utterances; for example, contrition would follow from rather than precede an act of apology. Prevalent among pious Muslims in Cairo, such an argument draws from (and elaborates) Aristotle's ideas about the cultivation of character through education and good deeds.

11. Alternatives thus come in the form of either/or and both/and. The tension between them exemplifies a central feature of human thought (Lambek 1998a, 2007b).

argument to the way ritual addresses the problem of the lie (How can we be reasonably sure that we are not lying to each other or establish commitments in the face of possible insincerity?) than to how it addresses alternatives. But in a sense the lie is a subspecies of alternative, and the focus in the subsequent argument on how ritual produces (relative) certainty is a way of reducing alternatives and specifying a particular path or set of criteria as much as it is one of assuring the truthfulness of any given utterance or set of propositions or, as noted above, of moving from the assertion's conformity to the facts to the conformity of the facts to the assertion.[12] Rituals commit their performers to taking up specific alternatives and therefore rejecting competing or contradictory ones (you cannot be simultaneously married and unmarried or alternate between these states at will) and to ignoring incommensurable ones (alternative views of what constitutes "marriage"). Moreover, rituals render such acts of commitment difficult, and sometimes impossible, to take back, as in acts of scarification, circumcision, and other forms of sacrifice (see chapter 9). (Cavell's problem of finding a voice is thus partially obviated by inhabiting and suffering a body.) A critical point here is that, while the unfolding of events enables us to reinterpret earlier events in light of subsequent ones through the ongoing construction of narrative, it is more difficult to reinterpret after the fact the commitments entered into and the moral conditions brought into effect through the performance of rituals and, indeed, of everyday performative utterances of all kinds.

Truthfulness and committing to specific ways of doing or being are fundamentally ethical matters. The questions are not only how human society responds to the possibility of the lie or adjudicates among competing alternatives, but how we accept specific statements, alternatives, responsibilities, and courses of action as *ours*, how we become committed to them (such that they become a part of us and we of them), and how we demonstrate and acknowledge to ourselves and to others that we (and that others) mean what they say. The broader issues are less ones of distinguishing lies from truth than of enacting and recognizing acceptance of (or accepting one's nomination to) certain positions and committing to one's utterances, to the courses of action established and initiated in public moments, and to the criteria by which such courses of action are identified as such and the means by which they are taken up and evaluated. Temporality is critical—whether we

12. The most salient and succinct form of the question of commitment is that of making a pledge or promise, a matter that, as noted in Lambek 2010b, is central to and often materialized as the gift.

stick with things long enough to make our statements and actions coherent and reasonably predictable, available for development, interpretation, evaluation, and response. Ultimately we must acknowledge our identification with the person we have, through a series of marked and unmarked acts and utterances, become.

From Performance of Ritual to Performance of Everyday Speech and Action

For Rappaport, ritual lies at one end of a continuum of formality. Yet many of his arguments apply to acts and events of lesser formality. While the "conjunction of the indexical and canonical," and especially the invocation of relatively unchanging "canonical" phrases (like *b'ismillah*) and sequences of action (like the Catholic communion), are depicted as characterizing ritual, in fact virtually all speaking entails a similar conjunction. What Rappaport calls the indexical dimension is each time original, linear, and consequential—a threshold crossed and an act that happens and cannot readily be retracted (my words uttered, the "reply all" button fatefully pushed), while what he calls the canonical dimension is highly iterative or citational, comprising words or phrases that have been said before, and will be again, by other people.[13] Many ordinary utterances bring the performative and iterative dimensions to the fore, so that Austin originally referred to them as performatives, as when I thank or introduce someone, or simply say "yes." As Austin subsequently realized, all utterances contain an illocutionary dimension, insofar as they make statements, describe a state of affairs, refer to a person or place, ask or respond to a question, and so forth. In so doing, and in announcing that they are statements or other specific acts of communication, all utterances entail simultaneously a commitment on the part of the speaker to be understood (somehow) and a commitment to stand by the message, semiotic code, and conversational implicatures (Grice 1976; Ochs Keenan 1976) that are ostensibly in use. We must, as Cavell puts it, mean what we say. Or, as Hent de Vries explicates Cavell's reading of Wittgenstein, "No a priori principles or axioms, no conventional maxims or norms, could ever relieve us of that responsibility—'commitment'—to the language and singular terms we use. . . . What holds true for promising and for moral judgment governs all actions and passions, events and encounters" (2008, 85).

13. Thus, ritual action entails the conjunction of what Lévi-Strauss (1972, 286) has called reversible and irreversible time.

Particular genres of speech and action in various cultural milieus refine such commitment—the ostensive relations between the speaker's intentionality and the code or message—in various ways. We can refer here to the field of metapragmatics as elaborated by Michael Silverstein (1976). Thus the displacement of intentionality is central to a practice like spirit possession, in which there are explicit shifts in voice (Boddy 1989; Lambek 1981). The perception of a possible gap between what is said and what is meant is also heightened in certain discursive regimes, such as Calvinist Protestantism, with respect to what Webb Keane (2007) has usefully identified as semiotic ideologies. Nevertheless, insofar as there is an illocutionary dimension, and it is felicitously enacted, so too the consequences that Austin and Rappaport attribute to performative utterances follow—namely, that they usher in a state of affairs (criteria) according to which the speakers, participants, and context are henceforth to be judged.

Language is central to the ethical and the ethical to language, both to language in the abstract, in the sense of grammar and semantics (*langue*), and to acts of speaking, pragmatics, and metapragmatics (*parole*)—to the names and pronouns that I take on, by which I am addressed and respond, by which I address others or refer to others, and which I link to specific actions. The ethical is intrinsic to utterances by which I acknowledge (or repudiate) words and acts as mine or yours, ours or theirs; by which I accuse, command, condemn, confess, congratulate, criticize, defer, defy, denounce, encourage, excuse, exonerate, honor, insult, ignore, injure, obey, praise, pronounce, refuse, swear, sympathize, and so on; but also by which I agree, answer, argue, denote, describe, disagree, exclaim, imply, question, refer, request, state, suggest, and so forth.[14] The ethical is embedded in the relations produced and presupposed among the nominative, the accusative, the dative, the ablative, and the genitive attributions of persons and things as the subjects and objects of action—as people nominate and accept nomination, accuse and receive accusation, act on and are acted upon directly and indirectly, toward and by means of other persons and things, and attribute similar actions and causes to others. Adverbs and adverbial phrases specifically refine aspects of means and intention, as memorably illustrated in Austin's (1970) elaboration of the distinction between shooting a donkey

14. In our joint seminar (2006), Jack Sidnell remarked on the large number of performative verbs in a single paragraph from Jane Austen. So far as I know, no one has investigated whether there has been a decline in the presence, number, or quality of explicitly performative verbs in English, whether and how their presence is related to such matters as genre and social class, what the implications are for infusing sociality with an ethical tenor (or whether this is mere propriety), or how closely the set of English performative verbs is replicated in other languages.

and dropping a tea tray by accident or by mistake. Ethics is grammatical; grammar, ethical.

Of course, the distinct verbs and adverbs of English or the nominal cases of Latin or Russian, no less than the speech genres in which they are embedded, express refinements of ethical stance and perspective that in other languages may be performed by means of other grammatical categories and functions, including modes of address (such as tecknonyms), allusion, metaphor, avoidance, shifts between transitive and intransitive or active and passive verbs, morphemes indicative of agency, authorship versus animation (Goffman 1981), evidentiality (Hill and Irvine 1993), indexical discernments of context (Hanks 1990), genres or modes of speaking that enable degrees of quotation or dequotation (Urban 1989), turn-taking, and various forms of oral and gestural punctuation.

Ethical Consequences of the Irreversibility of Action: Forgiveness and Acknowledgment

Taking speech to be a subcategory of acts (or, perhaps, acts to be a subcategory of speaking),[15] I turn to some of the general features of human action as discerned by Arendt, followed by some remarks on Cavell. Despite radical differences in style, sources, and temperament, there are interesting parallels between these two thinkers, each of whom attends to the irreversibility and ethical consequentiality of action. I begin with Arendt, even though, unlike Cavell, she writes without the benefit of speech act theory and hence introduces something of a break in my larger argument.[16]

Arendt celebrates the *vita activa,* in which public action is really the highest or best form of activity. The fundamental feature of an act is that it brings into play something new in the world. "To act" she says, "means to take an initiative, to begin" (1998, 177). She writes, "The life span of man running toward death would inevitably carry everything human to ruin and destruction if it were not for the faculty of interrupting it and beginning something new, a faculty which is inherent in action like an ever-present reminder that men, though they must die, are not born in order to die but in order to begin" (246). Arendt identifies "the principle of beginning" with

15. In chapter 3 I have described the maintenance of taboos as a kind of performative activity, in which speech may be largely irrelevant; gendered comportment would be another instance (Butler 1990). However, to ascribe an act as performative is to acknowledge its categorization in words.

16. My remarks on Arendt are restricted entirely to *The Human Condition.*

"the principle of freedom" (177). However, the condition of humanity is one of plurality. Hence she cautions that "because the actor always moves among and in relation to other acting beings, he is never merely a 'doer' but always and at the same time a sufferer. To do and to suffer are like opposite sides of the same coin" (190).

If human labor stems from necessity, and work is prompted by utility, by contrast, Arendt argues, speech and action spring from us as a kind of spontaneous disclosure of the agent. However, such disclosure retains a certain ambiguity insofar as action reveals its consequences only after the fact. Illuminating action is the province of the storyteller, not the agent; it cannot be captured in the intentionality of the actor. "This unpredictability of outcome is closely related to the revelatory character of action and speech, in which one discloses one's self without either knowing himself or being able to calculate beforehand whom he reveals" (1998, 192).[17] Hence the burden of the consequentiality of action is "the burden of irreversibility and unpredictability" (233).

Arendt honors the act more than the actor; indeed, for her, the relationship between the two is characterized by a kind of opacity: "Men have always known . . . that he who acts never quite knows what he is doing, that he always becomes 'guilty' of consequences he never intended or even foresaw, that no matter how disastrous and unexpected the consequences of his deed he can never undo it, that the process he starts is never consummated unequivocally in one single deed or event, and that its very meaning never discloses itself to the actor but only to the backward glance of the historian who himself does not act" (1998, 233).

This produces a paradox with respect to freedom insofar as it makes the actor appear "more the victim and the sufferer than the author and doer of what he has done" (1998, 234). Arendt remarks provocatively, "Nowhere, in other words, neither in labor, subject to the necessity of life, nor in fabrication, dependent upon given material, does man appear to be less free than in those capacities whose very essence is freedom and in that realm which owes its existence to nobody and nothing but man" (234).

The solution lies in the act and reception of the Other. Arendt writes, "The possible redemption from the predicament of irreversibility—of being unable to undo what one has done though one did not, and could not, have known what he was doing—is the faculty of forgiving" (1998,

17. This speaks directly to the condition of irony I discussed in Lambek 2010a and is illustrated in chapter 13 in the anecdote of the fallen granary.

237). Moreover, forgiving cannot be predicted and thus "is the only reaction [that] . . . retains . . . something of the original character of action"; indeed, forgiving is a new, unconditioned act (241). Furthermore, in a remark that returns us to Rappaport, "The remedy for unpredictability, for the chaotic uncertainty of the future, is contained in the faculty to make and keep promises" (237). In these two quintessential expressions of freedom—forgiving and promising—we are back to preeminently illocutionary acts and the criteria they establish.

Both forgiving and promising are performative acts, one retrospectively redressing the past and the other prospectively charting a future. Ethics in this vision is resolutely historical. It is not maintained by means of individual reason or internal self-control (Arendt 1998, 238), nor does it emerge directly from a form of Durkheimian social regulation or transcendence. Both promising and forgiving depend on the fact of human plurality, "for no one can forgive himself and no one can feel bound by a promise made only to himself" (237). In a striking phrase that distills the wisdom acquired by her own experience, Arendt writes that "men are unable to forgive what they cannot punish and . . . unable to punish what has turned out to be unforgivable" (241).

Arendt's ability to forgive was no doubt compromised by Martin Heidegger's inability to acknowledge his own actions. This weight of acknowledgment is a central subject for Cavell, who goes so far as to say that speaking is apt to become unbearable. Here Arendt's miracle of natality produces labor pains and struggles over both detachment from the words of others so as to find one's own voice and the weight of attachment to one's own words. Cavell advocates finding one's voice, yet recognizes that one "moves between owning one's words and being abandoned to them" (Szafraniec 2008, 379). We must mean what we say and yet recognize that we cannot always do so completely or consistently. The world would be incoherent if we did not stand by what we say, but to do so inflexibly leads inevitably to tragedy, so well exemplified in the figure of King Lear, or, for that matter, the unfolding of the *Hippolytus*.

Thus, if Cavell reads Austin as "affirming that I am abandoned to [my words]" (Szafraniec 2008, 371–72, quoting Cavell 1996, 125), Cavell himself would not exactly follow suit. Cavell would not condone Hippolytus for keeping his word to the bitter end:

> To live is to engage in a movement between controlling one's words and being controlled by them. To act as if these two sides of the movement were the

> same, as Hippolytus does, is to have, in Cavell's terms, a petrified imagination. To mean every word one says is to assume responsibility for the (criterial) implications of what one says, while in full awareness that these implications may change, that they remain in need of our future interventions, and that they are potentially infinite, so that what we say exceeds our control, so that we will always mean more and less than we do. (372)

That is to say, it is to acknowledge Arendt's "burden of irreversibility and unpredictability."

To take responsibility for one's words is not to refuse ever to take them back. But to redeem a change of direction, one must acknowledge it for what it is. We are faced with the challenges not only of keeping our commitments and answering to the names we have been given and accepted, but also of acknowledging our failures, thoughtlessness, infelicities, incontinence, and changes of heart and direction—and forgiving those of others, as well as accepting their forgiveness. As Stephen Mulhall helpfully puts it, it is not that a person is or isn't responsible for all the consequences of her utterances or actions, could have foreseen them all, and so forth, but that "she is then flatly responsible for determining her relation to them—whether and how to claim them as unforeseeable or simply unforeseen, to accept them as meant or excuse them as unintended" (1996, 17). The point is recognizing and living with the consequences of one's words.

Thus, whereas some thinkers focus on the lie, on promising, or on keeping one's promise, Cavell adds that, whether one promises or fails to keep a promise, the issue is acknowledging that one has done so. Whereas silence has its functions, sometimes speech is "essentially *owed*. Flowers are not a substitute" (Cavell 2005b, 191). Moreover, as he notes in *The Claim of Reason* (1999, 298; cited by de Vries 2008, 83), "There are any number of ways, other than promising, for committing yourself to a course of action: the expression or declaration of an intention, the giving of an impression, not correcting someone's misapprehension, . . . and so on."

I take the ethics of the ordinary to be entailed in these performative and practical qualities of speech and action, promising and beginning, forgiveness and acknowledgment. Not only are speaking and acting intrinsically or formally ethical (committing, executing, evaluating, and becoming subject to evaluation), but the particular substance of ethics (criteria, values, commitments) is specified, instantiated, and informed through specific utterances and acts. Original utterances nevertheless contain quotation or citation of some kind. Ritual performances may differ from everyday acts and utterances with respect to the degree of canonical citation, formality, legitimacy, publicity, conventionality, spectacle, consequentiality, and, as Rappaport (1999) argues, the relative certainty, perdurance, and sanctity of what is iterated. As noted, ritual performances establish and specify criteria for judgment more clearly than do less formal utterances, leaving less room for the kinds of qualifications that Cavell describes. However, the distinctions are not absolute, and all speaking carries some of the weight that Rappaport attributes to ritual, just as ritual carries the weight Cavell attributes to speaking. Moreover, certain relatively informal utterances, such as accusations and invective (*sale juif*), but also repeated praise or affirmations of love, may prove equally if not more momentous for addressees, and perhaps for speakers.[18] One implication of the work of Arendt, Cavell, and Rappaport is that the ethical is to be distinguished not only from what is specifically unethical but also, and perhaps more fundamentally, from simple indifference.

Finally, it is worth underlining that action finds its complement in passion; as Aristotle realized, virtue finds the right balance of passion and action to suit the circumstances. Arendt, as I have indicated, speaks of the complementarity of acting and suffering. Cavell (2005b) argues that the criteria for passionate utterances are not the same as those for performative utterances, emphasizing that a passionate utterance is one in which I do not know in advance how my statement will be received or what my standing is.[19] Radically to separate the ethical from the passionate would reproduce the Kantian dichotomy between reason and the senses as one between freedom and constraint. This is one of the places where a close analysis of spirit possession could prove instructive (Boddy 1989; Lambek 2010a).

From Performance to Practice and Back: Toward an Ethics of History

While ritual performance produces states of affairs, the descriptions under which people act, and the criteria for judgment, it cannot determine either who participates or the subsequent actions (including acts of evaluation) of the participants. How, when, and whether people act is a product of their exercise of judgment to fit the circumstances, an exercise that is in

18. In fact, invectives often carry the features of being low in informational content and high in meaning that Rappaport attributes to sacred utterances.

19. Thanks to Veena Das for clarifying the point. In addition, many emotion words or invocations carry ethical weight (see chapter 6; Lutz 1988; see also Lutz and Abu-Lughod 1990; Myers 1988; Hirschkind 2006; Stafford 2010; and Baker 2010).

turn related to character, acquired disposition, and accumulated wisdom.[20] Hence one may distinguish analytically the ethics of practice from that of performance. As a theorist of performance, Rappaport has relatively little to say about practice—how it is that *I* come to perform *this* ritual *now*, how I orient my conduct subsequently, whether or how I fulfill the obligations I have just committed myself to, or what happens if I do not. Bourdieu is the primary theorist of practice, discriminating the manner in which actions are undertaken and paying specific attention to response and timing. It is not simply a matter of playing by rules but, as Bourdieu puts it so well, of having a feel for the game, of simply doing the right or best thing under the circumstances (1977). If a theory of performativity describes the establishment of criteria, practice theory recognizes that criteria are not usually applied explicitly, as in following a set of rules or bureaucratic procedures, but are implicit in both the game and the disposition to exercise (and the ability to recognize) good judgment.

What counts as ethical is a matter not only of choosing freely or judging wisely but of sustaining commitment to a specific direction, order, goal, discipline, set of criteria, or Weberian "absolute value." Not to follow through on what one has committed to is, in at least some respect (but bearing in mind Cavell's strong qualifications), to place oneself in the wrong. Moreover, we are back to the problem of alternatives. To take up one alternative or to go down one path entails passing up opportunities that other paths could have afforded and even explicitly rejecting some. Having married one woman, given my blessing to one child, or shown my devotion to one jealous god, I cannot readily go ahead and pursue other alternatives.[21] Not only can we not explore all paths at once, or even in succession, but there is something to the fact that we ought to keep to certain paths or commitments once we have initiated or started to follow them, at least long enough for our companions to be able to count on us to be there. The freedom of starting something new entails the judgment of what kinds of compromises that will make with the old and reconciling the new direction with what is being left behind.

If performance establishes the criteria by which subsequent practice is engaged and evaluated, so too practical judgment generates new

20. Material constraints and political and discursive factors can also prevent people from carrying out certain desirable acts or from carrying them out in a specific manner.

21. Yet one should continuously exercise judgment; it would be unethical to be rigid, to stop thinking after one has made one's first commitment. The point is that subsequent acts need to be made with respect to or acknowledgment of previous commitments.

performances—that is, relatively formal acts and utterances that recalibrate the criteria and shift the ethical context. Thus there is a whole ethics to history and social change.

The emergence of new performances within the stream of practice may be understood with the assistance of a distinction made by Cavell.[22] Cavell describes appeals to criteria as having two moments, which he calls predication and proclamation—having something to say about something, and actually saying it: "In ordinary cases, a set of specifications or features is established that set the terms of, are the 'means' or basis of, the judgment; and then there are standards on the basis of which to assign the degree to which the object satisfies the criteria of judgment, or to determine whether an object *counts* under the criteria at all. We may think of the former moment as the judgment's *predication*, its saying something *about* something; we may think of the latter moment as the judgment's *proclamation*, its saying it out" (1979, 34). Further, "Whether to speak (proclaim) has two aspects: determining whether you are willing to count something as something; and determining when, if ever, you wish, or can, enter your accounting into a particular occasion" (35). Wittgenstein, says Cavell, moves between observing—"It is what human beings *say* that is true or false," the predicative moment—and communication as "agreement in judgments," the proclamatory moment (35).

A broad concern with acknowledging and reconciling with the past, as well as bearing witness to departures from it, has been evident in the practices of people I have encountered in fieldwork and hence has become a theme of my work (see chapter 4; Lambek 2002a, 2002c, 2004). Here, however, I offer two brief illustrations drawn from recent essays by younger scholars of the way that judgment is predicated in practice and proclaimed in performance, in acts of acknowledgment (as pointed to by Cavell) and in forgiveness and natality (as emphasized by Arendt).

Catherine Allerton reports the various ways that people of Manggarai in Western Flores, Indonesia, are performatively rooted in their localities through ritual acts performed as infants. As youths setting out to live elsewhere for high school or university, they perform another ritual, of "rooting the feet," acknowledging where they come from in order to travel safely forward. People of Manggarai must also formally say farewell to the dead. Allerton recounts how

22. In light of Cavell's account of opera as an exemplary locus of voice, I am tempted to speak of my ethnographic illustrations as a kind of *Cavelleria Rusticana*. Mascagni's *Cavalleria Rusticana* is itself a drama of failed acknowledgment.

> Maria . . . once described to me a time when she briefly visited a house in another village. As she sat down, she became aware of a terrible smell of rotting. She called out to the women of the house, "Quick, pass me a betel quid!" and then "offered betel" (*waré sepa*) to the ghost of a woman of that house. Maria told me that she had known this woman fairly well, but had not been able to visit the house to formally offer her "tears" (*waé lu'u*) [money] after the woman's death. The terrible smell was that of the corpse of the deceased woman, whom Maria had not yet formally "remembered." Finally remembering the woman by offering betel caused the smell to disappear, as the ghost returned to the realm of the ancestors. (2012, 187–88)

We see here both the named acts of conventional acknowledgment and the circumstantiality of initially having forgotten to carry them out. Maria both proclaims her omission (as manifest or predicated in the smell) and redresses it by acknowledging the deceased person. Her act is accepted, and the omission is forgiven as the smell disperses.

The second example illustrates how an act of acknowledgment resolves a traumatic historical event and a political stalemate. In 2002 a heavily laden ferry capsized en route from Ziguinchor in the Casamance region of Senegal to the capital, Dakar. As Ferdinand de Jong (n.d.) describes, after unsatisfactory attempts at memorializing the nearly two thousand people who drowned, some citizens of Ziguinchor began to feel that the cause of the accident was their unresolved struggle for independence of the Casamance. Women referred back to an earlier event, predicating the shipwreck as part of a moral state of struggle they had proclaimed in 1982. They then attempted to undo what they had begun, to terminate the state of being and close off the chapter. The women of the sacred groves, who twenty years earlier had assisted militants to utter oaths of commitment to the insurgent movement, now asked the men to take them back. As one of the women explained to de Jong, "*Il faut passer là ou tu es passé.* We have to return along the same path that has taken us here." Most remarkably, at the signing of the peace treaty that soon followed, the leader of the separatist movement publicly "apologized for the victims of the shipwreck" (n.d., 6).

These events indicate how Rappaport's account of ritual can be taken out of the structural and functionalist framework in which he largely places it and applied directly to specific historical occasions. The performance of taking back the oaths is a novel, historical event, actually making history, and doing so by publicly transforming the ethical state of affairs in Casamance so that new criteria apply. This offers another dimension to the much-discussed question of the relationship of structure to event (Sahlins 1985).

What is equally exciting and so productive of peace here is the performance of an apology. The actors in the conflict take responsibility for the tragedy rather than displacing it onto other people, actions, or forces (which one could readily imagine). There is a lesson of wide relevance here. Taking responsibility for historical events, acknowledging our role in them, is not only the way to make peace but also turns people from the victims of history into its agents and finds in suffering not resentment or *ressentiment* but forgiveness and conciliation. The simultaneous profundity and fragility of such acts leads directly to the final phase of my argument.

Skepticism

Rappaport argues that the clarity and certainty produced in the performance of ritual is necessary in light of the ambiguity and uncertainty that would reign in its absence; this is clearly illustrated in these ethnographic vignettes. But sometimes ambiguity appears more salient or powerful than what is achieved in ritual, persisting in the face of the performance or having no performance that could resolve it. Despite the evident and positive effects of acknowledgment, apology, and forgiveness, it sometimes rises to consciousness not only that the proclamation might be at odds with what we feel but that the very predication is difficult or impossible to make; that we cannot get to the bottom of where we stand or who we are, of our original or current intentions or deepest desires; that the right words or even the criteria for knowing, saying, or doing something are absent. An account of ethics must recognize limitations to acts of acknowledgment, the inevitable infelicities that accompany and undermine them, and the difficulties encountered in remaining consistent and complete with respect to one's criteria and acknowledgments.

Assuming we have the freedom or potential of which some philosophers speak, how shall we know what to do with it, what to choose, or how to recognize on what basis we have made our choice (or chosen to have it made for us)? Were we responsible for a given act of omission or commission? Where does responsibility begin and end? Did we know what we were doing or mean what we said? Are conventional words and actions sufficient to our meaning? Did we do it intentionally, seriously, unconsciously, by accident? Are your criteria commensurate with mine? How are we to recognize the meaning of our words or the consequences of our acts? How, at the end of the day, are we even to know who "we" are, or even that we are? Sometimes we simply feel the absence of criteria to know. Performance then takes place on thin ice, appearing as "mere" or "staged" performance, and sometimes the ice begins to melt.

In sum, what if skepticism creeps into performance or practice, if criteria are no longer unambiguous or disambiguating (or, conversely, too discriminating), if felicity conditions lose their authority, become fragmented or incoherent, if practices are no longer satisfying or sufficient, if there is a perceived rupture between means and ends, if competing or contradictory ends and means nominate us or override each other? These are problems not only of individual or collective incontinence and failure but also of genuine human paradox. Cavell describes the condition as "the absence or withdrawal of the world, that is, the withdrawal of my presentness to it; which for me means the withdrawal of my presentness to (the denial of our inheritance of) language" (1988, 174–75). Presence to the world is replaced by mourning its loss.

How could one have an answer for the disappointment of criteria? Only by concluding that ethical insight must *begin* in mourning the loss of the world—and thereby recognizing the courage entailed in speaking and acting at all, including the act of refusing to do so. (As Derrida indicates, disavowal is also an act of a kind of avowal.)

Most fundamentally, if ethics entails acknowledgment or avowal, who am *I* to make such acknowledgment? How is it that I find my voice or acknowledge myself, that I am who I say I am, who others say I am (or that I am other than who others say I am), that I hear my nomination, that I accept what has been entailed in that nomination, that I can be sure it is me who has been nominated, that I have not mistaken myself for another or been so mistaken by another? Reflecting on Abraham's answer to God's call to sacrifice his son, these are the questions with which Derrida begins a late essay.[23]

> The first Abrahamic teaching . . . [is] that if everything begins for us with the response, if everything begins with the "yes" implied in all responses ("yes, I respond," "yes, here I am,'" even if the response is "no"), then any response, even the most modest, the most mundane of responses, remains an acquiescence given to some self-presentation. Even if, during the response, in the

23. Derrida is drawing on a parable by Kafka, who imagines "another Abraham," who was unsure whether he was the one called and doesn't want to appear ridiculous by accepting the call too readily.

> determined content of a reply, I were to say "no"; even if I were to declare "no, no, and no. I am not here, I will not come, I am leaving, I withdraw, I desert, I'm going to the desert, I am not one of your own nor am I facing you," or "no, I deny, abjure, refuse, disavow, and so on," well then, this "no" will have said "yes," "yes, I am here to speak to you, I am addressing you in order to answer 'no,' here I am to deny, disavow, or refuse." (Derrida 2008, 313)

How Abraham should answer when he is called by God is not so different a question from how Derrida himself should answer the call of the Other, as a child in Algeria and since. What is it to be Jewish, or to be "a Jew," because others have called him Jew? And why him, rather than another? Derrida's "Jewish question" is at once exemplary and ordinary, applying to each of us.[24] This is because we come to be persons "under a description," hence ethical subjects, precisely by means of such nominations or interpellations, performative acts that begin even before we are born. For Derrida, to answer, to avow or disavow, provokes "an ethics of decision, an ethics of responsibility, exposed to the endurance of the undecidable, to the law of *my* decision as *decision of the other* in me" (2008, 324).

Derrida answers "yes," but he avows that he does not know what he means when he does so. He points to the "essential difficulty . . . in underwriting and in countersigning [*à soussigner et à contresigner*] an utterance of the type: 'Me, I am jew.' . . . To say 'I am jew,' as I do, while knowing and meaning what one says, is very difficult and vertiginous. One can only attempt to think it after having said it, and therefore, in a certain manner, without yet knowing what one does there, the *doing* [*le faire*] preceding the *knowing* [*le savoir*]" (2008, 333).[25]

Derrida answers "yes," but he refuses to choose or to authorize whether this answer (in response to Sartre) is authentic or inauthentic. Such undecidability, "far from being a suspending and paralyzing neutrality, I hold to be the very condition . . . within which decision, and any responsibility worthy of the name . . . must breathe" (2008, 335).

> Anyone responding to the call must continue to doubt, to ask himself whether he has heard right, whether there is no original misunderstanding; whether in fact it was his name that was heard, whether he is the only or the first

24. Cavell responds to his own "Jewish question" in a remarkable autobiographical essay in *A Pitch of Philosophy* (1996).

25. Note how Derrida addresses Cavell's fundamental question, "Must we mean what we say?" and places "proclamation" ahead of "predication."

> addressee of the call; whether he is not in the process of substituting himself violently for another; whether the law of substitution, which is also the law of responsibility, does not call for an infinite increase of vigilance and concern. It is possible that I have not been called, me, and it is not even excluded that no one, no One, nobody, ever called any One, any unique one, anybody. The possibility of an originary misunderstanding in destination is not an evil, it is the structure, perhaps the very vocation of any call worthy of that name, of all nomination, of all response and responsibility. (337)

In the beginning was the word, but the word was simultaneously a deed, an act, a call uttered without an intention we can fully understand, but the effects of whose proclamation we must continue to acknowledge.

Conclusion

In contrast to those who have seen the substance of ethics as either values or rules, or as the freedom to break away from the obligation of adhering to rules, I have argued that the ethical is intrinsic to human action, to meaning what one says and does, and to living according to the criteria thereby established. Ethics is a property of speech and action, as mind is a property of body (or, action is a manifestation of ethics as body is an extension of mind). Ethics is not a discrete object, not best understood as a kind or set of things. Taking such an approach has avoided explaining ethics in universal rational, instrumental, psychological, or biological terms. And while acknowledging cultural difference, it has equally avoided depicting such difference according to distinctive values and thus stumbling over problems of relativism.

If I have advocated the exercise of practical judgment at the expense of following (or rejecting) rules, that is in large part because it is a more accurate description of how we live. And if I have taken up the concept of virtue at the expense of values, that is largely because virtue pertains to the qualities of acts and practical judgment rather than to the depiction of discrete objects or cultures. The substance of a virtue is never fixed but is a function of contingent circumstances; virtues are attributions in context, not things in themselves.[26] Whether a specific act is to be described as virtuous is a matter not of adherence to a rule but of the quality of judgment it exhibits. The judgments entailed in ongoing practice (when and in what manner to act),

26. Of course, they often do become objectified as values. For an earlier and somewhat different attempt to articulate the relation of virtue to value, see chapter 10.

no less than the judgments entailed in evaluating acts and character after the fact, are rendered possible by the criteria at hand. Criteria are embedded in our use of language or established by means of the relatively formal orders of acts and utterances that anthropologists describe as ritual and that have as their core the illocutionary function of speech acts.[27] Criteria can be found in a hierarchy or continuum—from the fundamental, constant, comprehensive, or certain to those specific to the moral states, persons, and relations that have been brought into effect (under description) through immediate performances and acts of commitment. Criteria shape but do not determine how we act. We are never free insofar as we are always already spoken, spoken to, and spoken for; we are always free insofar as we are always already responsible for exercising our practical judgment.

Aristotle's conception of virtue as a function of ongoing practical judgment (*phronesis*) needs to be supplemented with an understanding of how criteria are established and how they come to apply to specific circumstances, contingencies, subjects, objects, and means of action. It is in the definitive acts and utterances we refer to as ritual that particular criteria are simultaneously established, acknowledged in principle, and rendered applicable in practice. To establish criteria is to acknowledge them both as valid generally and as relevant and relative to particular persons and circumstances. To live ethically is to accept specific criteria and nominations, to acknowledge such acceptance, to live in accord with such acceptance, to recognize the fragility of that acceptance and those criteria, and, finally, in the least felicitous circumstances, to acknowledge when one has failed and to forgive others their failures. Among the most significant and pervasive criteria are those that establish the basic humanity of persons—as beings mutually subject to criteria and hence to be acknowledged as ethical subjects in their own right, thereby, as Kant put it, having dignity, not price. However, this is also an area both subject to abuse and vulnerable to skepticism.

Speaking and acting entail the predication and appropriation of voice—speaking and acting as oneself (to someone, in the sight or hearing of someone, with reference to someone . . .)—and as such are intrinsically constitutive of ethical subjects and relations. We must (in this sense) mean what we say and do. In addition, we are required to acknowledge what we have said and done. And yet, at the same time, we cannot always mean what we say, insofar as we do not fully know the consequences of our actions, the depths of our intentions, the specificity of our path, or even that it is we

27. I have not addressed the place of criteria established through law, and hence do not discuss the struggle between ritual performance and legal act.

who are called upon to speak and act now. We must speak and act seriously and commit to the paths we have begun, to which we are held (and hold ourselves) accountable—and also recognize that full certainty and consistency are not possible. Ethics is vulnerable to—but also achieved in the face of—rupture, erosion, and skepticism.

Speech and action, understood as illocutionary performance, establish the criteria according to which practice, understood as the ongoing exercise of judgment, takes place. We are judged and we judge according to the commitments we make and have made (including those that others have made on our behalf). Ritual acts establish moral states in which new or renewed criteria apply. Ritual serves to increase clarity, certainty, consistency and completeness in what is accomplished in speech and action. Yet it can never fully overcome skepticism or the work of time.

Since every utterance entails a commitment to our words, we are continually put to the test to keep, as it were, our promises, But in the face of circumstance this is often hard to do, and so we are also faced with the challenges of acknowledging our failures, thoughtlessness, misdeeds, infelicities, and changes of heart—and forgiving those of others. It might be said, then, that promising, acknowledging, and forgiving are meta-ethical acts.

Such acts are intrinsically temporal and historical. Indeed, insofar as taking responsibility, rather than apportioning blame, serves as the motor of history, it not inconsequentially produces a subject position of agent rather than victim (except insofar as one is victim of one's own acts).

Insofar as these are features intrinsic to human speech and action, criteria of being human, they will be culturally recognized, a part of the store of human wisdom transmitted in distinctive traditions, cultivated through forms of discipline, embedded in the fine discriminations of ordinary language, and enunciated more explicitly in proverbs and narratives, and sometimes in the rationalized bodies of argument we call philosophy, theology, and even *ethics*.

TWELVE

Ethics Out of the Ordinary

In her review of Ordinary Ethics, *Rena Lederman regretted the absence of a chapter on the ethics of anthropology. This is my attempt to turn what I learned from the anthropology of ethics back on the field, and specifically on fieldwork. The essay was originally solicited by the wonderful Olivia Harris for the Methods section of the* ASA Handbook of Social Anthropology. *I told her I could not write a "straight" piece on ethics as method, and the result is what follows. The essay is dedicated to her memory.*

> Critique, though indispensable, can occupy only a small part of a life that is lived sanely. It is nevertheless possible to be alert to the tension between the unconditional openness required by anthropological inquiry and the decisiveness demanded by ethical and political life. The two always go together but not easily.
>
> —Asad 2006, 207

A handbook usually offers answers to general queries and proposes models for performance. For this writer this is impossible with respect to ethics, despite the fact that ethics is commonly seen as a set of prescriptions, of do's and don'ts, perhaps enlivened by a few case studies of "difficult" situations.[1] Part of the story of anthropological ethics has been its increased

This chapter first appeared in Richard Fardon et al., ed., *ASA Handbook of Social Anthropology* (London: Sage, 2012), 2:141–52.

1. These first paragraphs draw heavily on correspondence with Olivia Harris, expressing my hesitation at accepting her invitation to write on anthropological ethics. She, of course, disarmed me, and I offer this essay in salute to her vigorously enthusiastic yet ironically tempered engagement with the world. *Ave atque vale*. The title is inspired by Stanley Cavell's "Something Out of the Ordinary" (2005c).

professionalization, rationalization, and routinization over the last two decades. The inclusion of chapters on ethics in a section entitled "Methods" is an illustration of that fact, as though ethics itself were a method. It is not! Insofar as ethics permeates the anthropological project, it is relevant for method as well, but it is neither a method nor should it be restricted to questions of method.[2] Indeed, ethics might be considered the very antithesis of method, insofar as the concept entails or presupposes an instrumental separation of means and ends, whereas ethics, in some accounts, is about a life or practices in which means and ends are one. In other words, the apparent rise of interest in ethics is actually a kind of victory of one kind or model of ethics—consequentialist—over others. These circumstances suggest that a closer acquaintance with the philosophy of ethics, as a complex tradition of reflection and argument, and with the anthropology of ethics, as a study of the salience of virtue and value in social life and the practical entailments of language and action, might offer clearer perspectives on the ethics of anthropology.

Anthropological ethics is now taught and overseen as part of the audit culture. Many people embrace these developments, and they are not entirely without merit. But, ultimately, the attraction *for institutions* of singling out "ethics" is as a means to avoid liability. Insofar as this is a bureaucratic strategy to download accountability from government funding organizations to the universities, from universities to researchers, and from researchers—via informed consent forms—to their subjects, hence from the more powerful to the less, it is, paradoxically, an unethical invocation of ethics. (Of what possible use is an assigned consent form except as a means to preempt a grievance or lawsuit on the part of the signer?) The attraction of "ethics" as an objectified subject *for researchers* is as a means to stave off anxiety. The anxiety addressed has multiple sources, including researchers' awareness of the great troubles in the world—poverty, violence, exploitation, and so forth—and especially the inequality between our subjects and ourselves. A second source of anxiety concerns the conduct of research itself, especially the ambiguity within any form of open-ended research with respect to both its conduct and its outcome. One thinks of George Devereux's famous title, *From Anxiety to Method* (1967)—to which the addition of ethics has become the latest step. However, I suggest that the objectification of ethics is largely a false solution. No amount of rules, recipes, or methods, as compiled in

2. Thanks to Jackie Solway for clarifying the point.

a handbook, are going to offset the existential dilemmas that being in the world or insinuating yourself into other peoples' worlds entails and provokes. As a subject matter, ethics should be understood not as a *solution*, but as *recognition* of the problem, which is the problematic nature of human existence. At the same time, nothing could be more ordinary.

Ethics receives a lot of attention today, not only as a concern of professional practice but also as a topic of anthropological investigation. How might the anthropology of ethics help us to understand the ethics of anthropology? One could attribute the attention to a heightened concern with agency as a result of both Protestant (and Protestant-influenced) concerns with individual responsibility and sincerity (Keane 2003), and actuarial concerns with the distribution of responsibility and the downloading of indemnity (Laidlaw 2010). At the same time, anthropology describes the prevalence of ethical criteria and concerns in ordinary life universally, indeed going so far as to argue, along with Wittgensteinian philosophers like Austin and Cavell, that ethics is intrinsic to ordinary life and language (see chapter 11).

Here it might be helpful to distinguish two senses of the term *ethics*. In ordinary usage, the ethical is what is right, good, just, and so on, whether universally, culturally relatively, or in the circumstances. But *ethical* refers also to the human situation, in which we are continuously faced with discerning what to do and acting upon it, and in which we are dependent upon the availability of criteria, means, and disposition for doing so.[3] The ethical is grounded in our existential condition and the very nature of intersubjectivity and of social action rather than pertaining simply to the application of specific values, rules, or content. Every situation and every human act and project, however small, is ethically constituted, whether it is carried out for good or bad, rightly or wrongly, carefully or carelessly, insofar as we have some degree of freedom with respect to how to construe it and what to do, and insofar as it entails some kind of regard or disregard for others. Moreover, it is always subject to evaluation after the fact (Arendt 1998).

3. I do not contrast "morality" and "ethics," since that distinction is highly variable among philosophers. Moreover, my point is not to contrast ordinary (conservative) observance of social obligations with extraordinary (radical) acts of individual initiative but to point to different levels of abstraction: from what is good and right to the exercise and accounting of good and right judgments, and from specific acts to the recognition that all acts and utterances entail judgment (chapter 11).

In addressing anthropological practice, we need to consider in which sense we are using the word *ethics*. In the first sense, ethics tends to be presented prescriptively and consequentially: know right from wrong and do what is right or what will have the best or least deleterious outcome. But knowing and doing what is right or best, I argue, is often less obvious than our ideology suggests and certainly less easy a matter to determine than any formal ethical guidelines could suggest. Ethics in the sense of simply doing what is good or right is not characteristic of fieldwork any more than it is of everyday life; we don't do right as consistently or completely as we'd like to think, and we usually don't do wrong as profoundly as our critics (or conscience) suggest. Moreover, there may be few ethical injunctions specific to anthropology. But what is interesting about anthropology is the way it is distinctive with respect to ethics in the second sense. Compared to the everyday, our consciousness of the ethical as intrinsic to action is heightened in any fieldwork worthy of the name, insofar as the situation impels us to continuously exercise judgment in the face of new, sometimes radically new, circumstances and criteria, and to come face to face with the contingency and limits of the ethical criteria, values, principles, and rationalized rules and guidelines we bring with us.

All this suggests that current anxiety over ethics within the profession is somewhat unreflexive and misplaced. Yes, anthropologists should act ethically; yes, there are always some practitioners who act unethically; yes, our research is linked (often problematically) to the policies and programs of funding agencies and to our class, historical, and political positions; and yes, students should be reminded of the issues and warned to stay away from such dubious enterprises as cooperation with the military. But it is not clear that there is any ethical improvement to be gained by submitting research proposals to bureaucratically established ethical review processes or obediently following all their subsequent instructions, creating and inculcating lists of obligations and prohibitions, or even teaching ethics as a distinct objective subject matter.

Anxiety is widespread—as noted, with respect to the acknowledgment of disparities of economic, political, and psychological well-being; with respect to the future—globally, nationally, and individually (e.g. with respect to finding a satisfying job); and with respect, also, to the anthropological project, whether it retains any relevance or clear goals, and with respect to the hubris entailed in beginning and pursuing any given ethnographic study, in both the fieldwork and the writing phases. But we should not mistake our anxiety or state of ethical confusion for the simple absence of a set of prescriptive ethics. Moreover, prescriptive ethics makes it all look too easy: simply follow the rules, and you don't have to think too hard or bear responsibility if things don't work out as planned.

By contrast, virtue ethics recognizes the continuous engagement with persons, events, and situations, the weighing and reweighing, attachment and commitment to specific courses of present, future, and past action. Some of this engagement is a product of relatively nondeliberative disposition, but fieldwork, insofar as it is an explicitly initiated project, and insofar as it truly takes us out of our comfort zone, will move ethical judgment from the tacit toward the reflected upon. Ethics, as James Laidlaw (2002) puts it (after Kant), is an index of human freedom, or, as I (in chapters 10 and 11, above) have argued (after Aristotle), expresses the human necessity for sustained exercise of judgment. The first lesson for fieldworkers is this: Expect ethics to be challenging. Sometimes the course of action is obvious, but more often it is ambiguous, as one is confronted with novel circumstances and criteria, or even the ostensible absence of criteria, and pulled between different sets and kinds of obligations and commitments. It is a mistake—an ethical blind spot—to expect that there is always an obvious, single, right, virtuous judgment to make or a correct path to follow in every situation. Not only is the enactment of every virtue a matter of situational judgment, but also at times one has to balance between different virtues and between the competing and equally compelling needs of different Others (as well as between our own needs and those of others).

Happily, one can turn this around and suggest that the challenges offered by anthropology provide a particular set of practices or discipline of ethical self-formation, in Foucault's sense (1990). To be ethical is a matter of becoming ethical, of honing one's character. Fieldwork itself is an ethical adventure, a trial or journey; in the course of encountering the ethical demands of fieldwork (including the criticism and laughter our actions provoke), we continue the cultivation of our own ethical dispositions. This could entail, in the first instance, challenging one's tendency to self-deception.[4] It might be unethical (in the first sense) if personal growth of this kind were the *only* benefit or outcome of fieldwork, unless it were equally open to everyone. But, phrased somewhat less egocentrically, by taking on ethnographic research, we become accountable to broader or more complex standards, modes, or sources of evaluation; these are ethical

4. In this respect those anthropologists who decades ago advocated psychoanalysis as a prerequisite for fieldwork were probably right. The fact is, however, that fieldwork conducted in an equally rigorous, disciplined, and reflective manner can itself be a kind of psychoanalysis—and, more importantly, an avenue for ethical cultivation.

as much as intellectual. Becoming accountable happens in the course of fieldwork (rather than simply being completed prior to it, in undergoing a proposal exam and an ethics review process), both because of what we do there and because of what we learn there, including learning to do better. Anthropology, and especially fieldwork, can also be seen as intrinsically and explicitly (if somewhat idealistically) ethical insofar as it attends to the Other (Evens 2008; Handelman, in press [after Levinas]).

These are insights that can't be directly taught or delivered by experts. You have to find out for yourself. In the lecture room or the supervisor's office (and maybe on this page), they come across as fatuous. From an Aristotelian perspective, ethical action is a product of situational judgment. Good judgment stems from (virtuous) character, and character is to be cultivated. We try to judge the character as well as the intellect of applicants to graduate programs and teaching and research positions (though our judgment sometimes fails), and we try to develop character in students by means of presenting the example of our own conduct and that of the anthropologists whose work we teach as models—not to exemplify ethical purity or perfection but to illustrate how we meet the challenges of our calling.

Thus, one vehicle for ethical formation is reading ethnography, as seminar participants put themselves in the shoes of Malinowski, Evans-Pritchard, Myerhoff, or other master craftsmen and appraise their strategies of both fieldwork and writing as demonstrated within the text. A classic narrative of fieldwork for my age cohort was *Return to Laughter* (Bowen 1964) (both fictionalized and written under a pseudonym, thus doubly dissociated and ironic); it might be compared today with the more literal-minded *Madumo* (Ashforth 2000). But there are many others, and witchcraft (the subject of both these books) is merely a metonym for the general issues entailed in encountering other models of and for the world, modes of being in the world, attributions of responsibility, and forms of violence, ambivalence, unfairness, and suffering.[5] One can also read fiction (Jane Austen and Alice Munro are as good primers on character as any abstract account) or works whose ethical challenge is formed through the very play with genre (e.g., Cavell 1996; Sebald 1996).[6] I start a Master's course with Jamaica Kincaid's *A Small Place* (1988), at once a fierce and subtle challenge to many assumptions, a superb exemplification of the writer's craft, and one of the few books to

5. Compare, among many others, the diverse approaches to ethics of Bailey (1994); Das (2007); Kleinman (2006); Scheper-Hughes (2004); and Smith (1999).

6. Jackson's anthropological memoir (2004) is modeled directly on Sebald.

match the didactic assertiveness of Malinowski by equally addressing the reader as *you*.

Anthropology's romantic heritage has largely evaporated into modern realism and postmodern cynicism or irony, but one area in which it persists is in the idea and ideal of fieldwork. In other words, if we no longer maintain illusions about the purity of cultural differences or the autonomy of better societies, we still emphasize the unique qualities of our own practice.[7] Whether to the South Seas, an inner-city neighborhood, or a biotech laboratory, the anthropologist travels bravely forward, enters a new world, inhabits it for a sufficient length of time, and returns to tell the tale. It is a quest with hazards and rewards, an adventure, and, like all adventures, both intensely real and not quite real at all. The anthropologist is there to experience, to have experiences (*Erlebnis*), and to grow in life experience (*Erfahrung*);[8] anthropological knowledge, as Sherry Ortner (2006), among others, has remarked, is filtered through the anthropologist's subjectivity. Yet, to become authorized as knowledge, it must be objectified, a process beginning with detached reflection and fieldnotes, and ending in refereed publications. Susan Sontag, writing of Lévi-Strauss, spoke of the anthropologist as hero (1966). In Lévi-Strauss's case it was the heroism simultaneously of the hazardous journey and of staying, cerebrally, at one remove from it and of drawing on the subjectivity of experience but managing ostensibly equally to transcend it in the magisterial intellectual endeavors accomplished on the return.

Lévi-Strauss's lone heroic detachment is actually at one end of a spectrum of fieldwork style,[9] which is characterized more commonly by its relational qualities. To begin with, the supervisor sends the apprentice on the quest and is the guarantor, monitor, and judge of its success. Supervisor/supervisee relations are likely to be fraught with transference, especially over issues of autonomy and dependence and in large part because of the ambiguity of what can be taught or learned within the relationship itself.[10]

7. For a recent example, see Borneman and Hammoudi 2009.

8. On the significance of the distinction, necessary in German and conflated in English, see Jay 2005.

9. This quality is itself partly a product of his text; it is only when he notes that his wife had to leave the field for reasons of ill health that the reader becomes aware of her existence. That is her sole appearance in 415 pages of *Tristes Tropiques* (Lévi-Strauss 1974).

10. This is surely a subject for an essay in its own right. For a start, see Reczkiewicz and Lambek (n.d.).

Despite her relative silence, the supervisor (and the larger projected readership for which she stands) triangulates and authorizes the relationships that the ethnographer engages with his research subjects. The Internet has had an enormous impact on the former relationship, enabling monitoring and mentoring of a different rhythm and intensity than in the days when letters took six weeks to arrive, and the crisis that had originated the initial message had been resolved by the time of the receipt of the response. Yet, anthropologists ideally still work things out for themselves in the field; they grow up. The situation changes again during the phase of writing up.

More significant, and more fraught, are the relationships of the ethnographer with the subjects of her research. As Malinowski long ago discovered in the Trobriands, one of the effects—since Malinowski's time, a deliberate one—of long-term fieldwork away from the ties of home is that the anthropologist becomes dependent on the "natives," developing emotional ties, relaxing, laughing, celebrating, complaining, and grieving along with them. At the same time, the good anthropologist must be alert to differences of feeling and to the effects of her own feelings on what she understands and comes to write about (Briggs 1970). Every anthropologist gets the culture he deserves, goes an old adage, but it is more that every successful anthropologist discovers what she needs or unconsciously seeks. This is decidedly not a matter of "going native," but of finding the right balance and perspective. While opinions differ, I personally advocate a relatively ascetic formulation of the anthropological calling that is skeptical of explicit attempts or even claims to being "changed in the field" and forgoes some of the pleasures of full participation for the distance of reflection and the loneliness of writing fieldnotes. At the same time, fieldwork entails finding and modulating a research persona along a continuum from a relatively passive or passionate stance, allowing oneself to be placed in other peoples' hands or swept along by events, toward a more active but relatively external stance, imposing a research agenda or interview protocol.[11]

---

11. Compare, for example, Evans-Pritchard's interventionist attempts to learn the secrets of Zande sorcery extraction (1937) with my own (frustrated) strategy of patience (1993b). I am not suggesting that one is ethically superior to the other, but that the very mode of inquiry is informed by ethical judgment. In that study I did imitate Evans-Pritchard in letting my questions emerge through the logic of local practice and describing how what I came to know was shaped in large part by the notions characteristic of respective traditions about how to teach. See also Solway 2005 and Lambek 1991a on modesty, Hirschkind 2001 on an ethics of listening, and, more generally, Gadamer 1975. I develop these issues further in Lambek 1997.

One of the curious features about ethical protocols is that they generally presume a rather thin and distant relationship with our subjects. Put another way, they focus on the ethics of observation rather than of participation, whereas the central problem of ethnographic ethics concerns subjects with whom we become very (too?) close. What are the risks and limits of intimacy? Intimacy takes many forms, but for the sake of expediency, I mention only one of the most salient. Thirty years ago prospective fieldworkers were warned against engaging in sexual relationships in the field. There is now a good deal less admonition, in part, no doubt, in the wake of occasional public confession and widespread tacit knowledge of infractions. Indeed, it is not unheard of for ethnographers to return home with partners or infants.[12] It is not entirely clear what this taboo was specifically meant to address, presumably it was as much methodological—maintain objectivity, avoid entanglements—as ethical. Like any taboo, it clarifies and maintains boundaries, but the larger point for which it stands is the fact that intimacy entails betrayal. The more intimate our relationships in the field, the richer our experience,[13] but also the more likely and the more intensely felt the eventual betrayal. It is not sufficient simply to assure interlocutors of our trustworthiness or to fool ourselves that being trustworthy is a simple matter of good will, since, in the end (and actually all along), we do two big things that challenge this: we leave and we write. Naturally this need not mean that we break off all ties or that we publish everything, but what else is it than a kind of betrayal to withdraw and to write frankly or from a critical angle about people whose lives one has shared?[14] Alongside our concern for (degrees of) betrayal, we should be on the lookout for bad faith, especially the bad faith that refuses to recognize betrayal or that assumes that telling people one is going to write about them or showing oneself in the act of writing fieldnotes is to maintain the boundaries sufficiently to preclude betrayal.

Anthropology is all very high-minded (sometimes even moralistic). It is how we attract students and how we position ourselves vis-à-vis other disciplines. But we need to acknowledge that all fieldwork is ethically ambiguous. My position here is not to champion the ethical purity of anthropology, nor to take up the superficial critique that, some students report, is

12. There is silence on the matter of infants conceived in the field and left there.

13. Possibly, then, the more intimate our relationships in the field, the deeper our understanding and the better our research—except for the fact that intimacy may weaken the critical detachment that is also a crucial part of knowledge construction.

14. The situation is not so different for memoirists or most writers of fiction.

to be found in certain women's studies and postcolonialism classrooms, criticism that merely lambastes anthropology for its colonialist associations and qualities and then goes on to offer in replacement thin imitations of the kind of positions that anthropology has in fact long since taken. I suggest that there are no easy or ready-made alternatives or prescriptive solutions for any of the obvious dilemmas associated with fieldwork and writing—for example, whether to be more an observer or an advocate (and if so, an advocate for which faction?); whether to grant voice to and recognize the identity of each informant (as oral historians do) or to protect identity through concealment; whether to speak "truthfully" or "sincerely" in fully reciprocal conversation with interlocutors or to privilege their positions.

One of the (ethical) lessons of fieldwork—one that contributes to the ethnographer's ethical self-formation, is the recognition that he cannot be consistently good or just, fully detached or fully committed, and that there is always a balance and compromise. Ethical action is never fully consistent or complete. (Saints, for example, or monks and nuns, must give up care for their immediate families.) The insights gained in fieldwork and the challenges faced are continued and possibly magnified in acts of writing.

Here are only a few situations encountered in fieldwork that demonstrate the pervasiveness of ethical ambiguity. A first point is that we can never stick fully to the outlooks that we attempt to grasp or that, by nods or silent acquiescence, we appear, for a time, to share with our interlocutors. This is both because of the critical distance necessary for social science and because our interlocutors do not all agree with each other. For all the talk in the anthropological literature about acknowledging the voice of "the Other," there is relatively little attention to the fact that there are many "Others" and that (being also Others to each other) they do not always agree among themselves. For example, in fieldwork in Madagascar not only did I have to disappoint expectations by not being able to provide a factual or authoritative account of Sakalava history and royal politics of the kind that some interlocutors seemed to expect from my inquiries, but also, had I tried to do so, I could not have met equally the expectations of the members of the various factions, each of whom tried earnestly to make me see the truth and justice of their own side of things (and which I could appreciate while I listened to each of them). It is not always easy to know on which side of a conflict to stand, with whom to show solidarity, or when to step out of the fray and become a neutral observer. When some of the spirit mediums who befriended me said bad things about each other, I found my loyalties and personal consistency tested. Much stronger expressions of this dilemma are to be found in highly stratified contexts in which some voices are silenced at the expense of others, and where the ethnographer is forced to take on the perspective of only one gender, class, or status group, and, if it is the dominant group, then to infringe on that understanding in the ensuing critical account.[15]

A second, related lesson concerns the prevalence and necessity of deceit. We often give an impression or fail to correct someone's misapprehension about such matters as our acceptance of certain practices or stances. For example, an anthropologist of religion who is an atheist (or a Christian) will often fail to make that explicit.[16] One could argue that refraining from expressing skepticism or superiority is often the right thing to do (not only for methodological reasons of maintaining openness but also out of simple politeness) but admit that it runs counter to an ethics of full disclosure. We are no doubt aware of this dilemma from our personal lives as well—and realize that it cannot be solved by following a rule; indeed, its experience as a dilemma is heightened insofar as we do conceive of the situation as one of potentially violating a rule.

Perhaps the central ethical dilemmas for anthropologists stem from the fact that, by its very definition, fieldwork is limited in time and space. This raises saliently the issues of forensic personhood and dissociation that have been central to philosophical debate over ethics (see chapter 14). Commitment (to specific people, values, and courses of action) and thus responsibility are central to ethical life and hence ought to be characterized with respect to both temporal continuity (as described by the forensic quality of personhood) and consistency or completeness (as indicated negatively by dissociation). On both counts the anthropological position is distinctly peculiar. Continuity is challenged by the fact that eventually we leave the field (whether provisionally or decisively), raising questions of abandonment and the breaking of ostensible commitments (betrayal, as referred to above). This suggests that attention to departures ought to be as central a subject of anthropological discussion as termination is with regard to psychoanalysis. But more to the point, the very foreknowledge of eventual

15. This raises also the relationship of the ethical to the political (or, as phrased in the chapter epigraph by Asad [2006], of anthropological inquiry to both the ethical and the political). My essay does not address the politics of anthropology: whether it is better to be a barefoot *compagnera* or a theoretical Marxist; to engage in grass-roots development or World Bank consultancy; and so on.

16. This point emerged in a discussion of ethics with post-Soviet scholars, led by Güzel Sabirova, in which I was privileged to participate.

departure and the fact of having a life outside the field cast a shadow over all the commitments entered into during the course of fieldwork, framing or bracketing them in a manner that implies a kind or degree of dissociation from one's own acts.

Following philosopher Alexander Nehamas, I associate this position with irony. There is irony entailed in leading a double life, but such doubling is often less a form of deliberate outright deception than of uncertainty.[17] As Nehamas puts it, irony "enables us to play at being someone, without forcing us to decide what we really are or, indeed, whether we really are anyone. . . . Irony always and necessarily postulates a double speaker and a double audience" (1998, 59–60). Dissociation conceived in this manner is by no means necessarily unethical (see chapter 7) but it renders ethics more complicated. Moreover, it may readily spill over from fieldwork into ordinary life, so that the latter is put into question as a kind of "field" itself and is no longer quite so "ordinary." The radical contingency of things is more apparent—not only cultural practices and criteria but also our own commitments to them.

Insofar as commitment to one way of life, system of thought, model of reality, religious order, social identity, community, or set of people entails rejection of others, the anthropologist is poised outside of any such ordinary commitment, a perch (detached, dissociated, doubled, distributed, or ironic) that is both precarious and implausible with respect to our lives taken in their entirety.[18] Within limits, it can be intellectually exhilarating, but it can also be ethically problematic or in need of specific ethical rationalization. I illustrate from my own practice. Insofar as spirit possession itself is characterized by dissociation, so has been my response to it. Readers of my work on spirit possession have accused me, on the one side, of naively accepting as real what (to these critics) is patently false, and, on the other side, of what one critic memorably called "ontological imperialism" insofar as I alluded to a mystified social construction. My attempt to wriggle (intellectually) out of the dilemma was to suggest that all strong cultural practices, my own included, entail some sort of mystification of social construction or legitimation. The point is that I am vulnerable neither to becoming possessed by an ostensibly autonomous Malagasy spirit nor to

17. Geertz elucidates what he calls "anthropological irony" precisely in an essay on the ethics of fieldwork. This remains an important and characteristically subtle discussion of "the inherent moral asymmetry of the fieldwork situation" (2000, 83).

18. Is it ethical to compartmentalize fieldwork? Is it ethical not to?

naively advocating for the authenticity of possession at large, nor am I about to reject spirit possession as false.

When I am in the field, and when I write about it, I accept the social reality of possession without question and am actively engaged in its reception (aesthetically, intellectually, ethically, and practically); in my everyday "personal life," "at home," spirit possession is nonexistent.[19] I am prepared to argue the merits of my (double) position; intellectually it represents what is valuable (difficult, exciting, insightful, perhaps even truthful and beautiful) about anthropology as a balancing act. Practically, such dissociation may not be so unusual and is certainly characteristic of numerous domains of social life (as when many Europeans move with ease between "science" and "religion" without worrying about consistency). The anthropological situation here epitomizes many highly intellectualized, detached, or skeptical positions or endeavors, albeit enriched and informed by deeply personal human encounters and presence (face-to-face encounters with spirits and spirit mediums, their presence and my presence, our mutual presence to each other). The anthropologist stands, in this regard, as both modernity's hero and its fool.[20]

Finally, I briefly add that not only fieldwork but also theory entails ethical judgment, especially in such matters as the balance we draw between structure and agency, human freedom and creativity, and biological, economic, or other forms of determinism; and the relative weight we give to power and interest. In other words, an ethical dimension of theory entails how we acknowledge the ethical insight, intention, responsibility, and constraints of others.

What I have been arguing is that the anthropological position is out of the ordinary in two, perhaps contradictory, respects. On one side, it is profoundly non-ethical or infra-ethical (I specifically do not call it *un*ethical) insofar as it precludes full (continuous, consistent, undissociated) commitment to a single given alternative, community, or way of life (though of course anthropology creates its own way of life). But on the other side, this renders the anthropological position supra-ethical, as it entails both a principled look at the existential abyss and a disciplined, ascetic rejection

19. Earlier reflections on the changing nature of "home and field" appear in Robbins and Bamford 1997. See my essay there (1997), and the response by Tehindrazanarivelo (1997).

20. On the "foolishness" of anthropology, I am indebted to Donna Young (2010 and forthcoming).

of any exclusive form of identity (or identity politics) at the same time as it understands and documents the value for a sane human life of commitment to a given cultural order and social community. Anthropological fieldwork is at once a kind of supra-ethical activity, in which one enables oneself to be "read" by the field and to be subject to exhilarating or excruciating challenges and calls for judgment, and an infra-ethical one, insofar as one does not fully commit to the indexical "I." One is never fully where one stands, or not exclusively there; one will leave one day, one is nosy and instrumental, and one will inevitably betray confidence and hospitality.

But in the end, anthropologists are also just ordinary human beings. Having made particular commitments, being given to particular and shifting attractions, friendships, and affinities rather than others, and subject as well to indignation and other ethical emotions (Strawson 2008; Stafford 2010), anthropologists cannot do better than anyone else at remaining calm or neutral or sticking to abstract principles, even when the right thing to do might appear relatively clear-cut. Our often self-conscious lapses of exemplary virtuous behavior Aristotelians translate by the awkward term of *incontinence*. While striving for virtue, we human beings have to be able to acknowledge our occasional incontinence as well as the unforeseen consequences of even our most virtuous acts. To act responsibly is not to protest our innocence, justify or rationalize our actions, or make excuses, but to apologize and ask forgiveness (and, in complementary circumstances, to forgive), as Hannah Arendt (1998) emphasized. Put more generally, and perhaps more strongly, following Stanley Cavell (1996), the thing to do about accidents or mistakes (Austin 1970 on the distinction between them) or shifts of commitment is simply to acknowledge them. As Stephen Mulhall articulates Cavell's position, it is not that a person is or isn't responsible for all the consequences of her utterances or actions, could have foreseen them all, and so forth, but that, "she is then flatly responsible for determining her relation to them—whether and how to claim them as unforeseeable or simply unforeseen, to accept them as meant or excuse them as unintended" (Mulhall 1996, 17).

I have emphasized the consistent challenges or tensions in living and working ethically, as anthropologists and in ordinary life. The ethical self cannot simply follow a rule or set of rules and established obligations; even were it possible, that would be a narrow, pinched existence. But equally, the ethical self is not simply open to a horizon of pure freedom. Instead, as we document in our ethnographic work, humans are constituted by prior commitments and open to further alternatives and other voices, acts and forms of interpellation, enticing or disturbing, more and less fully received, inhabited, or internalized. Anthropological fieldwork heightens the difficulty entailed in practical judgment between maintaining former or multiple commitments of identity and personhood, accepting interpellations, taking leaps into (or back from) new territory, or living in some degree of dissociation with both. Ethics can try to draw boundaries or exhort freedom, but inevitably it will escape them.

There is no set of rules that could offer a perfect or foolproof guide to ethical conduct, nor is it possible to act fully and consistently ethically. These are fantasies, attractive only to saints or prophets or to people whose work as professional ethicists overrides their imagination or life experience. This is not to say one should abandon a concern with ethics—in any case, this is no more possible than the enactment of a fully ethical practice—but to suggest a bit of realism. We need to face frankly the fact that anthropological practice may not be precisely ethical in the ordinary way of things. Moreover, it is probably as "ethical" to acknowledge inconsistency, incompleteness, incontinence, and just plain wrongdoing as to advocate perfection.

Each version of a handbook [such as the one in which this essay first appeared] is the product of its time. As the current period is one in which a great deal of anxiety has been expressed concerning ethics, it has seemed most useful to take a critical distance and suggest a bit of "lightening up." This has required judgment on the author's part. Whether good or bad, the judgment is one that can be ascribed to the broad field of the ethical.

THIRTEEN

The Value of (Performative) Acts

This has proved to be a controversial essay. The first draft was prepared for a workshop on value at James Cook University that, as it turned out, I could not attend but where apparently it was heavily criticized. It received positive scrutiny in seminars at Johns Hopkins, UCLA, and Toronto and during the review process at HAU, *where its "value" was also the subject of some debate between the editors in the introduction to the special issue (Otto and Willerslev 2013). As all this suggests—and as I note in my first sentence—the essay is a thought experiment. In any case, it continues an exploration of some of the ideas raised in chapter 10, as well as expanding on the ethnographic analysis presented in chapter 2.*

> With the increasing value of the world of things proceeds in direct proportion the devaluation of the world of men.
>
> —Karl Marx, *Economic and Philosophic Manuscripts of 1844*

This chapter is something of an experiment, a wager that there is value in examining the value of acts—that is, to think about action from the perspective of value or about value from the perspective of action. I argue that ethical value is to action (doing something) as material value is to production (making something). However, the objectification and hence circulation of ethical value is not the same as the objectification and circulation of economic value.

This chapter first appeared in a special double issue on value edited by Ton Otto and Rane Willerslev in *HAU* 3, no. 2 (2013): 141–60.

I

Marx's remark points to the fact that the economic and the ethical uses of value are inextricably connected. Hence it may be no accident of English that the same word extends from speaking about having "good values" to receiving "good value" for our money; from what is most important in life and could never be exchanged to the very basis and rate of exchange (Graeber 2001; see chapter 10).[1] Value is both substance and relation, absolute and relative. It brings together what in Western thought have been distinguished as the material and the ideal—indeed the materialistic and the idealistic—and also, perhaps, the earthly and the transcendent.

What would it mean to reconnect the investigation of the value of "the world of things" to the value of "the world of men"? This requires attending to value as applied to *activities* (acts, work, and practices) and to *objects*, the distinction, say, between the value of playing the violin and the value of the particular violin that a musician is playing. Marx distinguishes value as a function of labor, hence as an expression of an activity, from value as wages or price—when that activity and its products become objectified and placed on the market as commodities. There is a transvaluation from the activity to the object (Eiss and Pedersen 2002) and an objectification of value itself. Marx also gets at the matter through his distinction between use value (activity) and exchange value (objects). Marshall Sahlins (1976a) refines the idea of use value by distinguishing the semiotic values or cultural meanings that shape activities or practices from their ostensibly direct utilitarian functions. Here he conjoins the idea of the cultural mediation of human practice characteristic of American cultural anthropology, the mental mediation characteristic of Lévi-Straussian structuralism, and the critique of liberal political economy so beautifully exemplified in C. B. Macpherson's "view of man's essence not as a consumer of utilities but as a doer, a creator, an enjoyer of his [*sic*] human attributes. . . . Man is not a bundle of appetites seeking satisfaction but a bundle of conscious energies seeking to be exerted" (1973, 4–5). The nature of value shifts radically according to which of these latter two positions one takes.[2]

1. Questions remain regarding whether value is in some sense a transhistorical concept or particular to an economic system (capitalism) and to what degree parsing the economic from the ethical is peculiar to speakers of English.

2. Although Bronislaw Malinowski is famous for his utilities position, I have been inspired by his account of the value of the *kula* as an activity or set of activities (1922). Compare also the important contributions in Nancy Munn (1986) and David Graeber (2001).

In a somewhat similar and explicitly Aristotelian vein, Alasdair MacIntyre (1984) distinguishes between values internal to a practice and those external to it. Here one would distinguish the value of playing the violin for its own sake—that is, for the pleasures and challenges in drawing upon and stretching human capacities it brings—from the value of playing in order to make a living. As in Macpherson, the ethical sense of value is distinguished from the utilitarian one insofar as ends and means are conjoined in ethical value and separated in utilitarian or market value. You play the violin for the playing of it rather than simply as the means for an external end like fame or fortune. Scarcity applies only to external goods, to the object rather than the activity, as it were. Problems with this approach include how to distinguish the boundaries between one practice and another, and accounting for the fact that people are engaged in multiple practices. Indeed, some practices are embedded in one another, such that the ultimate practice is the living of life (the "art of living"), under a master value that might for some people be called happiness, well-being, or simply human flourishing (*eudaimonia*)—or, more reflectively, and perhaps chiefly for philosophers, moral perfectionism, that is, "the evaluation of a way of life, of a stance toward one's life as such rather than toward individual courses of conduct" (Cavell 2005b, 120). Thus the values external to one practice could be internal to another. Moreover, human flourishing in its totality entails the exercise of judgment between competing and incommensurable practices and values—for example, the time spent enjoying the violin or one's noisy children, never mind making a living to ensure the material well-being of those children.

In comparing the value of playing the violin to that of playing with one's children, there is no common measure one can apply, unlike in comparing the cost of a new violin with that of a children's toy. The former values are incommensurable with one another, while the latter are commensurable (chapter 10). Ethics concerns itself with incommensurable values; the market, with commensurable ones, or at least with what happens when one begins with a premise or goal of commensurability. When we turn activities into objects or put a price on things, we expand the realm of commensurable value and, as Georg Simmel (1978) observed, transform quality into quantity. This is not to say that money renders everything commensurable or that commensurable and incommensurable values do not intersect in practice. Comparing the price of two violins is different from deciding whether to purchase one for oneself or for one's child. Commensurability (or the premise of commensurability) of value or values enables and is enabled by quantification and ranking, hence calculative reasoning. Yet as Paul Bohannan famously showed (1959), there may be distinct spheres of exchange in operation. Exchanges within a sphere are commensurable; conversions between spheres are incommensurable and incite moral anxiety. In a bracing extension and critique of Bohannan, Jane Guyer observes that people may transact with multiple scales of value. She remarks that in Atlantic Africa "quantity was *a form* of quality" (2004, 12), in a sort of reversal of the process distinguished by Simmel and one that is visible in "tournaments of value" of many kinds.

The assumption of a single sphere of exchange is the basis for the abstraction and articulation of discrete variables in many economic and other positivist social scientific models, and if you "buy" (so to speak) the assumption, commensurability can be applied to anything. But ethnography shows how rarely this is the case; money itself may be divided between distinct spheres of exchange (Hutchinson 1996; Shipton 1989; Zelizer 1994).

Here a distinction between choice and judgment becomes relevant. Insofar as objects are commensurable to one another, that is, in relation to one or more standards of value, selection among them is a matter of choice. Whether one purchases one or another kind of breakfast cereal or cell phone contract could be a matter of simple choice (albeit complicated by the fact that a number of variables may be at issue). But ethical values are incommensurable to one another; they cannot be measured along any single standard and cannot be seen as mutually exclusive alternatives or as exchangeable for one another. A given act is a matter of balance between, say, justice and compassion, or responsibility to one's family and generosity to others. Achieving the balance is not a matter of simple calculation or preference but entails the exercise of judgment to fit the circumstances, according to cultivated disposition and prior commitments rather than rational choice. In sum, where choice entails selecting among commensurable alternatives or according to commensurable criteria, judgment entails the balancing of incommensurable values. While choice may be more or less easy, a salient characteristic of judgment is its difficulty; wisdom is not easily taught or achieved (neither for sale nor on sale).

That said, there are many ordinary circumstances or practices in which both choice and judgment are at stake or where they appear to blur together. Whereas a paradigmatic image of choice is that of *shopping*, when we look for the best deal (or marginal gain) according to one or more commensurable values along which we can compare, as an activity shopping itself is likely to be considerably more complex.[3] Hence Guyer (2004) is no doubt

3. In practice "shopping" entails judgments of many kinds: evaluating relative price in relation to various incommensurable criteria of need, taste, and so on.

correct to critique "conceptual binaries," whether those of mainstream economists or my own ideal types. Nevertheless, one can propose that what makes ethical and market models incommensurable to one another at the outset is precisely that one deals with incommensurable values, or value according to incommensurable criteria, while the other assumes commensurable value or value measured along a scale or according to criteria that produce commensurability.

One of the features of capitalist consumer culture and calculated effects of advertising is the confusion of these matters, so that complex questions of judgment are passed off as simple matters of choice, and questions of choice are aggrandized as matters of judgment. I suspect, but cannot show here, that forms of both neoliberal thought and evangelical Christianity do just this and owe their appeal to their ostensible ability to cover over deep incommensurabilities—if not outright contradictions—between market and ethical values. They respond to the sort of moral disquiet that Bohannan (1959) identified as accompanying conversions between spheres by setting strict limits in some areas (so-called family values) and denying incommensurability in others (so-called, by outsiders, fundamentalism). But obscuring or erasing distinctions between ethical and market value is likely only to increase disquiet.

II

Value is generated in human activity. For Marx this was primarily labor, but other forms of activity generate their own forms of value. I focus here on action as a relatively distinct but complementary kind of activity and potential source of value. The separation of action from labor as two forms of activity is grounded in Aristotle's (1976) distinction between making (*poiesis*) and doing (*praxis*) and informed by Hannah Arendt's (1998) elaboration of the distinctiveness of action (although here not by her distinction between work and labor).[4] Acts (in this sense) are activities whose primary outcomes are not products (objects) but consequences. Acts are also the subject of speech act theory, where J. L. Austin's specific point (1962) is how to do

4. Hannah Arendt distinguished work from labor in that only the former produces objects of real or lasting value, epitomized in durable *works* of art, like sculpture. Labor is ongoing, repetitive, and life-sustaining rather than object-creating. This is at once a protofeminist insight distinguishing unrewarding labor from unalienated or rewarding work and a "high" cultural valuing of the work of art over the shoddy, disposable commodity. Both Aristotle and Arendt add a further activity, namely, contemplation.

things with words rather than how to make things with words (the latter being the subject of the extensive literature on literary composition).

I realize that the distinction between making and doing is not always obvious (Is playing the violin a matter of *making* music or *performing* it? Are people in the various service industries or those carrying out "affective labor," making or doing?),[5] and that I am marching ever further into the land of ideal types. In fact, making and doing can be understood as distinctive perspectives on activities, as activities placed under, or seen in light of, different kinds of descriptions—whether these are products of structural forces, enunciated in the performance of their enactors, or conceptualized by analysts contemplating the nature of their activities.

The description under which we respectively place certain kinds of activities is one place where I part company with what is otherwise an extremely powerful and comprehensive model of value, namely, Pierre Bourdieu's account of forms of capital (1997). Bourdieu privileges labor and identifies what he calls capital, in all its varieties, as accumulated labor. For Bourdieu, scarcity is the basis of value, and, when necessary, value is manufactured in the symbolic realm through what he calls "the performative magic of the power of instituting, the power to show forth and secure belief or, in a word, to impose recognition" (1977, 51) or, more simply, "the alchemy of consecration" (52)—or what I am calling performative acts. Nevertheless, for Bourdieu such social acts of recognition are always secondary to labor; to fully distinguish or privilege them "reduces social exchanges to phenomena of communication and ignores the brutal fact of universal reducibility to economics" (54). Bourdieu's approach prioritizes scarcity, hence competition and exclusion, whereas I argue that certain acts are a different kind of activity from labor, not reducible to economics, but to the contrary, constitutive of ethics. Bourdieu's analysis of cultural and social capital is not wrong, just too narrow.

By *acts,* one can mean many things. Arendt idealized acts and saw them as political interventions whose consequences are unforeseen. For Arendt, acts are singular and unique, whereas I claim that most acts in social life could rather be called specific—that is, falling under a particular and culturally standardized description—and iterated. When I speak of acts in this chapter, I refer less to political acts (or political activism), to wild or singular acts, or acts of particular heroism or historical significance (the killing of Captain Cook, for example), than to specific and ordinary acts.

5. Thanks to Shiho Satsuka for the point.

Ordinary acts can be very ordinary. They include the following: calling someone by name and answering to a name, promising, apologizing, thanking, criticizing, praising, expressing condolences, declaring love or war, and so forth. As philosophers would say, these are happenings under a description; as anthropologists would say—if they ever properly considered acts, the way they consider things like kinship terms, plant taxonomies, and other nouns—they are culturally or semiotically shaped or mediated. The description can be uttered by the speaker as the explicit substance of the act ("I apologize") or can be implied ("Good morning"). Hence speakers themselves specify both that they are doing something and what it is, as acknowledged by respondents. These are what Austin (1962) called performative or illocutionary acts, that is, acts occurring under specified felicity conditions and that bring something conventional into being through the course of their enactment. I limit my discussion to acts in this sense. Hence, a gap in the argument is that I do not consider primarily physical acts (and hence many specifically destructive ones). Nevertheless, the category remains broad; in Stanley Cavell's redaction (1976), every utterance may carry the illocutionary entailment of meaning what we say.

Austin clarified what is entailed in explicitly performative utterances, and Roy Rappaport further developed the argument as he applied it to ritual (1999). At the heart of ritual are performative utterances—acts of deference, obeisance, praise, naming, blessing, baptism, sacrifice, sanctification (but also curses, insults, refusals), and so forth. Insofar as all such acts operate under a description, they are precisely not unique or singular in this respect but specific (cf. Chakrabarty 2000, 82–83), that is, of a specified kind. Yet at the same time, as Rappaport emphasizes, they conjoin this *canonical* dimension of iteration with an *indexical* dimension (who, when, where, etc.); in this sense, each act is also singular, taking place uniquely in time. Acts are consequential and categorical; either you bless your child or you do not; either you provide a Muslim funeral or you do not. They are also likely to be incommensurable to one another, if not outright contradictory. The acts of circumcising and baptizing your child cannot be fully measured against each other. Nor can the act of baptizing one child but not another. Much as Arendt argued for political acts, ritual acts are not easily retractable. Of all acts, sacrifice is perhaps the least retractable; indeed that is central to its import (chapter 9). Following Rappaport's hierarchy of sanctity, sacrifice could be the most profound of ritual acts, serving as the ultimate ground of value (chapter 10; cf. Otto and Willerslev 2013).

Arendt (1998) had profound things to say about irreversibility, and Cavell gives exquisite attention to it: "Human conduct and thought are inherently vulnerable to embarrassment. I can no more take back the word I have given you and you have acted on than I can take back my touch. Each has entered our history. Apology and reparation may be entered into that history, but they are subject to acceptance, hence to rejection" (2010, 322).

Many acts serve as kinds of acknowledgment of other acts or circumstances, whether putting events under a description after the fact, such as excuses with respect to "mistakes" and "accidents" (Austin 1970) or putting circumstances under a description before the fact, as in wagers and promises. Hence they act to place events and circumstances under a particular description (*this* was a mistake on my part; *that* was an accident). They form a kind of meta-action, action as text or commentary, the things people tell each other about themselves—thus, the sort of thing that interested Clifford Geertz (1973a), albeit here not taken in the abstract (any Balinese cockfight) but with respect to actual persons and events.

As we move from minute and tacit acts discernable through conversational analysis (Sidnell 2010) to those acts that announce themselves with much fanfare and formality and that anthropologists (and sometimes performers) label "ritual," the question of such action becomes more acute. Thus, Maurice Bloch (1989c) sees circumcision, for example, as secondary to and not really necessary for the maturation of boys. Yet I would argue that many such acts are fundamental to society or the person rather than extraneous or parasitic. Circumcision is not necessary for all human males, yet it is intrinsic to the re/production of specifically Muslim, Jewish, and (most) Malagasy males. Formalized acts of this kind are not merely representations of some prior state or action, after the fact, but are themselves socially constitutive and consequential—acts that create the facts. The gift, for example, does not merely represent social relations, it constitutes them; it *is* the social relation. In fact, insofar as ritual acts stand autonomous from the more material forms of intervention about which they speak—the warfare they promise to assist in, the damage they apologize for, the blessing they offer a child—they may be considered acts of the purest kind, accomplished immediately and completely in their saying and doing.

Acts of this general kind are necessary to—indeed constitutive of—society; indeed, they exemplify the working of society or sociality, and they put what would otherwise be chaotic and ambiguous interactions and conditions under a set of descriptions such that what follows is meaningful and interpretable by means of the criteria instantiated in the act (see chapter 11 for the argument). It is in this sense of instantiating criteria for the guidance and judgment of practice that performative acts intrinsically generate and carry ethical value. If culture mediates our world, letting us distinguish the trees from the forest, the bushes from the trees, and the rosemary from the rose bush, so the illocutionary force of utterances—language as action—puts social relations and conditions under descriptions and discriminates among kinds of acts (marriage/divorce/annulment) and consequences (peace/war, something unsettled between us/something now settled). At its most basic, even to say "I know" is a performative act, "*similar* to 'I promise' *in a specific respect*, . . . namely, that *you give others your word*" (Cavell 2010, 320). As Cavell continues, "*this* connection (this inner connection . . .) between claiming to know and making a promise . . . reveals human speech to be radically, in each uttered word, ethical. Speaking, or failing to speak, to another is as subject to responsibility, say to further response, as touching, or failing to touch, another" (320–21).

This does not imply a consistency or commensurability among all acts. Austin precisely did not anticipate a unified homogenous scheme for the doing of actions, even within a single language (1970, 203). It may well be that something akin to Bohannan's spheres of exchange operates with respect to acts in any given social system. Certain acts are located within an encompassing liturgical order (Rappaport 1999), whereas others fall outside it and within a different sphere, such as the market, or different language game, such as science.

III

Acts generate their own forms of value. To the degree that this value becomes objectified, that is, becomes detached from the doing (just as an *end*—or product—of work becomes detached from the means, that is, from the activity of making it, or as the end and even the very means are alienated from the producer), such objectified values might have their own properties, distinct from the use value and exchange value of the products of labor or from labor itself considered as an object.

Here the questions become what kinds of value or values are the consequences of action as a specific form or forms of activity and whether and how the value generated in such activity becomes objectified. Does it manifest in material objects or get stored in money? Or are there other forms and substances through which it is objectified? For example, can the value generated in social acts congeal and be stored in persons or relationships? In legislation and legal contracts? Or perhaps in religious forces such as intentionally minded deities or impersonal qualities like Malagasy *hasina* (whose analysis by Bloch [1989c] as the consequence of ritual acts exemplifies the kind of thing I am talking about)? Indeed, one could draw an analogy with the fetishization of commodities, if Marx's language were not already an analogy with the sphere of religion. Can such value circulate or be exchanged, and if so, through what means or media? Are the values generated through various kinds of incommensurable acts commensurable with one another, or can they be made so?[6] Does the objectification of the value generated in acts sometimes lend itself to commoditization or an equivalent form of standardization? I don't pretend I can fully answer these questions, and I do not even attempt to address them all, but I do assert that there is "value" simply in the *act* of posing them.[7]

Insofar as the mark of an illocutionary act is that it accomplishes its goal directly in the enactment, so we could say that means and ends are not distinguishable. Hence the most purely performative acts are valuable simply in, of, and for themselves. The conflation of means and ends is similar to what MacIntyre (1984) calls the goods internal to practice and, for nonutilitarian philosophers, a criterion of the ethical.

For Arendt, the value of an act is established only after the fact, that is, retrospectively, in historical narrative. Its value is ascertained through the kind of story into which it is placed, or its place in that story, how well it is remembered, how often repeated, and so on. I have recounted elsewhere (1993b) an event from Mayotte in which a granary collapsed on its owner, the richest man in the village, who was sleeping beneath it. During the night he cried in pain, but later he put a positive spin on the event, declaring his narrow escape and rescue as signs of God's grace. Villagers concurred in recognizing his blessings. That declaration was an act, and it seemed to satisfy the circumstances much better than my own assumption, informed by Evans-Pritchard, that the mishap would be declared witchcraft. Some months later, when the man's daughter died from complications following childbirth, the narrative was taken out of his hands, and the events at the granary reinterpreted. It was said that he had provoked his daughter's death while he was pinned under the granary. A grown man crying like a child inverts the moral order (*mañan antambo*), an act certain to bring on disaster.[8]

6. This kind of question is addressed by means of Louis Dumont's (1970) conception of hierarchy.

7. Further questions concern voice, who has the right to speak or act, and with what forcefulness. Hence, an additional analogy with Marx is the question of control over, or access to, the "means of action" and perhaps the identification of distinct "modes of action."

8. The primary inverted act of this kind is incest.

The crying was thus redescribed as an act of its own, and the illocutionary force or value shifted in relation to subsequent events as the narrative took on new coherence. The point is not the referential meaning of his words but the ascribed illocutionary force.

Thus if work produces objects—works—which can then be alienated and circulate apart from their producers, acts generate narratives, which too can circulate, or silences, which can settle (Das 2007). The value of the original act is determined by the narrative (or its absence), which is itself shaped by particular narrative conventions, theories of accountability, the power of certain voices, and a variety of contingent interests and circumstances. It is subject to alienation, revision, and in some instances entextualization and commoditization (in writing or film).

Conversely, specifically virtuous acts draw their value in part from the fact that (unlike the man pinned by the granary) they do not call attention to themselves. As the Malagasy proverb has it, "Full containers don't rattle" (*feno tsy mikobaña*). Their value is found in their immediate consequences for the others to whom they are directed (and eventually for social reproduction) and as they confirm or enlarge the characters of the protagonists. They may also inspire witnesses or bystanders. Hence, among the objects generated by acts are precisely the values and dispositions we call "ethical"—hope, faith, charity, compassion, and so forth (but also resentment, cynicism, etc.)—and ultimately the value of life itself. These culturally articulated values are themselves "valuable," stores of accumulated wisdom (or disaffection) and objectifications of value like the Malagasy proverb. Sometimes the objectified value gets alienated from the actors and the act, as in the case of American war amputees who are thanked by strangers for their "sacrifice" but do not see their service or injuries in that light (Wool 2011). In redescription as sacrifice value is recirculated in a discourse of patriotism. Values of this kind, of course, in turn shape further actions (as explored by authors in the Boasian and Weberian traditions).

Often the value of a performative act lies simply in the transformations it effects in the persons and conditions entailed by it, as does an apology that transforms relations with the aggrieved party. Equally important are the criteria such an act puts in place and by which subsequent actions are evaluated (chapter 11). The value of an apology is weakened, if not negated, if the person who apologized repeats his original offence; in fact, an offence after the apology takes on new weight. The value is also compromised if the felicity conditions are not all present; an apology offered too frequently, in the wrong tone of voice, or to the wrong person is weak or void. The value of various admissions of responsibility uttered in the course of the South

African Truth and Reconciliation Commission (and similar endeavors) and the public acts of forgiveness that followed them can be interpreted in this light (Ross 2010).

One effect of the market is that any object of a certain kind or equivalent value is substitutable for any other, but this is clearly not the case with respect to performative acts. My promise or apology is not substitutable for yours; I cannot stand at the altar in your stead or replace a wedding with a funeral. Nor can one place monetary value on the act of promising or apologizing, and although one can spend a lot of money on weddings or funerals, one cannot buy or sell acts of matrimony or dexiosis (farewell to the deceased).[9] The main point here is that values generated through acts are not usually mutually commensurable or quantifiable. Hence performative value is far less readily commoditized than productive value.

Perhaps the densest stores of the cumulative value of acts are what Rappaport refers to as ultimate sacred postulates, concise verbal utterances that are highly iterative, immutable, unquestionable, authoritative, and characterized by their historical longevity (1999, 314). To postulations I would add certain concise and reiterated acts like forms of prostration or cutting limes or kola nuts, as well as objects, such as relics, that are sacred in particular religious traditions. As Rappaport points out, ultimate sacred postulates are generally informationless and yet deeply meaningful. Their utterance sanctifies numerous other acts and utterances, and nothing can do this in their stead. They are thus, quite literally, both invaluable and stores and transmitters of "general-purpose value" (and, in this sense only, comparable to money). But in order to store and transmit value, they need to be invoked. When people no longer perform the rituals, the postulates lose their sanctifying powers and hence their value; we speak of religions like that of ancient Egypt as "dead."

I saw these issues manifest at a shrine in northwest Madagascar that houses the relics of ancestral figures of the northern Sakalava polity (Lambek 2002a). People come in large numbers to pay their respects and to receive blessings in return. Highly sacred, the relics cannot be approached directly. They are housed within a series of successively more restrictive enclosures and addressed through intermediaries. The ancestors can provide children, health, prosperity, jobs, and also discern truth from falsity, forming the ground and standard for value as well as its source. But the power of the relics is contingent upon the proper actions of the supplicants and

9. There are of course more complex issues here, such as the circulation of valuables at weddings or funerals or the different applications of gifts and payments for services.

the priestly guardians, and indeed of the whole community—contingent on maintaining the shrine in good order, generating generous offerings, and especially on maintaining the prohibitions associated with the temple and the persons of the relics. Throughout the twenty-year span of my visits, there has been anxiety over whether the restrictions are being maintained, the ancestors shown proper respect, and the annual purification ceremony carried out in good order: in sum, debate over the extent and fulfillment of felicitous action. As people explained, it is the acts of their subjects that maintain the power and sanctity of the royal ancestors. If the prohibitions were not maintained, the relics would lose their potency.[10]

In effect, to have, store, and emit value, the relics must be properly valued. Value, even that congealed as the sanctity of the ancestors, is understood here expressly as a consequence of human acts and attention. Value circulates through human activity, and it rapidly evaporates in the absence of such activity. Sacred value is in a sense the objectified consequence of collective and individual acts on the part of the faithful, to whatever degree that relationship is mystified to them (Bloch 1989c) and even where, as we have just seen, it is not. As alluded to above, the mystification of performative action is formally akin to Marx's discussion of the mystification of labor in commodity fetishism. And perhaps such value can collapse in a way similar to that of a financial institution when people no longer express their faith in its value through the regular performance of acts of buying, investing, or borrowing.

The value of human acts is stored in ultimate sacred postulates, icons, deities, and so forth, and would be depleted without the continued enactment of core rituals. Prayers must be regularly recited, irrespective of their objectification as scripture. Such recitations are acts, and value is not frozen or spent but lived and renewed, used but not used up. In fact, following the logic of the gift, expending value simultaneously generates more value (Hyde 1983). More precisely, certain core rituals (e.g., Catholic mass, Muslim *swala*, Sakalava *fanompoa*) felicitously (authoritatively) performed, regenerate the value congealed in the ultimate sacred postulates, gestures, and objects—and they and other rituals circulate value insofar as they invest new persons, relationships, and circumstances with sanctity and place them under new or renewed descriptions.

Acts are also necessary for the validation or authentication of objects, drawing sometimes on the previously established character or probity

10. In effect, Sakalava practitioners voice the same argument in practice that ethnographers of Madagascar (Bloch 1989c, Lambek 2002a) elevate to the level of general theory.

(value) of the authenticator. This is true for contracts, bonds, and even national currencies, which have two sides (Hart 1986), one indicating the numerical value and the other the ethical value (so to speak) stemming from the trustworthiness of the authenticating source. This holds in different ways for luxury objects—jewels, paintings, wine, and so on. The mark or brand adds to the monetary value of the object as the sign of acts of authentication during the design and production process. The value of objects is linked to acts of contract.[11]

If the value of embodied acts is objectified in words, signatures, or relics, it can also be found in such artifacts as a ring or headscarf, or in embodied traces such as a scar or the smear of white clay that Sakalava supplicants receive on their faces upon paying their respects at the shrine. In nearby Mayotte the value of the act of prayer on behalf of others, its substantiality and sweetness, is objectified in the pastries that are subsequently consumed or carried home and distributed to those who were not present but whose presence is post facto interpellated, so to speak, in the further act of consuming the sweet.

IV

The pastries lead to the final means I describe for ascertaining the value of acts, namely, by following the ways in which specific kinds of acts are reciprocated and their value circulated. That is to say, one can approach acts exactly along the lines laid out by Marcel Mauss (1990), namely, by following the gift. Indeed, I go further than mere analogy, since it is possible to argue that where Mauss speaks of the obligations to give, accept, and return gifts, he is discussing three kinds of acts, rather than rules. In the end I conclude that in fact it is these acts that are the gift and that the gift qua object is merely the materialization of the acts. The material gift, in effect, is the objectification of the value generated in acts of giving and receiving (including prior acts). Hence, whereas a commodity is an objectification of work placed on the market, a gift is an objectification of acts placed in social circulation (see also Gregory 1982; Strathern 1988).[12]

I am back in the magic land of ideal types, but I can illustrate and substantiate this argument through a small slice of ethnography from Mayotte

11. This paragraph draws on Paul Christopher Johnson's genealogical account of forensic persons (2011).

12. It is, of course, the case that buying, selling, lending, borrowing, and speculating are also acts, with their own relationships to objects.

(see also Lambek 1990b; 2000b; in press [b]). A steady progression of rituals takes place, some are deemed necessary for the life cycle, and others are not obligatory but nonetheless frequent. All entail the recitation of Islamic texts, and all are embedded within reciprocity scenarios.

The reciprocity scenario in Mayotte works as follows: I invite you to recite prayers on my behalf or on behalf of my community or my children or parents, and you, in turn, invite me to do the same on your behalf. For the act of praying for my kin you will receive recognition from God and also a substantial meal, pastries, and some cash from me; I will receive the equivalent for performing acts of prayer for you. Much as Erving Goffman (1981; cf. Sidnell 2009) distinguishes among the animator, author, principal, addressed and unaddressed recipients, overhearers, and eavesdroppers in a speech situation, so in these rituals one can minimally distinguish subjects (or principals), sponsors, performers/animators, addressed recipients, and witnesses.[13]

The cycle of reciprocity between sponsors and performers is articulated with a cycle of exchange between subjects and sponsors. If I sponsor rituals on behalf of my children today, after my death they will sponsor different ones on my behalf. Moreover, they can expect to sponsor the same rituals on behalf of their children that their parents have sponsored for them. Value thus circulates both within generational cohorts and between biological generations and in both of what Claude Lévi-Strauss (1969) called direct and generalized forms.

As kin are obligated to sponsor events for one another, so are community members obligated to perform at one another's events. Such reciprocal acts of recitation, witness, and sponsorship are valuable in reproducing persons and social relations. I am close to what an earlier generation spoke of as function here, but by *value* I refer to intentional, forceful, and recognized rather than simply necessary qualities and consequences, and to the exercise of human capacities (Macpherson 1973) rather than the satisfaction of appetites or needs. What I want to stress is that in a given community each person is an active participant in the well-being and transformation of every other. Sponsoring, witnessing, reciting, and subjecting oneself to be prayed over or transformed are roles that are exchanged and acts that implicate each person in the life and social being of every other. To be a complete citizen by the end of one's life is to have participated in the sponsorship of

13. Recipients might include saints, spirits, ancestors, angels, as well as God. The texts themselves have long-deceased authors; with respect to the Qur'an, Mohammed is its original human channel, followed by the chain of reciters from his time to the present.

numerous rituals and to have actively performed in the rituals of others—indeed, to have participated in the rituals of all those who have participated in one's own. Each person becomes who he is through the acknowledgment of others; as people say, "What makes a person a person is [other] persons, *mañka uluñu uluñu, uluñu.*"[14]

At most events, men recite while women cook and distribute food.[15] The labor-intensive activities of preparing, apportioning, and distributing food may be considered acts on the part of the women that are partially equivalent to those of the praying men; that is, they felicitously acknowledge, transform, and regenerate value. At each major event, women of the sponsoring household prepare pastries, drawing upon the assistance of kinswomen, friends, or the entire body of village women, according to the particular cycle of reciprocity at issue. Over the past three decades, they have prepared pastries of three kinds—*bañkora,* balls of coconut cream and rice flour that are squeezed into boiling oil, forming tails; *makarara,* rice-flour cakes that are rolled out on special wooden boards and elaborately crinkled before frying; and *biscuits,* made with condensed milk and spices and baked.[16] Huge quantities of pastries are elaborately divided according to the role and status of the participants and the nature of the occasion. At many events, performers are served tea or a full meal accompanied by platters of pastries, and they are always given additional bags—containing at least one of each kind of pastry—to take home. The pastries both add force to the act of prayer—the prayers of a satisfied reciter are said to move more swiftly and surely—and objectify and further circulate the value of the event. However these objects do not last much longer than the acts of recitation.

Insofar as acts of prayer (or pastries) are exchanged for one another, they are commensurable. However, they exist within a fairly narrow sphere of exchange. They can be exchanged for nothing but themselves (as Bohannan [1959] said of Tiv exchange of women).[17] Toward the end of the ritual season, people become quite tired of pastries, but they continue to be produced in large quantities. At other times one could sell *biscuits,* but not

14. To this, Sakalava add, *mañka ampanjaka ampanjaka, vahoaka,* "What makes a ruler a ruler is the people." This applies to the shrine scenario described above.

15. Men also collect and chop firewood, transport raw foodstuffs, slaughter animals, serve food to male guests, and, at some events, cook a portion of the meat (never the pastries). At some events women also recite prayers or sing and dance the text.

16. More recently, they have added to the repertoire *donuh* (doughnuts).

17. The production of the cakes from raw materials and the outlay of money and labor for ritual performances could be analyzed as conversions between spheres of exchange. This is another dimension of Lévi-Strauss's opposition of the raw and the cooked!

those produced for or received after a prayer event and not the act (or labor) of making them for a ritual.

For several decades one of the explicit values of these events was equivalence and hence equality. The male and female *chefs de village* had the responsibility to publicly measure the raw ingredients offered at each feast of a certain kind and to ensure that they were exactly equivalent to those offered at every other feast. Most salient and suspenseful was the measurement of raw rice; there were special wooden boxes for the purpose. Pastries were counted, and even the salt was measured. As one person put it, you couldn't add so much as a single extra tomato to your sauce (Lambek 1990b). This was established in explicit contrast to the practices among members of neighboring elite communities who used such events to reproduce status differences (Blanchy 2010; Breslar 1979).[18] Today some ritual acts remain governed by equivalence, while others have been opened to both inflation and a more selective guest list, thereby shifting from a systemic circulation and enhancement of value toward an individualized, scarcity-based exchange. As Guyer notes, the capacity to control and represent such conversions of value is highly relevant politically (2004, 39).

In the end, people in Mayotte exchange acts on behalf of one another and in recognition of others as persons like themselves. Food is valuable in itself (and its sensory qualities are not without significance) but the primary value lies elsewhere, in mutual acknowledgment as kin, fellow citizens, or simply fellow human beings, and in witnessing a circumcision or wedding, performing a prayer for well-being or protection, or simply expressing joy.[19] Such value is close to what Cavell describes as the unretractable and radically ethical nature of speaking: "What needs articulation is the sense that the root of morality is the fact of acknowledging shared human existence itself, that every utterance of the creature of speech is an exchange (if sometimes one-sided), an act of demanding a response, a confrontation that draws blood, or stops or boils or cools or heartens it" (2010, 447).

18. Sophie Blanchy's (2010) comprehensive account of contemporary hierarchical exchange on the Grande Comore (Ngazidja) is an outstanding recent exemplification of Mauss' "society of the gift."

19. Pierre Bourdieu makes the same point, albeit reversing the weight: "Exchange transforms the things exchanged into signs of recognition and, through the mutual recognition and the recognition of group membership which it implies, reproduces the group" (1997, 52). For an extended discussion of the materialization of recognition and its problems, see Webb Keane (1997).

V

As specific types of acts of acknowledgment and recognition, these prayer exchanges affirm the singularity, and hence the incommensurability, of each act and person, albeit within a larger order of acts and persons. Such recognition is a basic human end. Its consequence is what Immanuel Kant referred to as the dignity of persons and what he specifically contrasted with price.[20]

The elaboration of ritual formalizes the acknowledgment, renders it certain, public, lasting, and effectively irreversible, and establishes criteria to be recognized by all participants and the entire community. In materializing, objectifying, and displaying the value of acts, the publicity and formality of ritual approximate the way the market objectifies the value of work, but make the consequences impossible to commoditize. One might even say that ritual *de-commoditizes* value.

The thrust of this essay has been to conjoin Marx and Mauss, not to oppose them. Comprehensive theories of value must describe whether and how the human energies exerted in both production and action are condensed and possibly occluded in their ends or objects. Above all, theory must not collude in that occlusion by reducing value to its objectified and material or functional dimension or by collapsing the value of acts into the value of productive labor. The world seems a considerably broader place than a shop floor or a shopping mall when we remember that there is also value in what we say and do, and in the saying and doing themselves.[21]

Although Marx founded his theory of value on labor, most anthropological accounts of value, influenced no doubt by both a certain reading of *The Gift* and the prevalence of commodity capitalism (as well, perhaps, as the Marxist distinction between use and exchange value), have focused on the value of objects. This has led to elegant comparisons of gifts and commodities in the sphere of exchange (Gregory 1982; Strathern 1988). The focus on objects is also part of a broader contemporary interest in materiality. But the new emphasis on materiality sometimes obscures the very premise

20. "In the kingdom of ends everything has either a *price* or a *dignity*. If it has a price, something else can be put in its place as an *equivalent*; if it is exalted above all price and so admits of no equivalent, then it has a dignity" (Kant 1964; quoted in Asad 2003b, 137, n. 21; his italics).

21. Such value is not always positive or excluded from the market sphere. Stock traders are not making anything; they are doing things with money—among other things, placing bets and cashing them in. Such actions precisely refuse to recognize the dignity of others and could be said to generate artificial or counterfeit value rather than the real thing.

of materialist theory, which has to do as much with the work of production as with products or objects. Marx noted that it is only under capitalism that work becomes commodified, that is, becomes an object rather than an activity. As Karl Polanyi (1971) subsequently argued, it may be a fictitious commodity. When labor is understood as an activity rather than always an object or a commodity, as a verb rather than a noun, as it were, the location and nature of value also shifts.[22]

Similarly, I have argued that one can read Mauss to say that what circulates is less gifts qua material objects than the acts of giving and receiving. What distinguishes ritual acts from everyday speaking may include the materialization of the acts in various objectifications, including material objects and dramatic displays, but at bottom the objects are simply signs of what is being done. The objects store (or symbolize) the value of the acts rather than being fully or purely valuable in and of themselves, let alone on the market. At base, the acts in question are ones of mutual acknowledgment (giving *and* receiving graciously)—and it is here, in acts of recognition, respect, and witness that the ground of human value is to be discovered.[23] Conversely, the core fault that Marx finds with capitalism, namely, exploitation, is at base the refusal of full acknowledgment or respect—treating persons (partially) as things and denying that their acts are those of full human beings whose labor time and activity are as valuable in the final instance as those of any other human being.

In the end, the value of such acts lies in what, whom, and how they acknowledge or affirm, in the way they serve as the means by which we acknowledge each other (or refuse to do so). At base, it is not the gift qua object that counts (though objects can have powerful meanings, high resale values, and interesting histories) but the acts of acknowledgment that it signifies. It is in their materialization of acts that gifts qua objects become not merely tokens of value but stores of value. The value they store is the *cumulation* of acknowledgments.

What might be critical then is not only the divide between precapitalist and capitalist social formations, but ritualized and postritualized societies, in which life transformations, rites of passage and their effects, and other forms of recognition are relatively absent, privatized, nonreciprocal, or

22. This is not to ignore the excellent literature on the anthropology of work, the dignity of labor, and so on.

23. This holds even in such instances as the inter-island *kula,* in which acts are marked by deliberate gracelessness and ostensible disdain for the value of what is exchanged (Malinowski 1922).

appropriated by the state (Lambek 2013b; cf. Dumont 1986).[24] The *value* of bureaucratic acts or legally constituted persons may not be the same as that of communal acts and ritually generated persons. Nevertheless, the divide is less sharp when the prevalence of ordinary illocutionary acts is considered; moreover, there are often articulations, dependencies, and reversible shifts between ritualized and nonritualized spheres or relations.

In sum, following *both* Marx and Mauss, I link the value of objects to the value of human activities. I argue that the value of objects should be understood with reference to this more encompassing field. I add action to work (production) as a human activity. Both making and doing—at least the kinds of doing addressed here—generate value. One of the consequences would be to think of exchange not only in terms of the contrast or relationship between commoditized and noncommoditized (gift) spheres, but also between ritual and legal-bureaucratic spheres of performative action. Another consequence would be to address the articulation of making and doing both in everyday life and in capitalist work environments (shop floor *and* trading floor). Following an insight of Lévi-Strauss and subsequent arguments of feminist theory, exchange cannot be disarticulated from reproduction. What underlies these activities is not simply biological need or appetites, nor simply human cognitive structures—say, in sum, "human nature"—but the expression and extension of human energies, capacities, and intentions, ethical criteria, judgment, and mutual acknowledgment—say, "the human condition."

24. What might have been the future of communist states had they not done away with everyday and popular ritual, imposing their own objectified and bureaucratized forms?

FOURTEEN

The Continuous and Discontinuous Person: Two Dimensions of Ethical Life

After forays into acts and values, the final chapter returns to the conceptualization and existence of persons but builds on what has come previously. It was written originally for a Sawyer seminar on personhood convened by Lesley Green and Hylton White at the University of Cape Town in 2009 and then considerably revised during a residency at the Rockefeller Foundation at Bellagio, with portions subsequently delivered at Toronto and UCLA. The theme was partly inspired by Paul Christopher Johnson's provocative rethinking of the genealogy of spirit possession (2011, 2014). The contrast between the forensic and mimetic dimensions is bluntly sketched here but has potential, if only to remind us to question the assumption of continuous accountability (forensic personhood) that underlies so much of Western thought about ethics.

> Sometimes the city is Leningrad, sometimes St. Petersburg; sometimes both at once; never now one without the other. We cannot separate the mistakes from our life; they are one and the same.
>
> —Michaels 2009, 333

> After December I become a different person.
>
> —Overheard from a colleague about to step down from an administrative position

It is inconceivable to think of ethics without consideration of persons—the beings conceived to act ethically and judged with respect to their actions

This chapter first appeared in the *Journal of the Royal Anthropological Institute* 19, no. 4 (2013): 837–58.

and character. The concept of the person is one that anthropologists have discussed at length, usually in order to emphasize cultural difference. Yet if, as I will argue, ethics is intrinsic to the human condition, to human speech and action, and hence in some respect universal, how do we reconcile that with cultural difference? Most attempts to do so have foundered in either ethnocentrism or relativism. I try to forge a different path.

There are many ways to think of persons, and no single one is likely to be accepted as definitive or comprehensive. In this chapter I offer a pair of ideal types that may prove useful for some kinds of questions. They were developed in the early modern period to describe two distinct kinds of persons, but I consider them as two alternative ways to conceptualize persons and finally as two dimensions of active personhood that have universal relevance but carry distinct relative weight or salience in different societies.[1]

Starting with the concept of person rather than the biological individual or psychological subject, my emphasis is on the social in two senses. First is the idea that personhood draws on public—that is, social or cultural—criteria, concepts, models, and vehicles for its realization. Hence I am attending more to what Stanley Cavell has called "participation in the order of law" than "improvisation in the disorders of desire" (2005a, 185). I share the wish to understand these together, but that is something beyond the scope of this particular essay. Second is the sense that the social is also the *inter*personal; persons are only persons in the context of and in relation to other persons. As the Kibushy saying goes, *mañka uluñu uluñu uluñu*, "What makes a person a person is other persons"; in other words, interaction, especially mutual acknowledgment, is central to personhood.[2]

Although my focus is on the public side of personhood rather than the interior and reflexive life of the self or subject, I do not make a sharp distinction between them; social constructs of personhood must draw upon psychological experiences and capacities for selfhood, and conversely, the latter are influenced by the social or cultural vehicles of personhood available (cf. Mead 1934). These questions are relevant but not the main issue here.[3] The

1. My types are offered in the same spirit as Carrithers's (1985) reformulation of Mauss's distinction between *personne* and *moi* (see Laidlaw 2013 for a lucid review) and Bloch's (2012) attempt at a unified theory, albeit I ground them in action rather than cognition.

2. Kibushy is the dialect of the Malagasy-speaking minority in Mayotte. This phrase is found elsewhere in Madagascar and Africa; in isiZulu it is *Umuntu ngumuntu ngabantu*.

3. This has led one reader to complain that my account is rather "bloodless" and conceals the role of persons as agents of history. In fact, my ideas draw from many encounters with individuals (e.g., chapters 7 and 8; Lambek 1993b; 2002a, 2002b; 2007a; 2011, 2014) that cannot be directly addressed here. I certainly do not discount the significance of motivation or

difference may be understood as one of perspective. The perspective in this chapter is how society describes or constitutes persons. A complementary perspective would start with individuals and how they establish their own persons or selves, drawing upon and contesting or undermining practices, models, and ideologies like those described here.

Two Constructs of the Person

In a recent article Paul Christopher Johnson has demonstrated how early modern political philosophers developed the concept of the self-possessed and accountable person by distinguishing it sharply from non-European persons, unduly susceptible to imitation, as exemplified by what the Europeans came to call spirit possession, and explicitly likened by John Locke to the quintessentially mimetic figure of the parrot (Johnson 2014, 37). Persons constituted through mimesis could not be accountable for their actions, could not therefore enter into contracts, and were better understood as a potential form of property (hence as slaves or, later, colonized subjects) than as proprietors.

It has given me some pause to realize that I too have been inspired by the observation of spirit possession to address the concept of person, but the lessons I draw are very different. My axis of comparison applies similar binary terms, albeit placing them at right angles to the philosophers of liberalism. I suggest two universal and intrinsic dimensions of the person. On one side, the person is understood as a unique, continuous, and unitary actor and cumulative product of the acts in which she has engaged or been engaged and for which she is held and holds herself accountable. Following Locke, I call this the forensic person, alluding here to identity over time, carrying moral responsibility for past and future deeds in the way that the law ascribes continuity to individuals with respect to such matters as intentionality, commission, and punishment.[4] On the other side, individuals

self-fashioning for ethics. On ethical subjects, see Faubion 2011 and Mahmood 2005. For psychoanalytic arguments that could articulate with my account of persons, see Loewald 1980 on introjection and S. Mitchell 1988 on object relations theory more broadly.

4. Locke put it as follows: "'Person' . . . is a forensic term, appropriating actions and their merit; and so belongs only to intelligent agents, capable of a law, and happiness, and misery. This personality extends itself beyond present existence to what is past, only by consciousness,—whereby it becomes concerned and accountable; owns and imputes to itself past actions, just upon the same ground and for the same reason as it does the present" (Locke 1975, II.27.xxvi). For my purposes, the Lockean term is preferable to Macpherson's "possessive individual," since

draw from a set of named *personnages*, or dramatis personae, that they "become," "inhabit," "play," "personify," "imitate," or "impersonate" alternately and discontinuously, or possibly successively or simultaneously, and for which different societies provide a variety of means and opportunities. These vehicles for subjection, as well as action and reflection, appear to produce discontinuous, dispersed, dividual, divided, uncontained, or nonunitary persons—a dimension I call mimetic.

Forensic and mimetic are not so much distinct persons as constructs of personhood. And although such constructs are differentially elaborated in local ideologies of the person (of which we may take Locke's as one), I argue that they refer to modes or dimensions of action that are relevant for all persons, everywhere, hence emphatically not mutually exclusive. They can also each respond to the aporias inherent in the other. On the surface, and especially in a context like modernity, in which a forensic ideology has prevailed, the two constructs might seem to produce or index discrepant relations to ethics, deep and shallow, respectively, but I argue that both dimensions are intrinsic to ethical life. I suggest that the forensic emphasizes the perspective on action that I single out as practice (continuous action), whereas the mimetic draws on what I distinguish as performance (discrete, discontinuous acts).

I follow an insight I derive from an early essay by Geertz (1973c) that it is a category mistake to clearly differentiate the particular from the universal when it comes to culture.[5] The point is that in illuminating the ostensibly exotic practices of Malagasy-speakers, my aim is precisely not to oppose "their" social or ethical world to "ours" or to distinguish their "traditional" world from their current "postcolonial" one, but to clarify a common

---

the emphasis is on notions of contract and responsibility rather than property—that is, of persons in relation to acts rather than objects. Thus philosopher William Uzgalis (2014) argues that "the whole force of Locke's definition of person as a thinking intelligent being that can know itself as the same thinking thing in different times and places is designed to account for the fact that we are creatures who are capable of operating the machinery of the law. When contemplating an action, we can think that in the future we will be the same being who will be punished or rewarded for the course of action which we choose. When being punished we can look back and see that we are the same being who committed the act for which we are being punished."

5. To recognize this is not to solve the problem of how to sound the universal in the particular. It is far easier to commit the category error than to find an alternative mode of procedure, and it may be that such category errors are themselves inevitably a part of the human condition, marking limits to the capacity for reason or to the commensurability of the world.

feature of human personhood, namely, its intrinsically ethical nature.[6] I argue that ethics entails a judicious balance between forensically maintaining commitments in continuous practice and mimetically initiating, accepting, or submitting to new ones in discontinuous performances.

My interest in the topic has emerged in part through attempts to develop a serious account of spirit possession and specifically of the practice of spirit mediums, acting both as themselves and as spirits, as I have encountered them on the island of Mayotte and in the city of Mahajanga in northwest Madagascar. When the medium is in trance, she is taken over by another being who speaks through her. The spirits are construed as persons in their own right, drawn from a set of publicly available "characters" (or *personnages*). To be actively possessed is for the medium to perform, temporarily and discontinuously, as someone else (and hence discontinuously as herself). Such performance is clearly mimetic, but it is not thereby play-acting or pretending. More to the point, such temporary discontinuities in personhood by no means vitiate the significance of the forensic dimension. The spirits themselves are understood as persons in a forensic sense, bearing singular and continuous identities and held accountable for their actions, despite their discontinuous and multiple appearances. Moreover, although possession disrupts the continuous personhood of the medium, in the end it does not diminish but highlights and enhances it.

Johnson writes that if in Locke's view contracts require "[first] authenticity, the assurance that contracts in fact express the actual wills of contracting partners; [second] identity, the assurance that contracts made today will still abide in the future; and [third] authority, an agreement as to the common power compelling and ensuring the contract's fulfillment, [then for liberal thinkers] possession by spirits throws all of these, and thus the contract itself, into question" (2014, 33).

However, possession in Mayotte and Madagascar does nothing of the kind so long as the persons of the host and of the spirit are clearly distinguished from one another—which is actually what the whole practice attempts to do. Additionally, possession serves as a kind of privileged site in which the making of forensic persons is rendered culturally explicit, and the ethical consequences and limitations are made salient for participants and observers (Lambek 1981).[7]

6. The ethical is, of course, only one transection or formulation of personhood. Others might highlight reason, desire, existence, and so on.

7. When spirits first come into presence, the initial tasks are to greet, identify, and socialize them. When they are called up for the first time in a given host, they must be coaxed into social

I have addressed specific ethical entailments, capacities, and resonances of spirit possession in other essays. In this chapter I forgo further inspection of possession itself, seeing it as one of a larger set of cultural institutions that draw upon what Mauss (1985) referred to as *personnages* and that highlight or elaborate the mimetic dimension. My presentation proceeds in three segments. In the first, I summarize and extend the argument developed in previous chapters that ethics is entailed in the articulation of practice with performative action. In the second section I rapidly survey a range of mimetic vehicles other than spirit possession evident in the ethnographic literature. In the final section I develop an ideal-typical model of the forensic and mimetic dimensions of the person.

A large question this chapter raises but does not pretend to answer is the following: How do our views of human being, reason, truth, and ethics shift if we take the mimetic dimension seriously and if we see mimesis not merely as a human capacity (or incapacity) but as intrinsic to human sociality? Moreover, how can ethics address discontinuity? To put this another way, what is the relationship between the perduring and the contingent in ethical action and judgment? "Jack" is a good person, but now he has done a bad thing; is he still a good person? If not, can he recover the person he was? Or, more strikingly, "Jill" has been a very good person for thirty years, but then it is discovered that in her youth she policed a concentration camp; how should we revise our opinion of her? How do we determine the criteria for ascertaining and ascribing which are the continuous and which the discontinuous traits, attributions, responsibilities, and descriptions of persons? How do we acknowledge, describe, and evaluate the continuous, consistent, and possibly essential in relation to the discontinuous, contingent, ostensibly inconsistent, and relatively superficial? What is the place of distinctive cultural vehicles in this process?

The Constitution of Ethical Persons

By *ethics* I do not mean goodness or justice per se, or simply the dispositions toward them, and certainly not normative injunctions and prescriptive rules, but the condition in the first instance of being subject to judgment (in the broad sense of discernment); that is, to the conditions under which

engagement. A critical moment is reached when a spirit first announces its name in public in a given host and that relationship is acknowledged by all who witness it, both other humans and fellow spirits. This establishes the basis for forensic accountability. A further theme of possession concerns the opacity of persons and ultimately the limits of acknowledgment (Lambek 1981).

criteria of goodness or justice and the like become relevant, necessary, and particular.[8] Performative acts establish criteria according to which practice and circumstances that follow are evaluated (chapter 11; Austin 1962; Cavell 1979; Rappaport 1999). That is to say, the participants in a performative act commit themselves to the criteria thereby instantiated (moreover, argues Rappaport, they accept the larger order that constitutes performative acts of a certain kind in the first place). The commitment could be to a state of war or peace or alliance, as described by Rappaport for the Maring in Papua New Guinea, or it could be something apparently trivial. If I make a commitment, say, to deliver a paper at a conference, my subsequent actions with respect to that commitment (Do I show up? With a paper? On topic?) are subject to evaluation, indexing whether I have kept my word and eventually whether I am the kind of person who *can* keep his word.[9]

Since performative acts, understood as entailed in the illocutionary force or dimension of all utterances, are pervasive, so too is ethics. This is evident in Cavell's discussion of our accountability for, and hence the immense consequentiality of, every word we utter (1976, 1996). Performativity and its consequentiality are highlighted through formalization and elaboration in those acts we refer to specifically as ritual. Ritual thus is not simply a secondary representation and possible mystification of underlying social relations or values (as some British social anthropologists have thought), but is, at least in this respect, constitutive of them. As Andrew Walsh (2002) has put it, rituals do not only fulfill responsibility, they produce it. Ritual produces a world in which practice and behavior are explicit, definable, and available for discernment and judgment according to the criteria the rituals instantiate. From such a perspective, ethics is intrinsic to human social worlds.

Ethics is entailed in human speech, construed as carrying illocutionary force, and is as inseparable from acts of speaking as mind is from body. (Hence it would be a category error to attempt to distinguish ethics from action as distinct commensurate phenomena or provinces of analysis.) Again, what I mean by *ethics* here is the availability, acceptance of, and susceptibility to criteria, not only or necessarily doing what is right or good, rationalizing the right and good, or theorizing about them. Acts have a temporal dimension, since those who enter into them have been shaped by prior acts

8. For lack of space, I do not compare the range of perspectives now understood by "ethics" in anthropology or philosophy.

9. Additional criteria would apply to the quality of the presentation itself and whether a poor presentation would be attributed to an ethical lapse, such as laziness or disregard for the organizers, or to intellectual inability.

and the criteria and commitments engaged therein, and since performative acts, as noted, cast their consequences forward, shaping the evaluation of subsequent practice—and presumably, to a degree, the practice itself, by means of the criteria they put into place. Actors are rendered persons through performative acts and gain thereby a (socially) temporal existence: commitments entail the continuity of those who commit or are committed to or through them.[10]

The question is how long such continuity lasts and whether and how it can be terminated or disrupted. What are the criteria that justify new acts or setting aside old ones? Persons are discontinuous insofar as they successively take on new commitments or commitments of a different kind, as in religious conversion or remarriage; break or acknowledge their relinquishment of past commitments, as in resigning from service or asking for forgiveness; or are reassigned criteria, as in psychiatric diagnoses or legal pronouncements. Do such discontinuities justify their being labeled different persons? What cultural vehicles and mechanisms are available for producing, enforcing, and legitimating various framings of continuity and discontinuity, or consistency and inconsistency? Any given society will have ideas or principles as to which illocutionary effects or commitments can be broken or put aside—how, and with what meaning or consequence—and which cannot. Likewise, over time, the ethical context in which any group of humans subsists will inevitably become highly complex, dense with multiple and possibly conflicting or incommensurable, continuous and discontinuous performative vehicles, criteria, and specific effects and commitments, some of which may be subject to misrecognition.

Such matters of the continuity of persons are culturally or humanly universal insofar as they are intrinsic to speech, social action, temporality, and the fact that we inhabit relatively discrete bodies (not to mention innate or developmental dispositions, capacities, and limits; cf. Bloch 2012; Mauss 1985). Nevertheless, it is evident that human acts and utterances take place under particular descriptions and with respect to specific felicity conditions and criteria, and such descriptions, conditions, and criteria vary across culture, language, and time and within any given society. Hence persons are not identical to one another. They are not the same not simply because their bodies and minds are distinct from one another, but also because the performative acts in which they engage or are engaged differ in their conditions, meaning, force, criteria, and effects. I say "are engaged" because many

10. Compare Ricoeur 1992 on the temporality and ethics of the self.

acts are performed over us without our direct intention, as in infant baptism or circumcision. It is of considerable interest that the Church of England faces a group of atheists who call for a rite of "debaptism," much as there exists a collection of men in the United States who claim their foreskins back.[11] Insofar as the states of social and bodily being to which we commit and are committed and the criteria for evaluating our being or practice with respect to those states vary enormously, so too does the substance of personhood and whether, as in these instances, it is meant as continuous and permanent, albeit indelibly, if privately, marked in the one case and not the other.

In addition to the differences produced by specific performative acts, there are larger differences according to how such acts are articulated with one another across society and over the lifetime; the degree to which they are imposed, given, or freely initiated, and how they are authorized; as well as the range of persons they engage—whether, for example, initiations are collective or individual, in what respects they are gender-specific and gender-specifying, whether initiation is a step linked intrinsically to marriage, and so forth. Rappaport was much taken by his cousin Robert Levy's (1973) account of Tahiti, where boys were responsible for initiating their own circumcisions. Very broadly, one could say that social orders can frame personhood with respect to kinds and degrees of responsibility (or "agency") and with respect to continuity over the life span or transition and discontinuity (and anthropologists, likewise, can follow either emphasis). Additionally, a given social order could emphasize the connectedness of persons to one another, their unity or reciprocity in acting or being acted upon in common or in relation, or their separateness, distinctiveness, and autonomy.

It was part of the transformation in European society over the last few hundred years, as well as the explicit argument of a number of European political theorists, later supported by the professional experts described by Foucault, to emphasize the temporally continuous and maximally accountable person (in various forms of essentialism and by means of various technologies, including the new ones today of forensic science and genetics) over dispersed or diffuse forms of agency and the manifest discontinuities within a single life—and yet simultaneously to emphasize the discontinuities over the continuities between persons (e.g., the celebration of birthdays rather than saints' days). Hence the rise of the modern monadic individual.

11. On baptism, see Pigott 2009. The two cases are not strictly parallel, since not all American foreskins were removed performatively in the same manner or with similar ethical entailments.

One could say that the maximally socially distinct and temporally continuous individual is the ideological exemplar of the modern person.[12]

Along with parallel transformations in the religious sphere, broadly speaking, and notably a change in what Keane (2007) has called the semiotic ideology, whereby speakers and actors are understood to be linked to their words and acts in particular ways, there is the emergence of a particular kind of ethical subjects, held as solely responsible not only for their acts but possibly for ascertaining the relevant criteria. Such subjects are either blithely untroubled by prior commitments to others or given to anxious self-scrutiny. These subjects are also citizens of liberal states to whose laws they are accountable, in part because the state has largely taken over authority for the order of the performative acts that constitute the person (as a citizen, for example), which were formerly in the sphere of religion, kinship, or the community and whose performativity is now largely concealed from its own participants (Lambek 2013b; cf. Bloch 1986). Bureaucracy has encroached on religious and family ritual, and law has overshadowed ethics.

In this way, the person is simultaneously rendered anonymous and placed firmly under the control and gaze of the state through its various apparatuses and discourses. Moreover, insofar as they no longer participate bodily and explicitly in rituals, people are no longer as fully constituted by, or as constitutive of, encompassing liturgical orders that authorize and substantiate ethical values and orientation (Rappaport 1999). Ethics becomes abstracted and objectified as something at arm's length, to be acquired as discrete knowledge of rules rather than assimilated and embodied as part of life. With the decline of formerly hegemonic orders of performatively established personhood in the arenas of kinship, community, and congregation, discourses of the individual self, and hence of self-help, and also of individual achievement and fame, rush in to fill their place. I suggest this is symptomatic of a gap in or thinning out of the ritually performative realization of ethical persons.[13] We still do have the ethics entailed in ordinary speaking, of course, and I am on weaker ground if I suggest as well a decline

12. This section is highly schematic and somewhat idiosyncratic. I remain agnostic about the role of Christianity relative to other sources of these developments and do not enter into discussion with such thinkers as Nietzsche, Mauss, Dumont, or Bernard Williams on the subject.

13. My argument and diagnosis here have some similarities to MacIntyre's (1981) account of the confusion entailed by the decline or collapse of tradition, but I see this as a product more of the disappearance of ritual order than of the disintegration of a coherent system of ethical thought. Hylton White (personal communication) notes that labor power under capitalism forms an additional "mode of social integration that does not accord with performative bases of personhood."

in the everyday use of ordinary, explicitly performative utterances—say from Jane Austen's world to that of our texting children. Even to raise the idea is controversial, and I leave it to linguists to answer.[14]

To speculate further, the popularity of charismatic Christianity may reside in part in its ability to offer a public form and forum for establishing emotionally and ethically charged non- or anti-bureaucratic and somewhat less individuated and vigorously performative means of personhood, and shifting the emphasis from the relentlessly forensic to the mimetic (explicitly "born again"). Islam, too, offers an encompassing liturgical order that grants legitimacy to particular performative acts engaged within its framework and hence provides a kind of uniformity and consistency, in which individuals are identified with ethical order—it becomes an embodied part of them, and they become an embodied part of it—rather than experiencing a detached, externalized engagement with or against it (Hirschkind 2006).

I have recounted this story breathlessly and too broadly, but let me emphasize one further twist. It is part of the ideology of this transformation that modern persons are rendered free to exercise their rational faculties and especially the faculty of choice (whether this choice is described by liberals as "free" or exalted by existentialists as terrifying and authentic). From such a perspective, those who submit to the rituals of their communities of kinship or religion are conceptualized as "unfree" insofar as they are not given choice (witness the imposed baptisms and circumcisions); moreover, they are ostensibly mystified, not understanding the human sources of the performative acts in which they engage or find themselves engaged. They mistake illocutionary acts that construct the world for locutionary statements that describe or refer to it, and yet conversely assume that illocutionary acts can have material rather than simply conventional effects.

It is anthropological wisdom (or deconstructive foolishness) to suggest that it is equally we moderns who are mystified by supposing that such mystification is necessarily a bad, superficial, or unnecessary thing, as if it could be replaced by purely rational thought and transparent, unmediated procedures; as if all utterances could and should be merely constative, individual, "freely" given statements and hence only acceptable if "true"; and as if we, too, are not partially already formed or informed by performative acts and the orders of which they are a part; as if we could be fully and exclusively forensic persons, fully accountable not only for each of our actions but for the descriptions they get placed under or the criteria they entail. I

14. One reason for its complexity has to do with the relation of language to class and social distinction.

would call this the mystification of the constative. I mean by this that insofar as our semiotic ideology has assumed that our utterances are or should be constative—locutionary, referential, rational, fully intentional, and sincere declarations of what is the case—it has misled us.[15] It was not until Austin (in the wake of Wittgenstein) that it became (re)apparent that utterances are not identical to referential statements, that they do not all carry truth value in the same way, that utterances have illocutionary force as well as locutionary and perlocutionary dimensions, and hence (Cavell 1976; Rappaport 1999) that we are embedded in our successive performatively engaged commitments in the manner I stated earlier.[16] If the Rest mystifies the illocutionary basis of ritual utterances and their effects, the West mystifies the reach and powers of the constative. Hence, insofar as one wants to draw that imaginary line between West and Rest (or modern and nonmodern), one might do it according to the complementary ways in which our personhood is respectively mystified rather than opposing the rational *to* the mystified.

Whatever the source, kind, or degree of mystification, ethical personhood is constituted through an interplay of performance and practice. Performance instantiates the criteria that organize and evaluate practice, while it is from the stream of practice that new performances are enacted. By *performance*, I refer primarily to the illocutionary acts or force of ordinary language; in ritual these performative acts are put more fully "on stage," thereby taking on some of the connotations we associate with the idea of explicit performances. Illocutionary acts may explicitly perform deference to the authority of a liturgical or legal order, or they may mark consistency with internal intention. In the latter instance, sincerity becomes a more salient felicity condition than conformity to external scenarios or modes of comportment. In each case, acts are assessed as more or less successful according to their ability to satisfy the felicity conditions associated with them. Practice is shaped and interpreted in light of the criteria established by means of performative acts, but practice is also the field in which new performative acts are generated and new criteria brought into play. A simple illustration is the utterance of a promise followed by attention to whether it is kept or ignored in practice and subsequently whether a new act, such as an apology or a denial, is performed.

15. Such assumptions are found in varying loci, from formal truth-conditional semantics of representation through much academic writing. I am not positing "mystification of the constative" as a mirror image of "mystification of the performative." Indeed, it partakes of the latter insofar as it ignores the prevalence of illocutionary force.

16. Cavell 2005a importantly distinguishes the performative and the passionate utterance; for outstanding interpretations, see Das 2012, 2014.

If persons are subject to criteria established in performance, they must find ways to live with them in practice. This raises a number of challenges insofar as criteria may not fit changing circumstances, interests, or intentions; criteria may be incommensurable with one another; commitments may conflict or compete with one another; and the attempt to be consistent and complete may present significant difficulties. Ethical practice requires the sustained, judicious balancing of commitments and criteria, including when to engage in new performative acts.[17] Virtuous wisdom (*phronesis*) entails not only meaning what we say as an entailment of a given performance but balancing that with the entailments of other performances, knowing when and how to say what we mean and to whom in ongoing practice, and when to let it go. Wisdom also entails recognizing our own and others' inability to be fully consistent and sometimes the limits of any criteria. In most human circumstances there is a complex play of judgment, desire, and discretion that does not lend itself to literal transcription. There is always a slippage between the clarity of ethical criteria established in single performances and the heterogeneity and ambiguity of circumstances (including past performances) and hence what is realizable in practice. As Cavell shows in his discussions of *Lear* (1976) and *Hippolytus* (1996), inflexible adherence to a given criterion or commitment is liable to provoke tragedy.[18]

A person is accountable in the first instance to and for herself in light of the illocutionary acts in which she engages or is engaged. However, the understanding and experience of being accountable is not uniform but depends on the prevalent semiotic ideology—for example, on whether one attends to one's accounting primarily internally and psychologically (and then whether in a Protestant fashion or a Freudian one) or by means of the body (through visceral responses like blushing, nausea, or paralysis), or by bearing; or externally, whether interpersonally by means of a simple apology or on the public stage within one's community of practice, perhaps by means of appropriate sacrifice or penance, that is, by means of further elaborate and highly visible or audible performative acts. From the perspective of each semiotic ideology (and corresponding emotional nexus), the practices authorized under the others are ethically suspect. Ritualists can

17. Otherwise put, virtuous practice entails the disposition to follow the Aristotelian mean between being overly ready to take responsibility and not ready enough, or between being rigid, literal-minded, and overly consistent and being indecisive, inconsistent, unreliable, and too ready to rationalize such behavior.

18. As ethical disposition approximates character, it is surely no accident that tragedies are so frequently named for the persons of their protagonists.

accuse non-ritualists of indecorous and idiosyncratic, if not chaotic, behavior, while being vulnerable in turn to accusations of insincerity or mere conformity.[19]

In sum, personhood is both an entailment and cumulative product of a series of acts, acts committed toward, over, with respect to, and by the individual concerned. These include acts of naming or interpellation and of accepting and answering to names, as well as acts that bear consequences and are committed in or under those names. Persons are human beings under a set of descriptions, criteria, and commitments put into place by means of successive performative acts. These descriptions render them in the first instance as ethical subjects. Again, I do not mean they are inherently or consistently good or just or honorable, but that they are subject to recognition and to evaluation, not least self-recognition and self-evaluation, according to the criteria to which they have committed or been committed. Phrased in somewhat different language, persons are granted a certain dignity by being placed performatively under a description;[20] moreover, one of the chief criteria for maintaining that dignity entails granting dignity reciprocally to others by recognizing them as persons under comparable kinds of descriptions, by witnessing their performances, by standing by one's word to them, acknowledging one's lapses (including performing excuses), and generally submitting oneself to the criteria established by means of the acts one has undergone or undertaken and acknowledging the engagements of others. The necessity, availability, production, recognition, and application of such criteria are the grounds of what I mean by *ethics*; the intrinsic nature of subjection and accountability to criteria is what I mean by *persons*. Note that to be subject to criteria does *not* mean that persons are determined by them, forced or "caused" to act in certain ways.[21]

I close this section by emphasizing that all this leaves persons immensely vulnerable, both to a lack of positive recognition by others (shame) and to the sense of having failed sufficiently to recognize others (guilt). We are

19. The ambivalence and double meaning of the word *performance* in English is indicative of the fact. How do we distinguish an authentic mode of being oneself from *mere* performance? This is a question whose salience and resolution are relative to the particular semiotic ideology and mode of performance in question. Under a different semiotic ideology, the more relevant question might be, How do I ensure a *felicitous* performance (Keane 2007; chapter 8)?

20. I do not address here the question of being performatively condemned to lesser dignity, as in the case of slaves or forms of social hierarchy based on "race," gender, sexuality, age, pathology, or relative competence.

21. Rappaport, on whom much of this argument is built, distinguishes sharply between acceptance and behavior (1999, 123–24).

also subject to the contingencies of history, notably to acts of violence and disruption, but also to the inability, for economic or political reasons, to carry out sufficient or required rituals constitutive of personhood and acknowledgment, and sometimes we even forget what these are. Such circumstances can produce enormous anxiety and anomie, sometimes misdiagnosed as "trauma." A succinct example of the failure of recognition may be seen in Adam Ashforth's (2000) portrayal of a resident of Soweto who is vulnerable both to being attacked by witchcraft and to being considered a witch (it is a considerable merit of his book to show the proximity and even ambiguity between these two subject positions), in large part because he has failed to acknowledge his own ancestors and because they, too, have failed to fully recognize him and to be present in his life. Finally and conversely, people are vulnerable at times to an excess of criteria and expectations and may need to effect avenues of partial escape into privacy.

The *Personnage*

The idea of unity in continuity (*contin-unity*) as a kind of permanent identification between the person and the body is epitomized in the forensic person of modern law no less than in the science of forensics. I think there is something deeply universal about this sense of distinctive self-sameness. But if it does not correspond exclusively to the modern individual, how is it accommodated by different ethnographic facts, arguments, or ideologies concerning relational, discontinuous, and possibly even multiple and dispersed persons that are a feature of so many nonmodern societies (including the virtual worlds of postmodernity)? The difference is first elucidated in Mauss's (1985) concept of the *personnage*. The *personnage* is, then, a second sense of the term *person* circulating in anthropology.

Where the ideology of the modern West emphasizes the preeminence of the unique, self-continuous, bounded, forensic, and "possessive" individual (Macpherson 1962), certain other societies may highlight a relatively fixed set of distinct, socially recognized positions that individuals successively come to inhabit or among which they may alternate. These can be considered dramatis personae, a socially recognized, possibly permanent cast of characters whose performance successive actors take up. They are the characters that comprise the life of a certain kind of society or community. Whereas Westerners might be inclined to say that individuated actors impersonate such characters and would grant a lesser status to *impersonation* than to directly *being* a single person (despite the cult of film stars), as though the former were less authentic or less real than the latter, and as though the latter did not entail performance of its own, such distinctions would not arise in a society with *personnages*. Performance in a Maussian world is neither excessively strategic nor somehow make-believe, but constitutive. To be or become a person in this sense is to fit the title of Ricoeur's book *Oneself as Another* (1992), or perhaps to fit the phrase *another as oneself*.

Mauss's model fits Malagasy spirit possession, insofar as mediums are possessed by one or another of a set of spirits,[22] but possession is only one of the more florid exemplifications of *personnages*. Mauss himself was drawing from Pueblo and West Coast Amerindians, where it is the circulation of names and titles or, rather, the circulation of individuals into these names and titles (Mauzé 1994) that is critical. A comparable system is found among the British aristocracy in the tradition of succession to a named landed estate and title, with associated house, income, and political office. A more complex form in central Africa is "positional succession," as described by Cunnison for the Luapula. I quote at length Karin Barber's lucid summary of the ethnography:

> In "positional succession," . . . a successor steps completely into a predecessor's role, taking over his name, property, social identity, relationships and responsibilities.[23] In the Luapula valley in northern Zambia, every married man occupied a position which, if he died, had to be taken over by a junior member of the matrilineage. The successor took over the widow, the deceased's name, role and status. "One in heart with my uncle, I succeed him. I am just exactly as my uncle was" (Cunnison 1956, 33). "It is the names rather than any particular incumbents of them that achieve fame and gain currency in traditions. . . ." (1956, 33). It is not that there is a *real* Magumbe whose name is *fictitiously* taken over by a successor: for the person you succeed himself succeeded someone else, and what we are looking at is an endless succession of shells or inhabitable slots, with individuals moving up through them. Children are not sons of an individual but of a position, "whose mark

22. The set is not closed; new spirits emerge, and older ones sometimes disappear. Nevertheless many spirits remain active in the community, possessing a new medium just before or sometime after the death of a previous medium. Mediums possess more than one spirit, and most spirits possess more than one medium. On the seriousness of iterative performance and the acquisition of conviction, see chapter 8.

23. The following is Barber's original note from the quoted passage. "For examples of positional succession, see Miller (1977) on the Imbangala of Angola, Richards (1951) on the Bemba, and Wilson (1951) on the Nyakyusa. . . . Among the Nyakyusa, 'death does not break a family and its relationships, but simply alters the particular people between whom these relationships obtain; . . . nearly always someone is substituted in place of the one who has died' (Wilson 1951, 265)" (Barber 2007, 233, n. 4).

> is the name which is at any time the label of the man occupying the position" (ibid). When positional succession is combined with "perpetual kinship," relationships between pairs of positions whose "names" have been inherited through the generations are held to remain fixed. What is taken over is not just a name but the relationships that attend the name. Living people step into pre-existing genealogical slots in an unchanging structure.
>
> These relations of equivalence may suggest an effacement of individual agency in impersonal, external social structures. Yet the peoples of the Luapula valley, as described in Cunnison's beautiful ethnography (Cunnison 1959), were intensely entrepreneurial, quick to adapt, worked alone or in small groups and were keen on individual success. (Barber 2007, 111–12; her emphasis)

Barber goes on to discuss the role of praise poems and other literary genres as "modes of making persons" (2007, 134) and argues that "it is in the playing field of textuality that the relational nature of personhood is most fully disclosed" (134). Such genres work by locating the person in an external form, such as a name, ox, mask, or feature of the landscape. "Names and their expansions are the kernel of social reputation, the index of self-realisation, and the vehicle of survival beyond death. Names are the nodes through which multiple links and affiliations with other names pass" (135).[24]

A converse form of personhood is found in societies where it is a nonmaterial aspect of the person that circulates through new bodies. Reincarnation has been a pervasive consideration in many Inuit communities, where the birth of an infant is recorded as the reappearance of someone who has recently died.[25] The infant thus begins life as both herself and another. She is child of the family into which she is born but also takes the kinship position of the formerly deceased person. She is thus a double person, living life as her own person but equally reproducing another. A question is how these positions articulate in practice. The circumstances offer much room for play or "freedom" as well, perhaps, as some hard choices of loyalty in particular situations of conflict.[26]

24. One wonders about the relevance of this for evaluating political office-holders in contemporary African states. On names more generally, see vom Bruck and Bodenhorn (2006).

25. My depiction draws especially from Nuttall's (1992) ethnography of Greenland.

26. Yet another kind of mimetic doubling is characteristic of Amazonian animistic perspectivism as elucidated by Viveiros de Castro (1998), in which souls shift between human and nonhuman bodies in an alternation of perspectives as predator and prey and see themselves as human within each different body. The contrast between animism and naturalism parallels at the cosmological level the contrast between mimetic and forensic apprehensions of the person (cf. Costa and Fausto 2010).

Reincarnation takes on a different valence in different societies. There is a quiet presence of reincarnation, behind the scenes and far from universal, in Switzerland. In the cases I have encountered, reincarnation enables imaginative and retrospective identifications and connections between historical periods. The *personnages* in question are neither regularly circulating names or titles nor family or community members, but individuals. Like Malagasy spirits, they are "characters" in a *poiesis* of history who exemplify a past epoch—an ordinary woman who resisted the Nazis in a German village (Lambek 2007a) or a well-known Jewish writer who committed suicide during the Second World War. They may be social types derived from popular culture, like a martial arts figure in a medieval Himalayan monastery.[27] These dramatis personae distance people from their ordinary circumstances, doubling or multiplying personhood, even if relatively privately.[28]

These examples reinforce two points made in Geertz's famous essay "Person, Time and Conduct in Bali" (1973e): first, that personhood and temporality or historicity are intrinsically related; and, second, that every biological individual is ascribed multiple forms of personhood by means of such things as names (first names, family names, nicknames, tecknonyms, kinship terms, etc.) and titles.[29] It thus becomes evident that the line between the forensic person and mimetic *personnage* is not easy to draw, and it is even possible that their relative weight shifts over the life cycle. This is true with respect not only to titles or office-holders (like named professorships or district commissioners) but also to kinship itself.[30]

Kinship worlds are intrinsically perspectival, and persons are multiply refracted: a given individual may be concurrently and alternately daughter and mother, sister and wife, and so forth. The individual operates within an indexically shifting relational matrix. Moreover, the relationship between two individuals can often be construed in multiple ways, sister-in-law and cross-cousin, for example, and these can be redoubled in practices like joking relationships in which grandparents address grandchildren as spouses.[31]

27. Malagasy share this culture; a spirit recently arrived in Madagascar is Burushly (Bruce Lee).

28. On public, personal, and private, see Obeyesekere (1981). On the therapeutic aspect of recontextualizing an "over-determined" self, see Boddy (1988).

29. Like the Balinese calendar, mimetic personhood is multiple, punctual, and recurring rather than single, continuous, and linear.

30. To be clear, I am *not* suggesting that mimetic and forensic persons map respectively or exclusively on contrasting institutional domains like kinship and law.

31. For a different example, in Mayotte when their parents die, one of a sibling set may come to be called "father" and another "mother" by the other siblings. This is not positional succession; it is optional, context-specific, and occurs without relinquishing former attributes of personhood. It acknowledges an expansion of responsibility and care (Lambek 2011).

In societies like the Inuit of Greenland (Nuttall 1992) or the !Kung San (Lee 2003), the relational matrix across the whole range of persons can be doubled or tripled, whereas in other kinds of societies accession to a title can serve to extract the individual from the ordinary perspectival flux and execute a shift from multiple forms of interpellation to a single one of higher saliency or authority.

One of the things that made Bali appear so harmonious, and perhaps so claustrophobic, was that the various modes of naming seemed to draw on the same underlying model or structure and hence fit well with one another, like the cycles of the multiple calendars. In many societies, however, modes of interpellation are incommensurable, or even conflicting, subject to differing social forces or differentially subject to historical change.

A contemporary locus for alternate personhood is the Internet. It is available in elaborate games like Second Life (Boelstorff 2008) and in possibilities for creative disguise on dating sites, e-mail solicitations, and blogs, such as that of the Syrian lesbian in Damascus who turned out to be (also? really?) an American man in Scotland. We call these hoaxes or frauds, and sometimes prosecute them, in part because we draw such a sharp line between continuous and discontinuous dimensions of personhood. Roughly analogous issues appear with respect to gender reassignment and perhaps to gender itself (cf. Butler 1990). At the same time, many American Protestants characterize successive personhood positively in the practice of being "born again," while popular Catholicism has encouraged mimetic identification with particular saints (Orsi 2005). Whatever the salience of discontinuity for Christianity more broadly (Robbins 2007), I hope it is evident that these examples erode the line between West and Rest, not least because there is a great deal of heterogeneity on both sides of the (straw) line, and not only insofar as the dominant ideology of the Western person was constructed (partly) in opposition, and hence relation, to what came to be perceived as its radical Other (Johnson 2014).

Forensic and Mimetic Dimensions of the Person

Because my explication remains largely at the level of ideal types and cultural constructs, I want to emphasize at the outset that I consider the forensic and mimetic to have qualities that are phenomenologically and psychologically real. The forensic and mimetic are complementary and intrinsic dimensions of selfhood and subjectivity; however, the particular shape, salience, and degree of objectification vary with place and period. Hence the public *personnage* is a cultural elaboration of the mimetic dimension.

It is not my intention to draw on all the connotations and intellectual baggage that the terms carry. In particular, I have no wish to embroil myself in theories of mimesis.[32] *Mimetic* here simply codes the dimension of difference, iteration, and imitation, while *forensic* codes identity in the sense of self-sameness and unfolding over time. I use *mimesis* in the sense of an aesthetic, embodied realization of likeness (Auerbach 1953), drawing from conventions of genre and authorization and evidenced in such things as answering to a name, cultural scenarios, comportment, dress, and styles of speaking. Mimesis often implies an embodied articulation unmediated by conscious reason, but it need not entail the depth of dissociation found in spirit possession.[33] It is characteristic of play, imagination, and fantasy but can also be serious. The forensic implies conscious intention and recognition (whether or not they are actually present). Linguists can track shifting modes evident in speech; the mimetic can be found in practices of quotation and de-quotation (Urban 1989), whereas the forensic maintains or asserts stability of pronominal reference, among numerous other syntactic and pragmatic markers.

The forensic model entails the linear constitution of the person as a being in time who is accountable both for past acts and for living up to future commitments.[34] Whereas the mimetic entails the ways in which what a person says and does draw from what other people have said or done or serve in turn as examples or foils for others, the forensic emphasizes how what a person says and does follows from what that person herself has already said and done and anticipates what she will do subsequently. Psychoanalytically, the mimetic entails identification (or competition) with and introjection of others (or being projected upon); sociologically, it concerns assuming status and role. The forensic entails the psychological unity and boundedness of the maturing self or ego; sociologically, it concerns singular identity.[35]

32. I abstain from discussion of Girard's (1977) influential theory. Incisive anthropological accounts include Kramer (1993) and Taussig (1993).

33. There is even a neurological level at which, "as we interact, our brains synchronise, and thus understanding or watching another person's actions involves much the same neurological activity as doing them oneself" (Rizzolatti et al. 1996). In other words, "at levels which are normally below consciousness, we are continually echoing each other" (Bloch 2012, 179).

34. Significantly, Hannah Arendt (1998) singles out the key acts of beginning, promising, and forgiving, temporally keyed, respectively, to present, future, and past.

35. A comparable distinction to that of the forensic and mimetic is found in George Herbert Mead's (1934) dialectic of the "I" and the "me," in which the singular "I" holistically transcends but also refracts back into the multiple "me's" of social ascription, performance, and psychological identification ("me" the anthropologist, son, father, Canadian, etc.). See also Goffman (1959).

Viewed mimetically, the person is a subject, informed by others and their representations, and susceptible to the passions. Viewed forensically, the person is an agent, characterized by her own actions and accountable for them. The mimetic dimension is ostensibly relational, dividual, specific (kinded), and iterative; the forensic is ostensibly autonomous, individual, singular, and original. The forensic person is more or less narrativized and appears in the context of or as the product of narration. The mimetic person is more or less dramatized and appears in the context of or as the product of explicit performance. The forensic voice draws on tropes of intention and consistency, whereas the mimetic draws on irony and ambiguity. The narrative or drama can be of suffering or victimization as well as of heroic action and responsibility. The two dimensions clash in discursive spaces like the South African Truth and Reconciliation Commission, where, as Sue Williamson (2011) has put it, the idea was that if you just tell (perform) the truth, then you have no more accountability. As can be imagined, this formula led to a variety of results, some quite unsatisfying.[36]

Yet more abstractly, the distinction can be understood as roughly analogous to that between the syntagmatic and paradigmatic or between metonymy and metaphor—here transferred from the structural analysis of language or texts to the social life of persons.[37] As in linguistic or poetic analysis, these refer not to mutually exclusive alternatives but to intersecting dimensions, although one can be highlighted at the expense of another. Hence, if in Mayotte spirits are mimetically realized as persons through name, dress, comportment, dissociation, and performance as distinct from their hosts and from other spirits, they are also forensically realized through their individual names, acts, and commitments. Conversely, where the forensic dimension is salient, as in North America, persons are nonetheless

36. Of the Truth and Reconciliation Commission, Fiona Ross astutely notes, "Remembering and recounting harm is never simple or neutral. Alongside the value that may be derived from public processes, we would do well to remember that subject position is not uniform, and the social and cultural locations from which to speak may be fraught, saturated with discomforting customs that mould patterns of speech. They may render testifiers vulnerable. . . . Legalistic interventions may result in a strangulation of desired forms of voice" (2003, 332). Ross's work is original in following through with women the consequences of their testimonies and their responses to the public response of that testimony. She thus traces accounts of violence from the subjective to the public and back, offering a sober counterpoint to assumptions that narrating one's experience of violence is a straightforward matter and unequivocally beneficial. Ross points to contexts of reception and local ideas of responsibility, reticence, and modes of narration, showing that testimony is never a purely individual matter but is social from its inception to its consequences.

37. Further analogies may be made with diachronic and synchronic perspectives and, perhaps most interestingly, with correspondence and poetic conceptions of truth.

constituted partly through mimesis, in everyday performative iteration, and by way of education, the media, taste, and fashion. Many working- and middle-class people shift between distinct public and domestic personas.[38] Ethnographers are different persons in the field than they are at home.

A central point is that the forensic dimension manifests temporal continuity in the life of the individual while relatively disregarding continuity with other persons. The mimetic dimension manifests continuity with other persons while relatively disregarding temporal continuity in the life of the person.

Western thought has at times explicitly disparaged the mimetic. I have already noted Johnson's account of the forging of the modern person through contrast with spirit possession. Nineteenth-century psychiatry consigned the mimetic to pathology. In the grand rounds of Charcot, hysterical patients were put on display and made to perform. Hypnosis became both an analogy of their condition and a form of treatment. As Ruth Leys (2000) has shown, psychiatrists have been divided ever since between upholding what she calls mimetic and anti-mimetic theories of etiology and treatment of trauma (respectively unmediated and mediated by conscious reason)—theories that, she argues, inevitably collapse into one another. It may well be that something like this tension applies as well to the nonpathologized self and, in effect, to constructs of the social person.

For early modern political philosophers, possession appeared to obviate the three features of free will as discerned by Leibniz: "the spontaneity of action, the assurance that action originates from the one who acts; the contingency of action, the fact that other courses not taken were possible; and the rationality of action, the guarantee that it follows from the deliberation of alternatives" (Johnson 2014, 34). In fact, what spirit possession does is raise the skeptical question of whether free will in this strong sense is ever fully (completely and consistently) possible (chapter 7). The spirits perform in a manner that, far from obviating these criteria of free will, plays ironically, knowingly, and sometimes humorously on their ambiguity. Elsewhere mimesis challenges unilateral conceptions of personal autonomy and private property, as is evident in lawsuits about impersonation and intellectual property (Coombe 1998).

Mimetic performance is sometimes multilayered, as when spirit mediums in the Caribbean imitate possession during performances for tourists. Conversely, child spirits in Mayotte pretend to be their unpossessed

38. Personas are not formally established in the way that spirit possession or positional succession are.

mediums (Lambek 1981). Sometimes there are ruptures across frames, as during a "folkloric" performance of spirit possession in Puerto Rico observed by Raquel Romberg (2014), in which one of the players became actively possessed, and the spirit rushed from the stage. Consider also the nineteenth-century American intersection of spiritualism and blackface, where white men performed as southern blacks, while spirit mediums were possessed by southern blacks and eventually also by blackface performers, who returned the favor by also performing as possessed spirit mediums (Polk 2014).

As noted, the kind of possession found in Mayotte and Madagascar illustrates the intersection of both dimensions of personhood. Spirits are themselves constituted as persons in the continuous sense, bearing responsibility for prior acts and utterances and subject to acknowledging them in much the way that Cavell suggests we must all mean what we say, although they also have more license for departing from expectations in a way that highlights by contrast the obligations of ordinary persons. A spirit is often quite explicitly taught to make and honor a commitment to the well-being of the host.[39] The spirit is understood as a continuous person not only despite his discontinuous appearance in the body of a single medium but also with respect to his appearances in multiple mediums. Thus, when a medium grows ill or dies, clients are advised to seek the same spirit in other mediums, from whose mouths the spirit should take up with the clients where they had left off in the previous medium.

Yet, possession and dissociation mean that the host is not tethered to what the spirit says through her, and indeed part of the drama of possession (and a tacit means of legitimating it) is that host and spirit are of quite different voice and often do not agree or share all their knowledge with one another. For example, consider the following: a spirit who at first does not have its host's best interests at heart, a spirit who warns a host to improve her behavior or warns her that she is at risk from a third party, a spirit who comments in fluent French on his host's evident lack of facility in that language.

39. A typical scenario at the onset of possession is that the spirit is accused of making the host ill. The spirit agrees to make her well and even to protect her once he has received assurances that he will receive public recognition in return. A contract is negotiated with the end of turning a relative stranger into a supportive member of the family. Thereafter the spirit is reminded that he is expected to conform to his word. Once the name of a given spirit has been publicly legitimated, his identity is firm and not subject to change, though he may stop visiting the host or be displaced by new arrivals.

An important point is that although a host and her spirits exhibit discontinuous voices, any given host (spirit medium) is also constituted as a continuous person who must return to herself after episodes of overt possession and who is accountable more broadly for how she addresses and articulates the presence of spirits in her life. An ethically competent spirit medium is someone who can perform appropriately as a given spirit but also can exercise tacit judgment as to when to enter and leave trance, by which spirits to become actively possessed, and how to manage clients who come to her or her spirits for assistance (Lambek 1993b). The medium is accountable for the articulation of the spirits in her everyday life; this is made evident with respect to maintaining the taboos associated with each spirit. A medium possessed of many spirits has to be continuously aware of such matters as the day of the week, the composition of her meals, and the identities of other mediums. Additionally, she should be available for performing as the spirit at public events or private consultations. She must also ensure that her possession articulates with the needs and desires of other family members who may have claims on the same spirits (Lambek 2011).

Exemplary mediums, such as Mme Doso or Kassim Tolondraza in Mahajanga (Lambek 2002a), act as generous patrons or advocates, both extending their actions to the public and enabling the person of the spirit to permeate their everyday acts and outlook, and with respect not only to immediate social circumstances but also to the broader evaluation of an entire way of life, hence exemplifying what Cavell calls moral perfectionism (Cavell 2005b, 120). They—and their spirits—become the vehicles of historical consciousness and the exemplars of historical conscience. Complementary to being responsive to the social world and the changing times, each medium has the ethical task of integrating her possession into the larger course of her life and ensuring that the breaks in personhood are subsumed at some higher level of consistency.

In sum, both spirits and spirit mediums are constituted as ethical subjects. The ethical subjectivity of spirit mediums is enhanced by the ways they address discontinuity—for example, through the disagreements between the host and spirit. In effect, this discontinuity or mimetic dimension can be drawn upon to amplify, augment, or enrich the forensic dimension, seen here as the course of a whole life.

A forensic model must confront the fact that people are often undecided, ambivalent, or face difficult choices; they do inconsistent things or confront an ostensible absence of criteria; they can and do change, fantasize, experience regret, but they can also move on from a sense of responsibility, guilt, or grief to achieve complacency or equanimity. The courts serve to clarify and authorize forensic forms of personhood, yet even the law affords a statute of limitations for most crimes and a fixed term for most punishments. While the courts aim for conclusive judgments, the difference between first- and second-degree murder, for example, is often slippery. The forensic model has to address the limits of personal intention and agency. If we can be blamed for wrong actions, we can also understand contributing factors, such as a bad childhood or various financial or psychological circumstances. A commonly heard excuse is that "I was not myself at the time." To take an extreme example, in what sense is the normally loving father subject to a brain tumor responsible for the murder of his child (Laidlaw 2010, 152–53)? Are the juridical, normative, ethical, and psychological responses here equivalent?[40] As James Laidlaw (2010) notes, similar questions are raised in Evans-Pritchard's (1937) account of the Azande: is the potter able to blame witchcraft for his shoddy work? More saliently, is the witch to be blamed for his unconscious actions, or is he to be exonerated for his earnest apologies? Indeed, *might we understand the witch on the lines of a discontinuous mimetic personnage?*

People sometimes feel that personal accountability does not satisfy justice, full accountability cannot be known, or that justice cannot be reached or served.[41] The question arises whether we can have a complete and consistent account of agency or speak decisively about it (chapter 7; Laidlaw 2010). Forensic accountability eventually reaches aporias with respect to continuous (complete and consistent), autonomous, and unitary personal identity.

The limits of the forensic are offset by the mimetic constructs that highlight temporal discontinuity and difference within the person, acknowledging that we are not always fully whole, single, consistent, or sealed off from those around us. Whether it provides distinct alternative persons to inhabit discontinuously or successively, mimesis recognizes that sometimes one is "not oneself," "not fully oneself," or not only oneself, and that we cannot ever fully or consistently know or be accountable for ourselves. The mimetic dimension is always potentially ironic, both insofar as it enables speaking with more than one voice (Burke 1945) and as it acknowledges that persons are partially opaque to themselves (chapter 7; Nehamas 1998). Mimesis affirms the heterogeneity of experience.

Earlier I described the articulation of performance and practice in ethical action. Now I can suggest that performance exemplifies the mimetic and

40. The question is drawn from Matthew Pettit's (2011) analysis of the concept of the will in treatments for alcoholism.

41. For a captivating illustration with respect to a recent trial, see Malcolm (2011).

practice the forensic mode, or at least that performance is to practice as mimetic personhood is to forensic. This last analogy reinforces the point that forensic and mimetic are not mutually exclusive; both are necessary components of lived, ethical personhood, two modes or dimensions of personhood, just as performance and practice are two modes or dimensions of action. As we offer a greeting, make a promise, or conduct a ritual, we are acting mimetically, reiterating in our words and bodies a formula, script, or scenario that has been uttered and enacted by others before us (Rappaport 1999). But the practical provocations, entailments, and consequences of the performance are forensic; each successive performative act binds us to the criteria it establishes. Thus, the act of naming someone or answering to a name is mimetic, while the consequences of carrying that name are forensic.

Conclusion

The distinction I have been drawing between continuity and discontinuity is less about the mutually exclusive opposition that the terms might imply than about two ways of looking at the same phenomenon. We are each continuous and discontinuous persons; continuity and discontinuity presuppose each other. Explicit vehicles of discontinuity are a kind of cultural artifice, but so too are those that deny it. In the end, what happens to experienced spirit mediums is that the host is partially present as her spirit speaks and the spirit is partially present in the life of the host. This is neither full dissociation nor full integration. It is an ironic, possibly playful, possibly resigned recognition of the continuous presence of multiple but not fully discontinuous persons. It is a way one can live with oneself.

If early accounts argued that mimetic personhood evades or challenges ethics, my observations are quite the reverse. This is because, first, mimetic vehicles also leave room for forensic notions of responsibility and may even highlight or double them (Lambek 2010a); second, there is a mimetic dimension embedded in, and necessary to, the forensic constitution of the person, in every instantiation of commitment and criteria. Whatever the cultural ideology or objectification of individuals or *personnages*, in practice the forensic and mimetic dimensions are interdependent.

To take the first point, while mimetic vehicles may offset the weight placed on the forensic, societies with *personnages* also draw on forensic accounts of responsibility. Spirits are distinguished as forensic persons even while discontinuously present and are held to account. In religion more generally we mimetically produce ostensibly forensic persons in the form of ancestors, saints, and deities; they exist insofar as they are acknowledged, prayed to, or worshipped, and they are deemed to acknowledge our address and to be answerable to their commitments, or else are understood as so powerful and autonomous as to be beyond ordinary morality.[42]

Regarding the second point, if the decisions to conduct performative acts and the consequences of having performed them are forensic, performative acts themselves are iterative, hence mimetic. Without discontinuous, iterated, performative acts, persons and their subsequent acts and practice would have no instantiated criteria by which they could be described, acknowledged, and evaluated. Hence there could be no ethics.

42. Literature, too, is a prime site for the mimetic construction of and identification with forensically developed characters. Witness the popularity of the detective novel.

REFERENCES

Abinal, Antoine, and V. Malzac. 1987 [1888]. *Dictionnaire Malgache-Français*. Fianarantsoa: n.p.

Ackrill, J. L. 1980. "Aristotle on Action." In Rorty 1980, 93–101.

Agamben, Giorgio. 1998. *Homo Sacer: Sovereign Power and Bare Life*. Translated by D. Heller-Roazen. Stanford, CA: Stanford University Press.

———. 1999. *The Man without Content*. Translated by G. Albert. Stanford, CA: Stanford University Press.

Ahern, Emily Martin. 1979. "The Problem of Efficacy: Strong and Weak Illocutionary Acts." *Man* (n. s.) 14 (1): 1–17.

Allerton, Catherine. 2012. "Visible Relations and Invisible Realms: Speech, Materiality and Two Manggarai Landscapes." In *Landscapes Beyond Land: Routes, Aesthetics, Narratives*. Edited by A. Árnason, N. Ellison, J. Vergunst, and A. Whitehouse. New York: Berghahn.

Anderson, Benedict. 1991. *Imagined Communities*. 2nd ed. London: Verso.

Anscombe, G. E. M. 1957. *Intention*. Oxford: Blackwell.

Antze, Paul. 1996. "Telling Stories, Making Selves: Memory and Identity in Multiple Personality Disorder." In Antze and Lambek 1996, 3–23.

———. 2003. "Illness as Irony in Psychoanalysis." In Antze and Lambek 2003, 102–21.

———. 2010. "On the Pragmatics of Empathy in the Neurodiversity Movement." In Lambek 2010c, 310–27.

Antze, Paul, and Michael Lambek, eds. 1996. *Tense Past: Cultural Essays in Trauma and Memory*. New York: Routledge.

———, eds. 2003. *Illness and Irony: On the Ambiguity of Suffering in Culture*. New York: Berghahn.

Appadurai, Arjun. 1986. *The Social Life of Things: Commodities in Cultural Perspective*. Cambridge: Cambridge University Press.

Arendt, Hannah. 1998 [1958]. *The Human Condition*. Chicago: University of Chicago Press.

Arens, William, and Ivan Karp, eds. 1989. *Creativity of Power*. Washington, DC: Smithsonian Institution Press.

Aristotle. 1947. "Poetics." In *Introduction to Aristotle*, edited by R. McKeon, 624–67. New York: Random House.

———. 1976. *Nichomachaean Ethics*. Translated by J. A. K. Thomson. Edited by H. Tredennick. Harmondsworth: Penguin.

Asad, Talal. 1993a [1983]. "The Construction of Religion as an Anthropological Category." In *Genealogies of Religion: Discipline and Reasons of Power in Christianity and Islam*, 27–54. Baltimore, MD: Johns Hopkins University Press.

———. 1993b [1988]. "Toward a Genealogy of the Concept of Ritual." In *Genealogies of Religion: Discipline and Reasons of Power in Christianity and Islam*, 55–79. Baltimore, MD: Johns Hopkins University Press.

———. 2003a. *Formations of the Secular: Christianity, Islam, Modernity*. Stanford, CA: Stanford University Press.

———. 2003b. "Thinking about Agency and Pain." In Asad 2003a.

———. 2006. "Responses." In *Powers of the Secular Modern: Talal Asad and His Interlocutors*, 206–42, edited by D. Scott and C. Hirschkind. Stanford, CA: Stanford University Press.

Ashforth, Adam. 1998. "Reflections on Spiritual Insecurity in a Modern African City (Soweto)." *African Studies Review* 41 (3): 39–67.

———. 2000. *Madumo: A Man Bewitched*. Chicago: University of Chicago Press.

Astuti, Rita. 1995. *People of the Sea*. Cambridge: Cambridge University Press.

Audi, Robert, ed. 1999. *The Cambridge Dictionary of Philosophy*. Cambridge: Cambridge University Press.

Auerbach, Erich. 1953. *Mimesis: The Representation of Reality in Western Literature*. Translated by W. R. Trask. Princeton, NJ: Princeton University Press.

Austin, J. L. 1962 [1955]. *How to do Things with Words*. Cambridge, MA: Harvard University Press.

———. 1970 [1956–57]. "A Plea for Excuses." In *Austin, Philosophical Papers*, edited by J. O. Urmson and G. J. Warnock, 175–204. New York: Oxford University Press.

Babb, Lawrence. 2003. "Thwarted Sacrifice: On the Origin Myths of Jain Castes." In *Jainism and Early Buddhism: Essays in Honor of Padmanabh S. Jaini*, edited by O. Qvarnström, 29–46. Fremont, CA: Asian Humanities Press.

Bailey, Frederick. 1994. *The Witch-Hunt; or, The Triumph of Morality*. Ithaca, NY: Cornell University Press.

Baker, Judith. 2010. "Philosophical Comments on Charles Stafford and Francesca Merlan." In Lambek 2010c, 225–34.

Bakhtin, Mikhail. 1981. *The Dialogic Imagination*. Translated by C. Emerson and M. Holquist. Edited by M. Holquist. Austin: University of Texas Press.

Barber, Karin. 1999. "Quotation in the Constitution of Yorùbá Oral Texts." *Research in African Literatures* 30 (2): 17–41.

———. 2007. *The Anthropology of Texts, Persons and Publics*. Cambridge: Cambridge University Press.

Bates, Stanley. 2003. "Stanley Cavell and Ethics." In *Stanley Cavell*. Edited by R. Eldridge, 15–47. Cambridge: Cambridge University Press.

Bateson, Gregory. 1972. "Style, Grace, and Information in Primitive Art." In Bateson, *Steps to an Ecology of Mind*. New York: Ballantine.

Becker, Alton. 1979. "Text-Building, Epistemology, and Aesthetics in Javanese Shadow Theatre." In *The Imagination of Reality*, edited by A. Becker and A. Yengoyan, 211–43. Norwood, NJ: Ablex.

Beidelman, T. O. 1993. *Moral Imagination in Kaguru Modes of Thought*. Washington, DC: Smithsonian Institution Press.

Bentham, Jeremy. 1931. *The Theory of Legislation*. Edited by C. K. Ogden. New York: Harcourt, Brace.

Berger, Peter, and Thomas Luckmann. 1971. *The Social Construction of Reality: A Treatise on the Sociology of Knowledge*. Hardmonsworth: Penguin.

Berlin, Isaiah. 2002. "Two Concepts of Liberty." In *Liberty*. Edited by H. Hardy. New York: Oxford University Press.

Berman, Marshall. 1988. *All That Is Solid Melts into Air: The Experience of Modernity*. New York: Viking Penguin.

Bernstein, Richard J. 1983. *Beyond Objectivism and Relativism: Science, Hermeneutics, and Praxis*. Philadelphia: University of Pennsylvania Press.

Besnier, Niko. 1995. *Literacy, Emotion, and Authority: Reading and Writing on a Polynesian Atoll*. Cambridge: Cambridge University Press.

Blanchy, Sophie. 2010. *Maisons des femmes, cités des hommes: Filiation, âge et pouvoir à Ngazidja (Comores)*. Nanterre: Société d'ethnologie.

Bloch, Maurice. 1971. *Placing the Dead*. London: Seminar Press.

———. 1986. *From Blessing to Violence: History and Ideology in the Circumcision Ritual of the Merina of Madagascar*. Cambridge: Cambridge University Press.

———. 1989a [1977]. "The Past and the Present in the Present." In Bloch 2004, 1–18.

———. 1989b [1974]. "Symbols, Song, Dance and Features of Articulation." In Bloch 2004, 19–45.

———. 1989c [1979]. "The Disconnection between Power and Rank as a Process." In Bloch 2004, 46–88.

———. 1989d. "The Ritual of the Royal Bath in Madagascar: The Dissolution of Death, Birth, and Fertility into Authority." In Bloch 2004, 187–211.

———. 1992. *Prey Into Hunter: The Politics of Religious Experience*. Cambridge: Cambridge University Press.

———. 1996. "Internal and External Memory: Different Ways of Being in History." In Antze and Lambek 1996, 215–33.

———. 1998. "Autobiographical Memory and the Historical Memory of the More Distant Past." In *How We Think They Think*, edited by M. Bloch, 114–27. Boulder, CO: Westview Press.

———. 1999. "'Eating' Young Men among the Zafimaniry." In Middleton 1999, 175–90.

———. 2004 [1989]. *Ritual History and Power: Selected Papers in Anthropology*. New York: Berg.

———. 2005. "Ritual and Deference." *In Essays on Cultural Transmission*, 123–38. Oxford: Berg.

———. 2012. *Anthropology and the Cognitive Challenge*. Cambridge: Cambridge University Press.

Boddy, Janice. 1988. "Spirits and Selves in Northern Sudan: The Cultural Therapeutics of Possession and Trance." *American Ethnologist* 15 (1): 4–27.

———. 1989. *Wombs and Alien Spirits: Women, Men, and the Zār Cult in Northern Sudan*. Madison: University of Wisconsin Press.

———. 1990. "Essential Texts: On Defending Uterine Blood in Northern Sudan." Paper presented at the American Ethnology Society, Atlanta, GA, April 27.

———. 1994 "Spirit Possession Revisited." *Annual Review of Anthropology* 23:407–34.

Boelstorff, Tom. 2008. *Coming of Age in Second Life*. Princeton, NJ: Princeton University Press.

Bohannan, Paul. 1959. "The Impact of Money on an African Subsistence Economy." *Journal of Economic History* 19 (4): 491–503.

Booth, Wayne. 1988. *The Company We Keep: An Ethics of Fiction*. Berkeley and Los Angeles: University of California Press.

Bordo, Susan. 1989. "The Body and the Reproduction of Femininity." In *Gender/Body/Knowledge: Feminist Reconstructions of Being and Knowing*, edited by A. Jaggar and S. Bordo, 13–33. New Brunswick, NJ: Rutgers University Press.

———. 1993. *Unbearable Weight: Feminism, Western Culture, and the Body*. Berkeley and Los Angeles: University of California Press.

Borneman, John, and Abdullah Hammoudi, eds. 2009. *Being There: The Fieldwork Encounter and the Making of Truth*. Berkeley and Los Angeles: University of California Press.

Bourdieu, Pierre. 1977. *Outline of a Theory of Practice*. Translated by R. Nice. Cambridge: Cambridge University Press.

———. 1984. *Distinction: A Social Critique of the Judgment of Taste*. Cambridge, MA: Harvard University Press.

———. 1997. "The Forms of Capital." In *Education: Culture, Economy, and Society*, edited by A. H. Halsey, H. Lauder, P. Brown, and A. S. Wells, 46–58. Oxford: Oxford University Press.

Bowen, Elenore Smith [Laura Bohannan]. 1964. *Return to Laughter*. New York: Doubleday.

Breslar, Jon. 1979. *L'habitat mahorais: Une perspective ethnologique*. Paris: Editions AGG.

Briggs, Jean. 1970. *Never in Anger: Portrait of an Eskimo Family*. Cambridge, MA: Harvard University Press.

Brown, Michael F. 1985. *Tsewa's Gift: Magic and Meaning in an Amazonian Society*. Washington, DC: Smithsonian Institution Press.

Burke, Kenneth. 1945. "Four Master Tropes." In *A Grammar of Motives*, 503–17. New York: Prentice Hall.

Burnyeat, Myles F. 1980. "Aristotle on Learning to be Good." In Rorty 1980, 69–92.

Burridge, Kenelm. 1969. *New Heaven, New Earth*. Oxford: Basil Blackwell.

———. 1970. *Mambu*. New York: Harper and Row.

Butler, Judith. 1990. *Gender Trouble: Feminism and the Subversion of Identity*. New York: Routledge.

Caillé, Alain. 2000. *Anthropologie du don*. Paris: Désclée de Brouwer.

Cannell, Fenella. 1999. *Power and Intimacy in the Christian Philippines*. Cambridge: Cambridge University Press.

Carrithers, Michael. 1985. "An Alternative Social History of the Self." In *The Category of the Person: Anthropology, Philosophy, History*, edited by M. Carrithers, S. Collins, and S. Lukes, 234–56. Cambridge: Cambridge University Press.

Casey, Edward. 1987. *Remembering: A Phenomenological Study*. Bloomington: Indiana University Press.

Cavell, Stanley. 1976. *Must We Mean What We Say?* Cambridge: Cambridge University Press.

———. 1979. "Criteria and Judgment." In Cavell 1999, 3–36.

———. 1988. "The Uncanniness of the Ordinary." In Cavell, *The Quest of the Ordinary: Lines of Skepticisim and Romanticism*, 153–78. Chicago: University of Chicago Press.

———. 1995. "What Did Derrida Want of Austin? In Cavell, *Philosophical Passages: Wittgenstein, Emerson, Austin, Derrida*. Oxford: Blackwell.

———. 1996. *A Pitch of Philosophy*. Cambridge, MA: Harvard University Press.

———. 1999. *The Claim of Reason: Wittgenstein, Skepticism, Morality and Tragedy*. New York: Oxford University Press.

———. 2005a. "Performative and Passionate Utterance." In *Philosophy the Day After Tomorrow*, 155–91. Cambridge, MA: Harvard University Press.

———. 2005b. "Philosophy the Day After Tomorrow." In *Philosophy the Day After Tomorrow*, 111–31. Cambridge, MA: Harvard University Press.

———. 2005c. "Something Out of the Ordinary." In *Philosophy the Day after Tomorrow*, 7–27. Cambridge, MA: Harvard University Press.

———. 2010. *Little Did I Know: Excerpts from Memory*. Stanford, CA: Stanford University Press.

Chakrabarty, Dipesh. 2000. *Provincializing Europe: Postcolonial Thought and Historical Difference*. Princeton, NJ: Princeton University Press.

Challenger, Douglas F. 1994. *Durkheim Through the Lens of Aristotle: Durkheimian, Postmodernist, and Communitarian Responses to the Enlightenment*. Lanham, MD: Rowman and Littlefield.

Chodorow, Nancy J. 1989. *Feminism and Psychoanalytic Theory*. New Haven, CT: Yale University Press.

Clay, Brenda J. 1977. *Pinikindu: Maternal Nurture, Paternal Substance*. Chicago: University of Chicago Press.

Cole, Jennifer. 1999. "Sacrifice, Narratives and Experience in East Madagascar." In Middleton 1999, 191–218.

Comaroff, Jean. 1985. *Body of Power, Spirit of Resistance*. Chicago: University of Chicago Press.

Comaroff, John, and Jean Comaroff. 1992. *Ethnography and the Historical Imagination*. Boulder, CO: Westview Press.

Comaroff, Jean, and John L. Comaroff. 1991. *Of Revelation and Revolution*. Vol. 1. Chicago: University of Chicago Press.

———. 1999. "Occult Economies and the Violence of Abstraction: Notes from the South African Postcolony." *American Ethnologist* 26 (2): 279–303.

Coombe, Rosemary. 1998. *The Cultural Life of Intellectual Properties*. Durham, NC: Duke University Press.

Costa, L., and Carlos Fausto. 2010. "The Return of the Animists: Recent Studies of Amazonian Ontologies." *Religion and Society* 1: 89–109.

Crapanzano, Vincent. 1977. "Introduction." In Crapanzano and Garrison 1977, 1–40.

———. 1980. *Tuhami*. Chicago: University of Chicago Press.

———. and V. Garrison, eds. 1977. *Case Studies in Spirit Possession*. New York: John Wiley & Sons.

Crisp, Roger. 1996. "Modern Moral Philosophy and the Virtues." In *How Should One Live? Essays on the Virtues*, edited by R. Crisp, 1–18. Oxford: Clarendon Press.

Critchley, Simon. 2005. "Cavell's 'Romanticism' and Cavell's Romanticism." In *Contending with Cavell*, edited by R. Goodman. Oxford: Oxford University Press.

Cunnison, Ian. 1956. "Perpetual Kinship: A Political Institution of the Luapula People." *Human Problems in British Central Africa (The Rhodes-Livingston Journal)* 20:28–48.

———. 1959. *The Luapula Peoples of Northern Rhodesia*. Manchester: Manchester University Press.

Dallmayr, Fred. 1993. *The Other Heidegger*. Ithaca, NY: Cornell University Press.

Daniel, Valentine. 1984. *Fluid Signs: Being a Person the Tamil Way*. Berkeley and Los Angeles: University of California Press.

Das, Veena. 2007. *Life and Words: Violence and the Descent into the Ordinary*. Berkeley and Los Angeles: University of California Press.

———. 2010. "Engaging the Life of the Other: Love and Everyday Life." In Lambek 2010c, 376–99.

———. 2012. "Ordinary Ethics." In *A Companion to Moral Anthropology*, edited by D. Fassin, 133–49. Boston: Wiley-Blackwell.

———. 2014. "Action, Expression, and Everyday Life: Recounting Household Events." In Das et al. 2014, 279–305.

Das, Veena, Michael D. Jackson, Arthur Kleinman, and Bhrigupati Singh, eds. 2014. *The Ground Between: Anthropologists Engage Philosophy*. Durham, NC: Duke University Press.

Daswani, Girish. 2015. *Looking Back, Moving Forward: Transformation and Ethical Practice in the Ghanaian Church of Pentecost*. Toronto: University of Toronto Press.

Dave, Naisargi. 2012. *Queer Activism in India: A Story in the Anthropology of Ethics*. Durham: Duke University Press.

de Boeck, Filip. 1995. "Bodies of Remembrance: Knowledge, Experience and the Growing of Memory in Luunda Ritual Performance." In *Rites et Ritualisation*, edited by G. Thinès and L. de Heusch, 113–38. Paris: J. Vrin.

de Boeck, Filip, and M.-F. Plissart. 2003. *Kinshasa: Tales of the Invisible City*. Ghent: Ludion.

de Heusch, L. 1985. *Sacrifice in Africa*. Bloomington: Indiana University Press.

de Jong, Ferdinand. N.d. "In Times of Catastrophe: Temporalities of Conflict and Peace in Senegal." Paper presented to the Conflicts in Time ESRC Seminar Number 1, University College London, May 17, 2008.

de Vries, Hent. 2008. "Why Still 'Religion'?" In *Religion: Beyond a Concept*, edited by Hent de Vries, 1–98. New York: Fordham University Press.

Derrida, Jacques. 2008. "Abraham, the Other." In *Religion: Beyond a Concept*, edited by H. de Vries, 311–38. New York: Fordham University Press.

Descola, Philippe. 2013. *Beyond Nature and Culture*. Translated by J. Lloyd. Chicago: University of Chicago Press.

Devereux, Georges. 1967. *From Anxiety to Method in the Behavioral Sciences*. New York: Humanities Press.

Dews, Peter. 1988. *Logics of Disintegration: Post-Structuralist Thought and the Claims of Critical Theory*. London: Verso.

Dirks, Nicholas B., Geoff Eley, and Sherry B. Ortner. 1994. "Introduction." In *Culture/Power/History: A Reader in Contemporary Social Theory*, edited by Nicholas Dirks, Geoff Eley, and Sherry Ortner. Princeton, NJ: Princeton University Press.

Douglas, Mary. 1966. *Purity and Danger*. Harmondsworth: Penguin.

———. 1970. *Natural Symbols*. New York: Pantheon.

Dreyfus, Hubert, and Stuart Dreyfus. 1986. *Mind Over Machine: The Power of Human Intuition and Expertise in the Era of the Computer*. New York: Free Press.

Dumont, Louis. 1970. *Homo Hierarchicus*. Translated by M. Sainsbury. Chicago: University of Chicago Press.

———. 1981. *Homo Hierarchicus: The Caste System and its Implications*. Translated by M. Sainsbury, L. Dumont, and B. Gulati. Chicago: University of Chicago Press.

———. 1986. *Essays on Individualism*. Chicago: University of Chicago Press.

Durham, Deborah. 1999. "In the Space of Death." Paper presented at the Satterthwaite Colloquium on African Ritual and Religion, 1999, Satterthwaite, UK.

Durkheim, Emile. 1965 [1915]. *The Elementary Forms of the Religious Life*. New York: The Free Press.

———. 1973. *On Morality and Society*. Chicago: University of Chicago Press.

Dwyer, Daisy H. 1978. *Images and Self Images: Male and Female in Morocco*. New York: Columbia University Press.

Dyring, Rasmus. 2013. "The Place of Ethics." Paper presented at the Philosophy and Anthropology of Moral Experience conference, Aarhus, Denmark, September 19, 2013.

Edel, May, and Abraham Edel. 2000 [1968]. *Anthropology and Ethics*. Edison, NJ: Transaction Books.

Eiss, Paul. 2002. "Hunting for the Virgin: Meat, Money and Memory in Tetiz, Yucatán." *Cultural Anthropology* 17 (3): 291–330.

———. 2007. "Beyond the Object: Of Rabbits, Rutabagas and History." *Anthropological Theory* 8 (1): 79–97.

Eiss, Paul, and David Pedersen. 2002. "Introduction: Values of Value." *Cultural Anthropology* 17 (3): 283–90.

Eldridge, Richard. 2003. "Between Acknowledgment and Avoidance." In *Stanley Cavell*, edited by R. Eldridge, 1–14. Cambridge: Cambridge University Press.

Evans-Pritchard, E. E. 1937. *Witchcraft, Oracles and Magic among the Azande*. Oxford: Clarendon Press.

———. 1940. *The Nuer: A Description of the Modes of Livelihood and Political Institutions of a Nilotic People*. Oxford: Clarendon Press.

Evens, T. M. S. 2008. *Anthropology as Ethics*. New York: Berghahn Books.

Fassin, Didier. 2012. "Introduction: Toward a Critical Moral Anthropology." In *A Companion to Moral Anthropology*, edited by D. Fassin, 1–17.Oxford: Wiley-Blackwell.

———. 2013. "On Resentment and *Ressentiment:* The Politics and Ethics of Moral Emotions." *Current Anthropology* 54 (3): 249–67.

———. 2014. "The Parallel Lives of Philosophy and Anthropology." In Das et al. 2014, 50–70.

Faubion, James. 2011. *An Anthropology of Ethics*. Cambridge: Cambridge University Press.

Feeley-Harnik, Gillian. 1984. "The Political Economy of Death: Communication and Change in Malagasy Colonial History." *American Ethnologist* 11 (1): 1–19.

———. 1991. *A Green Estate*. Washington, DC: Smithsonian Institution Press.

———. 2000. "Childbirth and the Affiliation of Children in Northwestern Madagascar." *Taloha* 13:135–72.

Felman, Shoshana, and Dori Laub. 1992. *Testimony: Crises of Witnessing in Literature, Psychoanalysis, and History*. New York: Routledge.

Fernandez, James. 1982. *Bwiti: An Ethnography of the Religious Imagination in Africa*. Princeton, NJ: Princeton University Press.

———. 1986. "Returning to the Whole." In *Persuasions and Performances: The Play of Tropes in Culture*, 188–213. Bloomington: Indiana University Press.

Fernandez, James, and Mary T. Huber, eds. 2001. *Irony in Action: Anthropology, Practice, and the Moral Imagination*. Chicago: University of Chicago Press.

Fingarette, Herbert. 1963. *The Self in Transformation: Psychoanalysis, Philosophy, and the Life of the Spirit*. New York: Basic Books.

———. 2000. *Self-Deception*, 2nd ed. Berkeley and Los Angeles: University of California Press.

Fleming, L., and Michael Lempert. 2014. "Poetics and Performativity." In *The Cambridge Handbook of Linguistic Anthropology*, edited by N. J. Enfield, P. Kockelman, and J. Sidnell, 485–515. Cambridge: Cambridge University Press.

Flyvbjerg, Bent. 2001. *Making Social Science Matter*. Cambridge: Cambridge University Press.

Fortes, Meyer. 1949. *The Web of Kinship among the Tallensi*. Oxford: Oxford University Press.

———. 1983 [1959]. *Oedipus and Job in West African Religion*. Cambridge: Cambridge University Press.

———. 1987a. *Religion, Morality and the Person: Essays on Tallensi Religion*. Cambridge: Cambridge University Press.

———. 1987b [1966]. "Totem and Taboo." In Fortes 1987a, 110–44.

Foucault, Michel. 1990. *The Uses of Pleasure*. Vol. 2 of *The History of Sexuality*. New York: Vintage.

Freud, Sigmund. 1958 [1913]. *Totem and Taboo: Some Points of Agreement between the Mental Lives of Savages and Neurotics*. In *The Standard Edition of the Complete Psychological Works of Sigmund Freud*, edited by James Strachey and Anna Freud, 13:ix–162. London: Hogarth.

———. 1974. *The Standard Edition of the Collected Works*. 24 vols. Translated by J. Strachey and A. Freud. Vol. 2. London: Hogarth Press.

Freud, Sigmund, and Josef Breuer. 1955 [1893–95]. *Studies on Hysteria*. Vol. 2 of *The Standard Edition of the Collected Works*,. London: Hogarth.

Friedman, Jonathan. 1990. "The Political Economy of Elegance." *Culture and History* 7:101–25.

Gadamer, Hans-Georg. 1975. *Truth and Method*. Translated by G. Borden and J. Cumming. New York: Seabury.

———. 1979. "The Problem of Historical Consciousness." In *Interpretive Social Science: A Reader*, edited by P. Rabinow and W. Sullivan. Berkeley and Los Angeles: University of California Press.

———. 1985 [1960]. *Truth and Method*. Translated by G. Borden and J. Cumming. New York: Crossroad.

Geertz, Clifford. 1973a. "Deep Play: Notes on the Balinese Cockfight." In Geertz 1973d, 412–53.

———. 1973b [1962]. "The Growth of Culture and the Evolution of Mind." In Geertz 1973d, 55–83.

———. 1973c [1966]. "The Impact of the Concept of Culture on the Concept of Man." In Geertz 1973d, 33–54.

———. 1973d. *The Interpretation of Cultures*. New York: Basic Books.

———. 1973e. "Person, Time, and Conduct in Bali." In Geertz 1973d, 360–411.

———. 1973f. "Religion as a Cultural System." In Geertz 1973d, 87–125.

———. 2000. "Thinking as a Moral Act: Ethical Dimensions of Anthropological Fieldwork in the New States." In *Available Light: Anthropological Reflections on Philosophical Topics*, 21–41. Princeton, NJ: Princeton University Press.

Gell, Alfred. 1979. "Reflections on a Cut Finger: Taboo in the Umeda Conception of the Self." In *Fantasy and Symbol: Studies in Anthropological Interpretation*, edited by R. H. Hook, 133–48. London: Academic Press.

Gibson, James J. 1977. "The Theory of Affordances." In *Perceiving, Acting, and Knowing: Toward an Ecological Psychology*, edited by R. Shaw and J. Bransford,67–82. Hillsdale, NJ: Lawrence Erlbaum.

Giddens, Anthony. 1984. *The Constitution of Society: Outline of the Theory of Structuration*. Berkeley and Los Angeles: University of California Press.

Giles, Linda. 1987. "Possession Cults on the Swahili Coast: A Re-Examination of Theories of Marginality." *Africa: Journal of the International African Institute* 57 (2): 234–57.

Girard, René. 1977. *Violence and the Sacred*. Translated by P. Gregory. Baltimore, MD: Johns Hopkins University Press.

Gluckman, Max. 1954. *Rituals of Rebellion in South-East Africa*. Manchester: Manchester University Press.

Goethe, J. W. V. 1992 [1797]. *Faust: A Tragedy*, pt. 1. Translated by M. Greenberg. New Haven, CT: Yale University Press.

Goffman, Erving. 1959. *The Presentation of Self in Everyday Life*. Garden City, NY: Doubleday.

———. 1981. "Footing." In *Forms of Talk*, 124–59. Philadelphia: University of Pennsylvania Press.

Goldman, Irving. 1975. *The Mouth of Heaven: An Introduction to Kwakiutl Religious Thought*. New York: John Wiley & Sons.

Goodenough, Ward. 1970. *Description and Comparison in Cultural Anthropology*. Chicago: Aldine.

Gould, Timothy. 2003. "The Names of Action." In *Stanley Cavell*, edited by R. Eldridge, 48–78. Cambridge: Cambridge University Press.

Graeber, David. 2001. *Toward an Anthropological Theory of Value*. New York: Palgrave Macmillan.

———. 2005. "Fetishism as Social Creativity." *Anthropological Theory* 5 (4): 407–38.

Gregory, Chris. A. 1982. *Gifts and Commodities*. London: Academic Press.

Grice, H. P. 1976. "Logic and Conversation." In *Syntax and Semantics*, edited by P. Cole and J. L. Morgan, 3:411–58. New York: Academic Press.

Guyer, Jane. 2004. *Marginal Gains: Monetary Transactions in Atlantic Africa*. Chicago: University of Chicago Press.

Guyer, Paul. 1999. "Cavell." *Cambridge Encyclopedia of Philosophy*. Cambridge: Cambridge University Press.

Hacking, Ian. 1990. *The Taming of Chance*. Cambridge: Cambridge University Press.

———. 1995. *Rewriting the Soul: Multiple Personality and the Sciences of Memory*. Princeton, NJ: Princeton University Press.

———. 1996. "Memory Sciences, Memory Politics." In Antze and Lambek 1996, 67–87.

Halbwachs, Maurice. 1980 [1950]. *The Collective Memory*. Translated by F. J. a.V. Y. Ditter. New York: Harper.

Hammer, Espen. 2002. *Stanley Cavell: Skepticism, Subjectivity, and the Ordinary*. Cambridge: Polity.

Hampshire, Stuart. 1983. *Morality and Conflict*. Oxford: Basil Blackwell.

Handelman, Don. In press. "The Ethics of Being Wrong: Levinas in the Field." In *Reflecting on Reflexivity*, edited by T. M. S. Evens, D. Handelman, and C. Roberts. Special issue of *Social Analysis*.

Handler, Richard. 1988. *Nationalism and the Politics of Culture in Quebec*. Madison: University of Wisconsin Press.

Hanks, William. 1990. *Referential Practice: Language and Lived Space among the Maya*. Chicago: University of Chicago Press.

Harding, Susan. 1987. "Convicted by the Holy Spirit: The Rhetoric of Fundamental Baptist Conversion. *American Ethnologist* 14 (1): 167–81.

Harpham, Geoffrey. G. 1995. "Ethics." In *Critical Terms for Literary Study*, edited by F. Lentricchia and T. McLaughlin, 387–405. Chicago: University of Chicago Press.

Hart, Keith. 1986. "Heads or Tails? Two Sides of the Coin." *Man* 21 (4): 637–56.

Hasan-Rokem, Galit. 2003. "Martyr vs. Martyr: The Sacred Language of Violence." *Ethnologia Europaea* 33 (2): 99–104.

Hastrup, Kirsten. 1978. "The Semantics of Biology: Virginity." In *Defining Females*, edited by S. Ardener, 49–65. London: Croom Helm.

Hatch, Elvin. 1963. *Culture and Morality*. New York: Columbia University Press.

Havelock, Eric A. 1963. *Preface to Plato*. Oxford: Basil Blackwell.

Hérault, Laurence. 2007. "Learning Faith: Young Christians and Catechism." In *Learning Religion: Anthropological Approaches*, edited by D. Berliner and R. Sarró, 161–76. New York: Berghahn Books.

Héritier, Françoise. 1982 [1979]. "The Symbolics of Incest and Its Prohibition." In *Between Belief and Transgression*, edited by M. Izard and P. Smith. Chicago: University of Chicago Press.

Heywood, Paulo. Forthcoming. "Freedom in the Code: The Anthropology of (Double) Morality." Submitted to *Anthropological Theory*.

Hill, Jane, and Judith Irvine, eds. 1993. *Responsibility and Evidence in Oral Discourse*. Cambridge: Cambridge University Press.

Hill, Thomas E., Jr. 1991. *Autonomy and Self-Respect*. Cambridge: Cambridge University Press.

Hirschkind, Charles. 2001. "The Ethics of Listening: Cassette Sermon Audition in Contemporary Egypt." *American Ethnologist* 28 (3): 623–49.

———. 2006. *The Ethical Soundscape*. New York: Columbia University Press.

Hobsbawm, Eric. 1992. "The Opiate Ethnicity." *Alphabet City* 2:8–11.

Hochschild, Arlie. 1983. *The Managed Heart: Commercialization of Human Feeling*. Berkeley and Los Angeles: University of California Press.

Hubert, Henri, and Marcel Mauss. 1964 [1888]. *Sacrifice: Its Nature and Function*. Translated by W. D. Halls. Chicago: University of Chicago Press.

Hugh-Jones, Stephen. 1994. "Shamans, Prophets, Priests and Pastors." In *Shamanism, History, and the State*, edited by N. Thomas and C. Humphrey. Ann Arbor: University of Michigan Press.

Humphrey, Caroline, and James Laidlaw. 1994. *The Archetypal Actions of Ritual*. Oxford: Oxford University Press.

Hutchinson, Sharon E. 1996. *Nuer Dilemmas: Coping with Money, War, and the State*. Berkeley and Los Angeles: University of California Press.

Hyde, Lewis. 1983. *The Gift: Imagination and the Erotic Life of Property*. New York: Vintage Books.

Jackson, Michael D. 1989. *Paths Toward a Clearing: Radical Empiricism and Ethnographic Inquiry*. Bloomington: Indiana University Press.

———. 2004. *In Sierra Leone*. Durham, NC: Duke University Press.

———. 2011. *Life within Limits: Well-being in a World of Want*. Durham, NC: Duke University Press.

———. 2013. *Lifeworlds: Essays in Existential Anthropology*. Chicago: University of Chicago Press.

Jackson, Michael D., and Albert Piette. In press. "Anthropology and the Existential Turn." In *What is Existential Anthropology?* edited by M. Jackson and A. Piette. Oxford: Berghahn.

James, Wendy. 1988. *The Listening Ebony: Moral Knowledge, Religion and Power among the Uduk of Sudan*. Oxford: Clarendon Press.

———. 1995. "Whatever Happened to the Enlightenment?" In *The Pursuit of Certainty*, 1–13. London: Routledge.

———. 2003. *The Ceremonial Animal: A New Portrait of Anthropology*. Oxford: Oxford University Press.

Janzen, John. 1992. *Ngoma: Discourses of Healing in Central and Southern Africa*. Berkeley and Los Angeles: University of California Press.

Jay, Martin. 2005. *Songs of Experience: Modern American and European Variations on a Universal Theme*. Berkeley and Los Angeles: University of California Press.

Joas, Hans. 1996 [1992]. *The Creativity of Action*. Translated by P. Keast and J. Gaines. Chicago: University of Chicago Press.

Johnson, Paul Christopher. 2011. "An Atlantic Genealogy of 'Spirit Possession.'" *Comparative Studies in Society and History* 53 (2): 393–425.

———. 2014. "Toward an Atlantic Genealogy of 'Spirit Possession.'" In *Spirited Things: The Work of "Possession" in Afro-Atlantic Religions*, edited by P. C. Johnson, 23–45. Chicago: University of Chicago Press.

Kagan, Jerome. 1987. "Introduction." In *The Emergence of Morality in Young Children*, edited by J. Kagan and S. Lamb, ix–xxxvi. Chicago: University of Chicago Press.

———. 1994. *The Nature of the Child*. 10th anniversary ed. Boston: Basic Books.

Kant, Immanuel. 1964. *Groundwork of the Metaphysics of Morals*. Translated by H. J. Paton. New York: Harper Torchbooks.

Kapferer, Bruce. 1983. *A Celebration of Demons: Exorcism and the Aesthetics of Healing in Sri Lanka*. Bloomington: Indiana University Press.

———. 1997. *The Feast of the Sorcerer: Practices of Consciousness and Power*. Chicago: University of Chicago Press.

Keane, Webb. 1997. *Signs of Recognition: Powers and Hazards of Representation in an Indonesian Society*. Berkeley and Los Angeles: University of California Press.

———. 2003. "Self-Interpretation, Agency, and the Objects of Anthropology: Reflections on a Genealogy." *Comparative Studies in Society and History* 45 (2): 222–48.

———. 2007. *Christian Moderns: Freedom and Fetish in the Mission Encounter*. Berkeley and Los Angeles: University of California Press.

———. 2008. "Others, Other Minds, and Others' Theories of Other Minds: An Afterword on the Psychology and Politics of Opacity Claims." *Anthropological Quarterly* 81 (2): 473–82.

———. 2010. "Minds, Surfaces, and Reasons in the Anthropology of Ethics." In Lambek 2010c, 64–83.

Kennedy, J. G. 1970. "Circumcision and Excision in Egyptian Nubia." *Man* 5 (2): 175–91.

Kierkegaard, Søren. 1968. *Fear and Trembling*. Translated by W. Lowrie. Princeton, NJ: Princeton University Press.

———. 2001. "The Concept of Irony," In *The Kierkegaard Reader*, edited by J. Chamberlain and J. Rée, 27–52. Oxford: Blackwell.

Kincaid, Jamaica. 1988. *A Small Place*. New York: Farrar, Straus, Giroux.

Kirmayer, Laurence. 1996. "Landscapes of Memory: Trauma, Narrative, and Dissociation." In Antze and Lambek 1996, 173–98.

Klaits, Frederick. 1999. "'A Visitor Does Not Mind': Mourning and Social Knowledge in Botswana." Paper presented at the Satterthwaite Colloquium on African Ritual and Religion, 1999, Satterthwaite, UK.

Kleinman, Arthur. 2006. *What Really Matters: Living a Moral Life Amidst Uncertainty and Danger*. New York: Oxford University Press.

Knauft, Bruce. 1979. "On Percussion and Metaphor." *Current Anthropology* 20 (1): 189–91.

Kohut, Heinz. 1977. *The Restoration of the Self*. New York: International University Press.

Kosman, L. A. 1980. "Being Properly Affected: Virtues and Feelings in Aristotle's *Ethics*." In Rorty 1980, 103–16.

Kramer, Fritz. 1993. *The Red Fez*. Translated by M. R. Green. London: Verso.

Kugelmass, Jack. 1996. "Missions to the Past: Poland in Contemporary Jewish Thought and Deed." In Antze and Lambek 1996, 199–214.

Kuhn, Thomas. 1970. *The Structure of Scientific Revolutions*. Chicago: University of Chicago Press.

Kwon, Heonik. 2008. *Ghosts of War in Vietnam*. Cambridge: Cambridge University Press.

Laidlaw, James. 1995. *Riches and Renunciation: Religion, Economy, and Society among the Jains*. New York: Clarendon Press.

———. 2002. "For an Anthropology of Ethics and Freedom." *Journal of the Royal Anthropological Institute* 8 (2): 311–32.

———. 2010. "Agency and Responsibility: Perhaps You Can Have Too Much of a Good Thing." In Lambek 2010c, 143–64.

———. 2013. "Ethics." In *A Companion to the Anthropology of Religion,* edited by M. Lambek and J. Boddy, 171–88. Boston: Wiley-Blackwell.

———. 2014. *The Subject of Virtue.* Cambridge: Cambridge University Press.

Lakoff, George, and Mark Johnson. 1980. *Metaphors We Live By.* Chicago: University of Chicago Press.

Lakoff, George, and Zoltan Kövecses. 1987. "The Cognitive Model of Anger Inherent in American English." In *Cultural Models in Language and Thought,* edited by D. Holland and N. Quinn, 195–221. Cambridge: Cambridge University Press.

Lambek, Michael. 1980. "Spirits and Spouses: Possession as a System of Communication among the Malagasy Speakers of Mayotte." *American Ethnologist* 7 (2): 318–31.

———. 1981. *Human Spirits: A Cultural Account of Trance in Mayotte.* Cambridge: Cambridge University Press.

———. 1983. "Virgin Marriage and the Autonomy of Women in Mayotte." *Signs* 9 (2): 264–81.

———. 1985. "Motherhood and Other Careers in Mayotte." In *In Her Prime: The Worlds of Middle-aged Women: A New View,* edited by J. K. Brown and V. Kerns, 76–92. South Hadley, MA: Bergin.

———. 1988a. "Graceful Exits: Spirit Possession as Personal Performance in Mayotte." *Culture* 8 (1): 59–69.

———. 1988b. "Spirit Possession/Spirit Succession: Aspects of Social Continuity in Mayotte."*American Ethnologist* 15:710–31.

———. 1989. "From Disease to Discourse: Remarks on the Conceptualization of Trance and Spirit Possession." In *Altered States of Consciousness and Mental Health: A Cross-Cultural Perspective,* edited by Colleen Ward, 36–61. Thousand Oaks, CA: Sage Press.

———. 1990a. "Certain Knowledge, Contestable Authority: Power and Practice on the Islamic Perpiphery." *American Ethnologist* 17:23–40.

———. 1990b. "Exchange, Time, and Person in Mayotte: The Structure and Destructuring of a Cultural System." *American Anthropologist* 92:647–61.

———. 1990c. "Toward a Pyschoanalytically Informed Reading of Spirit Possession in Mayotte." Paper presented at the Third Indo-Canadian Symposium, Mysore, January, 1990.

———. 1991a. *From Method to Modesty: Essays on Thinking and Making Ethnography Now.* Special section of *Culture* 11 (1–2), 3–133.

———. 1991b. "Tryin' to Make It Real But Compared to What?" *Culture* 11 (1–2): 29–38.

———. 1992a. "Like Teeth Biting Tongue: The Proscription and Practice of Spouse Abuse in Mayotte." In *Sanctions and Sanctuary: Cross-Cultural Perspectives on the Beating of Wives,* edited by J. K. Brown, D. Counts, and J. Campbell, 57–71. Boulder, CO: Westview Press.

———. 1992b. "Taboo as Cultural Practice among Malagasy Speakers." *Man* 27 (2): 245–66.

———. 1993a. "Cultivating Critical Distance: Oracles and the Politics of Voice." *PoLAR: Political and Legal Anthropology Review* 16 (2): 9–18.

———. 1993b. *Knowledge and Practice in Mayotte: Local Discourses of Islam, Sorcery and Spirit Possession.* Toronto: University of Toronto Press.

———. 1996. "The Past Imperfect: Remembering as Moral Practice." In Antze and Lambek 1996, 235–54.

———. 1997. "Pinching the Crocodile's Tongue: Affinity and the Anxieties of Influence in Fieldwork." *Anthropology and Humanism Quarterly* 22 (1): 31–53.

———. 1998a. "Body and Mind in Mind, Body and Mind in Body: Some Anthropological Interventions in a Long Conversation." In *Bodies and Persons: Comparative Perspectives from Africa and Melanesia*, edited by M. Lambek and A. Strathern, 103–23. Cambridge: Cambridge University Press.

———. 1998b. "The Sakalava Poiesis of History: Realizing the Past through Spirit Possession in Madagascar." *American Ethnologist* 25 (2): 106–27.

———. 2000a. "The Anthropology of Religion and the Quarrel between Poetry and Philosophy." *Current Anthropology* 41 (3): 309–20.

———. 2000b. "Localizing Islamic Performances in Mayotte. In *Islamic Prayer across the Indian Ocean: Inside and Outside the Mosque*, edited by D. Parkin and S. Headley, 63–97. Oxford: Curzon.

———. 2000c. "Nuriaty, the Saint, and the Sultan: Virtuous Subject and Subjective Virtuoso of the Post-Modern Colony." *Anthropology Today* 16 (2): 7–12.

———. 2001a. "Rappaport on Religion: A Social Anthropological Reading." In *Ecology and the Sacred: Engaging the Anthropology of Roy A. Rappaport*, edited by E. Messer and M. Lambek, 244–76. Ann Arbor: University of Michigan Press.

———. 2001b. "The Value of Coins in a Sakalava Polity: Money, Death, and Historicity in Mahajanga, Madagascar." *Comparative Studies in Society and History* 43 (4): 735–62.

———. 2002a. *The Weight of the Past: Living with History in Mahajanga, Madagascar*. New York: Palgrave Macmillan.

———. 2002b. "Fantasy in Practice: Projection and Introjection; or, the Witch and the Spirit-Medium." In *Beyond Rationalism: Rethinking Magic, Witchcraft and Sorcery*, edited by Bruce Kapferer, 198–214. New York: Berghahn.

———. 2002c. "Nuriaty, the Saint, and the Sultan: Virtuous Subject and Subjective Virtuoso of the Post-Modern Colony." In *Post-Colonial Subjectivities*, edited by Richard Werbner, 25–43. London: Zed Books.

———. 2003a. "Memory in a Maussian Universe." In *Regimes of Memory*, edited by K. Hodgkin and S. Radstone, 202–16. London: Routledge.

———. 2003b. "Rheumatic Irony: Questions of Agency and Self-Deception as Refracted Through the Art of Living with Spirits." In Antze and Lambek 2003, 40–59.

———. 2004. "The Saint, the Sea Monster, and an Invitation to a *Dîner-dansant:* Ethnographic Reflections on the Edgy Passage—and the Double Edge—of Modernity, Mayotte 1975–2001." *Anthropologica* 46 (1): 57–68.

———. 2007a. "The Cares of Alice Alder: Recuperating Kinship and History in Switzerland." In *Ghosts of Memory: Essays on Remembrance and Relatedness*, edited by J. Carsten, 218–40. Malden, MA: Blackwell.

———. 2007b. "How Do Women Give Birth?" In *Questions of Anthropology*, edited by R. Astuti, J. Parry, and C. Stafford, 197–226. Oxford: Berg.

———. 2007c. "Measuring—or Practising Well-Being?" In *Culture and Well-Being*, edited by A. C. Jiménez, 115–33. London: Pluto Press.

———. 2007d. "On Catching Up with Oneself: Learning to Know That One Means What One Does." In *Learning Religion*, edited by D. Berliner and R. Sarró, 65–81. Oxford: Berghahn.

———. 2007e. "Sacrifice and the Problem of Beginning." *Journal of the Royal Anthropological Institute* 13 (1): 19–38.

———. 2008a. "Provincializing God? Provocations from an Anthropology of Religion." In *Religion: Beyond a Concept*, edited by H. de Vries, 120–38. New York: Fordham University Press.

———. 2008b. "Value and Virtue." *Anthropological Theory* 8 (2): 133–57.

———. 2010a. "How to Make Up One's Mind: Reason, Passion, and Ethics in Spirit Possession." *University of Toronto Quarterly* 79 (2): 720–41.

———. 2010b. "Introduction." In Lambek 2010c, 1–36.

———. ed. 2010c. *Ordinary Ethics: Anthropology, Language, and Action*. New York City: Fordham University Press.

———. 2010d. "Toward an Ethics of the Act." In Lambek 2010c, 39–63.

———. 2011. "Kinship as Gift and Theft: Acts of Succession in Mayotte and ~~Ancient~~ Israel." *American Ethnologist* 38:1–15.

———. 2013a. "Introduction: What Is 'Religion' for Anthropology?" In *A Companion to the Anthropology of Religion*, edited by J. Boddy and M. Lambek, 1–32. Boston: Wiley-Blackwell.

———. 2013b. "Kinship, Modernity, and the Immodern." In *Vital Relations: Modernity and the Persistent Life of Kinship*, edited by F. Cannell and S. McKinnon, 241–60 . Santa Fe: School of Advanced Research Press.

———. 2014. "The Interpretation of Lives or Life as Interpretation: Person, Time and Conduct in the Western Indian Ocean." *America Ethnologist* 41 (3): 491–503.

———. In press (a). "Both/And." In *What Is Existential Anthropology?* edited by M. Jackson and A. Piette. Oxford: Berghahn.

———. In press (b). "Ritual as a Social Diagnostic and Lens of Comparison in Mayotte and Its Neighbours." *Etudes Rurales*. Special issue on Océan Indien, edited by Laurent Berger and Sophie Blanchy 194: 63–78.

Lambek, Michael, and Paul Antze. 1996. "Forecasting Memory." In Antze and Lambek 1996, xi–xxxviii.

Lambek, Michael, and Andrew Walsh. 1997. "The Imagined Community of the Antankaraña: Identity, History, and Ritual in Northern Madagascar." *Journal of Religion in Africa* 27 (3): 308–33.

Lan, David. 1985. *Guns and Rain*. London: J. Currey.

Lanthier, J. 2013. "Departing Provost Cheryl Misak: A Profile." *University of Toronto News*, August 27, 2013. Available online at http://news.utoronto.ca/provost-cherylmisak?utm_source=Bulletin&utm_medium=Email&utm_content=Staff.

Laugier, Sandra. 2005. "Rethinking the Ordinary: Austin *after* Cavell." In *Contending with Stanley Cavell*, edited by R. Goodman, 82–99. Oxford: Oxford University Press.

Leach, E. R. 1954. *Political Systems of Highland Burma*. Boston: Beacon Press.

———. 1961. "Two Essays Concerning the Symbolic Representation of Time." In *Rethinking Anthropology*, 124–36. London: Berg.

Lear, Jonathan. 1988. *Aristotle: The Desire to Understand*. Cambridge: Cambridge University Press.

———. 1990. *Love and Its Place in Nature*. New York: Farrar, Straus and Giroux.

———. 2000. *Happiness, Death, and the Remainder of Life*. Cambridge, MA: Harvard University Press.

———. 2003. *Therapeutic Action: An Ernest Plea for Irony*. New York: Other Press.

———. 2006. *Radical Hope: Ethics in the Face of Cultural Devastation*. Cambridge, MA: Harvard University Press

———. 2011. *A Case for Irony*. Cambridge, MA: Harvard University Press.

———. 2013. "Wisdom Won from Illness: The Psychoanalytic Grasp of Human Being." Paper presented at the Department of Philosophy, University of Toronto, September 26, 2013.

Leavitt, John. 1996. "Meaning and Feeling in the Anthropology of the Emotions." *American Ethnologist* 23 (3): 514–39.

Lee, Richard. 2003. *The Dobe Ju/'hoansi*. 3rd ed. South Melbourne: Wadsworth Thomson Learning.

Leenhardt, Maurice. 1979 [1947]. *Do Kamo: Person and Myth in a Melanesian World*. Translated by B. M. Gulati. Chicago: University of Chicago Press.

Lévi-Strauss, Claude. 1963 [1962]. *Totemism*. Translated by R. Needham. Boston: Beacon.

———. 1966. *The Savage Mind*. Chicago: University of Chicago Press.

———. 1969. *The Elementary Structures of Kinship*. Boston: Beacon Press.

———. 1970–81. *Mythologiques*. 4 vols. Translated by J. and D. Weightman. London: Cape.

———. 1972. *Structural Anthropology I*. Harmondsworth: Penguin.

———. 1974. *Tristes Tropiques*. Translated by J. and D. Weightman. New York: Atheneum.

Levy, Robert. 1973. *Tahitians: Mind and Experience in the Society Islands*. Chicago: University of Chicago Press.

Lewis, I. M. 1971. *Ecstatic Religion*. Harmondsworth: Penguin.

Leys, Ruth. 1996. "Traumatic Cures: Shellshock, Janet, and the Question of Memory." In Antze and Lambek 1996, 103–45.

———. 2000. *Trauma: A Genealogy*. Chicago: University of Chicago Press.

Lienhardt, Godfrey. 1961. *Divinity and Experience*. Oxford: Clarendon Press.

Locke, John. 1975 [1689]. *An Essay Concerning Human Understanding*, edited by P. H. Nidditch. Oxford: Oxford University Press.

Loewald, Hans. 1980. *Papers on Psychoanalysis*. New Haven, CT: Yale University Press.

Luhrmann, Tanya. 2000. *Of Two Minds: The Growing Disorder in American Psychiatry*. New York City: Alfred A. Knopf.

Lutz, Catherine. 1988. *Unnatural Emotions: Everyday Sentiments on a Micronesian Atoll and Their Challenge to Western Theory*. Chicago: University of Chicago Press.

Lutz, Catherine, and Lila Abu-Lughod, eds. 1990. *Language and the Politics of Emotion*. Cambridge: Cambridge University Press.

MacIntyre, Alasdair. 1981. *After Virtue: A Study in Moral Theory*. Notre Dame, IN: Notre Dame University Press.

———. 1984. *After Virtue: A Study in Moral Theory*. 2nd ed. Notre Dame, IN: University of Notre Dame Press.

———. 1988. *Whose Justice? Which Rationality?* Notre Dame, IN: University of Notre Dame Press.

Macpherson, C. B. 1962. *The Political Theory of Possessive Individualism*. London: Oxford University Press.

———. 1973. *Democratic Theory: Essays in Retrieval*. Oxford: Clarendon Press.

Mahmood, Saba. 2005. *Politics of Piety*. Princeton, NJ: Princeton University Press.

Malamoud, Charles. 1990. "Sans lieu ni date: Note sur l'absence de fondation dans l'Inde védique." In *Tracés de fondation*, edited by M. Detienne, 183–91. Louvain/Paris: Peeters.

Malcolm, Janet. 2011. *Iphigenia in Forest Hills: Anatomy of a Murder Trial*. New Haven, CT: Yale University Press.

Malinowski, Bronislaw. 1922. *Argonauts of the Western Pacific*. London: Routledge.

Marx, Karl. 1971. *The Grundrisse*. Edited and translated by D. McLellan. New York: Harper & Row.

Mattingly, Cheryl. 2010. *The Paradox of Hope: Journeys through a Clinical Borderland*. Berkeley and Los Angeles: University of California Press.

———. 2012. "Two Virtue Ethics and the Anthropology of Morality." *Anthropological Theory* 12 (2): 161–84.

———. 2014. *Moral Laboratories: Family Peril and the Struggle for a Good Life*. Berkeley and Los Angeles: University of California Press.

Maurer, Bill. 2006. "The Anthropology of Money." *Annual Review of Anthropology* 35 (1): 15–36.

Mauss, Marcel. 1966. *The Gift*. Translated by I. Cunnison. London: Routledge and Kegan Paul.

———. 1985 [1938]. "A Category of the Human Mind: The Notion of Person, the Notion of Self." In *The Category of the Person: Anthropology, Philosophy, History*, edited by M. Carrithers, S. Collins, and S. Lukes, 1–25. Cambridge: Cambridge University Press.

———. 1990. *The Gift: The Form and Reason for Exchange in Archaic Societies*. Translated by W. D. Halls. New York: Routledge.

Mauzé, Marie. 1994. "The Concept of the Person and Reincarnation among the Kwakiutl Indians." In *Amerindian Rebirth*, edited by A. Mills and R. Slobodin, 177–91. Toronto: University of Toronto Press.

Mayblin, Maya. 2013. "The Untold Sacrifice." *Ethnos* 78 (3): 342–64. Special section entitled *The Other Side of Sacrifice*, edited by Maya Mayblin and Magus Course.

Mead, George Herbert. 1934. *Mind, Self, and Society*. Edited by C. W. Morris. Chicago: University of Chicago Press.

Menand, Louis. 2001. *The Metaphysical Club: A Story of Ideas in America*. New York: Farrar, Straus and Giroux.

Meneley, Anne. 1996. *Tournaments of Value: Sociability and Hierarchy in a Yemeni Town*. Toronto: University of Toronto Press.

Merleau-Ponty, Maurice. 1962. *The Phenomenology of Perception*. Translated by C. Smith. London: Routledge & Kegan Paul.

Michaels, Anne. 2009. *The Winter Vault*. Toronto: McLelland & Stewart.

Middleton, Karen, ed. 1999a. *Ancestors, Power and History in Madagascar*. Leiden: Brill.

———. 1999b. "Introduction." In Middleton 1999a, 1–36.

Miller, Daniel. 1998. *A Theory of Shopping*. Cambridge: Polity.

Miller, Joseph C. 1977. "Imbangala Lineage Slavery." In *Slavery in Africa: Historical and Anthropological Perspectives*, edited by S. Miers and I. Kopytoff, 205–33. Madison: University of Wisconsin Press.

Mitchell, Stephen A. 1988. *Relational Concepts in Psychoanalysis: An Integration*. Cambridge, MA: Harvard University Press.

Mitchell, Timothy. 1988. *Colonising Egypt*. Cambridge: Cambridge University Press.

Moore, Sally Falk. 1978. "Old Age in a Life-Term Social Arena." In *Life's Career—Aging*, edited by B. Myerhoff and A. Simic, 23–76. Beverly Hills: Sage.

Muehlebach, Andrea. 2012. *The Moral Neoliberal: Welfare and Citizenship in Italy*. Chicago: University of Chicago Press.

Mulhall, Stephen. 1996. "Introduction." In *The Cavell Reader*, edited by S. Mulhall. Malden, MA: Blackwell.

Munn, Nancy. 1986. *The Fame of Gawa: A Symbolic Study of Value Transformation in a Massim Society*. Cambridge: Cambridge University Press.

Murphy, Robert F. 1971. *The Dialectics of Social Life*. New York: Basic Books.

———. 1987. *The Body Silent*. New York: Henry Holt.

Myerhoff, Barbara. 1978. *Number Our Days*. New York: Simon and Schuster.

Myers, Fred. 1988. "The Logic and Meaning of Anger among Pintupi Aborigines." *Man* 23 (4): 589–610.

Myhre, Knut. 1998. "The Anthropological Concept of Action and Its Problems: A 'New' Approach Based on Marcel Mauss and Aristotle." *Journal of the Anthropological Society of Oxford* 29 (2): 121–34.

Needham, Rodney. 1967. "Percussion and Transition." *Man* 2 (4): 606–14.

Nehamas, Alexander. 1998. *The Art of Living*. Berkeley and Los Angeles: University of California Press.

Nelson, Eric Sean. 2009. "Traumatic Life: Violence, Pain, and Responsiveness in Heidegger." In *The Trauma Controversy: Philosophical and Interdisciplinary Dialogues*, edited by K. B. Golden and B. G. Bergo, 189–204. Albany, NY: SUNY Press.

Nussbaum, Martha. 1980. "Shame, Separateness, and Political Unity: Aristotle's Criticism of Plato." In Rorty 1980, 395–435.

———. 1994. *The Therapy of Desire*. Princeton, NJ: Princeton University Press.

Nuttall, Mark. 1992. *Arctic Homeland: Kinship, Community and Development in Northwest Greenland*. Toronto: University of Toronto Press.

Obeyesekere, Gananath. 1981. *Medusa's Hair*. Chicago: University of Chicago Press.

Ochs Keenan, Elinor. 1976. "The Universality of Conversational Postulates." *Language in Society* 5 (1): 67–80.

Orsi, Robert. 2005. *Between Heaven and Earth*. Princeton, NJ: Princeton University Press.

Ortner, Sherry. 1978. *Sherpas Through Their Rituals*. Cambridge: Cambridge University Press.

———. 2006. *Anthropology and Social Theory: Culture, Power, and the Acting Subject*. Durham, NC: Duke University Press.

Ottenheimer, Martin, and Harriet Ottenheimer. 1979. "Matrilocal Residence and Non-sororal Polygyny: A Case from the Comoro Islands." *Journal of Anthropological Research* 35 (3): 328–35.

Otto, Ton, and Rane Willerslev. 2013. "Prologue: Value *as* Theory: Values, Action, and Critique." *HAU: Journal of Ethnographic Theory* 3 (2): 1–10.

Parry, Jonathan. 1986. "The Gift, the Indian Gift and the 'Indian Gift.'" *Man* (n. s.) 21 (3): 453–73.

———. 1989. "On the Moral Perils of Exchange." In *Money and the Morality of Exchange*, edited by J. Parry and M. Bloch, 64–93. Cambridge: Cambridge University Press.

———. 1994. *Death in Banaras*. Cambridge: Cambridge University Press.

Pigott, R. 2009. "Atheists Call for 'Debaptism.'" BBC News, March 14. Available online at http://news.bbc.co.uk/2/hi/uk_news/7941817.stm (accessed 23 September 2013).

Polanyi, Karl. 1971. "The Self-Regulating Market and the Fictitious Commodities: Labour, Land, and Money." In *Primitive, Archaic and Modern Economies: Essays of Karl Polanyi*, edited by G. Dalton, 26–37. Boston: Beacon Press.

———. 2001 [1944]. *The Great Transformation: The Political and Economic Origins of Our Time*. 2nd ed. Boston: Beacon.

Polk, Patrick. 2014. "'Who's Dat Knocking at the Door?' A Tragi-comic Ethiopian Delineation in Three Parts." In *Spirited Things: The Work of "Possession" in Afro-Atlantic Religions*, edited by P. C. Johnson, 79–97. Chicago: University of Chicago Press.

Putnam, Hilary. 1992. *Renewing Philosophy*. Cambridge, MA: Harvard University Press.

Ramonet, Ignacio. 2000. "The Control of Pleasure." *Le Monde Diplomatique* (May).

Rappaport, Roy. 1979a. *Ecology, Meaning, and Religion*. Richmond, CA: North Atlantic.

———. 1979b. "The Obvious Aspects of Ritual." In Rappaport 1979a, 173–221.

———. 1999. *Ritual and Religion in the Making of Humanity*. Cambridge: Cambridge University Press.

Reczkiewicz, Mark, and Michael Lambek. n.d. "Cultivating the Art of Fieldwork in an Age of Professional Reproduction." Unpublished paper.

Reddy, William. 1999. "Emotional Liberty: Politics and History in the Anthropology of the Emotions." *Cultural Anthropology* 14 (2): 256–88.

Reminick, Ronald A. 1976. "The Symbolic Significance of Ceremonial Defloration among the Amhara of Ethiopia." *American Ethnologist* 3 (4): 751–63.

Richards, Audrey. 1951. "The Bemba of North-eastern Rhodesia." In *Seven Tribes of British Central Africa*, edited by E. Colson and M. Gluckman, 164–93. London: Oxford University Press for Rhodes-Livingstone Institute.

———. 1956. *Chisungu*. London: Faber & Faber.

Ricoeur, Paul. 1971. "The Model of the Text: Meaningful Action Considered as a Text." *Social Research* 38:529–62.

———. 1992. *Oneself as Another*. Chicago: University of Chicago Press.

Rizzolatti, Giacomo, L. Fadiga, L. Fogassi, and V. Gallese. 1996. "Premotor Cortex and the Recognition of Motor Actions." *Cognitive Brain Research* 3:131–41.

Robbins, Joel. 2004. *Becoming Sinners: Christianity and Moral Torment in a Papua New Guinea Society*. Berkeley and Los Angeles: University of California Press.

———. 2007. "Continuity Thinking and the Problem of Christian Culture." *Current Anthropology* 48 (1): 5–17.

Robbins, Joel, and Sandra Bamford, eds. 1997. "Fieldwork Revisited: Changing Contexts of Ethnographic Practice in the Era of Globalization." Special issue of *Anthropology and Humanism* 22 (1).

Romberg, Raquel. 2014. "Corporeality, Discourse, and Indeterminacy in Spirit Possession." In *Spirited Things: The Work of "Possession" in Afro-Atlantic Religions*, edited by P. C. Johnson, 225–56. Chicago: University of Chicago Press.

Rorty, A. O., ed. 1980. *Essays on Aristotle's Ethics*. Berkeley and Los Angeles: University of California Press.

Rosaldo, Michelle. 1980. *Knowledge and Passion: Ilongot Notions of Self and Social Life*. Cambridge: Cambridge University Press.

Rosaldo, Renato. 1984. "Grief and a Headhunter's Rage: On the Cultural Force of Emotions." In *Text, Play and Story*, edited by E. Bruner, 178–95. Washington, DC: American Anthropological Association.

Ross, Fiona. 2010. "An Acknowledged Failure: Women, Voice, Violence and the South African Truth and Reconciliation Commission." In *Localizing Transitional Justice: Interventions and Priorities after Mass Violence*, edited by R. Shaw, L. Waldorf, and P. Hazan, 69–91. Stanford, CA: Stanford University Press.

Ruel, Malcolm. 1990. "Non-Sacrificial Ritual Killing." *Man* 25 (2): 323–35.

———. 1997. *Belief, Ritual and the Securing of Life: Reflexive Essays on a Bantu Religion*. Leiden: E. J. Brill.

Rumsey, Alan. 2010. "Ethics, Language, and Human Sociality." In Lambek 2010c, 105–22.

Ruud, J. 1960. *Taboo: A Study of Malagasy Customs and Beliefs*. London: Allen & Unwin.

Ryle, Gilbert. 1949. *The Concept of Mind*. London: Hutchinson.

Sacks, Oliver. 1993. "Making Up the Mind." *New York Review of Books*, April 8, 42–49.

Sahlins, Marshall. 1976a. *Culture and Practical Reason*. Chicago: University of Chicago Press.

———. 1976b. *The Use and Abuse of Biology*. Ann Arbor: University of Michigan Press.

———. 1985. *Islands of History*. Chicago: University of Chicago Press.

______. 1995. *How "Natives" Think: About Captain Cook, for Example*. Chicago: University of Chicago Press.

———. 1996. "The Sadness of Sweetness: The Native Anthropology of Western Cosmology." *Current Anthropology* 37 (3): 395–428.

Said, Edward. 1975. *Beginnings: Intention and Method*. Baltimore, MD: Johns Hopkins University Press.

Sandis, C. 2013. "Basic Actions and Individuation." In *A Companion to the Philosophy of Action*, edited by T. O'Connor and C. Sandis. Malden, MA: Wiley-Blackwell.

Sartre, Jean Paul. 1956 [1943]. *Being and Nothingness*. Translated by H. Barnes. New York: Philosophical Library.

Schafer, Ralph. 1976. *A New Language for Psychoanalysis*. New Haven, CT: Yale University Press.

———. 1978. *Language and Insight*. New Haven, CT: Yale University Press.

Schapera, Isaac. 1971 [1940]. *Married Life in an African Tribe*. Harmondsworth: Penguin.

Scheper-Hughes, Nancy. 2004. "Parts Unknown: Undercover Ethnography of the Organs-Trafficking Underworld." *Ethnography* 5 (1): 29–73.

Schneider, Jane. 1971. "Of Vigilance and Virgins." *Ethnology* 10 (1): 1–24.

Schutz, Alfred. 1964. "The Well-Informed Citizen." In *Collected Papers*. Vol. 2. The Hague: Martinus Nijhoff.

Schwimmer, Eric. 1973. *Exchange in the Social Structure of the Orokaiva*. London: Hurst.

Sebald, W. G. 1996. *The Emigrants*. London: Harvill Press.

Seligman, Adam B., Robert P. Weller, Michael Puett, and Bennett Simon. 2008. *Ritual and Its Consequences: An Essay on the Limits of Sincerity*. Oxford: Oxford University Press.

Sharp, Lesley. 1989. "Spirit Possession as Ethnohistory." Paper presented at the American Ethnological Society annual meeting, Santa Fe, New Mexico

———. 1993. *The Possessed and the Dispossessed*. Berkeley and Los Angeles: University of California Press.

Shepherd, Gillian. 1977. "Two Marriage Forms in the Comoro Islands." *Africa* 47 (4): 344–59.

Shiner, Roger. 1986. "Canfield, Cavell, and Criteria." In *Criteria*, edited by J. Canfield, 353–72. London: Garland.

Shipton, Parker. 1989. *Bitter Money: Cultural Economy and Some African Meanings of Forbidden Commodities*. Washington, DC: American Anthropological Association.

Shohet, Merav. 2013. "Everyday Sacrifice and Language Socialization in Vietnam: The Power of a Respect Particle." *American Anthropologist* 115 (2): 203–17.

Sider, Gerald, and Gavin Smith, eds. 1997. *Between History and Histories: The Making of Silences and Commemorations*. Toronto: University of Toronto Press.

Sidnell, Jack. 2009. "Participation. In *The Pragmatics of Interaction*, edited by S. D'hondt, J.-O. Östman, and J. Verschueren, 125–56. Amsterdam: John Benjamins.

———. 2010. "The Ordinary Ethics of Everyday Talk." In Lambek 2010c, 125–39.

Silver, Daniel. 2011. "The Moodiness of Action." *Sociological Theory* 29 (3): 199–222.

Silverstein, Michael. 1976. "Shifters, Linguistic Categories, and Cultural Descriptions." In *Meaning in Anthropology*, edited by K. Basso and H. Selby, 2–55. Albuquerque: University of New Mexico Press.

Silverstein, Michael, and Greg Urban, eds. 1996. *Natural Histories of Discourse*. Chicago: University of Chicago Press.

Simmel, Georg. 1978 [1907]. *The Philosophy of Money*. Translated by T. Bottomore and D. Frisby. London: Routledge & Kegan Paul.

———. 2011 [1918]. *The View of Life: Four Metaphysical Essays*. Chicago: University of Chicago Press.

Smith, Gavin. 1997. "Pandora's History: Central Peruvian Peasants and the Re-covering of the Past." In *Between History and Histories: The Production of Silences and Commemorations*, edited by G. Sider and G. Smith, 80–97. Toronto: University of Toronto Press.

———. 1999. *Confronting the Present: Towards a Politically Engaged Anthropology*. Oxford: Berg.

Solway, Jacqueline. 1994. "Drought as a Revelatory Crisis: An Exploration of Shifting Entitlements and Hierarchies in the Kalahari." *Development and Change* 25 (3): 471–96.

———. 2005. "Anthropologist and Accomplice in Botswana." In *Auto-Ethnographies: The Anthropology of Academic Practices*, edited by A. Meneley and D. Young, 113–25. Peterborough, Ontario: Broadview.

———. 2007. "Branding Diamonds and Branding Bushmen: The Central Kalahari Game Reserve Case." Paper presented at the American Anthropological Association Annual Meeting, November 30, 2007, Washington, DC.

———. 2009. "Human Rights and NGO 'Wrongs'; Conflict Diamonds, Culture Wars and the 'Bushman Question.'" *Africa* 79 (3): 321–46.

Solway, Jacqueline, and Michael Lambek. 2001. "Just Anger: Scenarios of Indignation in Botswana and Madagascar." *Ethnos* 66 (1): 1–23.

Sontag, Susan. 1966. "The Anthropologist as Hero." In *Against Interpretation, and Other Essays*, 77–89. New York: Farrar, Straus, and Giroux.

Sorabji, Richard. 1980. "Aristotle on the Role of Intellect in Virtue." In Rorty 1980, 201–19.

Stafford, Charles. 2010. "The Punishment of Ethical Behaviour." In Lambek 2010c, 187–206.

———, ed. 2013. *Ordinary Ethics in China*. London: Bloomsbury.

Steedman, Carolyn. 1986. *Landscape for a Good Woman*. London: Virago.

Steiner, Franz. 1956. *Taboo*. New York: Philosophical Library.

Steiner, George. 1978. "On Heidegger's "'Way.'" In *Martin Heidegger*. New York: Viking.

Strathern, Marilyn. 1988. *The Gender of the Gift: Problems with Women and Problems with Society in Melanesia*. Berkeley and Los Angeles: University of California Press.

Strawson, Peter F. 2008 [1962]. "Freedom and Resentment." In *Freedom and Resentment and Other Essays*, 1–28. London: Routledge.

Streumer, Bart. 2013. "Practical Reasoning." In *A Companion to the Philosophy of Action*, edited by T. O'Connor and C. Sandis, 244–51. Malden, MA: Wiley-Blackwell.

Suleri, Sara. 1992. "Woman Skin Deep: Feminism and the Postcolonial Condition." *Critical Inquiry* 18 (Summer): 756–69.

Szafraniec, Asja. 2008. "Inheriting the Wound: Religion and Philosophy in Stanley Cavell." In *Religion: Beyond a Concept*, edited by Hent de Vries, 368–79. New York: Fordham University Press.

Tambiah, Stanley. J. 1973. "Form and Meaning in Magical Acts." In *Modes of Thought*, edited by R. Horton and R. Finnegan, 199–229. London: Faber.

———. 1985. *Culture, Thought, and Social Action: An Anthropological Perspective*. Cambridge, MA: Harvard University Press.

———. 1990. *Magic, Science, Religion, and the Scope of Rationality*. New York: Cambridge University Press.

Taussig, Michael. 1980. *The Devil and Commodity Fetishism in South America*. Chapel Hill: University of North Carolina Press.

———. 1993. *Mimesis and Alterity: A Particular History of the Senses*. New York: Routledge.

______. 2003. "Viscerality, Faith, and Skepticism." In *Magic and Modernity: Interfaces of Revelation and Concealment*, edited by B. Meyer and P. Pels. Stanford, CA: Stanford University Press.

Tavris, Carol. 1982. *Anger: The Misunderstood Emotion*. New York: Simon and Schuster.

Taylor, Charles. 1989. *Sources of the Self: The Making of the Modern Identity*. Cambridge, MA: Harvard University Press.

Tehindrazanarivelo, Emmanuel. 1997. "Fieldwork: The Dance of Power." *Anthropology and Humanism Quarterly* 22 (1): 54–60.

Terdiman, Richard. 1993. *Present Past: Modernity and the Memory Crisis*. Ithaca, NY: Cornell University Press.

Thompson, E. P. 1971. "The Moral Economy of the English Crowd." *Past and Present* 50:76–136.

Throop, Jason. 2014. "Moral Moods." *Ethos* 42 (1): 65–83.

Trilling, Lionel. 1971. *Sincerity and Authenticity*. Cambridge, MA: Harvard University Press.

Turner, Bryan S. 1984. *The Body and Society: Explorations in Social Theory*. Oxford: Basil Blackwell.

Turner, Victor. 1967. *The Forest of Symbols: Aspects of Ndembu Ritual*. Ithaca, NY: Cornell University Press.

———. 1969. *The Ritual Process: Structure and Anti-Structure*. Chicago: Aldine.

———. 1974. *Dramas, Fields, and Metaphors*. Ithaca, NY: Cornell University Press.

———. 1982. "Acting in Everyday Life and Everyday Life in Acting." In *From Ritual to Theatre*. New York: Performing Arts Journal Press.

Urban, Greg. 1989. "The 'I' of Discourse." In *Semiotics, Self, and Society*, edited by B. Lee and G. Urban, 27–52. Berlin: Walter de Gruyter.

Uzgalis, William. 2014. "John Locke." In *The Stanford Encyclopedia of Philosophy*, Winter 2014 ed., edited by Edward N. Zalta. Available online at http://plato.stanford.edu/archives/win2014/entries/locke/supplement.html (accessed 29 September 2014).

Vallely, Anne. 2002. *Guardians of the Transcendent: An Ethnography of a Jain Ascetic Community*. Toronto: University of Toronto Press.

van de Port, Mattijs. 1998. *Gypsies, Wars and Other Instances of the Wild: Civilisation and Its Discontents in a Serbian Town*. Amsterdam: Amsterdam University Press.

van Gennep, Arnold. 1904. *Tabou et totémisme à Madagascar: Étude descriptive et théorique*. Paris: Ernest Leroux.

———. 1960 [1908]. *The Rites of Passage*. Translated by M. B. Vizedom and G. L. Caffee. Chicago: University of Chicago Press.

Verdery, Katherine. 1999. *The Political Lives of Dead Bodies*. New York: Columbia University Press.

Vérin, Pierre, and Narivelo Rajaonarimanana. n.d. "Divination in Madagascar: The Antemoro Case and the Diffusion of Divination." (MS) Paris: Institut National des Langues et Civilisations Orientales.

Viveiros de Castro, Eduardo. 1998. "Cosmological Deixis and Amerindian Perspectivism." *Journal of the Royal Anthropological Institute* 4: 469–88.

vom Bruck, G., and B. Bodenhorn, eds. 2006. *The Anthropology of Names and Naming*. Cambridge: Cambridge University Press.

Walsh, Andrew. 1998. *Constructing "Antankarana": History, Ritual and Identity in Northern Madagascar*. PhD diss. Department of Anthropology, University of Toronto.

———. 2002. "Responsibility, Taboos and the 'Freedom to do Otherwise' in Northern Madagascar." *Journal of the Royal Anthropological Institute* 8: 451–68.

———. 2004. "In the Wake of Things: Speculating in and about Sapphires in Northern Madagascar." *American Anthropologist* 106 (2): 225–37.

Weber, Max. 1958 [1904–5]. *The Protestant Ethic and the Spirit of Capitalism*. Translated by T. Parsons. New York: Scribner.

Weiner, Annette. 1976. *Women of Value, Men of Renown*. Austin: University of Texas Press.

———. 1992. *Inalienable Possessions*. Berkeley and Los Angeles: University of California Press.

Wentzer, Thomas Schwarz. 2014. "'I Have Seen Königsberg Burning': Philosophical Anthropology and the Responsiveness of Historical Experience." *Anthropological Theory* 14 (1): 27–48.

Werbner, Pnina. 1996. "Allegories of Sacred Imperfection: Magic, Hermeneutics, and Passion in *The Satanic Verses*." *Current Anthropology* 37:S55–86.

Werbner, R. 1989. *Ritual Passage, Sacred Journey: The Process and Organization of Religious Movement*. Washington, DC: Smithsonian Institution Press.

White, Hayden. 1973. *Metahistory*. Baltimore, MD: Johns Hopkins University Press.

———. 1987. *The Content of the Form: Narrative Discourse and Historical Representation*. Baltimore, MD: Johns Hopkins University Press.

Whitehead, Harry. 2000. "The Hunt for Quesalid: Tracking Lévi-Strauss's Shaman." *Anthropology and Medicine* 7 (2): 149–68.

Wikan, Unni. 1990. *Managing Turbulent Hearts: A Balinese Formula for Living*. Chicago: University of Chicago Press.

Williams, Bernard. 1981. *Moral Luck*. Cambridge: Cambridge University Press.

Williams, Raymond. 1976. *Keywords*. London: Fontana.

Williamson, Sue. 2011. Presentation to Residents at Bellagio. June 2011.

Wilson, Godfrey. 1951. "The Nyakyusa of South-western Tanganyika." In *Seven Tribes of British Central Africa*, edited by E. Colson and M. Gluckman. Oxford: Oxford University Press.

Wilson, Peter J. 1977. "The Problem with Simple Folk." *Natural History* 86 (10): 26–32.

———. 1992. *Freedom by a Hair's Breadth: Tsimihety in Madagascar*. Ann Abor: University of Michigan Press.

Wittgenstein, Ludwig. 1973 (1958). *Philosophical Investigations*. Translated by G. E. M. Anscombe. Oxford: Blackwell.

———. 1979 [1931]. *Remarks on Frazer's Golden Bough*. Translated by A. Miles. Edited by R. Rhees. Nottingham: Brynmill Press.

Wool, Zoe. 2011. *Emergent Ordinaries at Walter Reed Army Medical Center*. PhD diss. Department of Anthropology, University of Toronto.

Wrong, Dennis. 1961. "The Oversocialized Conception of Man in Modern Sociology." *American Sociological Review* 26 (2): 183–93.

Yang, Mayfair M.-H. 1994. *Gifts, Favors, and Banquets: The Art of Social Relationships in China*. Ithaca, NY: Cornell University Press.

Young, Donna. 2010. "Engaging Others: Religious Conviction and Irony in the Holy Lands." In Lambek 2010c, 351–67. New York: Fordham.

———. Forthcoming. *The Bridge to Nowhere: An Ethnographic Account of Memory*. Toronto: University of Toronto Press.

Zelizer, Viviana. 1994. *The Social Meaning of Money: Pin Money, Paychecks, Poor Relief, and Other Currencies*. New York: Basic Books.

Zempleni, Andras. 1977. "From Symptom to Sacrifice: The Story of Khady Fall." In Crapanzano and Garrison 1977, 87–139.

INDEX